MUSEUM OF ANTHROPOLOGY, THE UNIVERSITY OF MICHIGAN

TECHNICAL REPORTS

Number 14

RESEARCH REPORTS IN ARCHAEOLOGY

Contribution 9

ARCHAEOLOGICAL SETTLEMENT PATTERN DATA FROM THE CHALCO, XOCHIMILCO, IXTAPALAPA, TEXCOCO AND ZUMPANGO REGIONS, MEXICO

D1606900

by

Jeffrey R. Parsons

Keith W. Kintigh

Susan A. Gregg

ANN ARBOR
1983

TABLE OF CONTENTS

LIST OF TABLES

LIST OF MAPS

INTRODUCTION

This report is a descriptive tabulation of settlement pattern data collected by University of Michigan projects in the Valley of Mexico between 1967 and 1973. It is intended to facilitate analyses of these data and does not attempt any analysis of its own. The decision to make such a report available grew out of periodic requests for unpublished settlement pattern data from a variety of people over the years. There was usually no easy way to provide such information, except to graduate students at the University of Michigan who had direct access (because they were just down the hall) to the original notes and field maps (e.g., Brumfiel 1976; Earle 1976; Alden 1979; Steponaitis 1981). Furthermore, even though final publications have now appeared for the Texcoco (Parsons 1971), the Ixtapalapa (Blanton 1972), and the Chalco-Xochimilco (Parsons et al. 1982) regions, it remains difficult to make some types of quantitative analyses of these materials. This difficulty is partly due to the lack of complete standardization of chronology and site classification. Perhaps more significant has been the omission of precise locational coordinates and rainfall data in the original monographs. Another problem has been the scattering of the major publications in time and space: they have not always been conveniently available to all who might be interested.

This report attempts to remedy these problems by making the information available in a single, standardized format. Recent advances in the application to archaeology of computer technology have greatly facilitated this effort. It should be emphasized, however, that this report does not constitute a complete or independent description of the sites and features discussed in the monographs. This publication is complementary to the latter, since only data which were readily reducible to a few numbers, a few symbols, or a few words could be tabulated here. Thus, we have not been able to incorporate details on architectural remnants, intra-site variability of surface pottery, the intricacies of site topography, etc. Neither do we repeat here the important details of survey methodology, site classification, ceramic chronology, or natural environment. We have simply assumed that people who use this report will do so in conjunction with the detailed monographs.

After some agonizing, we decided against including details of the surface ceramic collections originally made from most sites. We have been criticized for failing to do this in the past (Tourtellot 1973; Blanton et al. 1982). Nevertheless, we are still convinced that since these collections were not systematically made, they should not serve as the base for anything more than general chronology. Attempts to use

1

them for rigorous quantitative analyses could easily produce misleading results.

One of the principal shortcomings of these data tabulations has been our inability to find a reasonable way to make legible maps with site numbers. Hence, to connect any specific symbol on a map with a site number, it is necessary to work from the UTM locational coordinates. We recognize that this detracts from the utility of this report.

We have made no attempt to include Late Aztec (Late Horizon) sites which are known from ethnohistoric sources to have existed at the time of European contact, but which were invisible to our surveys because of dense modern occupation in the same localities. Examples would include Xochimilco, Mixquic, and Chiautla, and there are many more. Any attempt to use this report for analysis of Late Aztec occupation should make proper allowance for this.

Finally, it should be remembered that settlement pattern data from the Zumpango Region in the far northwestern Valley of Mexico (Map 1) remain incompletely analyzed. Unlike the Texcoco, Ixtapalapa and Chalco-Xochimilco Regions, the Zumpango Region materials have not yet been fully described and are still subject to some revision and re-interpretation.

We anticipate that this report will be most useful for persons interested in working with data from the contiguous survey regions in the eastern and southern Valley of Mexico: the Texcoco, Ixtapalapa, and Chalco-Xochimilco Regions. Here surface survey is largely complete and continuous (although there are two gaps in the Texcoco Region where intensive survey was not carried out; these gaps were nevertheless covered by extensive surveys, and most significant sites were located). Ideally, this report should also have included data from the surveys carried out by Pennsylvania State University projects in the Teotihuacan, Cuauhtitlan, and Temascalapa Regions. This would have provided continuous longitudinal data from the far southeastern to the far northwestern valley. Although it has not been possible for us to provide such a complete data compilation at this time, we do plan to eventually publish a compendium report with these latter data.

GENERAL GUIDELINES FOR THE USE OF THIS REPORT

This report consists of a long data tabulation and eight general settlement pattern maps (Maps 2-9). The tabulated data are arranged in chronological order, in eight periods (Table 1): Early Formative (Early Horizon), Middle Formative (First Intermediate Phase One), Late Formative (First Intermediate Phase Two), Terminal Formative (First Intermediate Phases Three and Four), Classic (Middle Horizon), Early Toltec (Second Intermediate Phase One), Late Toltec (Second Intermediate Phase Two), and Aztec (Second Intermediate Phase Three and Late Horizon). The map of Early Formative (Early Horizon) has been omitted because of the existence of so few sites and their restriction to the far south (see Blanton 1972 and Parsons et al. 1982).

Within each period, the data are presented by survey area, moving from south to north: first, the Chalco-Xochimilco Region; second, the Ixtapalapa Region; third, the Texcoco Region; and fourth, the Zumpango Region (Map 1; Table 2). Within each survey area, the data have been separated into two subdivisions: "environmental data" and "settlement data." The report is arranged so that data from both subdivisions occur on opposing pages as the book is opened. The environmental data subdivision contains columns giving the site number, environmental zone, Universal Transverse Mercator (UTM) coordinates for the mid-point of each site, site elevation (for the approximate mid-point of each site), modern soil depth, modern erosion, and modern land use.

The settlement data subdivision contains columns giving site number, site classification, environmental zone (we felt this was important enough to warrant repetition), site area, site population (the maximum end of our estimated range), a listing of other-period occupations at the site locality, the temporary site number assigned during our original fieldwork, the name of the survey supervisor, and the year in which the survey was carried out. Additional clarification of some data is provided below.

Chronology (Table 1)

Classic-period sites from the Texcoco, Ixtapalapa, and Zumpango Regions are separated into Early and Late sub-periods. We have at present only limited confidence in our separation of Early and Late Classic for the Texcoco and Ixtapalapa Regions--these separations were made early in the course of our research, before we fully understood the Classic-period ceramic chronology. We have preserved the two-fold Classic division only in order to conform with the original published

4

Table 1: Valley of Mexico Prehispanic Chronology.
Adapted from Sanders, Parsons and Santley 1979:93.

Approx. Absolute Chronology	Major Period		Phases	
	Newer System	Older System	This Report	General
1520 / 1400 — Late Horizon		Late Postclassic	Late Aztec	Tlatelolco/ Az IV / Tenochtitlan/ Az III
Second Intermediate	Phase Three		Early Aztec	Tenayuca/ Az II / Culhuacan/ Az I
1000 — Second Intermediate	Phase Two	Early Postclassic	Late Toltec	Mazapan
	Phase One	Early Postclassic	Early Toltec	Coyotlatelco
Middle Horizon	Phase Two	Classic	Late Classic	Metepec / Xolalpan
500 — Middle Horizon	Phase One	Classic	Early Classic	Tlamimilolpa
	Phase Five			Miccaotli
A.D. 0 — First	Phase Four	Terminal Formative	Terminal Formative	Tzacualli
B.C. — First	Phase Three	Terminal Formative	Terminal Formative	Patlachique
500 — Intermediate	Phase Two	Late Formative	Late Formative	Ticoman
	Phase One	Middle Formative	Middle Formative	La Pastora
1000				El Arbolillo
				Bomba
Early Horizon	Phase Two	Early Formative	Early Formative	Manantial
	Phase One	Early Formative	Early Formative	Ayotla
1500				Coapexco

5

Table 2. Key to Site Designations. Each Site Designation Contains Three Parts: Sub-region, Chronological Period, and Number Within the Sub-region for a Particular Period.

Sub-Region	Chronological Period	Number
Ch = Chalco	EF = Early Formative	For each time period, site numbers are assigned sequentially within each sub-region. The numbering sequence begins in the NE corner of the sub-region (with the number "1") and terminates in the SW corner.
Xo = Xochimilco	MF = Middle Formative	
Ix = Ixtapalapa	LF = Late Formative	
Tx = Texcoco	TF = Terminal Formative	
Zu = Zumpango	Cl = Classic	
	EC = Early Classic	
	LC = Late Classic	
	ET = Early Toltec	
	LT = Late Toltec	
	Az = Aztec	
	EA = Early Aztec	
	LA = Late Aztec	

6

reports (Parsons 1971; Blanton 1972). We now believe the "Early Classic" division offers a reasonable general picture for overall Classic-period occupation in both the Texcoco and Ixtapalapa Regions. Our analogous subdivision of the Zumpango Region Classic is substantially more accurate and can be taken fairly seriously. For the Chalco-Xochimilco Region, Classic occupation is undifferentiated by site number, although Early and Late components are designated in the "Other Occupations" column.

A special problem exists for the Early Aztec period (Second Intermediate Phase Three) in the Zumpango Region at the far northwestern corner of the Valley of Mexico. This report shows only two Early Aztec sites for this survey area (Zu-Az-259 and Zu-Az-276). However, we strongly suspect that there is actually considerably more occupation than this, most of which is at present unrecognizable because of inadequate knowledge about this part of the ceramic sequence in this area. Our present guess is that most SI-3 occupation in the Zumpango Region is camouflaged by a ceramic assemblage closely related to that of the Tula Region to the north and which is very similar to our Late Toltec pottery in this northern area (see Parsons et al. 1982:371-72, for additional discussion). For the present, we can only recognize this problem and caution against any uncritical acceptance of our apparent near-lack of sites for the Early Aztec period.

A somewhat comparable state of affairs appears to exist for the later part of the Terminal Formative period: the Tzacualli phase (First Intermediate Phase Four). Small quantities of recognizable Tzacualli phase pottery occur in both the Texcoco and Ixtapalapa Regions. Virtually no Tzacualli material was found in the Chalco-Xochimilco Region. For the Texcoco, Ixtapalapa, and Chalco-Xochimilco Regions, occupation from the earlier part of the Terminal Formative period (Patlachique phase, or First Intermediate Phase Three) occurs in great abundance. In the Teotihuacan Valley, both Patlachique and Tzacualli pottery occur in quantity (Sanders et al. 1979). Significant quantities of Tzacualli material have been found in the west-central Valley of Mexico (Rattray 1968) and apparently in eastern Morelos, to the south of the Valley of Mexico (Hirth 1983). Our present interpretation is that the dearth of Tzacualli pottery in the southern Valley of Mexico implies a very small population there during FI-4 times. However, we cannot at present actually demonstrate that spatial ceramic variation, analogous to that which we suggest above for SI-3 times (Early Aztec), was not also characteristic of the later part of the Terminal Formative era.

To further complicate the Terminal Formative picture, it appears that Patlachique phase pottery is lacking in the Zumpango Region. All of the modest Terminal Formative occupation in that area is Tzacualli phase. In any event, in this report all Terminal Formative sites are lumped together, and no differentiation is made between the great majority, which have Patlachique phase pottery, and the small minority, with Tzacualli phase ceramics.

Environmental Zone (Table 3)

These zones are generally identical to those defined in some detail in the longer monographs (Parsons 1971; Blanton 1972; Parsons et al. 1982). In a few cases we have slightly modified our original terminology: (1) by the notation of a site's location on an island or isolated hill in lakebed, lakeshore, or piedmont settings; (2) by a simplification to "Lower Piedmont - Smooth" or "Upper Piedmont - Smooth" of sites in the Ixtapalapa Region originally designated "Cerro Pino Lower Slopes" and "Cerro Pino Upper Slopes," respectively; and (3) by a simplification to "Lower Piedmont - Rugged" or "Upper Piedmont - Rugged" of sites in the Ixtapalapa Region originally designated "Lomas and Hoyas." The terms "Lower Piedmont - Smooth" and "Lower Piedmont - Rugged" are employed only for the southern area (the Chalco-Xochimilco and Ixtapalapa Regions, where Late Pleistocene vulcanism has produced a very contorted piedmont landscape). Elsewhere, the unmodified terms "Lower Piedmont" and "Upper Piedmont" are used exclusively. In the latter cases, the designations "Lower Piedmont" and "Upper Piedmont" are generally environmentally equivalent to "Lower Piedmont - Smooth" and "Upper Piedmont - Smooth," respectively, as these terms are used for the Chalco-Xochimilco and Ixtapalapa Regions. The only significant exception is that the "Lower Piedmont" category for the Zumpango Region also includes land well below 2200 meters, in the upper Rio Salado drainage along the southern edge of the Mezquital (minimal elevation in the Valley of Mexico proper is approximately 2240 meters above sea level).

Site Classification (Table 4)

The terminology used here is essentially that employed by the recent monograph for the Chalco-Xochimilco Region (Parsons et al. 1982:70-71). This is a slightly modified version of earlier terminologies for the Texcoco and Ixtapalapa Regions (Parsons 1971; Blanton 1972), as indicated in Table 4. Site terminology from the latter two areas have been appropriately modified so as to provide a standardized nomenclature for all survey areas.

Universal Transverse Mercator Coordinates

The Universal Transverse Mercator east and north coordinates are given to locate the sites precisely. The coordinates are given in kilometers, to the nearest 0.01 km (10 m). All UTM coordinates given are in Zone 14 (96-102 degrees). The UTM coordinates of the southeast corner of the best available settlement pattern base map were determined through a comparison with 1: 25,000 topographic maps (Secretaria de la Defensa Nacional 1959) with the UTM grid marked. On the base maps, the distance of each site east and north of the southeast corner was measured and added to the corner coordinates yielding the UTM coordinates of the sites. Because of varying quality of the base maps,

Table 3. Environmental Concordances for the Valley of Mexico Settlement Pattern Surveys.

This Report	Parsons et al. 1982	Blanton 1972	Parsons 1971
Lakebed	Lakebed	Lakebed	Lakebed
Lakeshore Plain	Lakeshore Plain	Lakeshore Plain	Lakeshore Plain
Island - Lakeshore Plain			
Lower Piedmont Smooth	Smooth Lower Piedmont	Lower Piedmont Cerro Pino- Lower Slopes	Lower Piedmont
Low Piedmont Hill			
Lower Piedmont Rugged	Rugged Lower Piedmont	Lomas and Hoyas (below 2500 m)	- -
Upper Piedmont Smooth	Smooth Upper Piedmont	Upper Piedmont Cerro Pino- Upper Slopes	Upper Piedmont
Upper Piedmont Rugged	Rugged Upper Piedmont	Lomas and Hoyas (above 2500 m)	- -
Amecameca Sub-Valley	Amecameca Sub-Valley	- -	- -

Table 4. Site Classification Terminology

This Report	Parsons et al. 1982	Blanton 1972	Parsons 1971
Regional Center	Regional Center	Primary Regional Center	Primary Regional Center
Local Center	Local Center	Secondary Regional Center	Secondary Regional Center
Large Nucleated Village	Large Nucleated Village	Village	Large Nucleated Village
Small Nucleated Village	Small Nucleated Village		Small Nucleated Village
Large Dispersed Village	Large Dispersed Village		Large Dispersed Village
Small Dispersed Village	Small Dispersed Village		Small Dispersed Village
Hamlet	Hamlet	Hamlet	Hamlet
Small Hamlet	Small Hamlet	Isolated Residence	
Ceremonial Center	Isolated Ceremonial Precinct	- -	Isolated Ceremonial Precinct
Questionable	Questionable	- -	Camp
Large Elite District	- -	- -	Segregated Elite District
Small Elite District	- -	- -	

UTM coordinates from the Chalco-Xochimilco and Zumpango regions will be more accurate than those from Texcoco and Ixtapalapa.

Site Surface Area

In this report, site area is recorded to the nearest tenth of a hectare. No site is recorded as less than 0.1 hectare, even though, in a few cases, it may actually extend over a smaller area. This duplicates our procedure in the Chalco-Xochimilco Region (Parsons et al. 1982). However, in the original Texcoco and Ixtapalapa reports (Parsons 1971; Blanton 1972), very small sites were simply recorded as "less than 1 hectare." We have gone back over the two latter monographs and made a more precise estimate of these small-site areas, and in this report they are listed at between 0.1 and 0.9 hectares.

For Classic-period sites in the Chalco-Xochimilco Region, where no differentiation between Early and Late sub-periods is made, it is reasonable to assume that site areas for the two components are about the same when they occur together. However, such is not the case for the Early vs. Late Aztec periods. When the latter two co-occur (as can be recognized in the "Other Occupations" column for Aztec sites) the surface area is always that of the dominant component (which is usually, although not always, Late Aztec). Because Early Aztec sites are almost always so overwhelmed by Late Aztec occupation, it has proved difficult for us to measure surface area adequately for most Early Aztec sites. This difficulty is compounded by the fact that Early Aztec utilitarian wares remained poorly defined through the 1970s, and we were usually forced to work with a comparatively small number of low-frequency decorated sherds in defining this occupation.

Other Occupations

This section states how many sites of other periods occur within the borders of any specific site. Although the site numbers of these other-period sites are maintained in the project records, for the sake of compactness only a count is given in the table. By definition, there will be no other sites of the same time period, since sites are defined on the basis of chronology. Thus, for example, site Ch-TF-14 contains no Early Formative site, two Middle Formative sites, one Late Formative site, no other Terminal Formative site (by definition), no Early Classic site, no Late Classic site, one Early Toltec site, no Late Toltec site, no Early Aztec site, and no Late Aztec site.

Temporary Site Number and Survey Supervisor

These data will be of little interest except to those who in the future might have occasion to utilize our original site reports or surface collections. The temporary site numbers were assigned to facilitate field operations, and were not intended for any enduring use. Thus, we employed a series of chronological and geographic referents that were not meant to appear in published form (Table 5). Often these provisional numbers reflect our initial uncertainty about precise chronological placement. For example, the site whose final, published designation was Ch-ET-1, was originally assigned a temporary number of Ch-T-16. This signified that we recognized it as belonging to the general Toltec period, but that we were originally uncertain about its assignment to the Early or Late subdivision of that era. Our temporary site numbers were assigned sequentially by each survey supervisor, to sites as they were encountered and processed during each field season. Thus, the same temporary site numbers could be repeated as many times as there were survey supervisors during any given field season--e.g., the temporary site number Am-LF-5 was assigned twice during the 1972 field season, once by R. Wenke to a site which was subsequently designated Ch-LF-30 in our final report, and once by M. Parsons to a site finally designated as Ch-LF-50.

In some cases the temporary site number was assigned before a site's chronological placement was securely made--thus, the site whose final number is Ch-TF-1 was originally labeled Ch-Cl-10. This was either because it was originally mistakenly identified as a Classic-period occupation, or, more likely, because the Terminal Formative component was not recognized until somewhat later (usually as a result of closer examination of our surface collections). In some cases there were no temporary site numbers assigned to localities which were ultimately designated as sites (e.g., Ch-TF-49). This was usually because a belated decision was made to recognize a site on the basis of examination of the completed field maps rather than during the actual field reconnaissance. This almost always occurred with small, unobtrusive sites whose status was not fully appreciated during ground survey, but whose significance became more apparent after tracing of the original survey airphotos had been completed.

There are no temporary site numbers listed for any sites in the Ixtapalapa Region. They were assigned, of course, but we did not have access to the original records during the period when we were tabulating data for this report.

Site Elevation

Elevations, in meters above sea level, were taken from 1: 25,000 topographic maps (Secretaria de la Defensa Nacional 1959). These maps had a contour interval of 10 meters, and we generally calibrated by eye to the nearest 5 meters, although precision to the nearest meter was occasionally attempted when we felt we could do it adequately. The elevation listed is that of a site's mid-point. Many piedmont sites, of course, actually extend over a considerable vertical range.

Table 5. Guide to Referents in Temporary Site Numbers.

Designation	Significance
	I. Geographic Referents
Ch	Chalco Region (except for Amecameca sub-valley)
Am	Amecameca sub-valley (SE corner of the Chalco Region)
XE	Xochimilco Region, eastern section
XW	Xochimilco Region, western section
Tx	Texcoco Region
Zu	Zumpango Region
	II. Chronological Referents
F	Formative (no specification as to subdivision)
EF	Early Formative
MF	Middle Formative
LF	Late Formative
TF	Terminal Formative
C	Classic (unspecified as to Early or Late)
Cl	Classic (unspecified as to Early or Late)
T	Toltec (unspecified as to Early or Late)
ET	Early Toltec
LT	Late Toltec
A	Aztec (unspecified as to Early or Late)
Az	Aztec (unspecified as to Early or Late)

Site Rainfall

These figures were obtained by superimposing rainfall isohyets from 1: 500,000 climatic maps (Comision de Estudios del Territorio Nacional y Planeacion 1970) onto our 1: 25,000 survey maps, and extrapolating to obtain average annual rainfall for each site locality. This was a fairly straightforward process, accompanied by only minimal uncertainty on our part. The published isohyets were 100 mm, and we attempted to calibrate to the nearest 10 mm (occasionally even a little finer). We are aware that these average rainfall figures do not take evapotranspiration into account, and thus probably fail to make a clear enough climatic distinction between the drier, and sunnier northern valley (Zumpango Region) and the wetter, cloudier south (Chalco-Xochimilco Region).

13

Modern Soil Erosion and Modern Soil Depth (Tables 6 and 7)

These closely related characteristics are subjective categories, determined simply by general "eyeball" appraisal of the site area in the course of recording archaeological features. These data give some indication of how badly the archaeological materials may have been disturbed by physical weathering or obscured by alluviation.

Table 6. Modern Soil Depth Characteristics.

Term	Approximate Depth
Shallow	0-25 cm
Medium	25-100 cm
Deep	>100 cm

Table 7. Severity of Modern Erosion.

Term	Meaning
None	Almost always on flat terrain, with deep soil cover.
Slight	Generally level or very gently sloping terrain, although some protected piedmont areas also occur. Soil depth medium to deep, with little or no active downcutting.
Moderate	Intermediate between slight and deep.
Deep	Generally sloping terrain. Maximum soil depth is shallow, with much exposed subsoil or bedrock. Active downcutting.

THE DATA

CHALCO-XOCHIMILCO REGION - ENVIRONMENTAL DATA
Early Formative Sites

Site Number	Environmental Zone	UTM Coordinates East	North	Elev (in m)	Rainfall (in mm)	Modern Soil Depth	Modern Erosion	Modern Land use
CH-EF-1	Amecameca Sub-Valley	527.64	2114.79	2570	1125	Medium	Slight	Agricultural
CH-EF-2	Amecameca Sub-Valley	527.99	2114.71	2585	1125	Shallow	Moderate-Deep	Agricultural
XO-EF-1	Lakebed	497.23	2132.60	2240	675	Deep	None	Agricultural
XO-EF-2	Lakebed	497.51	2132.06	2240	690	Deep	None	Agricultural

CHALCO-XOCHIMILCO REGION - PREHISPANIC SETTLEMENT DATA
Early Formative Sites

SITE NUMBER	CLASSIFICATION	ENVIRONMENTAL ZONE	AREA (in ha)	POP.	OTHER OCCUPATIONS										SURVEY RECORDS		
					EF	MF	LF	TF	EC	LC	ET	LT	EA	LA	TEMPORARY SITE NO.	SUPERVISOR	YEAR
CH-EF-1	Sm Nucl Village	Amecameca Sub-Valley	8.5	250	0	0	0	0	0	0	0	0	0	0	AM-EF-1	E. PRAHL	1972
CH-EF-2	Sm Nucl Village	Amecameca Sub-Valley	5.2	200	0	0	0	0	0	0	0	0	0	0	AM-EF-2	E. PRAHL	1972
XO-EF-1	Small Hamlet	Lakebed	0.9	10	0	0	0	0	0	0	0	0	0	0	XE-EF-2	M. PARSONS	1972
XO-EF-2	Hamlet	Lakebed	3.7	80	0	0	0	0	0	0	0	0	0	0	XE-EF-1	M. PARSONS	1972

CHALCO-XOCHIMILCO REGION - ENVIRONMENTAL DATA
Middle Formative Sites

Site Number	Environmental Zone	UTM Coordinates East	UTM Coordinates North	Elev (in m)	Rainfall (in mm)	Modern Soil Depth	Modern Erosion	Modern Land use
CH-MF-1	Low Piedmont-Smooth	518.35	2136.13	2390	770	Shallow	Deep	Grazing
CH-MF-2	Low Piedmont-Smooth	518.65	2135.35	2450	780	Medium	Moderate	Agricultural
CH-MF-3	Low Piedmont-Smooth	514.05	2133.75	2280	690	Deep	Slight-Moderate	Agricultural
CH-MF-4	Low Piedmont-Smooth	516.07	2131.47	2300	735	Medium-Deep	Slight-Moderate	Agricultural
CH-MF-5	Low Piedmont-Smooth	518.00	2130.43	2310	775	Medium	Moderate	Agricultural
CH-MF-6	Low Piedmont-Smooth	520.72	2125.38	2410	940	Medium	Moderate	Agricultural
CH-MF-7	Low Piedmont-Smooth	521.30	2125.47	2370	960	Medium	Moderate	Agricultural
CH-MF-8	Low Piedmont-Smooth	517.95	2125.70	2295	830	Medium-Deep	Slight-Moderate	Agricultural
CH-MF-9	Low Piedmont-Rugged	512.20	2122.83	2280	700	Medium-Deep	Moderate	Grazing & Agri
CH-MF-10	Lakeshore Plain	512.95	2124.56	2260	690	Deep	None	Agricultural
CH-MF-11	Lakebed	507.30	2128.28	2240	675	Deep	None	Agricultural
CH-MF-12	Low Piedmont-Rugged	506.20	2123.51	2275	740	Medium	Slight	Agricultural
CH-MF-13	Low Piedmont-Rugged	503.18	2121.58	2440	900	Shallow	Moderate	Agricultural
CH-MF-14	Low Piedmont-Rugged	500.06	2125.33	2310	730	Medium	Slight	Agricultural
CH-MF-15	Lakeshore Plain	499.81	2128.28	2245	710	Medium	Slight-Moderate	Grazing & Agri
XO-MF-1	Lakebed	497.78	2132.35	2240	675	Deep	None	Agricultural
XO-MF-2	Low Piedmont-Rugged	489.73	2127.41	2305	780	Shallow-Med	Moderate	Agricultural

CHALCO-XOCHIMILCO REGION - PREHISPANIC SETTLEMENT DATA
Middle Formative Sites

SITE NUMBER	CLASSIFICATION	ENVIRONMENTAL ZONE	AREA (in ha)	POP.	OTHER OCCUPATIONS EF	MF	LF	TF	EC	LC	ET	LT	EA	LA	TEMPORARY SITE NO.	SURVEY RECORDS SUPERVISOR	YEAR
CH-MF-1	Sm Disp Village	Low Piedmont-Smooth	7.9	160	0	0	0	0	0	0	0	0	0	1	CH-F-18	J. PARSONS	1969
CH-MF-2	Small Hamlet	Low Piedmont-Smooth	2.2	20	0	0	0	0	0	0	0	0	1	1	CH-F-17	J. PARSONS	1969
CH-MF-3	Hamlet	Low Piedmont-Smooth	4.3	40	0	0	1	0	0	0	0	0	0	0	CH-F-15	J. PARSONS	1969
CH-MF-4	Sm Disp Village	Low Piedmont-Smooth	16.9	160	0	0	1	0	0	1	0	0	0	0	CH-F-10	J. PARSONS	1969
CH-MF-5	Lg Nucl Village	Low Piedmont-Smooth	52.8	2160	0	0	0	1	1	0	1	0	0	0	CH-F-4	J. PARSONS	1969
CH-MF-6	Hamlet	Low Piedmont-Smooth	6.2	80	0	0	1	1	0	0	0	0	0	0	CH-F-24	J. PARSONS	1969
CH-MF-7	Hamlet	Low Piedmont-Smooth	3.3	40	0	0	0	1	0	0	0	0	0	0	CH-F-24	J. PARSONS	1969
CH-MF-8	Sm Disp Village	Low Piedmont-Smooth	14.0	150	0	0	1	1	0	0	0	0	0	1	CH-F-13	J. PARSONS	1969
CH-MF-9	Lg Nucl Village	Low Piedmont-Rugged	42.1	1600	0	0	1	1	0	0	0	0	0	0	AM-MF-1	M. PARSONS	1972
CH-MF-10	Small Hamlet	Lakeshore Plain	0.2	10	0	0	1	1	0	0	0	0	0	0	AM-MF-2	M. PARSONS	1972
CH-MF-11	Hamlet	Lakebed	2.8	30	0	0	0	1	0	0	0	0	0	0	CH-F-2	J. PARSONS	1969
CH-MF-12	Hamlet	Low Piedmont-Rugged	3.7	80	0	0	0	0	0	0	0	0	0	0	CH-MF-3	J. PARSONS	1972
CH-MF-13	Small Hamlet	Low Piedmont-Rugged	0.7	10	0	0	0	0	0	0	0	0	0	0	CH-MF-4	J. PARSONS	1972
CH-MF-14	Small Hamlet	Low Piedmont-Rugged	0.7	10	0	0	1	0	1	1	0	0	0	0	CH-MF-2	J. PARSONS	1972
CH-MF-15	Lg Nucl Village	Lakeshore Plain	17.4	700	0	0	0	1	0	0	1	0	1	1	CH-MF-1	J. PARSONS	1972
XO-MF-1	Small Hamlet	Lakebed	0.4	10	0	0	1	1	0	1	0	0	0	0	XE-LF-2	M. PARSONS	1972
XO-MF-2	Lg Nucl Village	Low Piedmont-Rugged	20.3	800	0	0	0	1	1	1	0	0	0	0	XW-MF-1	J. PARSONS	1972

CHALCO-XOCHIMILCO REGION - ENVIRONMENTAL DATA
Late Formative Sites

Site Number	Environmental Zone	UTM Coordinates East	North	Elev (in m)	Rainfall (in mm)	Modern Soil Depth	Modern Erosion	Modern Land use
CH-LF-1	Low Piedmont-Smooth	514.18	2133.88	2275	690	Deep	Slight	Agricultural
CH-LF-2	Low Piedmont-Smooth	516.43	2131.60	2315	740	Medium-Deep	Slight-Moderate	Agricultural
CH-LF-3	Low Piedmont-Smooth	519.05	2133.13	2400	800	Fully Eroded	Deep	None
CH-LF-4	Low Piedmont-Smooth	517.95	2130.55	2310	775	Medium	Moderate	Agricultural
CH-LF-5	Low Piedmont-Smooth	521.30	2125.50	2405	960	Medium	Moderate	Agricultural
CH-LF-6	Low Piedmont-Smooth	518.30	2125.45	2305	840	Medium-Deep	Slight-Moderate	Agricultural
CH-LF-7	Low Piedmont-Smooth	519.10	2123.72	2360	875	Medium	Moderate	Agricultural
CH-LF-8	Low Piedmont-Smooth	519.18	2124.10	2380	890	Medium	Moderate	Agricultural
CH-LF-9	Low Piedmont-Smooth	520.43	2124.03	2365	925	Medium-Deep	Moderate	Agricultural
CH-LF-10	Low Piedmont-Smooth	523.35	2123.57	2440	1030	Deep	Slight	Agricultural
CH-LF-11	Low Piedmont-Smooth	523.43	2122.68	2440	1030	Deep	Slight	Agricultural
CH-LF-12	Low Piedmont-Smooth	515.55	2123.10	2340	780	Medium-Deep	Moderate	Agricultural
CH-LF-13	Low Piedmont-Smooth	515.65	2122.57	2340	800	Medium	Moderate	Agricultural
CH-LF-14	Low Piedmont-Smooth	515.05	2122.32	2290	750	Medium-Deep	Slight-Moderate	Agricultural
CH-LF-15	Low Piedmont-Smooth	516.28	2118.58	2435	840	Shallow	Moderate-Deep	Agricultural
CH-LF-16	Low Piedmont-Smooth	515.60	2117.29	2390	840	Medium	Moderate	Agricultural
CH-LF-17	Low Piedmont-Smooth	516.32	2117.04	2400	860	Shallow-Med	Moderate	Agricultural
CH-LF-18	Low Piedmont-Smooth	517.28	2116.96	2450	900	Medium	Moderate	Agricultural
CH-LF-19	Low Piedmont-Smooth	516.32	2117.04	2450	925	Shallow-Med	Moderate	Agricultural
CH-LF-20	Low Piedmont-Smooth	518.97	2115.86	2425	955	Shallow-Med	Deep	Agricultural
CH-LF-21	Low Piedmont-Smooth	520.28	2116.33	2460	970	Shallow	Deep	Agricultural
CH-LF-22	Upr Piedmont-Rugged	512.03	2113.76	2530	950	Very Shallow	Deep	Agricultural
CH-LF-23	Low Piedmont-Smooth	515.97	2115.04	2440	890	Medium	Slight-Moderate	Agricultural
CH-LF-24	Low Piedmont-Smooth	517.12	2114.63	2420	930	Medium	Moderate	Agricultural
CH-LF-25	Low Piedmont-Rugged	514.60	2113.54	2450	900	Medium	Moderate	Agricultural
CH-LF-26	Upr Piedmont-Rugged	513.95	2113.21	2510	930	Shallow	Moderate	Agricultural
CH-LF-27	Upr Piedmont-Rugged	513.78	2112.26	2550	975	Medium	Moderate	Agricultural
CH-LF-28	Upr Piedmont-Rugged	514.85	2111.88	2540	975	Medium	Moderate	Agricultural
CH-LF-29	Upr Piedmont-Rugged	515.32	2112.11	2510	960	Medium	Moderate	Agricultural
CH-LF-30	Upr Piedmont-Rugged	516.03	2112.21	2550	960	Shallow	Deep	Agricultural
CH-LF-31	Upr Piedmont-Rugged	515.22	2111.56	2550	975	Very Shallow	Deep	Agricultural
CH-LF-32	Low Piedmont-Rugged	518.90	2113.88	2440	990	Fully Eroded	Deep	Agricultural
CH-LF-33	Upr Piedmont-Rugged	519.95	2112.88	2500	1010	Medium	Moderate	Agricultural
CH-LF-34	Low Piedmont-Rugged	520.28	2113.21	2490	1010	Shallow	Deep	Settlement
CH-LF-35	Upr Piedmont-Rugged	520.18	2112.36	2510	1020	Medium	Moderate	Agricultural
CH-LF-36	Amecameca Sub-Valley	522.22	2117.48	2470	1020	Medium	Slight	Agricultural
CH-LF-37	Amecameca Sub-Valley	526.29	2108.46	2520	1130	Medium	Moderate	Agricultural
CH-LF-38	Amecameca Sub-Valley	524.82	2107.88	2440	1100	Shallow-Med	Moderate-Deep	Agricultural
CH-LF-39	Amecameca Sub-Valley	523.97	2107.96	2400	1100	Deep	Moderate	Agricultural
CH-LF-40	Amecameca Sub-Valley	525.00	2108.58	2400	1100	Deep	Moderate	Agricultural
CH-LF-41	Low Piedmont-Rugged	522.95	2108.41	2400	1080	Deep	Moderate	Agricultural
CH-LF-42	Low Piedmont-Rugged	521.60	2107.88	2400	1070	Medium	Moderate	Grazing & Agri

CHALCO-XOCHIMILCO REGION - PREHISPANIC SETTLEMENT DATA
Late Formative Sites

SITE NUMBER	CLASSIFICATION	ENVIRONMENTAL ZONE	AREA (in ha)	POP.	OTHER OCCUPATIONS EF	MF	LF	TF	EC	LC	ET	LT	EA	LA	SURVEY RECORDS TEMPORARY SITE NO.	SUPERVISOR	YEAR
CH-LF-1	Lg Nucl Village	Low Piedmont-Smooth	59.7	2400	0	1	0	0	1	3	0	2	1	1	CH-F-15	J. PARSONS	1969
CH-LF-2	Lg Nucl Village	Low Piedmont-Smooth	67.0	2700	0	1	0	0	0	1	0	1	1	1	CH-F-10	J. PARSONS	1969
CH-LF-3	Small Hamlet	Low Piedmont-Smooth	0.3	10	0	0	0	0	0	0	0	0	0	0	CH-LF-4	J. PARSONS	1972
CH-LF-4	Lg Nucl Village	Low Piedmont-Smooth	34.8	1000	0	1	0	0	1	1	0	1	0	0	CH-F-4	J. PARSONS	1969
CH-LF-5	Local Center	Low Piedmont-Smooth	130.0	5200	0	2	0	1	0	0	1	0	0	0	CH-F-24	J. PARSONS	1969
CH-LF-6	Local Center	Low Piedmont-Smooth	86.0	3400	0	1	0	1	2	2	0	0	1	1	CH-F-13	J. PARSONS	1969
CH-LF-7	Hamlet	Low Piedmont-Smooth	7.2	70	0	0	0	0	0	0	0	0	0	0	CH-F-34	J. PARSONS	1969
CH-LF-8	Small Hamlet	Low Piedmont-Smooth	1.0	10	0	0	0	0	0	0	0	0	0	0	CH-F-33	J. PARSONS	1969
CH-LF-9	Sm Disp Village	Low Piedmont-Smooth	17.8	300	0	0	0	1	0	0	0	1	0	0	CH-F-24	J. PARSONS	1969
CH-LF-10	Small Hamlet	Low Piedmont-Smooth	1.9	10	0	0	0	0	0	0	0	0	0	0	CH-F-28	M. PARSONS	1969
CH-LF-11	Small Hamlet	Low Piedmont-Smooth	1.6	15	0	0	0	0	0	0	0	0	0	0	CH-F-29	M. PARSONS	1969
CH-LF-12	Lg Nucl Village	Low Piedmont-Smooth	43.2	1700	0	0	0	1	0	0	0	1	0	0	CH-F-31	M. PARSONS	1969
CH-LF-13	Hamlet	Low Piedmont-Smooth	3.5	40	0	0	0	1	0	0	0	0	0	0	CH-F-32	M. PARSONS	1969
CH-LF-14	Hamlet	Low Piedmont-Smooth	4.2	50	0	0	0	1	0	0	0	0	1	1	CH-F-35	M. PARSONS	1969
CH-LF-15	Sm Nucl Village	Low Piedmont-Smooth	14.0	500	0	0	0	0	0	0	0	0	1	1	AM-F-2	M. PARSONS	1972
CH-LF-16	Sm Disp Village	Low Piedmont-Smooth	19.7	400	0	0	0	1	0	0	0	0	0	1	AM-F-3	M. PARSONS	1972
CH-LF-17	Small Hamlet	Low Piedmont-Smooth	1.3	20	0	0	0	0	0	0	0	0	0	0	AM-F-11	M. PARSONS	1972
CH-LF-18	Hamlet	Low Piedmont-Smooth	4.5	50	0	0	0	0	0	0	0	0	0	0	AM-F-12	M. PARSONS	1972
CH-LF-19	Small Hamlet	Low Piedmont-Smooth	1.0	20	0	0	0	0	0	0	1	0	0	1		M. PARSONS	1972
CH-LF-20	Lg Nucl Village	Low Piedmont-Smooth	73.6	3000	0	0	0	1	0	0	0	0	0	0	AM-LF-16	M. PARSONS	1972
CH-LF-21	Small Hamlet	Low Piedmont-Smooth	0.6	10	0	0	0	0	0	0	0	0	0	0	AM-LF-6	E. PRAHL	1972
CH-LF-22	Small Hamlet	Upr Piedmont-Rugged	1.3	10	0	0	0	0	0	0	0	0	0	0	AM-LF-1	M. PARSONS	1972
CH-LF-23	Hamlet	Low Piedmont-Smooth	2.3	50	0	0	0	1	0	0	0	0	1	1	AM-F-14	M. PARSONS	1972
CH-LF-24	Small Hamlet	Low Piedmont-Smooth	0.6	10	0	0	0	0	0	0	0	0	0	0	AM-F-9	M. PARSONS	1972
CH-LF-25	Small Hamlet	Low Piedmont-Rugged	0.6	10	0	0	0	0	0	0	0	0	0	0	AM-F-6	M. PARSONS	1972
CH-LF-26	Hamlet	Upr Piedmont-Rugged	1.9	20	0	0	0	1	0	0	0	0	0	0	AM-F-8	M. PARSONS	1972
CH-LF-27	Small Hamlet	Upr Piedmont-Rugged	3.5	20	0	0	0	0	0	0	0	0	0	0	AM-LF-4	R. WENKE	1972
CH-LF-28	Small Hamlet	Upr Piedmont-Rugged	2.5	20	0	0	0	0	0	0	0	0	0	0	AM-LF-3	R. WENKE	1972
CH-LF-29	Small Hamlet	Upr Piedmont-Rugged	1.0	20	0	0	0	1	0	0	0	0	1	1	AM-LF-1	R. WENKE	1972
CH-LF-30	Small Hamlet	Upr Piedmont-Rugged	1.3	10	0	0	0	1	0	0	0	0	0	0	AM-LF-5	R. WENKE	1972
CH-LF-31	Small Hamlet	Upr Piedmont-Rugged	2.8	20	0	0	0	0	0	0	0	0	0	0	AM-LF-2	R. WENKE	1972
CH-LF-32	Hamlet	Low Piedmont-Rugged	4.5	50	0	0	0	1	0	0	0	0	0	0	AM-LF-3	M. PARSONS	1972
CH-LF-33	Small Hamlet	Upr Piedmont-Rugged	2.6	20	0	0	0	0	0	0	0	0	0	0	AM-LF-4	E. PRAHL	1972
CH-LF-34	Small Hamlet	Low Piedmont-Rugged	0.9	10	0	0	0	1	0	0	0	0	0	0	AM-LF-2	E. PRAHL	1972
CH-LF-35	Small Hamlet	Upr Piedmont-Rugged	3.4	20	0	0	0	1	0	0	0	0	0	0	AM-LF-3	E. PRAHL	1972
CH-LF-36	Sm Disp Village	Amecameca Sub-Valley	10.0	200	0	0	0	0	0	0	0	0	0	0	AM-LF-1	E. PRAHL	1972
CH-LF-37	Sm Disp Village	Amecameca Sub-Valley	7.8	160	0	0	0	0	0	0	0	0	0	0		E. PRAHL	1972
CH-LF-38	Hamlet	Amecameca Sub-Valley	7.6	100	0	0	0	0	0	0	0	0	0	0	AM-LF-8	E. PRAHL	1972
CH-LF-39	Small Hamlet	Amecameca Sub-Valley	2.0	20	0	0	0	0	0	0	0	0	0	0	AM-LF-12	E. PRAHL	1972
CH-LF-40	Small Hamlet	Amecameca Sub-Valley	1.0	10	0	0	0	0	0	0	0	0	0	0	AM-LF-13	E. PRAHL	1972
CH-LF-41	Small Hamlet	Low Piedmont-Rugged	0.5	10	0	0	0	0	0	0	0	0	0	0	AM-LF-11	E. PRAHL	1972
CH-LF-42	Small Hamlet	Low Piedmont-Rugged	1.4	10	0	0	0	0	0	0	0	0	0	0	AM-LF-9	E. PRAHL	1972

CHALCO-XOCHIMILCO REGION - ENVIRONMENTAL DATA
Late Formative Sites

Site Number	Environmental Zone	UTM Coordinates East	North	Elev (in m)	Rainfall (in mm)	Modern Soil Depth	Modern Erosion	Modern Land Use
CH-LF-43	Low Piedmont-Rugged	520.95	2108.19	2450	1060	Medium	Moderate	Grazing & Agri
CH-LF-44	Low Piedmont-Rugged	519.10	2107.91	2415	1050	Medium	Moderate	Agricultural
CH-LF-45	Low Piedmont-Rugged	518.70	2108.01	2440	1050	Medium	Moderate	Agricultural
CH-LF-46	Low Piedmont-Rugged	510.75	2122.66	2270	715	Medium	Moderate	Grazing & Agri
CH-LF-47	Lakeshore Plain	512.80	2124.54	2255	690	Deep	None	Agricultural
CH-LF-48	Low Piedmont-Smooth	514.43	2127.53	2280	695	Deep	Slight	Agricultural
CH-LF-49	Lakeshore Plain	509.50	2126.13	2245	690	Deep	None	Agricultural
CH-LF-50	Low Piedmont-Rugged	508.38	2123.71	2275	725	Medium	Deep	Agricultural
CH-LF-51	Lakebed	507.40	2128.35	2240	670	Deep	None	Agricultural
CH-LF-52	Island-Lakesh Plain	507.20	2129.70	2248	665	Medium-Deep	Slight-Moderate	Agricultural
CH-LF-53	Lakeshore Plain	499.73	2128.23	2248	720	Medium	Moderate	Agricultural
CH-LF-54	Lakebed	500.16	2129.95	2240	675	Deep	None	Agricultural
CH-LF-55	Upr Piedmont-Rugged	513.10	2121.13	2690	860	Shallow	Moderate	Grazing & Agri
XO-LF-1	Lakeshore Plain	497.96	2132.85	2245	675	Deep	None	Agricultural
XO-LF-2	Lakebed	497.48	2132.45	2240	680	Deep	None	Agricultural
XO-LF-3	Lakebed	498.08	2132.03	2240	680	Deep	None	Agricultural
XO-LF-4	Low Piedmont-Hill	486.12	2129.18	2400	750	Very Shallow	Deep	Grazing
XO-LF-5	Lakeshore Plain	485.72	2129.23	2265	780	Deep	Slight	Agricultural

CHALCO-XOCHIMILCO REGION - PREHISPANIC SETTLEMENT DATA
Late Formative Sites

SITE NUMBER	CLASSIFICATION	ENVIRONMENTAL ZONE	AREA (in ha)	POP.	OTHER OCCUPATIONS										TEMPORARY SITE NO.	SURVEY RECORDS	
					EF	MF	LF	TF	EC	LC	ET	LT	EA	LA		SUPERVISOR	YEAR
CH-LF-43	Small Hamlet	Low Piedmont-Rugged	0.9	10	0	0	0	0	0	0	0	0	0	1	AM-LF-10	E. PRAHL	1972
CH-LF-44	Hamlet	Low Piedmont-Rugged	3.5	50	0	0	0	0	0	0	0	0	0	0	AM-LF-7	R. WENKE	1972
CH-LF-45	Small Hamlet	Low Piedmont-Rugged	0.8	10	0	0	0	0	0	0	0	0	0	0	AM-LF-6	R. WENKE	1972
CH-LF-46	Hamlet	Low Piedmont-Rugged	5.3	100	0	1	0	0	0	0	0	0	0	0	AM-LF-4	M. PARSONS	1972
CH-LF-47	Small Hamlet	Lakeshore Plain	0.2	10	0	1	0	0	0	0	0	0	0	0	AM-LF-6	M. PARSONS	1972
CH-LF-48	Sm Nucl Village	Low Piedmont-Smooth	11.8	480	0	0	0	1	1	1	0	0	0	0	CH-F-6	J. PARSONS	1969
CH-LF-49	Small Hamlet	Lakeshore Plain	0.7	10	0	0	0	1	1	1	1	0	0	0	CH-LF-3	J. PARSONS	1972
CH-LF-50	Lg Nucl Village	Low Piedmont-Rugged	17.8	800	0	0	0	1	1	1	1	0	0	0	AM-LF-5	M. PARSONS	1972
CH-LF-51	Hamlet	Lakebed	2.8	40	0	1	0	0	0	0	0	0	0	0	CH-F-2	J. PARSONS	1969
CH-LF-52	Hamlet	Island-Lakesh Plain	5.2	50	0	0	0	1	1	1	1	0	0	0	CH-F-1	J. PARSONS	1969
CH-LF-53	Lg Nucl Village	Lakeshore Plain	20.5	840	0	1	0	1	1	1	0	1	0	1	CH-LF-1	J. PARSONS	1972
CH-LF-54	Small Hamlet	Lakebed	0.6	20	0	0	0	0	0	0	0	0	0	0	CH-LF-4	R. WENKE	1972
CH-LF-55	Ceremonial Ctr	Upr Piedmont-Rugged	0.6	0	0	0	0	0	0	0	0	0	0	0	CH-LF-2	J. PARSONS	1972
XO-LF-1	Small Hamlet	Lakeshore Plain	0.2	5	0	0	0	0	0	0	0	0	0	0		M. PARSONS	1972
XO-LF-2	Sm Nucl Village	Lakebed	8.6	350	0	1	0	0	0	0	0	0	0	0	XE-LF-2	M. PARSONS	1972
XO-LF-3	Small Hamlet	Lakebed	0.7	20	0	0	0	0	0	0	0	0	1	1	XE-LF-1	M. PARSONS	1972
XO-LF-4	Questionable	Low Piedmont-Hill	1.1	0	0	0	0	1	0	0	0	0	0	0	XW-LF-3	J. PARSONS	1972
XO-LF-5	Hamlet	Lakeshore Plain	2.0	50	0	0	0	0	0	0	0	0	0	0	XW-LF-1	J. PARSONS	1972

CHALCO-XOCHIMILCO REGION - ENVIRONMENTAL DATA
Terminal Formative Sites

Site Number	Environmental Zone	UTM Coordinates East	North	Elev (in m)	Rainfall (in mm)	Modern Soil Depth	Modern Erosion	Modern Land use
CH-TF-1	Low Piedmont-Smooth	514.50	2133.15	2280	690	Deep	Slight-Moderate	Agricultural
CH-TF-2	Low Piedmont-Smooth	520.55	2130.72	2410	900	Shallow-Med	Moderate-Deep	None
CH-TF-3	Low Piedmont-Smooth	520.65	2129.10	2370	1000	Very Shallow	Deep	Grazing
CH-TF-4	Lakeshore Plain	514.32	2129.28	2260	700	Deep	Slight	Agricultural
CH-TF-5	Lakeshore Plain	514.32	2128.63	2260	695	Deep	Very Slight	Agricultural
CH-TF-6	Lakeshore Plain	512.43	2128.25	2245	680	Deep	None	Agricultural
CH-TF-7	Low Piedmont-Smooth	513.70	2126.55	2275	695	Medium-Deep	Slight	Agricultural
CH-TF-8	Low Piedmont-Hill	514.22	2126.95	2420	685	Shallow	Moderate-Deep	Grazing
CH-TF-9	Low Piedmont-Smooth	514.82	2126.93	2315	695	Medium-Deep	Slight-Moderate	Agricultural
CH-TF-10	Lakeshore Plain	515.65	2127.50	2265	720	Deep	Very Slight	Agricultural
CH-TF-11	Low Piedmont-Smooth	520.18	2127.80	2305	900	Shallow-Med	Moderate-Deep	Agricultural
CH-TF-12	Low Piedmont-Smooth	520.47	2127.30	2335	920	Medium	Moderate	Agricultural
CH-TF-13	Low Piedmont-Smooth	520.62	2126.88	2340	920	Medium	Moderate	Agricultural
CH-TF-14	Low Piedmont-Smooth	521.32	2125.47	2405	960	Medium	Moderate	Agricultural
CH-TF-15	Low Piedmont-Smooth	520.37	2123.95	2365	925	Medium-Deep	Moderate	Agricultural
CH-TF-16	Low Piedmont-Smooth	518.30	2125.45	2305	850	Medium-Deep	Slight-Moderate	Agricultural
CH-TF-17	Low Piedmont-Smooth	517.62	2126.32	2270	820	Deep	Very Slight	Agricultural
CH-TF-18	Low Piedmont-Smooth	516.60	2126.35	2270	780	Deep	Very Slight	Agricultural
CH-TF-19	Low Piedmont-Smooth	515.52	2125.63	2285	720	Medium-Deep	Slight-Moderate	Agricultural
CH-TF-20	Low Piedmont-Smooth	515.55	2123.10	2360	775	Medium-Deep	Moderate	Agricultural
CH-TF-21	Low Piedmont-Smooth	515.65	2122.57	2340	790	Medium	Moderate	Agricultural
CH-TF-22	Low Piedmont-Smooth	515.15	2122.28	2290	760	Medium-Deep	Slight-Moderate	Agricultural
CH-TF-23	Low Piedmont-Smooth	514.47	2119.63	2330	780	Shallow-Med	Moderate	Agricultural
CH-TF-24	Low Piedmont-Smooth	516.28	2118.26	2425	1100	Shallow	Moderate-Deep	Agricultural
CH-TF-25	Low Piedmont-Smooth	515.30	2117.31	2390	800	Medium	Moderate	Agricultural
CH-TF-26	Upr Piedmont-Rugged	511.20	2116.08	2640	875	Medium	Slight-Moderate	Agricultural
CH-TF-27	Upr Piedmont-Rugged	511.05	2113.61	2550	1000	Shallow	Moderate-Deep	Agricultural
CH-TF-28	Low Piedmont-Rugged	514.00	2115.54	2440	850	Medium	Slight-Moderate	Agricultural
CH-TF-29	Low Piedmont-Rugged	513.28	2114.73	2470	860	Shallow	Deep	Grazing & Agri
CH-TF-30	Low Piedmont-Rugged	514.03	2113.63	2470	900	Medium	Moderate	Agricultural
CH-TF-31	Upr Piedmont-Rugged	513.95	2113.16	2520	925	Medium	Moderate	Agricultural
CH-TF-32	Low Piedmont-Smooth	514.62	2115.71	2430	850	Medium	Moderate	Agricultural
CH-TF-33	Low Piedmont-Smooth	515.47	2115.51	2430	880	Medium	Moderate	Agricultural
CH-TF-34	Low Piedmont-Smooth	515.80	2115.29	2440	890	Medium	Moderate	Agricultural
CH-TF-35	Low Piedmont-Smooth	515.95	2114.71	2440	900	Medium	Slight	Agricultural
CH-TF-36	Low Piedmont-Smooth	516.95	2115.51	2440	1100	Shallow	Deep	Grazing
CH-TF-37	Low Piedmont-Smooth	516.97	2115.01	2450	980	Medium	Moderate	Agricultural
CH-TF-38	Low Piedmont-Smooth	517.55	2115.23	2420	880	Shallow	Moderate	Grazing & Agri
CH-TF-39	Low Piedmont-Smooth	518.45	2116.06	2440	950	Medium	Moderate-Deep	Agricultural
CH-TF-40	Low Piedmont-Smooth	518.70	2115.46	2400	960	Medium	Moderate	Agricultural
CH-TF-41	Low Piedmont-Smooth	519.25	2115.81	2420	950	Shallow	Moderate-Deep	Agricultural
CH-TF-42	Low Piedmont-Smooth	518.43	2115.04	2410	950	Shallow	Moderate-Deep	Agricultural

CHALCO-XOCHIMILCO REGION - PREHISPANIC SETTLEMENT DATA
Terminal Formative Sites

SITE NUMBER	CLASSIFICATION	ENVIRONMENTAL ZONE	AREA (in ha)	POP.	EF	MF	LF	TF	EC	LC	ET	LT	EA	LA	TEMPORARY SITE NO.	SUPERVISOR	YEAR
CH-TF-1	Hamlet	Low Piedmont-Smooth	2.5	30	0	0	0	0	0	0	1	0	0	0	CH-CL-10	J. PARSONS	1969
CH-TF-2	Hamlet	Low Piedmont-Smooth	3.9	50	0	0	0	0	1	1	0	0	0	0	CH-F-20	J. PARSONS	1969
CH-TF-3	Hamlet	Low Piedmont-Smooth	3.4	30	0	0	0	0	0	0	1	0	1	1	CH-F-22	M. PARSONS	1969
CH-TF-4	Hamlet	Lakeshore Plain	4.1	50	0	0	0	0	0	0	0	0	0	0	CH-F-9	M. PARSONS	1969
CH-TF-5	Hamlet	Lakeshore Plain	8.5	100	0	0	0	0	0	0	1	0	1	0	CH-F-8	J. PARSONS	1969
CH-TF-6	Sm Disp Village	Lakeshore Plain	20.9	400	0	0	0	0	0	0	0	0	1	1	CH-F-3	J. PARSONS	1969
CH-TF-7	Questionable	Low Piedmont-Smooth	11.1	300	0	0	0	0	0	0	0	0	0	0	CH-F-14	J. PARSONS	1969
CH-TF-8	Ceremonial Ctr	Low Piedmont-Hill	2.0	0	0	0	0	0	0	0	0	0	0	1	CH-F-5	J. PARSONS	1969
CH-TF-9	Local Center	Low Piedmont-Smooth	75.0	3000	0	0	0	0	1	1	0	0	0	0	CH-F-6	J. PARSONS	1969
CH-TF-10	Hamlet	Lakeshore Plain	5.2	80	0	0	0	0	0	0	0	0	0	0	CH-F-7	J. PARSONS	1969
CH-TF-11	Sm Disp Village	Low Piedmont-Smooth	10.6	200	0	0	0	0	0	0	1	1	0	0	CH-F-19	M. PARSONS	1969
CH-TF-12	Hamlet	Low Piedmont-Smooth	4.1	40	0	0	0	0	0	0	1	0	1	1	CH-F-27	M. PARSONS	1969
CH-TF-13	Hamlet	Low Piedmont-Smooth	4.7	40	0	0	0	0	0	0	0	0	0	0	CH-F-25	M. PARSONS	1969
CH-TF-14	Local Center	Low Piedmont-Smooth	129.0	4000	0	2	1	0	0	0	1	0	0	0	CH-F-24	J. PARSONS	1969
CH-TF-15	Sm Disp Village	Low Piedmont-Smooth	23.6	240	0	1	0	0	0	0	1	1	0	0	CH-F-4	J. PARSONS	1969
CH-TF-16	Local Center	Low Piedmont-Smooth	74.6	2200	0	1	1	0	2	2	1	1	1	1	CH-F-13	J. PARSONS	1969
CH-TF-17	Small Hamlet	Low Piedmont-Smooth	0.9	10	0	0	0	0	0	0	0	0	0	0	CH-F-12	J. PARSONS	1969
CH-TF-18	Small Hamlet	Low Piedmont-Smooth	0.8	10	0	0	0	0	1	0	0	0	0	0	CH-C-7	J. PARSONS	1969
CH-TF-19	Lg Nucl Village	Low Piedmont-Smooth	35.2	1200	0	0	0	0	0	0	0	0	1	1	CH-F-11	J. PARSONS	1969
CH-TF-20	Hamlet	Low Piedmont-Smooth	8.7	100	0	1	0	0	0	0	1	0	0	0	CH-F-31	M. PARSONS	1969
CH-TF-21	Small Hamlet	Low Piedmont-Smooth	2.0	20	0	1	0	0	0	0	0	0	0	0	CH-F-32	M. PARSONS	1969
CH-TF-22	Hamlet	Low Piedmont-Smooth	4.2	40	0	1	0	0	0	0	1	0	1	0	CH-F-35	M. PARSONS	1969
CH-TF-23	Sm Disp Village	Low Piedmont-Smooth	12.3	240	0	0	0	0	0	0	0	0	0	0	AM-F-1	M. PARSONS	1972
CH-TF-24	Sm Disp Village	Low Piedmont-Smooth	12.7	250	0	1	0	0	0	0	1	0	1	1	AM-F-2	M. PARSONS	1972
CH-TF-25	Sm Disp Village	Low Piedmont-Smooth	7.3	150	0	0	0	0	0	0	0	0	0	1	AM-F-3	M. PARSONS	1972
CH-TF-26	Hamlet	Upr Piedmont-Rugged	1.7	30	0	0	0	0	0	0	0	0	0	0	AM-TF-1	M. PARSONS	1972
CH-TF-27	Small Hamlet	Upr Piedmont-Rugged	0.3	10	0	0	0	0	0	0	0	0	0	1	AM-LT-6	M. PARSONS	1972
CH-TF-28	Small Hamlet	Low Piedmont-Rugged	1.2	15	0	0	0	0	0	0	0	0	0	0	AM-F-7	M. PARSONS	1972
CH-TF-29	Small Hamlet	Low Piedmont-Rugged	1.5	10	0	0	0	0	1	0	0	0	0	0	AM-F-10	M. PARSONS	1972
CH-TF-30	Small Hamlet	Low Piedmont-Rugged	0.9	10	0	0	0	0	0	1	0	0	0	0	AM-CL-6	M. PARSONS	1972
CH-TF-31	Hamlet	Upr Piedmont-Rugged	1.8	30	0	1	0	0	1	0	0	0	1	0	AM-F-8	M. PARSONS	1972
CH-TF-32	Hamlet	Low Piedmont-Smooth	5.7	100	0	0	0	0	0	0	0	0	0	1	AM-F-4	M. PARSONS	1972
CH-TF-33	Hamlet	Low Piedmont-Smooth	2.6	30	0	0	0	0	0	0	0	0	0	1	AM-F-5	M. PARSONS	1972
CH-TF-34	Small Hamlet	Low Piedmont-Smooth	0.9	10	0	0	0	0	0	0	0	0	0	0	AM-CL-10	M. PARSONS	1972
CH-TF-35	Hamlet	Low Piedmont-Smooth	2.3	50	0	1	0	0	1	0	0	0	1	0	AM-F-14	M. PARSONS	1972
CH-TF-36	Small Hamlet	Low Piedmont-Smooth	2.4	20	0	0	0	0	0	0	0	0	0	0	AM-F-13	M. PARSONS	1972
CH-TF-37	Small Hamlet	Low Piedmont-Smooth	0.7	10	0	1	0	0	1	0	0	0	1	0	AM-F-15	M. PARSONS	1972
CH-TF-38	Small Hamlet	Low Piedmont-Smooth	1.3	10	0	0	0	0	1	0	0	0	1	1	AM-CL-11	M. PARSONS	1972
CH-TF-39	Small Hamlet	Low Piedmont-Smooth	1.7	20	0	0	0	0	0	0	0	0	0	0	AM-TF-5	M. PARSONS	1972
CH-TF-40	Hamlet	Low Piedmont-Smooth	7.5	60	0	1	0	0	0	0	0	0	1	0	AM-LF-16	M. PARSONS	1972
CH-TF-41	Small Hamlet	Low Piedmont-Smooth	1.2	15	0	0	0	0	0	0	1	0	0	0	AM-LF-16	M. PARSONS	1972
CH-TF-42	Small Hamlet	Low Piedmont-Smooth	0.8	10	0	1	0	0	0	0	0	0	0	0	AM-LF-16	M. PARSONS	1972

CHALCO-XOCHIMILCO REGION - ENVIRONMENTAL DATA
Terminal Formative Sites

Site Number	Environmental Zone	UTM Coordinates East	North	Elev (in m)	Rainfall (in mm)	Modern Soil Depth	Modern Erosion	Modern Land use
CH-TF-43	Low Piedmont-Rugged	519.15	2113.83	2450	1000	Shallow-Med	Moderate-Deep	Agricultural
CH-TF-44	Low Piedmont-Rugged	519.47	2113.54	2460	1000	Medium	Moderate	Agricultural
CH-TF-45	Low Piedmont-Rugged	520.30	2113.19	2500	1000	Shallow	Deep	Agricultural
CH-TF-46	Amecameca Sub-Valley	521.70	2113.79	2470	1020	Medium	Moderate	Agricultural
CH-TF-47	Amecameca Sub-Valley	524.55	2116.21	2470	1060	Deep	Slight	Agricultural
CH-TF-48	Amecameca Sub-Valley	525.40	2115.83	2480	1060	Deep	Slight	Agricultural
CH-TF-49	Amecameca Sub-Valley	523.97	2111.56	2480	1070	Medium	Moderate	Agricultural
CH-TF-50	Upr Piedmont-Rugged	520.22	2112.61	2520	1000	Medium	Moderate	Agricultural
CH-TF-51	Low Piedmont-Rugged	518.10	2111.26	2480	1010	Medium	Moderate	Agricultural
CH-TF-52	Upr Piedmont-Rugged	516.05	2112.08	2510	975	Shallow	Deep	Agricultural
CH-TF-53	Upr Piedmont-Rugged	515.28	2112.01	2500	980	Medium	Moderate	Agricultural
CH-TF-54	Upr Piedmont-Rugged	511.93	2112.66	2540	1000	Medium	Moderate	Agricultural
CH-TF-55	Low Piedmont-Rugged	512.07	2122.48	2280	700	Medium	Slight	Grazing & Agri
CH-TF-56	Lakeshore Plain	512.55	2122.83	2260	700	Deep	Slight	Agricultural
CH-TF-57	Lakeshore Plain	509.55	2126.23	2245	690	Deep	None	Agricultural
CH-TF-58	Island-Lakesh Plain	507.25	2129.78	2248	665	Deep	Slight	Agricultural
CH-TF-59	Low Piedmont-Rugged	508.68	2123.61	2280	725	Medium	Moderate	Agricultural
CH-TF-60	Lakeshore Plain	502.45	2124.38	2245	730	Deep	None	Agricultural
CH-TF-61	Low Piedmont-Rugged	501.55	2123.56	2305	760	Shallow-Med	Slight-Moderate	Agricultural
CH-TF-62	Low Piedmont-Rugged	500.11	2125.03	2300	740	Medium	Moderate	Agricultural
CH-TF-63	Lakeshore Plain	499.38	2127.98	2273	790	Medium-Deep	Slight-Moderate	Agricultural
XO-TF-1	Low Piedmont-Rugged	496.51	2128.43	2300	780	Medium	Moderate	Agricultural
XO-TF-2	Low Piedmont-Rugged	493.48	2127.75	2360	750	Medium	Moderate	Agricultural
XO-TF-3	Low Piedmont-Rugged	490.61	2127.41	2330	780	Shallow-Med	Moderate	Agricultural
XO-TF-4	Low Piedmont-Rugged	489.73	2127.41	2315	780	Shallow-Med	Moderate	Agricultural
XO-TF-5	Low Piedmont-Hill	485.77	2129.35	2470	780	Very Shallow	Deep	Grazing
XO-TF-6	Low Piedmont-Rugged	484.74	2131.06	2270	790	Deep	Slight	Agricultural
XO-TF-7	Low Piedmont-Rugged	484.39	2130.88	2280	795	Medium	Moderate	Agricultural
XO-TF-8	Low Piedmont-Rugged	484.74	2131.58	2270	790	Deep	Slight	Agricultural
XO-TF-9	Low Piedmont-Rugged	480.69	2132.25	2270	890	Shallow	Moderate-Deep	Grazing & Agri

CHALCO-XOCHIMILCO REGION - PREHISPANIC SETTLEMENT DATA
Terminal Formative Sites

SITE NUMBER	CLASSIFICATION	ENVIRONMENTAL ZONE	AREA (in ha)	POP.	OTHER OCCUPATIONS										SURVEY RECORDS		
					EF	MF	LF	TF	EC	LC	ET	LT	EA	LA	TEMPORARY SITE NO.	SUPERVISOR	YEAR
CH-TF-43	Sm Disp Village	Low Piedmont-Rugged	7.5	150	0	0	0	1	0	0	0	0	0	0	AM-TF-4	M. PARSONS	1972
CH-TF-44	Small Hamlet	Low Piedmont-Rugged	2.7	20	0	0	0	0	0	0	0	0	0	0	AM-TF-2	E. PRAHL	1972
CH-TF-45	Small Hamlet	Low Piedmont-Rugged	0.9	20	0	0	1	0	0	0	0	0	0	0	AM-LF-2	E. PRAHL	1972
CH-TF-46	Sm Disp Village	Amecameca Sub-Valley	11.2	200	0	0	0	0	0	0	0	0	0	0	AM-TF-1	E. PRAHL	1972
CH-TF-47	Hamlet	Amecameca Sub-Valley	4.2	50	0	0	0	0	0	0	0	0	0	0	AM-TF-3	E. PRAHL	1972
CH-TF-48	Small Hamlet	Amecameca Sub-Valley	1.5	20	0	0	0	0	0	0	0	1	0	0	AM-TF-7	J. PARSONS	1972
CH-TF-49	Small Hamlet	Amecameca Sub-Valley	0.8	10	0	1	0	0	0	0	0	0	0	0		E. PRAHL	1972
CH-TF-50	Small Hamlet	Upr Piedmont-Rugged	0.6	10	0	0	1	0	0	0	0	0	0	0	AM-LF-3	E. PRAHL	1972
CH-TF-51	Small Hamlet	Low Piedmont-Rugged	0.5	10	0	0	0	1	0	0	0	0	0	0	AM-CL-5	R. WENKE	1972
CH-TF-52	Small Hamlet	Upr Piedmont-Rugged	0.5	10	0	0	1	0	0	0	0	0	0	0	AM-LF-5	R. WENKE	1972
CH-TF-53	Small Hamlet	Upr Piedmont-Rugged	0.6	10	0	0	0	0	0	0	0	0	1	0	AM-LF-1	R. WENKE	1972
CH-TF-54	Hamlet	Upr Piedmont-Rugged	10.4	50	0	0	0	2	0	0	0	0	0	0	AM-TF-2	R. WENKE	1972
CH-TF-55	Sm Disp Village	Low Piedmont-Rugged	14.0	280	0	1	1	0	0	0	0	0	0	0	AM-TF-3	M. PARSONS	1972
CH-TF-56	Small Hamlet	Lakeshore Plain	0.4	10	0	1	0	0	0	1	0	0	0	0	AM-LT-17	M. PARSONS	1972
CH-TF-57	Small Hamlet	Lakeshore Plain	0.7	10	0	0	1	1	1	1	0	0	0	0	CH-LF-3	J. PARSONS	1972
CH-TF-58	Hamlet	Island-Lakesh Plain	8.7	100	0	0	0	1	1	1	0	1	0	0	CH-TF-9	J. PARSONS	1969
CH-TF-59	Lg Nucl Village	Low Piedmont-Rugged	43.4	1800	0	0	1	0	1	1	0	0	0	0	AM-TF-6	M. PARSONS	1972
CH-TF-60	Hamlet	Lakeshore Plain	3.8	50	0	0	0	0	0	0	0	0	0	0	CH-TF-4	J. PARSONS	1972
CH-TF-61	Lg Nucl Village	Low Piedmont-Rugged	33.8	1350	0	1	0	0	0	0	0	0	1	1	CH-TF-5	J. PARSONS	1972
CH-TF-62	Hamlet	Low Piedmont-Rugged	4.3	100	0	0	0	0	0	0	0	0	0	0	CH-TF-2	J. PARSONS	1972
CH-TF-63	Lg Nucl Village	Lakeshore Plain	74.0	2500	0	1	1	1	1	1	0	0	0	0	CH-TF-1	J. PARSONS	1972
XO-TF-1	Hamlet	Low Piedmont-Rugged	11.9	100	0	0	0	0	0	0	0	0	0	0	XE-TF-1	M. PARSONS	1972
XO-TF-2	Sm Disp Village	Low Piedmont-Rugged	14.7	200	0	1	0	0	0	0	0	0	0	0	XE-TF-2	M. PARSONS	1972
XO-TF-3	Small Hamlet	Low Piedmont-Rugged	1.2	10	0	0	0	0	0	0	0	1	1	1	XW-TF-2	J. PARSONS	1972
XO-TF-4	Lg Nucl Village	Low Piedmont-Rugged	22.0	880	0	1	0	0	1	0	1	0	1	1	XW-CL-6	J. PARSONS	1972
XO-TF-5	Ceremonial Ctr	Low Piedmont-Hill	0.8	0	0	0	1	0	0	0	0	0	0	0	XW-TF-1	J. PARSONS	1972
XO-TF-6	Hamlet	Low Piedmont-Rugged	3.5	30	0	0	0	0	1	0	1	0	0	0	XW-CL-1	J. PARSONS	1972
XO-TF-7	Small Hamlet	Low Piedmont-Rugged	1.8	20	0	0	0	0	0	1	1	0	0	0	XW-ET-1	J. PARSONS	1972
XO-TF-8	Hamlet	Low Piedmont-Rugged	2.5	30	0	0	0	0	0	1	1	0	0	1	XW-ET-2	J. PARSONS	1972
XO-TF-9	Questionable	Low Piedmont-Rugged	0.9	0	0	0	0	0	0	0	0	0	0	0	XW-LF-2	J. PARSONS	1972

CHALCO-XOCHIMILCO REGION - ENVIRONMENTAL DATA
Classic Sites

Site Number	Environmental Zone	UTM Coordinates East	North	Elev (in m)	Rainfall (in mm)	Modern Soil Depth	Modern Erosion	Modern Land use
CH-CL-1	Low Piedmont-Smooth	514.12	2134.35	2270	685	Medium-Deep	Slight	Agricultural
CH-CL-2	Lakeshore Plain	513.90	2133.70	2260	685	Deep	Very Slight	Agricultural
CH-CL-3	Low Piedmont-Smooth	514.47	2133.22	2280	690	Medium-Deep	Slight	Agricultural
CH-CL-4	Low Piedmont-Smooth	515.47	2131.30	2280	725	Deep	Very Slight	Agricultural
CH-CL-5	Low Piedmont-Smooth	516.57	2131.43	2300	740	Medium-Deep	Slight-Moderate	Agricultural
CH-CL-6	Low Piedmont-Smooth	517.62	2130.53	2300	760	Deep	Slight	Agricultural
CH-CL-7	Low Piedmont-Smooth	520.60	2130.72	2400	900	Shallow-Med	Moderate-Deep	Grazing & Agri
CH-CL-8	Low Piedmont-Smooth	519.35	2127.00	2300	860	Deep	Slight-Moderate	Agricultural
CH-CL-9	Low Piedmont-Smooth	518.55	2125.00	2305	875	Deep	Slight-Moderate	Agricultural
CH-CL-10	Low Piedmont-Smooth	517.95	2125.78	2290	825	Deep	Slight-Moderate	Agricultural
CH-CL-11	Low Piedmont-Smooth	516.02	2124.07	2330	765	Medium-Deep	Moderate	Agricultural
CH-CL-12	Low Piedmont-Smooth	516.00	2124.97	2310	750	Medium	Moderate	Agricultural
CH-CL-13	Lakeshore Plain	516.60	2126.32	2270	780	Deep	Slight-Moderate	Agricultural
CH-CL-14	Lakeshore Plain	513.93	2127.60	2270	690	Deep	Slight	Agricultural
CH-CL-15	Lakeshore Plain	513.05	2126.70	2250	680	Deep	Very Slight	Agricultural
CH-CL-16	Low Piedmont-Rugged	512.15	2123.04	2270	700	Medium	Moderate	Grazing & Agri
CH-CL-17	Low Piedmont-Rugged	512.75	2121.69	2280	710	Medium	Slight	Agricultural
CH-CL-18	Low Piedmont-Rugged	512.93	2121.46	2280	710	Medium	Slight	Agricultural
CH-CL-19	Low Piedmont-Rugged	513.97	2119.81	2350	780	Shallow-Med	Moderate	Agricultural
CH-CL-20	Low Piedmont-Rugged	513.72	2118.26	2380	780	Shallow-Med	Moderate	Grazing & Agri
CH-CL-21	Low Piedmont-Rugged	514.30	2116.98	2400	800	Shallow-Med	Moderate	Grazing & Agri
CH-CL-22	Low Piedmont-Rugged	513.00	2116.71	2460	810	Shallow	Moderate	Grazing & Agri
CH-CL-23	Low Piedmont-Rugged	515.55	2115.33	2430	900	Shallow	Moderate	Agricultural
CH-CL-24	Upr Piedmont-Rugged	512.25	2114.54	2500	900	Shallow-Med	Moderate	Grazing & Agri
CH-CL-25	Upr Piedmont-Rugged	511.63	2112.66	2550	1000	Medium	Moderate	Agricultural
CH-CL-26	Upr Piedmont-Rugged	512.00	2112.46	2540	990	Medium	Moderate	Agricultural
CH-CL-27	Low Piedmont-Rugged	513.35	2114.66	2460	895	Shallow	Deep	Grazing & Agri
CH-CL-28	Low Piedmont-Rugged	513.47	2114.46	2460	890	Shallow	Moderate	Grazing
CH-CL-29	Low Piedmont-Rugged	514.05	2113.73	2460	900	Medium	Moderate	Agricultural
CH-CL-30	Low Piedmont-Smooth	513.97	2114.31	2440	900	Shallow	Moderate-Deep	Grazing
CH-CL-31	Low Piedmont-Smooth	516.20	2113.46	2440	930	Medium	Moderate	Grazing
CH-CL-32	Low Piedmont-Smooth	516.90	2114.88	2445	930	Medium	Moderate	Agricultural
CH-CL-33	Low Piedmont-Smooth	517.35	2115.29	2420	915	Shallow	Moderate	Grazing & Agri
CH-CL-34	Low Piedmont-Smooth	520.82	2115.23	2430	1000	Medium	Moderate	Agricultural
CH-CL-35	Amecameca Sub-Valley	523.57	2116.41	2470	1040	Medium	Slight	Grazing & Agri
CH-CL-36	Amecameca Sub-Valley	523.32	2115.56	2460	1035	Deep	Slight	Agricultural
CH-CL-37	Amecameca Sub-Valley	522.95	2114.44	2460	1040	Medium-Deep	Slight-Moderate	Agricultural
CH-CL-38	Amecameca Sub-Valley	523.25	2113.31	2460	1050	Medium-Deep	Slight	Agricultural
CH-CL-39	Amecameca Sub-Valley	521.75	2113.48	2490	1020	Medium	Moderate	Grazing & Agri
CH-CL-40	Low Piedmont-Smooth	517.90	2113.08	2440	960	Medium	Slight	Agricultural
CH-CL-41	Low Piedmont-Rugged	519.22	2111.73	2490	1015	Medium	Moderate	Agricultural
CH-CL-42	Amecameca Sub-Valley	522.12	2107.88	2410	1080	Medium-Deep	Moderate	Agricultural

CHALCO-XOCHIMILCO REGION - PREHISPANIC SETTLEMENT DATA
Classic Sites

SITE NUMBER	CLASSIFICATION	ENVIRONMENTAL ZONE	AREA (in ha)	POP.	EF	MF	LF	TF	EC	LC	ET	LT	EA	LA	TEMPORARY SITE NO.	SUPERVISOR	YEAR
CH-CL-1	Sm Disp Village	Low Piedmont-Smooth	6.7	140	0	1	1	0	1	1	0	1	0	0	CH-C-12	M. PARSONS	1969
CH-CL-2	Hamlet	Lakeshore Plain	2.4	25	2	1	1	0	0	1	0	0	0	1	CH-C-11	J. PARSONS	1969
CH-CL-3	Hamlet	Low Piedmont-Smooth	2.6	30	0	0	0	0	1	0	1	1	0	0	CH-C-10	J. PARSONS	1969
CH-CL-4	Small Hamlet	Low Piedmont-Smooth	0.9	10	0	0	0	0	1	1	0	0	0	0	CH-C-3	J. PARSONS	1969
CH-CL-5	Hamlet	Low Piedmont-Smooth	3.4	30	0	1	1	0	0	1	0	0	1	1	CH-C-4	J. PARSONS	1969
CH-CL-6	Hamlet	Low Piedmont-Smooth	2.9	30	0	1	1	0	1	1	1	0	0	0	CH-F-4	J. PARSONS	1969
CH-CL-7	Hamlet	Low Piedmont-Smooth	6.2	100	0	0	0	1	1	1	0	0	0	0	CH-C-14	J. PARSONS	1969
CH-CL-8	Small Hamlet	Low Piedmont-Smooth	1.4	10	0	0	0	0	0	1	1	0	0	0	CH-C-13	J. PARSONS	1969
CH-CL-9	Sm Disp Village	Low Piedmont-Smooth	9.5	150	0	0	1	1	1	1	0	1	1	1	CH-C-9	J. PARSONS	1969
CH-CL-10	Hamlet	Low Piedmont-Smooth	5.8	60	0	0	1	0	1	1	0	1	1	1	CH-C-8	J. PARSONS	1969
CH-CL-11	Small Hamlet	Low Piedmont-Smooth	1.4	15	0	0	0	1	0	0	0	0	0	0	CH-C-15	J. PARSONS	1969
CH-CL-12	Hamlet	Low Piedmont-Smooth	2.5	30	0	0	0	0	1	1	0	1	1	1	CH-C-6	J. PARSONS	1969
CH-CL-13	Small Hamlet	Lakeshore Plain	1.1	15	0	0	0	0	1	1	0	0	0	0	CH-C-7	J. PARSONS	1969
CH-CL-14	Sm Disp Village	Lakeshore Plain	33.4	500	0	0	1	1	1	1	0	0	1	0	CH-C-2	J. PARSONS	1969
CH-CL-15	Sm Nucl Village	Lakeshore Plain	11.3	340	0	0	0	0	1	1	0	0	1	1	CH-C-5	J. PARSONS	1969
CH-CL-16	Small Hamlet	Low Piedmont-Rugged	0.8	10	0	1	1	1	1	1	0	1	0	0	AM-CL-17	M. PARSONS	1972
CH-CL-17	Small Hamlet	Low Piedmont-Rugged	2.1	20	0	0	0	0	1	1	0	0	0	0	AM-CL-13	M. PARSONS	1972
CH-CL-18	Hamlet	Low Piedmont-Rugged	1.7	30	0	0	0	0	1	1	0	0	0	0	AM-CL-14	M. PARSONS	1972
CH-CL-19	Sm Nucl Village	Low Piedmont-Rugged	6.6	200	0	0	0	0	0	1	0	1	1	1	AM-CL-1	M. PARSONS	1972
CH-CL-20	Hamlet	Low Piedmont-Rugged	7.1	70	0	0	0	0	1	1	0	0	1	1	AM-CL-2	M. PARSONS	1972
CH-CL-21	Hamlet	Low Piedmont-Rugged	2.0	40	0	0	0	0	1	1	0	0	1	1	AM-CL-3	M. PARSONS	1973
CH-CL-22	Hamlet	Low Piedmont-Rugged	1.6	30	0	0	0	0	0	1	0	1	1	1	AM-CL-4	M. PARSONS	1972
CH-CL-23	Hamlet	Low Piedmont-Smooth	3.2	60	0	0	0	0	1	0	0	0	1	0	AM-CL-10	M. PARSONS	1972
CH-CL-24	Sm Disp Village	Upr Piedmont-Rugged	15.5	400	0	0	0	0	1	1	0	1	1	1	AM-CL-12	M. PARSONS	1972
CH-CL-25	Small Hamlet	Upr Piedmont-Rugged	0.5	10	0	0	0	1	0	1	0	0	0	0	AM-CL-1	R. WENKE	1972
CH-CL-26	Small Hamlet	Upr Piedmont-Rugged	2.6	20	0	0	0	0	1	0	0	0	1	1	AM-CL-2	R. WENKE	1972
CH-CL-27	Small Hamlet	Low Piedmont-Rugged	0.9	10	0	0	0	1	1	1	0	0	0	0	AM-F-10	M. PARSONS	1972
CH-CL-28	Small Hamlet	Low Piedmont-Rugged	0.7	10	0	0	0	0	0	1	0	0	1	1	AM-CL-9	M. PARSONS	1972
CH-CL-29	Hamlet	Low Piedmont-Rugged	4.8	100	0	0	0	1	0	1	0	0	0	0	AM-CL-6	M. PARSONS	1972
CH-CL-30	Hamlet	Low Piedmont-Smooth	1.0	10	0	0	0	0	0	0	0	0	1	1	AM-CL-5	M. PARSONS	1972
CH-CL-31	Hamlet	Low Piedmont-Smooth	2.1	40	0	0	0	1	1	1	0	0	1	1	AM-CL-7	M. PARSONS	1972
CH-CL-32	Sm Disp Village	Low Piedmont-Smooth	7.4	150	0	0	0	0	0	1	0	0	0	1	AM-CL-8	M. PARSONS	1972
CH-CL-33	Small Hamlet	Low Piedmont-Smooth	2.1	20	0	0	0	1	1	0	0	0	1	1	AM-CL-11	M. PARSONS	1972
CH-CL-34	Small Hamlet	Low Piedmont-Smooth	0.4	10	0	0	0	1	1	1	0	0	1	1	AM-CL-1	E. PRAHL	1972
CH-CL-35	Hamlet	Amecameca Sub-Valley	4.1	50	0	0	0	0	0	1	0	0	0	1	AM-CL-1	E. PRAHL	1972
CH-CL-36	Hamlet	Amecameca Sub-Valley	3.3	100	0	0	0	0	0	1	0	0	1	0	AM-CL-2	E. PRAHL	1972
CH-CL-37	Small Hamlet	Amecameca Sub-Valley	0.9	10	0	0	0	0	1	0	0	0	1	1	AM-AZ-8	E. PRAHL	1972
CH-CL-38	Sm.Disp Village	Amecameca Sub-Valley	6.7	200	0	0	0	1	1	1	0	0	1	1	AM-CL-3	E. PRAHL	1972
CH-CL-39	Small Hamlet	Amecameca Sub-Valley	1.9	20	0	0	0	0	0	1	0	0	0	0	AM-CL-4	E. PRAHL	1972
CH-CL-40	Small Hamlet	Low Piedmont-Smooth	0.4	10	0	0	0	0	1	0	0	0	1	1	AM-CL-15	M. PARSONS	1972
CH-CL-41	Small Hamlet	Low Piedmont-Rugged	1.7	10	0	0	0	0	0	0	0	0	0	0		E. PRAHL	1972
CH-CL-42	Hamlet	Amecameca Sub-Valley	2.2	60	0	0	0	0	1	1	0	0	0	0	AM-CL-5	E. PRAHL	1972

Early Classic and Late Classic occupations are tabulated on a presence-absence basis.

CHALCO-XOCHIMILCO REGION - ENVIRONMENTAL DATA

Classic Sites

Site Number	Environmental Zone	UTM Coordinates East	UTM Coordinates North	Elev (in m)	Rainfall (in mm)	Modern Soil Depth	Modern Erosion	Modern Land use
CH-CL-43	Low Piedmont-Rugged	517.60	2107.71	2450	1100	Medium	Moderate	Agricultural
CH-CL-44	Low Piedmont-Rugged	518.03	2111.38	2490	1010	Medium-Deep	Moderate	Agricultural
CH-CL-45	Upr Piedmont-Rugged	512.50	2109.38	2550	1050	Medium	Moderate	Agricultural
CH-CL-46	Lakeshore Plain	510.38	2124.38	2245	700	Deep	None	Agricultural
CH-CL-47	Lakeshore Plain	510.95	2125.26	2245	690	Deep	None	Agricultural
CH-CL-48	Lakeshore Plain	510.03	2125.46	2245	690	Deep	None	Agricultural
CH-CL-49	Lakeshore Plain	509.40	2125.91	2245	690	Deep	Very Slight	Agricultural
CH-CL-50	Low Piedmont-Rugged	508.38	2123.48	2270	725	Medium	Slight	Agricultural
CH-CL-51	Island-Lakesh Plain	507.45	2130.25	2250	660	Medium-Deep	Slight-Moderate	Agricultural
CH-CL-52	Low Piedmont-Rugged	501.22	2123.51	2290	775	Medium	Moderate	Agricultural
CH-CL-53	Low Piedmont-Rugged	500.85	2124.13	2270	766	Medium	Slight	Agricultural
CH-CL-54	Low Piedmont-Rugged	500.07	2125.08	2295	750	Medium	Moderate	Agricultural
CH-CL-55	Low Piedmont-Rugged	500.03	2127.08	2250	750	Medium	Slight	Grazing & Agri
CH-CL-56	Lakeshore Plain	499.66	2128.20	2250	725	Medium	Moderate	Agricultural
XO-CL-1	Lakebed	497.31	2133.10	2240	660	Deep	None	Agricultural
XO-CL-2	Low Piedmont-Rugged	496.31	2127.83	2325	790	Medium	Moderate	Agricultural
XO-CL-3	Low Piedmont-Rugged	490.76	2127.75	2270	785	Medium	Moderate	Agricultural
XO-CL-4	Low Piedmont-Rugged	489.73	2127.41	2280	780	Shallow-Med	Moderate	Agricultural
XO-CL-5	Lakebed	489.88	2134.75	2240	665	Deep	None	Agricultural
XO-CL-6	Low Piedmont-Rugged	484.69	2131.10	2280	790	Medium	Slight	Agricultural

CHALCO-XOCHIMILCO REGION - PREHISPANIC SETTLEMENT DATA
Classic Sites

SITE NUMBER	CLASSIFICATION	ENVIRONMENTAL ZONE	AREA (in ha)	POP.	EF	MF	LF	TF	EC	LC	ET	LT	EA	LA	TEMPORARY SITE NO.	SUPERVISOR	YEAR
CH-CL-43	Small Hamlet	Low Piedmont-Rugged	1.0	20	0	0	0	0	0	0	0	0	0	0	AM-CL-6	R. WENKE	1972
CH-CL-44	Hamlet	Low Piedmont-Rugged	3.0	30	0	0	0	1	1	1	0	0	0	0	AM-CL-5	R. WENKE	1972
CH-CL-45	Small Hamlet	Upr Piedmont-Rugged	2.4	20	0	0	0	0	1	0	0	0	0	0	AM-CL-3	R. WENKE	1972
CH-CL-46	Sm Disp Village	Lakeshore Plain	17.3	400	0	0	0	0	1	1	1	1	0	0	AM-CL-16	M. PARSONS	1972
CH-CL-47	Small Hamlet	Lakeshore Plain	0.6	10	0	0	0	0	1	1	0	0	0	0	CH-CL-9	J. PARSONS	1972
CH-CL-48	Small Hamlet	Lakeshore Plain	2.2	20	0	0	0	0	1	1	0	.1	0	0	CH-CL-7	J. PARSONS	1972
CH-CL-49	Hamlet	Lakeshore Plain	5.5	100	0	0	1	1	1	1	1	0	0	0	CH-CL-6	J. PARSONS	1972
CH-CL-50	Small Hamlet	Low Piedmont-Rugged	0.2	10	0	0	1	1	1	1	0	0	0	0	AM-LF-5	M. PARSONS	1972
CH-CL-51	Hamlet	Island-Lakesh Plain	4.7	50	0	0	1	1	1	1	1	0	0	0	CH-CL-8	J. PARSONS	1969
CH-CL-52	Hamlet	Low Piedmont-Rugged	1.7	30	0	0	0	0	1	1	0	0	0	0	CH-TF-5	J. PARSONS	1972
CH-CL-53	Hamlet	Low Piedmont-Rugged	3.0	50	0	0	0	0	0	0	0	0	0	0	CH-CL-5	J. PARSONS	1972
CH-CL-54	Sm Disp Village	Low Piedmont-Rugged	18.3	360	0	0	0	1	1	1	0	1	0	1	CH-CL-1	J. PARSONS	1972
CH-CL-55	Hamlet	Low Piedmont-Rugged	3.3	50	0	1	0	0	0	1	1	0	0	0	CH-CL-2	J. PARSONS	1972
CH-CL-56	Hamlet	Lakeshore Plain	8.5	100	0	1	1	1	1	1	0	1	0	0	CH-CL-4	J. PARSONS	1972
XO-CL-1	Questionable	Lakebed	0.4	0	0	0	0	0	0	1	1	1	0	0	XE-CL-1	M. PARSONS	1972
XO-CL-2	Small Hamlet	Low Piedmont-Rugged	1.3	10	0	0	0	0	1	0	0	0	0	0	XE-CL-4	M. PARSONS	1972
XO-CL-3	Small Hamlet	Low Piedmont-Rugged	0.7	10	0	0	0	0	1	1	0	0	1	1	XW-CL-5	J. PARSONS	1972
XO-CL-4	Lg Disp Village	Low Piedmont-Rugged	31.5	700	0	1	0	1	1	1	0	0	0	1	XW-CL-6	J. PARSONS	1972
XO-CL-5	Small Hamlet	Lakebed	5.5	5	0	0	0	0	1	1	1	0	0	0	XW-CL-2	J. PARSONS	1972
XO-CL-6	Hamlet	Low Piedmont-Rugged	4.5	100	0	0	0	0	0	0	0	0	0	0	XW-CL-1	J. PARSONS	1972

Early Classic and Late Classic occupations are tabulated on a presence-absence basis.

32

CHALCO-XOCHIMILCO REGION – ENVIRONMENTAL DATA
Early Toltec Sites

Site Number	Environmental Zone	UTM Coordinates East	North	Elev (in m)	Rainfall (in mm)	Modern Soil Depth	Modern Erosion	Modern Land use
CH-ET-1	Low Piedmont-Smooth	517.15	2134.31	2360	740	Very Shallow	Deep	Grazing & Agri
CH-ET-2	Low Piedmont-Smooth	514.70	2133.16	2280	700	Medium-Deep	Slight-Moderate	Agricultural
CH-ET-3	Low Piedmont-Smooth	520.28	2130.58	2380	900	Shallow-Med	Moderate-Deep	Agricultural
CH-ET-4	Low Piedmont-Smooth	520.43	2129.01	2350	920	Shallow	Deep	Grazing & Agri
CH-ET-5	Low Piedmont-Smooth	521.07	2129.04	2370	940	Very Shallow	Deep	Grazing
CH-ET-6	Low Piedmont-Smooth	520.72	2128.51	2350	930	Shallow	Deep	Grazing & Agri
CH-ET-7	Low Piedmont-Smooth	520.32	2127.76	2330	920	Medium	Moderate	Grazing & Agri
CH-ET-8	Low Piedmont-Smooth	520.05	2127.23	2360	900	Medium	Moderate	Agricultural
CH-ET-9	Low Piedmont-Smooth	519.82	2126.94	2310	900	Medium	Moderate	Agricultural
CH-ET-10	Low Piedmont-Smooth	519.40	2127.21	2300	880	Medium-Deep	Moderate	Agricultural
CH-ET-11	Low Piedmont-Smooth	521.72	2125.94	2415	1000	Medium	Moderate	Agricultural
CH-ET-12	Low Piedmont-Smooth	518.47	2125.11	2310	860	Medium-Deep	Moderate	Agricultural
CH-ET-13	Upr Piedmont-Smooth	520.53	2121.61	2500	970	Medium	Moderate	Grazing & Agri
CH-ET-14	Upr Piedmont-Smooth	520.28	2121.16	2530	950	Medium	Moderate	Grazing & Agri
CH-ET-15	Upr Piedmont-Smooth	519.55	2120.66	2550	940	Medium-Deep	Moderate	Agricultural
CH-ET-16	Amecameca Sub-Valley	522.18	2117.69	2470	1010	Deep	Slight	Grazing & Agri
CH-ET-17	Low Piedmont-Smooth	520.65	2117.06	2485	990	Medium	Moderate	Agricultural
CH-ET-18	Low Piedmont-Smooth	520.00	2116.33	2450	960	Medium	Moderate	Agricultural
CH-ET-19	Low Piedmont-Smooth	519.60	2115.91	2460	960	Medium	Moderate	Agricultural
CH-ET-20	Low Piedmont-Smooth	518.62	2116.44	2430	920	Medium	Moderate	Agricultural
CH-ET-21	Low Piedmont-Smooth	518.22	2116.48	2460	910	Medium	Moderate	Agricultural
CH-ET-22	Low Piedmont-Smooth	518.22	2116.21	2450	910	Medium	Moderate	Agricultural
CH-ET-23	Lakeshore Plain	510.15	2124.08	2245	700	Deep	Slight	Agricultural
CH-ET-24	Lakeshore Plain	509.78	2125.66	2245	690	Deep	None	Agricultural
CH-ET-25	Lakeshore Plain	510.30	2126.66	2245	680	Deep	None	Agricultural
CH-ET-26	Lakeshore Plain	508.52	2126.85	2245	680	Deep	None	Agricultural
CH-ET-27	Lakeshore Plain	509.57	2127.65	2245	675	Deep	None	Agricultural
CH-ET-28	Island-Lakesh Plain	507.22	2130.22	2250	665	Medium-Deep	Slight-Moderate	Agricultural
CH-ET-29	Island-Lakesh Plain	506.57	2129.90	2290	665	Medium-Deep	Moderate	Agricultural
CH-ET-30	Low Piedmont-Rugged	501.22	2124.21	2270	750	Medium	Moderate	Agricultural
CH-ET-31	Low Piedmont-Rugged	500.53	2125.86	2260	733	Shallow-Med	Slight-Moderate	Agricultural
CH-ET-32	Low Piedmont-Rugged	499.80	2127.31	2250	740	Medium	Slight-Moderate	Agricultural
XO-ET-1	Lakebed	497.23	2133.00	2240	665	Deep	None	Agricultural
XO-ET-2	Lakebed	493.19	2133.38	2240	670	Deep	None	Agricultural
XO-ET-3	Lakeshore Plain	496.38	2129.68	2245	725	Deep	None	Agricultural
XO-ET-4	Lakeshore Plain	497.11	2129.10	2250	725	Deep	None	Agricultural
XO-ET-5	Lakeshore Plain	495.44	2129.06	2245	720	Deep	None	Agricultural
XO-ET-6	Lakeshore Plain	494.96	2128.63	2250	720	Deep	None	Agricultural
XO-ET-7	Low Piedmont-Rugged	490.61	2127.41	2300	775	Medium	Moderate	Agricultural
XO-ET-8	Lakebed	490.01	2134.98	2240	670	Deep	None	Agricultural
XO-ET-9	Lakebed	489.83	2134.45	2240	665	Deep	None	Agricultural
XO-ET-10	Lakeshore Plain	486.24	2129.13	2260	730	Deep	Slight	Settlement

CHALCO-XOCHIMILCO REGION - PREHISPANIC SETTLEMENT DATA
Early Toltec Sites

SITE NUMBER	CLASSIFICATION	ENVIRONMENTAL ZONE	AREA (in ha)	POP.	EF	MF	LF	TF	EC	LC	ET	LT	EA	LA	TEMPORARY SITE NO.	SUPERVISOR	YEAR
							OTHER OCCUPATIONS									SURVEY RECORDS	
CH-ET-1	Hamlet	Low Piedmont-Smooth	3.4	30	0	0	0	0	0	0	0	0	1	1	CH-T-16	J. PARSONS	1969
CH-ET-2	Sm Disp Village	Low Piedmont-Smooth	9.4	200	0	0	0	1	0	0	1	0	0	0	CH-T-14	J. PARSONS	1969
CH-ET-3	Small Hamlet	Low Piedmont-Smooth	0.5	10	0	0	0	0	0	0	1	0	1	1	CH-A-27	J. PARSONS	1969
CH-ET-4	Hamlet	Low Piedmont-Smooth	3.3	60	0	0	0	0	0	0	0	0	0	0	CH-T-26	M. PARSONS	1969
CH-ET-5	Sm Disp Village	Low Piedmont-Smooth	9.1	180	0	0	0	1	0	0	0	0	1	1	CH-T-27	M. PARSONS	1969
CH-ET-6	Hamlet	Low Piedmont-Smooth	3.6	40	0	0	0	0	0	0	0	0	1	1	CH-T-25	M. PARSONS	1969
CH-ET-7	Lg Nucl Village	Low Piedmont-Smooth	42.1	1200	0	0	0	1	0	0	0	0	0	0	CH-T-22	M. PARSONS	1969
CH-ET-8	Hamlet	Low Piedmont-Smooth	3.0	50	0	0	0	0	0	0	0	0	0	0	CH-T-31	M. PARSONS	1969
CH-ET-9	Hamlet	Low Piedmont-Smooth	3.3	50	0	0	0	0	0	0	0	0	1	1	CH-T-30	M. PARSONS	1969
CH-ET-10	Sm Disp Village	Low Piedmont-Smooth	10.2	150	0	0	0	0	1	0	1	0	1	1	CH-T-29	M. PARSONS	1969
CH-ET-11	Hamlet	Low Piedmont-Smooth	2.6	40	0	0	1	1	0	0	0	0	0	0	CH-F-24	J. PARSONS	1969
CH-ET-12	Sm Disp Village	Low Piedmont-Smooth	15.8	300	0	0	1	1	1	0	1	0	0	0	CH-T-9	J. PARSONS	1969
CH-ET-13	Small Hamlet	Upr Piedmont-Smooth	0.8	20	0	0	0	0	0	0	0	0	1	1	CH-A-34	J. PARSONS	1969
CH-ET-14	Hamlet	Upr Piedmont-Smooth	1.6	40	0	0	0	0	0	0	0	0	1	1	CH-A-35	J. PARSONS	1969
CH-ET-15	Hamlet	Upr Piedmont-Smooth	3.1	30	0	0	0	0	0	0	0	0	1	1	CH-A-36	J. PARSONS	1969
CH-ET-16	Small Hamlet	Amecameca Sub-Valley	0.6	10	0	0	0	0	0	0	0	0	0	1	AM-AZ-1	E. PRAHL	1972
CH-ET-17	Hamlet	Low Piedmont-Smooth	3.2	100	0	0	0	0	0	0	0	0	0	0	AM-ET-1	E. PRAHL	1972
CH-ET-18	Small Hamlet	Low Piedmont-Smooth	0.8	10	0	0	0	0	0	0	1	0	0	0	AM-LT-4	E. PRAHL	1972
CH-ET-19	Small Hamlet	Low Piedmont-Smooth	0.4	10	0	0	0	0	0	0	0	0	0	0	AM-LT-5	E. PRAHL	1972
CH-ET-20	Small Hamlet	Low Piedmont-Smooth	0.4	10	0	0	0	0	0	0	1	0	0	0	AM-LT-5	M. PARSONS	1972
CH-ET-21	Small Hamlet	Low Piedmont-Smooth	0.4	10	0	0	0	0	0	0	1	0	0	0	AM-LT-3	M. PARSONS	1972
CH-ET-22	Hamlet	Low Piedmont-Smooth	1.1	30	0	0	1	0	1	0	1	0	0	1	AM-LT-3	M. PARSONS	1972
CH-ET-23	Hamlet	Lakeshore Plain	7.6	80	0	0	0	0	1	0	1	0	1	0	AM-ET-1	M. PARSONS	1972
CH-ET-24	Local Center	Lakeshore Plain	77.2	2400	0	0	1	1	1	0	2	1	1	1	CH-ET-2	J. PARSONS	1972
CH-ET-25	Hamlet	Lakeshore Plain	4.6	100	0	0	0	0	0	0	0	0	0	0	CH-ET-3	J. PARSONS	1972
CH-ET-26	Hamlet	Lakeshore Plain	6.4	80	0	0	0	0	0	0	0	0	1	1	CH-ET-5	J. PARSONS	1969
CH-ET-27	Hamlet	Lakeshore Plain	5.4	50	0	0	0	0	0	0	0	0	1	1	CH-ET-4	J. PARSONS	1969
CH-ET-28	Local Center	Island-Lakesh Plain	102.3	3500	0	0	0	0	1	0	1	0	1	1	CH-T-1	J. PARSONS	1969
CH-ET-29	Questionable	Island-Lakesh Plain	0.1	10	0	0	0	0	0	0	0	0	0	1	CH-ET-2	J. PARSONS	1969
CH-ET-30	Small Hamlet	Low Piedmont-Rugged	0.7	10	0	0	0	0	0	0	1	0	0	0	CH-LT-5	J. PARSONS	1972
CH-ET-31	Lg Nucl Village	Low Piedmont-Rugged	35.5	800	0	0	0	0	0	0	2	0	0	0	CH-ET-1	J. PARSONS	1972
CH-ET-32	Hamlet	Low Piedmont-Rugged	2.4	50	0	0	0	0	0	1	0	0	0	0	CH-CL-2	J. PARSONS	1972
XO-ET-1	Small Hamlet	Lakebed	1.0	10	0	0	0	0	0	1	0	0	0	1	XE-CL-1	M. PARSONS	1972
XO-ET-2	Small Hamlet	Lakebed	0.8	10	0	0	0	0	0	0	0	0	0	0	XE-ET-3	M. PARSONS	1972
XO-ET-3	Hamlet	Lakeshore Plain	2.5	30	0	0	0	0	0	0	0	0	0	0	XE-CL-2	M. PARSONS	1972
XO-ET-4	Lg Nucl Village	Lakeshore Plain	32.3	1000	0	0	0	0	0	0	1	0	0	0	XE-ET-2	M. PARSONS	1972
XO-ET-5	Hamlet	Lakeshore Plain	3.1	60	0	0	0	0	0	0	0	0	0	0	XE-ET-1	M. PARSONS	1972
XO-ET-6	Sm Disp Village	Lakeshore Plain	13.7	150	0	0	0	0	0	0	0	0	0	0	XE-ET-4	M. PARSONS	1972
XO-ET-7	Small Hamlet	Low Piedmont-Rugged	1.0	10	0	0	0	0	0	0	0	0	1	1	XW-CL-4	J. PARSONS	1972
XO-ET-8	Hamlet	Lakebed	2.4	70	0	0	0	0	0	0	0	0	0	0	XW-CL-3	J. PARSONS	1972
XO-ET-9	Sm Nucl Village	Lakebed	6.3	200	0	0	0	0	0	0	1	0	0	0	XW-CL-2	J. PARSONS	1972
XO-ET-10	Questionable	Lakeshore Plain	1.0	0	0	0	0	0	0	0	0	0	0	0	XW-ET-4	J. PARSONS	1972

| | | UTM Coordinates | | Elev | Rainfall | Modern | Modern Erosion | Modern |
Site Number	Environmental Zone	East	North	(in m)	(in mm)	Soil Depth		Land use
XO-ET-11	Lakeshore Plain	484.97	2131.66	2260	890	Medium	Moderate	Agricultural
XO-ET-12	Low Piedmont-Rugged	484.42	2131.08	2290	790	Medium	Slight-Moderate	Agricultural
XO-ET-13	Low Piedmont-Rugged	483.92	2131.33	2280	800	Medium	Moderate	Agricultural

CHALCO-XOCHIMILCO REGION - ENVIRONMENTAL DATA
Early Toltec Sites

CHALCO-XOCHIMILCO REGION - PREHISPANIC SETTLEMENT DATA
Early Toltec Sites

SITE NUMBER	CLASSIFICATION	ENVIRONMENTAL ZONE	AREA (in ha)	POP.	OTHER OCCUPATIONS										TEMPORARY SITE NO.	SURVEY RECORDS	
					EF	MF	LF	TF	EC	LC	ET	LT	EA	LA		SUPERVISOR	YEAR
XO-ET-11	Hamlet	Lakeshore Plain	3.0	60	0	0	0	1	0	0	0	1	0	1	XW-ET-2	J. PARSONS	1972
XO-ET-12	Small Hamlet	Low Piedmont-Rugged	1.9	20	0	0	0	1	0	0	0	1	0	0	XW-ET-1	J. PARSONS	1972
XO-ET-13	Small Hamlet	Low Piedmont-Rugged	1.4	20	0	0	0	0	0	0	1	1	0	0	XW-ET-3	J. PARSONS	1972

CHALCO-XOCHIMILCO REGION - ENVIRONMENTAL DATA
Late Toltec Sites

Site Number	Environmental Zone	UTM Coordinates East	North	Elev (in m)	Rainfall (in mm)	Modern Soil Depth	Modern Erosion	Modern Land use
CH-LT-1	Low Piedmont-Smooth	514.12	2134.60	2270	690	Deep	Very Slight	Agricultural
CH-LT-2	Low Piedmont-Smooth	516.25	2134.30	2360	700	Very Shallow	Deep	Grazing & Agri
CH-LT-3	Low Piedmont-Smooth	514.50	2133.25	2280	695	Deep	Slight-Moderate	Agricultural
CH-LT-4	Low Piedmont-Smooth	515.75	2133.35	2325	720	Medium	Moderate	Agricultural
CH-LT-5	Low Piedmont-Smooth	516.32	2133.03	2360	725	Very Shallow	Deep	Grazing & Agri
CH-LT-6	Low Piedmont-Smooth	516.30	2132.00	2305	730	Medium-Deep	Slight-Moderate	Agricultural
CH-LT-7	Low Piedmont-Smooth	519.25	2133.45	2430	800	Medium	Moderate	Grazing & Agri
CH-LT-8	Low Piedmont-Smooth	518.95	2133.15	2410	800	Medium	Moderate	Agricultural
CH-LT-9	Low Piedmont-Smooth	519.32	2132.82	2410	810	Medium	Moderate	Grazing & Agri
CH-LT-10	Low Piedmont-Smooth	519.20	2132.56	2390	810	Shallow	Deep	Agricultural
CH-LT-11	Low Piedmont-Smooth	520.47	2132.71	2460	900	Very Shallow	Deep	None
CH-LT-12	Low Piedmont-Smooth	519.57	2132.36	2410	850	Very Shallow	Deep	Agricultural
CH-LT-13	Island-Lakesh Plain	507.05	2130.40	2250	660	Medium-Deep	Slight-Moderate	Agricultural
CH-LT-14	Upr Piedmont-Smooth	523.00	2130.40	2550	975	Medium	Moderate-Deep	Grazing
CH-LT-15	Low Piedmont-Smooth	520.18	2130.65	2380	860	Shallow-Medi	Moderate-Deep	Agricultural
CH-LT-16	Low Piedmont-Smooth	519.75	2130.20	2350	850	Shallow-Med	Moderate-Deep	Agricultural
CH-LT-17	Low Piedmont-Smooth	517.68	2130.50	2300	770	Medium	Moderate	Agricultural
CH-LT-18	Low Piedmont-Smooth	518.80	2129.80	2300	800	Medium	Moderate	None
CH-LT-19	Lakeshore Plain	514.65	2128.50	2260	700	Deep	Very Slight	Agricultural
CH-LT-20	Low Piedmont-Smooth	519.62	2127.80	2295	860	Medium-Deep	Slight-Moderate	Agricultural
CH-LT-21	Low Piedmont-Smooth	519.25	2127.15	2300	850	Medium-Deep	Moderate	Agricultural
CH-LT-22	Low Piedmont-Smooth	520.10	2127.50	2310	900	Medium	Moderate	Grazing & Agri
CH-LT-23	Low Piedmont-Smooth	519.32	2126.60	2310	870	Medium	Moderate	Agricultural
CH-LT-24	Low Piedmont-Smooth	518.80	2126.05	2290	860	Deep	Slight	Agricultural
CH-LT-25	Low Piedmont-Smooth	519.15	2125.82	2290	870	Deep	Slight	Agricultural
CH-LT-26	Low Piedmont-Smooth	519.30	2125.35	2300	880	Medium-Deep	Moderate	Agricultural
CH-LT-27	Low Piedmont-Smooth	520.90	2124.22	2365	950	Medium-Deep	Moderate	Agricultural
CH-LT-28	Low Piedmont-Smooth	518.43	2125.38	2300	850	Medium-Deep	Moderate	Agricultural
CH-LT-29	Low Piedmont-Smooth	517.57	2125.60	2290	825	Medium	Moderate	Agricultural
CH-LT-30	Low Piedmont-Smooth	517.30	2125.07	2300	810	Medium	Moderate	Agricultural
CH-LT-31	Low Piedmont-Smooth	516.00	2123.88	2310	760	Medium	Moderate	Grazing & Agri
CH-LT-32	Low Piedmont-Smooth	514.80	2124.00	2290	710	Deep	Slight	Agricultural
CH-LT-33	Low Piedmont-Smooth	515.00	2123.70	2300	725	Medium	Moderate	Agricultural
CH-LT-34	Low Piedmont-Smooth	515.45	2122.13	2350	775	Medium	Moderate	Grazing & Agri
CH-LT-35	Low Piedmont-Smooth	513.57	2122.13	2290	710	Deep	Slight-Moderate	Agricultural
CH-LT-36	Lakeshore Plain	512.95	2122.01	2260	700	Medium-Deep	Moderate	Agricultural
CH-LT-37	Low Piedmont-Smooth	514.05	2121.75	2290	740	Deep	Slight	Agricultural
CH-LT-38	Low Piedmont-Smooth	513.68	2121.38	2290	735	Deep	Slight	Agricultural
CH-LT-39	Low Piedmont-Smooth	513.90	2121.20	2300	750	Medium	Moderate	Grazing & Agri
CH-LT-40	Low Piedmont-Smooth	515.15	2115.88	2420	850	Medium	Slight	Agricultural
CH-LT-41	Low Piedmont-Smooth	515.07	2115.29	2450	870	Shallow-Med	Moderate	Agricultural
CH-LT-42	Low Piedmont-Smooth	517.15	2116.33	2420	900	Shallow-Med	Moderate	Agricultural

CHALCO-XOCHIMILCO REGION - PREHISPANIC SETTLEMENT DATA
Late Toltec Sites

SITE NUMBER	CLASSIFICATION	ENVIRONMENTAL ZONE	AREA (in ha)	POP.	OTHER OCCUPATIONS EF	MF	LF	TF	EC	LC	ET	LT	EA	LA	TEMPORARY SITE NO.	SURVEY RECORDS SUPERVISOR	YEAR
CH-LT-1	Hamlet	Low Piedmont-Smooth	3.2	60	0	0	1	0	1	1	0	0	0	0	CH-T-15	M. PARSONS	1969
CH-LT-2	Lg Disp Village	Low Piedmont-Smooth	37.8	760	0	0	0	0	0	0	1	0	1	1	CH-T-16	J. PARSONS	1969
CH-LT-3	Sm Disp Village	Low Piedmont-Smooth	6.8	140	0	0	0	1	0	1	1	0	0	0	CH-T-14	J. PARSONS	1969
CH-LT-4	Lg Disp Village	Low Piedmont-Smooth	38.2	760	0	0	0	0	0	0	0	0	1	1	CH-T-13	J. PARSONS	1969
CH-LT-5	Hamlet	Low Piedmont-Smooth	6.2	120	0	0	0	0	0	0	0	0	1	1	CH-T-18	J. PARSONS	1969
CH-LT-6	Sm Disp Village	Low Piedmont-Smooth	21.9	400	0	0	1	0	0	0	0	0	1	1	CH-T-17	J. PARSONS	1969
CH-LT-7	Hamlet	Low Piedmont-Smooth	2.8	60	0	0	0	0	0	0	0	0	0	0	CH-T-20	J. PARSONS	1969
CH-LT-8	Hamlet	Low Piedmont-Smooth	1.5	40	0	0	0	0	0	0	0	0	0	0	CH-T-19	J. PARSONS	1969
CH-LT-9	Hamlet	Low Piedmont-Smooth	2.0	30	0	0	0	0	0	0	0	0	0	0	CH-T-21	J. PARSONS	1969
CH-LT-10	Small Hamlet	Low Piedmont-Smooth	0.2	10	0	0	0	0	0	0	0	0	0	0	CH-LT-17	J. PARSONS	1972
CH-LT-11	Small Hamlet	Low Piedmont-Smooth	1.8	20	0	0	0	0	0	0	0	0	0	0	CH-LT-11	J. PARSONS	1972
CH-LT-12	Small Hamlet	Low Piedmont-Smooth	0.5	10	0	0	0	0	0	0	0	0	0	0	CH-LT-16	J. PARSONS	1972
CH-LT-13	Local Center	Island-Lakesh Plain	43.3	2000	0	0	0	0	0	0	1	0	0	0	CH-T-1	J. PARSONS	1969
CH-LT-14	Small Hamlet	Upr Piedmont-Smooth	0.2	5	0	0	0	0	0	0	0	0	0	0	CH-LT-48	J. PARSONS	1969
CH-LT-15	Small Hamlet	Low Piedmont-Smooth	0.5	10	0	0	0	0	0	0	1	0	0	1	CH-A-27	J. PARSONS	1969
CH-LT-16	Small Hamlet	Low Piedmont-Smooth	0.6	10	0	0	0	0	0	0	0	0	0	1	CH-A-28	J. PARSONS	1969
CH-LT-17	Sm Disp Village	Low Piedmont-Smooth	11.1	200	0	1	1	0	1	1	0	0	0	0	CH-T-6	J. PARSONS	1969
CH-LT-18	Small Hamlet	Low Piedmont-Smooth	1.9	20	0	0	0	0	0	0	0	0	0	1	CH-T-7	J. PARSONS	1969
CH-LT-19	Hamlet	Lakeshore Plain	3.5	30	0	0	0	1	0	0	0	0	0	0	CH-F-8	J. PARSONS	1969
CH-LT-20	Hamlet	Low Piedmont-Smooth	4.8	100	0	0	0	0	0	0	0	0	0	0	CH-T-23	M. PARSONS	1969
CH-LT-21	Sm Disp Village	Low Piedmont-Smooth	9.0	180	0	0	0	0	0	1	1	0	1	1	CH-T-29	M. PARSONS	1969
CH-LT-22	Hamlet	Low Piedmont-Smooth	4.1	40	0	0	0	0	0	0	1	0	0	0	CH-T-22	M. PARSONS	1969
CH-LT-23	Small Hamlet	Low Piedmont-Smooth	2.4	20	0	0	0	0	0	0	0	0	0	1	CH-T-28	M. PARSONS	1969
CH-LT-24	Hamlet	Low Piedmont-Smooth	4.0	80	0	0	0	0	0	0	0	0	0	0	CH-T-12	J. PARSONS	1969
CH-LT-25	Hamlet	Low Piedmont-Smooth	1.7	30	0	0	0	0	0	0	0	0	0	0	CH-T-12	J. PARSONS	1969
CH-LT-26	Hamlet	Low Piedmont-Smooth	1.7	30	0	0	0	0	0	0	0	0	0	0	CH-LT-32	J. PARSONS	1969
CH-LT-27	Sm Disp Village	Low Piedmont-Smooth	10.1	200	0	0	1	1	0	0	0	0	0	0	CH-T-32	J. PARSONS	1969
CH-LT-28	Sm Disp Village	Low Piedmont-Smooth	12.2	240	0	0	1	1	1	1	1	0	0	1	CH-T-9	J. PARSONS	1969
CH-LT-29	Small Hamlet	Low Piedmont-Smooth	0.6	10	0	0	1	1	0	0	0	0	0	0	CH-T-11	J. PARSONS	1969
CH-LT-30	Hamlet	Low Piedmont-Smooth	4.9	100	0	0	1	1	0	0	0	0	0	0	CH-T-8	J. PARSONS	1969
CH-LT-31	Hamlet	Low Piedmont-Smooth	2.7	50	0	0	0	0	0	0	0	0	0	0	CH-T-37	J. PARSONS	1969
CH-LT-32	Questionable	Low Piedmont-Smooth	0.6	0	0	0	0	0	0	0	0	0	0	0	CH-T-33	M. PARSONS	1969
CH-LT-33	Hamlet	Low Piedmont-Smooth	2.7	40	0	0	0	0	0	0	0	0	0	0	CH-T-34	M. PARSONS	1969
CH-LT-34	Hamlet	Low Piedmont-Smooth	2.6	30	0	0	0	0	0	0	0	0	0	0	CH-T-35	M. PARSONS	1969
CH-LT-35	Hamlet	Low Piedmont-Smooth	4.4	80	0	0	0	0	0	0	0	0	1	1	CH-T-36	M. PARSONS	1969
CH-LT-36	Small Hamlet	Lakeshore Plain	0.5	10	0	0	0	0	0	0	0	0	0	1	AM-AZ-48	M. PARSONS	1972
CH-LT-37	Small Hamlet	Low Piedmont-Smooth	1.1	20	0	0	0	0	0	0	0	0	1	1	CH-T-38	M. PARSONS	1969
CH-LT-38	Hamlet	Low Piedmont-Smooth	3.0	60	0	0	0	0	0	0	0	0	0	1	CH-T-39	M. PARSONS	1969
CH-LT-39	Hamlet	Low Piedmont-Smooth	5.7	100	0	0	0	0	0	0	0	0	0	1	CH-T-40	M. PARSONS	1969
CH-LT-40	Sm Disp Village	Low Piedmont-Smooth	6.8	140	0	0	0	0	0	0	0	0	0	0	AM-LT-1	M. PARSONS	1972
CH-LT-41	Small Hamlet	Low Piedmont-Smooth	0.8	10	0	0	0	0	0	0	0	0	1	0	AM-LT-4	M. PARSONS	1972
CH-LT-42	Small Hamlet	Low Piedmont-Smooth	1.1	10	0	0	0	0	0	0	0	0	0	0	AM-LT-2	M. PARSONS	1972

38

CHALCO-XOCHIMILCO REGION - ENVIRONMENTAL DATA
Late Toltec Sites

Site Number	Environmental Zone	UTM Coordinates East	North	Elev (in m)	Rainfall (in mm)	Modern Soil Depth	Modern Erosion	Modern Land use
CH-LT-43	Low Piedmont-Smooth	518.22	2116.56	2460	915	Shallow-Med	Moderate	Agricultural
CH-LT-44	Low Piedmont-Smooth	517.93	2116.16	2430	910	Shallow-Med	Deep	Agricultural
CH-LT-45	Low Piedmont-Smooth	518.55	2116.33	2460	940	Shallow	Moderate	Agricultural
CH-LT-46	Low Piedmont-Smooth	518.45	2115.41	2410	950	Medium-Deep	Moderate	Agricultural
CH-LT-47	Low Piedmont-Smooth	519.25	2115.94	2430	950	Shallow	Deep	Agricultural
CH-LT-48	Low Piedmont-Smooth	520.05	2116.41	2450	960	Medium-Deep	Moderate	Agricultural
CH-LT-49	Amecameca Sub-Valley	520.55	2117.33	2510	980	Medium-Deep	Moderate	Agricultural
CH-LT-50	Amecameca Sub-Valley	520.72	2117.66	2510	980	Medium	Moderate-Deep	Grazing & Agri
CH-LT-51	Amecameca Sub-Valley	522.95	2118.36	2470	1030	Deep	Slight	Agricultural
CH-LT-52	Amecameca Sub-Valley	521.95	2116.63	2460	1020	Deep	Slight	Agricultural
CH-LT-53	Amecameca Sub-Valley	525.32	2115.88	2480	1060	Deep	Slight	Agricultural
CH-LT-54	Amecameca Sub-Valley	528.24	2114.46	2610	1130	Medium	Moderate	Grazing & Agri
CH-LT-55	Upr Piedmont-Rugged	510.47	2113.91	2560	1000	Shallow-Med	Moderate	Agricultural
CH-LT-56	Upr Piedmont-Rugged	509.57	2115.08	2700	1000	Very Shallow	Deep	None
CH-LT-57	Upr Piedmont-Rugged	511.32	2118.08	2560	800	Medium	Moderate	Grazing & Agri
CH-LT-58	Lakeshore Plain	512.53	2122.69	2265	700	Deep	None	Agricultural
CH-LT-59	Lakeshore Plain	512.78	2123.21	2260	690	Deep	None	Agricultural
CH-LT-60	Lakeshore Plain	512.70	2124.08	2255	690	Deep	None	Agricultural
CH-LT-61	Lakeshore Plain	512.03	2124.44	2250	690	Deep	None	Agricultural
CH-LT-62	Lakeshore Plain	511.25	2123.16	2255	705	Medium-Deep	Slight	Agricultural
CH-LT-63	Lakeshore Plain	510.90	2125.31	2245	690	Deep	None	Agricultural
CH-LT-64	Lakeshore Plain	510.18	2124.41	2245	690	Deep	None	Agricultural
CH-LT-65	Lakeshore Plain	509.93	2125.54	2245	690	Deep	None	Agricultural
CH-LT-66	Lakeshore Plain	509.70	2125.98	2245	690	Deep	None	Agricultural
CH-LT-67	Lakeshore Plain	510.80	2126.91	2245	680	Deep	None	Agricultural
CH-LT-68	Lakeshore Plain	511.57	2127.60	2245	675	Deep	None	Agricultural
CH-LT-69	Lakeshore Plain	512.12	2129.10	2245	675	Deep	None	Agricultural
CH-LT-70	Island-Lakesh Plain	505.30	2128.90	2245	670	Deep	Very Slight	Grazing
CH-LT-71	Lakebed	507.30	2127.95	2240	675	Deep	None	Agricultural
CH-LT-72	Low Piedmont-Rugged	507.75	2123.29	2300	740	Medium-Deep	Slight	Agricultural
CH-LT-73	Low Piedmont-Rugged	507.05	2123.21	2300	750	Shallow-Med	Moderate	Agricultural
CH-LT-74	Low Piedmont-Rugged	505.05	2123.26	2260	775	Medium	Moderate	Grazing
CH-LT-75	Lakebed	504.78	2128.88	2240	675	Deep	None	Agricultural
CH-LT-76	Lakebed	505.15	2127.71	2240	675	Deep	None	Agricultural
CH-LT-77	Lakebed	504.25	2128.46	2240	675	Deep	None	Agricultural
CH-LT-78	Lakebed	503.93	2127.88	2240	680	Deep	None	Agricultural
CH-LT-79	Lakebed	503.43	2127.94	2240	680	Deep	None	Agricultural
CH-LT-80	Lakebed	503.13	2127.48	2240	680	Deep	None	Agricultural
CH-LT-81	Low Piedmont-Rugged	501.80	2123.44	2280	760	Medium	Moderate	Agricultural
CH-LT-82	Low Piedmont-Rugged	501.43	2123.66	2270	760	Medium	Moderate	Agricultural
CH-LT-83	Low Piedmont-Rugged	501.07	2123.91	2270	765	Medium	Moderate	Agricultural
CH-LT-84	Low Piedmont-Rugged	501.55	2123.91	2270	750	Medium	Moderate	Agricultural

CHALCO-XOCHIMILCO REGION - PREHISPANIC SETTLEMENT DATA
Late Toltec Sites

SITE NUMBER	CLASSIFICATION	ENVIRONMENTAL ZONE	AREA (in ha)	POP.	EF	MF	LF	TF	EC	LC	ET	LT	EA	LA	TEMPORARY SITE NO.	SUPERVISOR	YEAR
CH-LT-43	Small Hamlet	Low Piedmont-Smooth	0.5	10	0	0	0	0	0	0	1	0	0	0		E. PRAHL	1972
CH-LT-44	Hamlet	Low Piedmont-Smooth	3.9	80	0	0	0	0	0	0	1	0	1	1	AM-LT-3	M. PARSONS	1972
CH-LT-45	Hamlet	Low Piedmont-Smooth	4.0	80	0	0	0	0	0	0	1	0	1	0	AM-LT-5	M. PARSONS	1972
CH-LT-46	Small Hamlet	Low Piedmont-Smooth	1.4	10	0	0	1	0	0	0	0	0	0	0	AM-LT-9	M. PARSONS	1972
CH-LT-47	Small Hamlet	Low Piedmont-Smooth	0.4	10	0	0	1	1	0	0	0	0	0	0	AM-LF-16	E. PRAHL	1972
CH-LT-48	Small Hamlet	Low Piedmont-Smooth	0.5	10	0	0	0	0	0	0	0	0	0	0	AM-LT-4	E. PRAHL	1972
CH-LT-49	Hamlet	Amecameca Sub-Valley	4.4	80	0	0	0	0	0	0	0	0	1	0	AM-LT-1	E. PRAHL	1972
CH-LT-50	Small Hamlet	Amecameca Sub-Valley	1.2	20	0	0	0	0	0	0	0	0	0	0	AM-LT-3	E. PRAHL	1972
CH-LT-51	Small Hamlet	Amecameca Sub-Valley	0.6	10	0	0	0	0	0	0	0	0	0	0		E. PRAHL	1972
CH-LT-52	Hamlet	Amecameca Sub-Valley	1.9	50	0	0	0	0	0	0	0	0	0	0	AM-LT-2	E. PRAHL	1972
CH-LT-53	Small Hamlet	Amecameca Sub-Valley	0.5	20	0	0	0	1	0	0	0	0	0	0	AM-LT-7	J. PARSONS	1972
CH-LT-54	Small Hamlet	Amecameca Sub-Valley	0.1	10	0	0	0	0	0	0	0	0	0	0	AM-LT-6	E. PRAHL	1972
CH-LT-55	Small Hamlet	Upr Piedmont-Rugged	1.8	20	0	0	0	0	0	0	0	0	0	1	AM-LT-7	M. PARSONS	1972
CH-LT-56	Questionable	Upr Piedmont-Rugged	0.1	0	0	0	0	0	0	0	0	0	0	0		M. PARSONS	1972
CH-LT-57	Small Hamlet	Upr Piedmont-Rugged	0.8	10	0	0	0	0	0	0	1	0	1	1	AM-LT-8	M. PARSONS	1972
CH-LT-58	Hamlet	Lakeshore Plain	8.1	100	0	1	0	0	0	0	0	0	0	0	AM-LT-17	M. PARSONS	1972
CH-LT-59	Hamlet	Lakeshore Plain	3.5	60	0	0	0	0	0	0	0	0	0	1	AM-LT-16	M. PARSONS	1972
CH-LT-60	Small Hamlet	Lakeshore Plain	0.4	10	0	0	0	0	0	0	0	0	0	0		M. PARSONS	1972
CH-LT-61	Small Hamlet	Lakeshore Plain	0.3	10	0	0	0	0	0	0	0	0	0	0	AM-LT-13	M. PARSONS	1972
CH-LT-62	Small Hamlet	Lakeshore Plain	0.7	10	0	0	0	0	0	0	1	0	1	0	AM-LT-12	M. PARSONS	1972
CH-LT-63	Small Hamlet	Lakeshore Plain	0.7	10	0	0	0	0	0	0	1	0	0	0	CH-LT-15	J. PARSONS	1972
CH-LT-64	Hamlet	Lakeshore Plain	2.8	30	0	0	0	0	1	1	1	0	0	0	AM-LT-15	M. PARSONS	1972
CH-LT-65	Hamlet	Lakeshore Plain	7.6	100	0	0	0	0	1	1	1	0	0	0	CH-LT-13	J. PARSONS	1972
CH-LT-66	Small Hamlet	Lakeshore Plain	0.9	20	0	0	0	0	0	0	1	0	0	0	CH-LT-12	J. PARSONS	1972
CH-LT-67	Small Hamlet	Lakeshore Plain	1.7	10	0	0	0	0	0	0	0	0	0	0	CH-LT-14	J. PARSONS	1969
CH-LT-68	Sm Disp Village	Lakeshore Plain	6.5	130	0	0	0	0	0	0	0	0	1	0	CH-T-4	J. PARSONS	1969
CH-LT-69	Small Hamlet	Lakeshore Plain	0.5	10	0	0	0	0	0	0	0	0	0	1	CH-LT-17	J. PARSONS	1969
CH-LT-70	Small Hamlet	Island-Lakesh Plain	0.5	10	0	0	0	0	0	0	0	0	1	1	CH-T-2	J. PARSONS	1969
CH-LT-71	Small Hamlet	Lakebed	0.3	10	0	0	0	0	0	0	0	0	1	0	CH-A-12	J. PARSONS	1969
CH-LT-72	Small Hamlet	Low Piedmont-Rugged	0.1	10	0	0	0	0	0	0	0	0	0	0	AM-LT-14	M. PARSONS	1972
CH-LT-73	Small Hamlet	Low Piedmont-Rugged	1.4	20	0	0	0	0	0	0	0	0	0	0	CH-LT-11	J. PARSONS	1972
CH-LT-74	Hamlet	Low Piedmont-Rugged	4.9	100	0	0	0	0	0	0	0	0	0	0	CH-LT-10	J. PARSONS	1972
CH-LT-75	Small Hamlet	Lakebed	0.7	20	0	0	0	0	0	0	0	0	0	0	CH-LT-1	R. WENKE	1972
CH-LT-76	Small Hamlet	Lakebed	0.8	10	0	0	0	0	0	0	0	0	1	1	CH-LT-12	R. WENKE	1972
CH-LT-77	Small Hamlet	Lakebed	0.4	10	0	0	0	0	0	0	0	0	0	0	CH-LT-2	R. WENKE	1972
CH-LT-78	Small Hamlet	Lakebed	0.4	10	0	0	0	0	0	0	0	0	0	0	CH-LT-3	R. WENKE	1972
CH-LT-79	Small Hamlet	Lakebed	0.8	10	0	0	0	1	0	0	0	0	0	1	CH-LT-6	R. WENKE	1972
CH-LT-80	Hamlet	Lakebed	8.5	100	0	0	0	0	0	0	0	0	1	0	CH-LT-7	R. WENKE	1972
CH-LT-81	Hamlet	Low Piedmont-Rugged	2.1	30	0	0	0	0	0	0	0	0	0	0	CH-LT-9	J. PARSONS	1972
CH-LT-82	Small Hamlet	Low Piedmont-Rugged	0.5	10	0	0	0	1	0	0	0	0	0	0	CH-LT-8	J. PARSONS	1972
CH-LT-83	Small Hamlet	Low Piedmont-Rugged	0.4	10	0	0	0	0	0	0	0	0	0	0	CH-LT-6	J. PARSONS	1972
CH-LT-84	Small Hamlet	Low Piedmont-Rugged	1.0	10	0	0	0	1	0	0	0	0	0	0	CH-LT-7	J. PARSONS	1972

OTHER OCCUPATIONS columns: EF MF LF TF EC LC ET LT EA LA. Columns under SURVEY RECORDS: TEMPORARY SITE NO., SUPERVISOR, YEAR.

CHALCO-XOCHIMILCO REGION - ENVIRONMENTAL DATA
Late Toltec Sites

Site Number	Environmental Zone	UTM Coordinates East	North	Elev (in m)	Rainfall (in mm)	Modern Soil Depth	Modern Erosion	Modern Land use
CH-LT-85	Low Piedmont-Rugged	501.05	2124.21	2270	750	Medium	Slight	Agricultural
CH-LT-86	Low Piedmont-Rugged	500.44	2125.28	2290	730	Medium	Moderate	Agricultural
CH-LT-87	Low Piedmont-Rugged	500.03	2125.83	2300	740	Medium	Moderate	Agricultural
CH-LT-88	Low Piedmont-Rugged	500.63	2125.56	2270	735	Medium-Deep	Moderate	Agricultural
CH-LT-89	Lakeshore Plain	499.66	2128.20	2255	720	Medium	Slight-Moderate	Grazing & Agri
CH-LT-90	Lakebed	500.95	2130.79	2240	680	Deep	None	Agricultural
XO-LT-1	Lakebed	498.41	2132.03	2240	680	Deep	None	Agricultural
XO-LT-2	Lakeshore Plain	497.41	2129.13	2253	730	Deep	Slight	Agricultural
XO-LT-3	Lakeshore Plain	497.41	2128.20	2255	775	Deep	Slight	Agricultural
XO-LT-4	Low Piedmont-Rugged	490.53	2127.33	2270	775	Medium	Moderate	Agricultural
XO-LT-5	Low Piedmont-Rugged	489.56	2127.73	2270	780	Medium	Moderate	Agricultural
XO-LT-6	Lakeshore Plain	488.31	2128.28	2245	750	Deep	Slight	Agricultural
XO-LT-7	Lakeshore Plain	487.88	2128.23	2245	750	Deep	None	Agricultural
XO-LT-8	Lakeshore Plain	487.01	2129.06	2250	730	Deep	Slight	Agricultural
XO-LT-9	Lakeshore Plain	484.92	2131.63	2260	780	Medium-Deep	Slight	Agricultural
XO-LT-10	Low Piedmont-Smooth	484.34	2131.00	2300	900	Shallow	Slight	Agricultural
XO-LT-11	Low Piedmont-Rugged	483.97	2131.20	2280	800	Medium	Slight	Agricultural

CHALCO-XOCHIMILCO REGION - PREHISPANIC SETTLEMENT DATA
Late Toltec Sites

SITE NUMBER	CLASSIFICATION	ENVIRONMENTAL ZONE	AREA (in ha)	POP.	EF	MF	LF	TF	EC	LC	ET	LT	EA	LA	TEMPORARY SITE NO.	SUPERVISOR	YEAR
CH-LT-85	Small Hamlet	Low Piedmont-Rugged	0.7	10	0	0	0	0	0	0	1	0	0	0	CH-LT-5	J. PARSONS	1972
CH-LT-86	Hamlet	Low Piedmont-Rugged	2.0	50	0	0	0	0	0	0	1	0	1	1	CH-LT-4	J. PARSONS	1972
CH-LT-87	Hamlet	Low Piedmont-Rugged	1.7	40	0	0	0	0	0	0	0	0	0	0	CH-LT-3	J. PARSONS	1972
CH-LT-88	Hamlet	Low Piedmont-Rugged	4.2	80	0	0	0	0	0	0	1	0	0	0	CH-LT-2	J. PARSONS	1972
CH-LT-89	Sm Disp Village	Lakeshore Plain	9.4	200	0	1	1	1	1	0	0	0	0	0	CH-LT-1	J. PARSONS	1972
CH-LT-90	Small Hamlet	Lakebed	1.1	10	0	0	0	0	0	0	0	0	1	1	CH-LT-11	R. WENKE	1972
XO-LT-1	Hamlet	Lakebed	1.1	30	0	0	0	0	0	0	6	0	0	0	XE-LT-1	M. PARSONS	1972
XO-LT-2	Sm Disp Village	Lakeshore Plain	12.1	200	0	0	0	0	0	0	1	0	0	0	XE-LT-2	M. PARSONS	1972
XO-LT-3	Small Hamlet	Lakeshore Plain	1.5	20	0	0	0	0	0	0	0	0	0	1	XE-ET-4	M. PARSONS	1972
XO-LT-4	Small Hamlet	Low Piedmont-Rugged	0.8	10	0	0	0	1	0	0	0	0	1	1	XW-LT-8	J. PARSONS	1972
XO-LT-5	Small Hamlet	Low Piedmont-Rugged	1.1	20	0	0	0	1	1	1	0	0	0	1	XW-CL-6	J. PARSONS	1972
XO-LT-6	Small Hamlet	Lakeshore Plain	0.7	10	0	0	0	0	0	0	0	0	0	1	XW-LT-7	J. PARSONS	1972
XO-LT-7	Small Hamlet	Lakeshore Plain	0.4	10	0	0	0	0	0	0	0	0	0	0	XW-LT-6	J. PARSONS	1972
XO-LT-8	Hamlet	Lakeshore Plain	2.4	100	0	0	0	0	0	0	0	0	0	0	XW-LT-3	J. PARSONS	1972
XO-LT-9	Hamlet	Lakeshore Plain	3.7	70	0	0	0	1	0	0	1	0	0	1	XW-LT-3	J. PARSONS	1972
XO-LT-10	Small Hamlet	Low Piedmont-Smooth	1.4	10	0	0	0	1	0	0	1	0	0	0	XW-LT-10	J. PARSONS	1972
XO-LT-11	Small Hamlet	Low Piedmont-Rugged	1.1	10	0	0	0	0	0	0	1	0	0	0	XW-LT-5	J. PARSONS	1972

SURVEY RECORDS

OTHER OCCUPATIONS

CHALCO-XOCHIMILCO REGION - ENVIRONMENTAL DATA

Aztec Sites

Site Number	Environmental Zone	UTM Coordinates East	North	Elev (in m)	Rainfall (in mm)	Modern Soil Depth	Modern Erosion	Modern Land use
CH-AZ-1	Low Piedmont-Smooth	518.43	2136.15	2390	760	Very Shallow	Deep	Grazing
CH-AZ-2	Low Piedmont-Smooth	518.68	2135.38	2450	790	Medium	Moderate	Agricultural
CH-AZ-3	Low Piedmont-Smooth	516.27	2134.53	2350	700	Very Shallow	Deep	Grazing & Agri
CH-AZ-4	Low Piedmont-Smooth	513.95	2133.53	2270	690	Deep	Slight	Agricultural
CH-AZ-5	Low Piedmont-Smooth	516.35	2133.03	2330	730	Medium	Moderate-Deep	Grazing & Agri
CH-AZ-6	Upr Piedmont-Smooth	519.97	2133.58	2500	910	Fully Eroded	Deep	None
CH-AZ-7	Low Piedmont-Smooth	517.10	2131.47	2325	760	Shallow-Med	Moderate-Deep	Grazing & Agri
CH-AZ-8	Low Piedmont-Smooth	518.57	2131.20	2350	780	Medium	Moderate	Agricultural
CH-AZ-9	Low Piedmont-Smooth	518.75	2130.85	2345	790	Shallow-Med	Moderate-Deep	Grazing & Agri
CH-AZ-10	Low Piedmont-Smooth	519.75	2130.85	2360	830	Medium	Moderate	Agricultural
CH-AZ-11	Low Piedmont-Smooth	520.90	2131.25	2420	910	Very Shallow	Deep	Grazing
CH-AZ-12	Low Piedmont-Smooth	520.18	2130.63	2380	850	Shallow-Med	Moderate-Deep	Agricultural
CH-AZ-13	Low Piedmont-Smooth	519.72	2130.20	2350	850	Shallow-Med	Moderate-Deep	Agricultural
CH-AZ-14	Low Piedmont-Smooth	518.77	2129.75	2300	810	Medium	Moderate	None
CH-AZ-15	Low Piedmont-Smooth	520.72	2129.13	2375	900	Very Shallow	Deep	Grazing
CH-AZ-16	Low Piedmont-Smooth	520.77	2128.50	2350	910	Shallow	Deep	Grazing & Agri
CH-AZ-17	Low Piedmont-Smooth	520.02	2127.13	2310	900	Medium	Moderate	Agricultural
CH-AZ-18	Low Piedmont-Smooth	519.25	2127.10	2300	850	Medium-Deep	Moderate	Agricultural
CH-AZ-19	Low Piedmont-Smooth	519.35	2126.63	2310	875	Medium	Moderate	Agricultural
CH-AZ-20	Low Piedmont-Smooth	518.65	2125.70	2290	860	Medium-Deep	Moderate	Agricultural
CH-AZ-21	Low Piedmont-Smooth	517.82	2125.60	2295	830	Deep	Slight-Moderate	Agricultural
CH-AZ-22	Low Piedmont-Smooth	518.85	2125.30	2300	860	Medium-Deep	Slight-Moderate	Agricultural
CH-AZ-23	Low Piedmont-Smooth	520.65	2123.53	2385	940	Medium-Deep	Slight-Moderate	Agricultural
CH-AZ-24	Low Piedmont-Smooth	520.77	2122.45	2430	960	Medium	Moderate	Agricultural
CH-AZ-25	Upr Piedmont-Smooth	520.15	2121.75	2500	950	Medium	Moderate	Grazing & Agri
CH-AZ-26	Upr Piedmont-Smooth	520.02	2121.28	2530	950	Medium	Moderate	Grazing & Agri
CH-AZ-27	Upr Piedmont-Smooth	519.55	2120.75	2550	930	Medium	Moderate	Agricultural
CH-AZ-28	Low Piedmont-Smooth	516.60	2121.47	2430	830	Medium	Moderate	Agricultural
CH-AZ-29	Low Piedmont-Smooth	517.95	2120.78	2470	880	Shallow-Med	Moderate-Deep	Agricultural
CH-AZ-30	Amecameca Sub-Valley	522.10	2120.04	2550	1040	Shallow	Deep	Agricultural
CH-AZ-31	Amecameca Sub-Valley	522.68	2119.16	2490	1025	Medium-Deep	Slight	Agricultural
CH-AZ-32	Amecameca Sub-Valley	524.50	2118.66	2500	1050	Deep	Slight	Agricultural
CH-AZ-33	Amecameca Sub-Valley	524.78	2116.88	2480	1050	Deep	Slight-Moderate	Agricultural
CH-AZ-34	Amecameca Sub-Valley	522.53	2118.38	2490	1010	Medium	Moderate	Agricultural
CH-AZ-35	Amecameca Sub-Valley	522.22	2117.61	2480	1020	Medium-Deep	Slight	Agricultural
CH-AZ-36	Upr Piedmont-Smooth	520.40	2118.36	2610	1000	Deep	Slight	Grazing
CH-AZ-37	Amecameca Sub-Valley	520.68	2117.19	2500	1010	Medium	Moderate	Agricultural
CH-AZ-38	Amecameca Sub-Valley	523.80	2116.31	2470	1050	Medium-Deep	Slight	Grazing & Agri
CH-AZ-39	Amecameca Sub-Valley	523.47	2115.41	2470	1040	Deep	Slight	Agricultural
CH-AZ-40	Amecameca Sub-Valley	522.97	2114.29	2460	1040	Deep	Slight	Agricultural
CH-AZ-41	Amecameca Sub-Valley	523.30	2113.41	2470	1050	Medium-Deep	Moderate	Agricultural
CH-AZ-42	Amecameca Sub-Valley	522.40	2113.16	2460	1040	Medium-Deep	Slight-Moderate	Agricultural

CHALCO-XOCHIMILCO REGION - PREHISPANIC SETTLEMENT DATA
Aztec Sites

SITE NUMBER	CLASSIFICATION	ENVIRONMENTAL ZONE	AREA (in ha)	POP.	EF	MF	LF	TF	EC	LC	ET	LT	EA	LA	TEMPORARY SITE NO.	SUPERVISOR	YEAR
CH-AZ-1	Hamlet	Low Piedmont-Smooth	6.1	70	0	1	0	0	0	0	0	0	0	1	CH-F-18	J. PARSONS	1969
CH-AZ-2	Hamlet	Low Piedmont-Smooth	4.1	80	0	1	0	0	0	0	0	0	1	1	CH-A-25	J. PARSONS	1969
CH-AZ-3	Lg Disp Village	Low Piedmont-Smooth	64.0	1280	0	0	0	0	0	0	1	1	1	1	CH-A-45	J. PARSONS	1969
CH-AZ-4	Hamlet	Low Piedmont-Smooth	3.8	40	0	0	1	0	0	0	0	0	0	1	CH-F-15	J. PARSONS	1969
CH-AZ-5	Lg Disp Village	Low Piedmont-Smooth	70.6	1000	0	0	0	0	0	0	2	1	1	1	CH-A-44	J. PARSONS	1969
CH-AZ-6	Small Hamlet	Upr Piedmont-Smooth	0.5	10	0	0	0	0	0	0	0	0	1	0	CH-AZ-33	J. PARSONS	1972
CH-AZ-7	Lg Disp Village	Low Piedmont-Smooth	60.0	800	0	0	1	0	1	0	0	0	0	1	CH-AZ-7	J. PARSONS	1969
CH-AZ-8	Hamlet	Low Piedmont-Smooth	2.5	50	0	0	0	0	0	0	0	0	0	1	CH-AZ-8	J. PARSONS	1969
CH-AZ-9	Hamlet	Low Piedmont-Smooth	5.2	60	0	1	0	0	0	0	0	0	0	1	CH-F-4	J. PARSONS	1969
CH-AZ-10	Small Hamlet	Low Piedmont-Smooth	1.1	15	0	0	0	0	0	0	0	0	1	1	CH-A-26	J. PARSONS	1969
CH-AZ-11	Small Hamlet	Low Piedmont-Smooth	0.2	10	0	0	0	0	0	0	0	0	1	1	CH-A-29	J. PARSONS	1969
CH-AZ-12	Small Hamlet	Low Piedmont-Smooth	0.7	10	0	0	0	0	0	0	1	1	0	1	CH-A-27	J. PARSONS	1969
CH-AZ-13	Small Hamlet	Low Piedmont-Smooth	1.3	20	0	0	0	0	0	0	0	0	1	1	CH-A-28	J. PARSONS	1969
CH-AZ-14	Hamlet	Low Piedmont-Smooth	2.5	40	0	0	0	0	0	0	0	1	0	1	CH-A-20	J. PARSONS	1969
CH-AZ-15	Sm Disp Village	Low Piedmont-Smooth	13.9	140	0	0	0	1	0	0	0	0	1	0	CH-A-30	M. PARSONS	1969
CH-AZ-16	Hamlet	Low Piedmont-Smooth	3.0	30	0	0	0	0	0	0	0	0	0	1	CH-T-25	M. PARSONS	1969
CH-AZ-17	Hamlet	Low Piedmont-Smooth	4.3	30	0	0	0	0	0	0	0	0	1	1	CH-A-31	M. PARSONS	1969
CH-AZ-18	Hamlet	Low Piedmont-Smooth	8.3	80	0	0	0	0	1	0	1	1	1	1	CH-A-42	M. PARSONS	1969
CH-AZ-19	Small Hamlet	Low Piedmont-Smooth	0.7	10	0	0	0	0	0	0	0	0	0	1	CH-T-28	M. PARSONS	1969
CH-AZ-20	Hamlet	Low Piedmont-Smooth	4.3	90	0	1	1	1	0	0	1	1	1	1	CH-A-23	J. PARSONS	1969
CH-AZ-21	Hamlet	Low Piedmont-Smooth	6.0	60	0	0	1	1	0	0	0	1	0	1	CH-F-13	J. PARSONS	1969
CH-AZ-22	Sm Disp Village	Low Piedmont-Smooth	11.7	120	0	0	0	1	1	0	0	0	1	1	CH-F-13	J. PARSONS	1969
CH-AZ-23	Local Center	Low Piedmont-Smooth	80.0	4000	0	0	1	1	0	0	1	0	0	1	CH-A-43	J. PARSONS	1969
CH-AZ-24	Small Hamlet	Low Piedmont-Smooth	1.0	15	0	0	0	0	0	0	0	0	1	1	CH-A-40	J. PARSONS	1969
CH-AZ-25	Small Hamlet	Upr Piedmont-Smooth	0.9	20	0	0	0	0	0	0	0	0	1	1	CH-A-34	J. PARSONS	1969
CH-AZ-26	Small Hamlet	Upr Piedmont-Smooth	1.1	10	0	0	1	0	0	0	0	1	0	1	CH-A-35	J. PARSONS	1969
CH-AZ-27	Sm Disp Village	Upr Piedmont-Smooth	8.3	160	0	0	0	0	0	0	1	0	1	1	CH-A-36	J. PARSONS	1969
CH-AZ-28	Small Hamlet	Low Piedmont-Smooth	0.9	20	0	0	0	0	0	0	0	0	1	1	CH-A-38	J. PARSONS	1969
CH-AZ-29	Small Hamlet	Low Piedmont-Smooth	1.4	20	0	0	0	0	0	0	0	0	1	1	CH-A-37	J. PARSONS	1969
CH-AZ-30	Small Hamlet	Amecameca Sub-Valley	0.7	10	0	0	0	0	0	0	0	0	0	1	AM-AZ-3	E. PRAHL	1972
CH-AZ-31	Small Hamlet	Amecameca Sub-Valley	1.8	20	0	0	0	0	0	0	0	0	0	1	AM-AZ-6	E. PRAHL	1972
CH-AZ-32	Small Hamlet	Amecameca Sub-Valley	0.5	10	0	0	0	0	0	0	0	0	0	1	AM-AZ-7	E. PRAHL	1972
CH-AZ-33	Small Hamlet	Amecameca Sub-Valley	0.2	10	0	0	0	0	0	0	0	0	0	1		E. PRAHL	1972
CH-AZ-34	Small Hamlet	Amecameca Sub-Valley	0.5	10	0	0	0	0	0	0	0	0	0	1	AM-AZ-1	E. PRAHL	1972
CH-AZ-35	Hamlet	Amecameca Sub-Valley	2.7	30	0	0	1	0	0	0	1	0	0	1	AM-AZ-5	E. PRAHL	1972
CH-AZ-36	Small Hamlet	Upr Piedmont-Smooth	1.5	15	0	0	0	0	0	0	0	0	1	1	AM-LT-1	E. PRAHL	1972
CH-AZ-37	Small Hamlet	Amecameca Sub-Valley	0.7	20	0	0	0	0	0	0	1	0	1	0	AM-CL-1	E. PRAHL	1972
CH-AZ-38	Small Hamlet	Amecameca Sub-Valley	0.8	10	0	0	0	0	0	1	0	0	1	0	AM-AZ-4	E. PRAHL	1972
CH-AZ-39	Hamlet	Amecameca Sub-Valley	2.8	30	0	0	0	0	0	1	0	0	1	0	AM-AZ-8	E. PRAHL	1972
CH-AZ-40	Small Hamlet	Amecameca Sub-Valley	0.9	10	0	0	0	0	1	0	1	0	1	1	AM-AZ-8	E. PRAHL	1972
CH-AZ-41	Local Center	Amecameca Sub-Valley	400.0	10000	0	0	0	0	1	1	0	0	1	1	AM-AZ-9	E. PRAHL	1972
CH-AZ-42	Small Hamlet	Amecameca Sub-Valley	0.3	10	0	0	0	0	0	0	0	0	1	0		E. PRAHL	1972

Early Aztec and Late Aztec occupations are tabulated on a presence-absence basis.

CHALCO-XOCHIMILCO REGION - ENVIRONMENTAL DATA
Aztec Sites

Site Number	Environmental Zone	UTM Coordinates East	North	Elev (in m)	Rainfall (in mm)	Modern Soil Depth	Modern Erosion	Modern Land use
CH-AZ-43	Amecameca Sub-Valley	524.10	2113.01	2470	1070	Deep	Moderate	Agricultural
CH-AZ-44	Amecameca Sub-Valley	525.17	2112.61	2480	1075	Deep	Slight	Agricultural
CH-AZ-45	Amecameca Sub-Valley	525.56	2112.36	2490	1085	Medium-Deep	Slight-Moderate	Agricultural
CH-AZ-46	Amecameca Sub-Valley	526.59	2113.04	2500	1100	Deep	Slight	Agricultural
CH-AZ-47	Amecameca Sub-Valley	527.71	2113.63	2560	1120	Medium	Moderate	Grazing
CH-AZ-48	Amecameca Sub-Valley	526.59	2112.01	2510	1100	Medium	Moderate	Agricultural
CH-AZ-49	Amecameca Sub-Valley	526.36	2112.36	2505	1100	Medium	Moderate	Agricultural
CH-AZ-50	Amecameca Sub-Valley	526.17	2112.06	2500	1100	Medium	Moderate	Agricultural
CH-AZ-51	Amecameca Sub-Valley	526.29	2111.61	2520	1100	Deep	Slight	Agricultural
CH-AZ-52	Amecameca Sub-Valley	527.09	2111.51	2540	1120	Deep	Moderate	Agricultural
CH-AZ-53	Amecameca Sub-Valley	527.09	2111.19	2550	1120	Deep	Slight-Moderate	Agricultural
CH-AZ-54	Amecameca Sub-Valley	527.14	2110.46	2570	1110	Medium	Moderate	Agricultural
CH-AZ-55	Amecameca Sub-Valley	526.44	2110.46	2540	1100	Medium	Moderate	Agricultural
CH-AZ-56	Amecameca Sub-Valley	525.70	2109.04	2500	1100	Medium	Moderate	Agricultural
CH-AZ-57	Amecameca Sub-Valley	524.72	2107.88	2440	1110	Medium	Moderate	Agricultural
CH-AZ-58	Amecameca Sub-Valley	523.78	2111.04	2470	1070	Deep	Slight	Agricultural
CH-AZ-59	Upr Piedmont-Rugged	520.53	2108.86	2520	1060	Medium	Moderate	Agricultural
CH-AZ-60	Low Piedmont-Rugged	520.62	2108.41	2480	1060	Medium	Moderate	Agricultural
CH-AZ-61	Low Piedmont-Rugged	517.18	2107.83	2440	1060	Deep	Moderate	Agricultural
CH-AZ-62	Low Piedmont-Rugged	517.35	2107.86	2480	1060	Shallow-Med	Moderate	Grazing & Agri
CH-AZ-63	Upr Piedmont-Rugged	516.25	2107.61	2500	1040	Deep	Slight	Agricultural
CH-AZ-64	Upr Piedmont-Rugged	512.63	2107.83	2550	1050	Medium	Moderate	Grazing & Agri
CH-AZ-65	Upr Piedmont-Rugged	514.62	2110.58	2700	1000	Shallow	Moderate	Grazing & Agri
CH-AZ-66	Low Piedmont-Rugged	515.40	2112.01	2500	960	Medium	Moderate	Agricultural
CH-AZ-67	Low Piedmont-Rugged	519.40	2112.46	2480	1010	Medium	Moderate	Agricultural
CH-AZ-68	Low Piedmont-Rugged	519.12	2113.56	2450	990	Very Shallow	Deep	Agricultural
CH-AZ-69	Low Piedmont-Smooth	520.90	2115.06	2440	1010	Medium	Moderate	Agricultural
CH-AZ-70	Low Piedmont-Smooth	520.43	2116.33	2450	1000	Medium	Moderate	Agricultural
CH-AZ-71	Upr Piedmont-Smooth	519.15	2117.04	2540	950	Medium	Moderate	Agricultural
CH-AZ-72	Low Piedmont-Smooth	519.00	2114.96	2430	960	Shallow-Med	Slight-Moderate	Agricultural
CH-AZ-73	Low Piedmont-Smooth	518.00	2113.81	2440	990	Medium	Slight-Moderate	Agricultural
CH-AZ-74	Low Piedmont-Smooth	516.28	2113.31	2440	940	Medium	Moderate	Grazing
CH-AZ-75	Low Piedmont-Rugged	515.70	2113.66	2450	930	Shallow	Moderate	Agricultural
CH-AZ-76	Low Piedmont-Smooth	516.07	2114.01	2435	930	Medium	Moderate	Grazing
CH-AZ-77	Low Piedmont-Smooth	516.85	2114.46	2430	920	Medium	Moderate	Agricultural
CH-AZ-78	Low Piedmont-Hill	517.00	2114.88	2450	930	Medium	Moderate	Agricultural
CH-AZ-79	Low Piedmont-Smooth	517.50	2115.11	2420	920	Shallow	Deep	None
CH-AZ-80	Low Piedmont-Smooth	517.28	2115.46	2410	920	Medium	Moderate	Agricultural
CH-AZ-81	Low Piedmont-Smooth	518.32	2115.46	2400	950	Medium	Moderate	Agricultural
CH-AZ-82	Low Piedmont-Smooth	517.90	2115.96	2415	930	Medium	Moderate	Agricultural
CH-AZ-83	Low Piedmont-Smooth	518.15	2116.13	2450	930	Shallow	Moderate	Agricultural
CH-AZ-84	Low Piedmont-Smooth	518.28	2116.51	2480	930	Shallow-Med	Moderate-Deep	Grazing & Agri

CHALCO-XOCHIMILCO REGION – PREHISPANIC SETTLEMENT DATA
Aztec Sites

SITE NUMBER	CLASSIFICATION	ENVIRONMENTAL ZONE	AREA (in ha)	POP.	EF	MF	LF	TF	EC	LC	ET	LT	EA	LA	TEMPORARY SITE NO.	SUPERVISOR	YEAR
CH-AZ-43	Questionable	Amecameca Sub-Valley	1.2	15	0	0	0	0	0	0	0	0	0	1		E. PRAHL	1972
CH-AZ-44	Small Hamlet	Amecameca Sub-Valley	1.1	10	0	0	0	0	0	0	0	0	1	1		E. PRAHL	1972
CH-AZ-45	Small Hamlet	Amecameca Sub-Valley	1.3	10	0	0	0	0	0	0	0	0	0	1		E. PRAHL	1972
CH-AZ-46	Small Hamlet	Amecameca Sub-Valley	0.6	15	0	0	0	0	0	0	0	0	0	1		J. PARSONS	1972
CH-AZ-47	Ceremonial Ctr	Amecameca Sub-Valley	0.1	0	0	0	0	0	0	0	0	0	0	1		E. PRAHL	1972
CH-AZ-48	Small Hamlet	Amecameca Sub-Valley	1.2	10	0	0	0	0	0	0	0	0	0	1		E. PRAHL	1972
CH-AZ-49	Hamlet	Amecameca Sub-Valley	6.3	60	0	0	0	0	0	0	0	0	1	1		E. PRAHL	1972
CH-AZ-50	Small Hamlet	Amecameca Sub-Valley	0.8	10	0	0	0	0	0	0	0	0	0	1		E. PRAHL	1972
CH-AZ-51	Hamlet	Amecameca Sub-Valley	9.5	100	0	0	0	0	0	0	0	0	1	1	AM-AZ-11	E. PRAHL	1972
CH-AZ-52	Small Hamlet	Amecameca Sub-Valley	0.1	10	0	0	0	0	0	0	0	0	0	1		J. PARSONS	1972
CH-AZ-53	Small Hamlet	Amecameca Sub-Valley	0.1	10	0	0	0	0	0	0	0	0	0	1		J. PARSONS	1972
CH-AZ-54	Small Hamlet	Amecameca Sub-Valley	0.5	10	0	0	0	0	0	0	0	0	0	1		J. PARSONS	1972
CH-AZ-55	Small Hamlet	Amecameca Sub-Valley	0.9	10	0	0	0	0	0	0	0	0	0	1		E. PRAHL	1972
CH-AZ-56	Small Hamlet	Amecameca Sub-Valley	0.1	10	0	0	0	0	0	0	0	0	0	1		J. PARSONS	1972
CH-AZ-57	Small Hamlet	Amecameca Sub-Valley	0.9	10	0	0	1	0	0	0	0	0	0	1	AM-LF-8	E. PRAHL	1972
CH-AZ-58	Small Hamlet	Amecameca Sub-Valley	0.8	10	0	0	0	0	0	0	0	0	0	1		E. PRAHL	1972
CH-AZ-59	Hamlet	Upr Piedmont-Rugged	2.9	30	0	0	0	0	0	0	0	0	0	1	AM-AZ-13	E. PRAHL	1972
CH-AZ-60	Small Hamlet	Low Piedmont-Rugged	1.2	10	0	0	1	0	0	0	0	0	0	1	AM-AZ-12	E. PRAHL	1972
CH-AZ-61	Small Hamlet	Low Piedmont-Rugged	0.4	10	0	0	0	0	0	0	0	0	0	1	AM-LF-7	R. WENKE	1972
CH-AZ-62	Questionable	Low Piedmont-Rugged	0.1	10	0	0	0	0	0	0	0	0	0	1	AM-AZ-5	R. WENKE	1972
CH-AZ-63	Small Hamlet	Upr Piedmont-Rugged	1.0	20	0	0	0	0	0	0	0	0	0	1	AM-AZ-4	R. WENKE	1972
CH-AZ-64	Small Hamlet	Upr Piedmont-Rugged	1.1	10	0	0	0	0	0	0	0	0	0	1	AM-AZ-1	R. WENKE	1972
CH-AZ-65	Ceremonial Ctr	Upr Piedmont-Rugged	0.3	0	0	0	0	0	0	0	0	0	0	1	AM-AZ-3	R. WENKE	1972
CH-AZ-66	Hamlet	Low Piedmont-Rugged	4.1	100	0	0	0	0	0	0	0	0	1	1	AM-AZ-2	R. WENKE	1972
CH-AZ-67	Questionable	Low Piedmont-Rugged	0.7	30	0	0	0	0	0	0	0	0	0	1	AM-AZ-10	E. PRAHL	1972
CH-AZ-68	Small Hamlet	Low Piedmont-Rugged	0.8	10	0	0	0	1	0	1	0	0	0	1	AM-TF-4	M. PARSONS	1972
CH-AZ-69	Small Hamlet	Low Piedmont-Smooth	0.5	10	0	0	0	0	1	0	0	0	0	1		E. PRAHL	1972
CH-AZ-70	Small Hamlet	Low Piedmont-Smooth	0.4	10	0	0	0	0	0	0	0	0	0	1	AM-AZ-2	M. PARSONS	1972
CH-AZ-71	Small Hamlet	Upr Piedmont-Smooth	0.6	10	0	0	0	0	0	0	0	0	0	1	AM-AZ-51	M. PARSONS	1972
CH-AZ-72	Small Hamlet	Low Piedmont-Smooth	1.1	15	0	0	0	0	0	0	0	0	0	1	AM-LF-16	M. PARSONS	1972
CH-AZ-73	Small Hamlet	Low Piedmont-Smooth	0.5	10	0	0	0	0	1	0	0	0	0	1	AM-AZ-50	M. PARSONS	1972
CH-AZ-74	Small Hamlet	Low Piedmont-Smooth	1.5	20	0	0	0	0	1	0	0	0	0	1	AM-AZ-23	M. PARSONS	1972
CH-AZ-75	Small Hamlet	Low Piedmont-Rugged	0.7	10	0	0	0	0	1	0	0	0	0	1	AM-AZ-16	M. PARSONS	1972
CH-AZ-76	Hamlet	Low Piedmont-Smooth	8.5	90	0	0	0	0	1	0	0	0	0	1	AM-AZ-62	M. PARSONS	1972
CH-AZ-77	Small Hamlet	Low Piedmont-Smooth	0.6	10	0	0	0	0	1	0	0	0	0	1	AM-AZ-19	M. PARSONS	1972
CH-AZ-78	Small Hamlet	Low Piedmont-Hill	1.1	15	0	0	0	1	1	0	0	0	0	1	AM-AZ-20	M. PARSONS	1972
CH-AZ-79	Small Hamlet	Low Piedmont-Smooth	0.7	10	0	0	0	0	1	1	0	0	0	1	AM-AZ-21	M. PARSONS	1972
CH-AZ-80	Small Hamlet	Low Piedmont-Smooth	0.6	10	0	0	0	0	0	1	0	0	1	0	AM-AZ-22	M. PARSONS	1972
CH-AZ-81	Small Hamlet	Low Piedmont-Smooth	0.7	10	0	0	0	1	0	0	0	0	1	1	AM-TF-5	M. PARSONS	1972
CH-AZ-82	Small Hamlet	Low Piedmont-Smooth	1.5	20	0	0	0	0	0	0	0	1	1	1	AM-LT-3	M. PARSONS	1972
CH-AZ-83	Small Hamlet	Low Piedmont-Smooth	0.7	10	0	0	0	0	0	0	1	0	0	0	AM-LF-16	M. PARSONS	1972
CH-AZ-84	Small Hamlet	Low Piedmont-Smooth	0.3	10	0	0	0	0	0	0	0	0	0	1		M. PARSONS	1972

Early Aztec and Late Aztec occupations are tabulated on a presence-absence basis.

CHALCO-XOCHIMILCO REGION – ENVIRONMENTAL DATA
Aztec Sites

Site Number	Environmental Zone	UTM Coordinates East	North	Elev (in m)	Rainfall (in mm)	Modern Soil Depth	Modern Erosion	Modern Land use
CH-AZ-85	Low Piedmont-Hill	516.60	2114.83	2445	920	Very Shallow	Deep	Grazing & Agri
CH-AZ-86	Low Piedmont-Smooth	516.05	2114.91	2440	910	Medium-Deep	Slight-Moderate	Agricultural
CH-AZ-87	Low Piedmont-Smooth	515.40	2114.21	2440	900	Shallow	Moderate-Deep	Grazing
CH-AZ-88	Low Piedmont-Smooth	515.82	2115.41	2430	875	Shallow	Moderate	Agricultural
CH-AZ-89	Low Piedmont-Smooth	517.07	2117.04	2450	900	Medium	Moderate	Agricultural
CH-AZ-90	Upr Piedmont-Smooth	517.78	2117.46	2525	900	Very Shallow	Deep	None
CH-AZ-91	Upr Piedmont-Smooth	518.15	2118.83	2550	910	Shallow	Moderate	Grazing
CH-AZ-92	Low Piedmont-Smooth	517.05	2119.58	2495	850	Shallow	Deep	Grazing & Agri
CH-AZ-93	Low Piedmont-Smooth	517.03	2118.31	2475	875	Shallow	Moderate-Deep	Agricultural
CH-AZ-94	Low Piedmont-Smooth	516.30	2117.91	2430	860	Shallow	Deep	Agricultural
CH-AZ-95	Low Piedmont-Smooth	516.53	2118.83	2450	860	Very Shallow	Deep	Grazing
CH-AZ-96	Low Piedmont-Smooth	516.37	2119.58	2430	850	Shallow	Deep	Grazing
CH-AZ-97	Low Piedmont-Smooth	516.10	2118.96	2405	850	Very Shallow	Deep	Agricultural
CH-AZ-98	Low Piedmont-Smooth	515.62	2119.26	2360	830	Shallow	Moderate-Deep	Agricultural
CH-AZ-99	Low Piedmont-Smooth	515.37	2118.58	2370	810	Medium	Moderate	Agricultural
CH-AZ-100	Low Piedmont-Smooth	515.53	2117.16	2380	850	Medium	Slight-Moderate	Agricultural
CH-AZ-101	Low Piedmont-Smooth	515.28	2115.88	2410	850	Medium-Deep	Slight-Moderate	Agricultural
CH-AZ-102	Low Piedmont-Smooth	515.30	2115.29	2425	870	Medium-Deep	Slight-Moderate	Agricultural
CH-AZ-103	Low Piedmont-Smooth	514.78	2115.54	2430	860	Medium	Moderate	Agricultural
CH-AZ-104	Low Piedmont-Smooth	513.95	2115.29	2440	860	Medium	Moderate	Agricultural
CH-AZ-105	Low Piedmont-Rugged	513.43	2114.69	2470	900	Very Shallow	Deep	Agricultural
CH-AZ-106	Low Piedmont-Smooth	513.70	2116.36	2455	890	Shallow	Moderate	Grazing
CH-AZ-107	Low Piedmont-Smooth	514.25	2116.23	2435	840	Very Shallow	Deep	Grazing & Agri
CH-AZ-108	Low Piedmont-Smooth	514.97	2117.26	2380	820	Medium-Deep	Moderate	Agricultural
CH-AZ-109	Low Piedmont-Rugged	514.25	2117.13	2405	800	Shallow	Moderate	Agricultural
CH-AZ-110	Low Piedmont-Rugged	513.47	2117.08	2440	800	Shallow-Med	Moderate	Agricultural
CH-AZ-111	Upr Piedmont-Rugged	512.72	2116.21	2500	850	Shallow-Med	Moderate-Deep	Grazing & Agri
CH-AZ-112	Upr Piedmont-Rugged	512.13	2114.88	2510	925	Very Shallow	Deep	Grazing
CH-AZ-113	Upr Piedmont-Rugged	511.30	2113.66	2540	975	Deep	Slight	Agricultural
CH-AZ-114	Upr Piedmont-Rugged	510.47	2113.91	2570	975	Medium	Moderate	Agricultural
CH-AZ-115	Upr Piedmont-Rugged	511.47	2115.41	2600	925	Medium	Moderate	Agricultural
CH-AZ-116	Upr Piedmont-Rugged	510.75	2116.86	2640	875	Medium	Moderate	Agricultural
CH-AZ-117	Upr Piedmont-Rugged	509.82	2116.83	2700	900	Medium	Slight	None
CH-AZ-118	Upr Piedmont-Rugged	509.13	2117.01	2740	950	Medium	Moderate	Grazing
CH-AZ-119	Upr Piedmont-Rugged	509.05	2117.51	2750	925	Medium	Moderate	None
CH-AZ-120	Upr Piedmont-Rugged	509.47	2118.21	2710	900	Shallow-Med	Moderate	None
CH-AZ-121	Upr Piedmont-Rugged	510.18	2120.13	2500	780	Medium	Moderate	Grazing
CH-AZ-122	Upr Piedmont-Rugged	508.95	2118.01	2760	900	Medium	Slight-Moderate	Grazing & Agri
CH-AZ-123	Upr Piedmont-Rugged	508.07	2117.96	2760	925	Shallow-Med	Moderate	Grazing
CH-AZ-124	Upr Piedmont-Rugged	5C7.90	2118.81	2850	900	Medium	Moderate	None
CH-AZ-125	Upr Piedmont-Rugged	508.75	2119.56	2700	800	Medium	Moderate	Grazing & Agri
CH-AZ-126	Upr Piedmont-Rugged	509.93	2119.31	2605	800	Medium	Moderate	Grazing

CHALCO-XOCHIMILCO REGION – PREHISPANIC SETTLEMENT DATA
Aztec Sites

SITE NUMBER	CLASSIFICATION	ENVIRONMENTAL ZONE	AREA (in ha)	POP.	EF	MF	LF	TF	EC	LC	ET	LT	EA	LA	TEMPORARY SITE NO.	SUPERVISOR	YEAR
CH-AZ-85	Small Hamlet	Low Piedmont-Hill	2.0	20	0	0	0	0	0	0	0	0	0	1	AM-AZ-18	M. PARSONS	1972
CH-AZ-86	Hamlet	Low Piedmont-Smooth	7.0	80	0	0	0	1	0	0	0	0	1	1	AM-AZ-25	M. PARSONS	1972
CH-AZ-87	Small Hamlet	Low Piedmont-Smooth	0.7	10	0	0	0	0	1	0	0	0	1	1	AM-CL-5	M. PARSONS	1972
CH-AZ-88	Small Hamlet	Low Piedmont-Smooth	0.4	10	0	0	0	1	0	0	0	0	1	0	AM-CL-10	M. PARSONS	1972
CH-AZ-89	Small Hamlet	Low Piedmont-Smooth	0.5	10	0	0	0	0	0	0	0	0	0	1		M. PARSONS	1972
CH-AZ-90	Lg Disp Village	Upr Piedmont-Smooth	26.7	540	0	0	0	0	0	0	0	0	1	1	AM-AZ-7	M. PARSONS	1972
CH-AZ-91	Hamlet	Upr Piedmont-Smooth	5.7	40	0	0	0	0	0	0	0	0	1	1		E. PRAHL	1972
CH-AZ-92	Small Hamlet	Low Piedmont-Smooth	1.0	20	0	0	0	0	0	0	0	0	1	1	AM-AZ-6	M. PARSONS	1972
CH-AZ-93	Sm Disp Village	Low Piedmont-Smooth	19.1	300	0	0	0	0	0	0	0	0	1	1		M. PARSONS	1972
CH-AZ-94	Lg Disp Village	Low Piedmont-Smooth	41.8	840	0	0	1	1	0	0	0	0	1	1	AM-AZ-8	M. PARSONS	1972
CH-AZ-95	Small Hamlet	Low Piedmont-Smooth	1.8	20	0	0	0	0	0	0	0	0	1	1	AM-AZ-5	M. PARSONS	1972
CH-AZ-96	Hamlet	Low Piedmont-Smooth	0.9	30	0	0	0	0	0	0	0	0	1	0	AM-AZ-6	M. PARSONS	1972
CH-AZ-97	Hamlet	Low Piedmont-Smooth	6.0	100	0	0	0	0	0	0	0	0	1	1	AM-AZ-4	M. PARSONS	1972
CH-AZ-98	Hamlet	Low Piedmont-Smooth	2.5	30	0	0	0	0	0	0	0	0	1	1	AM-AZ-3	M. PARSONS	1972
CH-AZ-99	Small Hamlet	Low Piedmont-Smooth	1.2	10	0	0	0	0	0	0	0	0	1	1	AM-AZ-17	M. PARSONS	1972
CH-AZ-100	Questionable	Low Piedmont-Smooth	1.2	10	0	0	1	0	0	0	0	0	1	1	AM-F-3	M. PARSONS	1972
CH-AZ-101	Small Hamlet	Low Piedmont-Smooth	0.8	10	0	0	0	0	0	0	0	0	1	1		M. PARSONS	1972
CH-AZ-102	Hamlet	Low Piedmont-Smooth	7.3	70	0	0	0	1	0	0	0	1	1	0	AM-AZ-15	M. PARSONS	1972
CH-AZ-103	Sm Disp Village	Low Piedmont-Smooth	23.8	240	0	0	0	1	0	0	0	0	1	0	AM-AZ-14	M. PARSONS	1972
CH-AZ-104	Small Hamlet	Low Piedmont-Smooth	2.8	30	0	0	0	0	1	0	0	0	1	1	AM-AZ-13	M. PARSONS	1972
CH-AZ-105	Small Hamlet	Low Piedmont-Rugged	2.9	30	0	0	0	0	0	0	0	0	1	1	AM-AZ-31	M. PARSONS	1972
CH-AZ-106	Small Hamlet	Low Piedmont-Rugged	2.6	30	0	0	0	0	1	0	0	0	1	1	AM-AZ-24	M. PARSONS	1972
CH-AZ-107	Hamlet	Low Piedmont-Smooth	9.8	100	0	0	1	1	0	0	0	0	1	1	AM-AZ-12	M. PARSONS	1972
CH-AZ-108	Sm Disp Village	Low Piedmont-Smooth	7.5	150	0	0	0	0	0	0	0	0	1	1	AM-AZ-10	M. PARSONS	1972
CH-AZ-109	Hamlet	Low Piedmont-Rugged	8.3	80	0	0	0	0	1	1	0	0	1	1	AM-AZ-11	M. PARSONS	1972
CH-AZ-110	Small Hamlet	Low Piedmont-Rugged	0.8	10	0	0	0	0	0	0	0	0	1	1		M. PARSONS	1972
CH-AZ-111	Sm Disp Village	Upr Piedmont-Rugged	32.0	320	0	0	0	0	1	1	0	1	1	1	AM-AZ-26	M. PARSONS	1972
CH-AZ-112	Small Hamlet	Upr Piedmont-Rugged	1.0	15	0	0	0	0	0	0	1	0	1	1	AM-AZ-30	M. PARSONS	1972
CH-AZ-113	Small Hamlet	Upr Piedmont-Rugged	0.2	10	0	0	0	0	0	0	0	0	1	1	AM-AZ-28	M. PARSONS	1972
CH-AZ-114	Small Hamlet	Upr Piedmont-Rugged	2.6	20	0	0	0	0	0	0	0	0	1	1	AM-AZ-29	M. PARSONS	1972
CH-AZ-115	Small Hamlet	Upr Piedmont-Rugged	1.0	10	0	0	0	0	0	0	0	0	0	1	AM-AZ-27	M. PARSONS	1972
CH-AZ-116	Small Hamlet	Upr Piedmont-Rugged	2.2	20	0	0	0	0	0	0	0	0	0	1	AM-AZ-34	M. PARSONS	1972
CH-AZ-117	Small Hamlet	Upr Piedmont-Rugged	0.7	10	0	0	0	0	0	0	0	0	0	1	AM-AZ-32	M. PARSONS	1972
CH-AZ-118	Small Hamlet	Upr Piedmont-Rugged	0.7	10	0	0	0	0	0	0	0	0	0	1	AM-AZ-33	M. PARSONS	1972
CH-AZ-119	Small Hamlet	Upr Piedmont-Rugged	0.8	15	0	0	0	0	0	0	0	0	0	1	AM-AZ-35	M. PARSONS	1972
CH-AZ-120	Sm Disp Village	Upr Piedmont-Rugged	21.0	200	0	0	0	0	0	0	0	0	0	1	AM-AZ-40	M. PARSONS	1972
CH-AZ-121	Small Hamlet	Upr Piedmont-Rugged	0.4	10	0	0	0	0	0	0	0	0	0	1		M. PARSONS	1972
CH-AZ-122	Small Hamlet	Upr Piedmont-Rugged	0.4	10	0	0	0	0	0	0	0	0	0	1	AM-AZ-64	M. PARSONS	1972
CH-AZ-123	Small Hamlet	Upr Piedmont-Rugged	0.4	10	0	0	0	0	0	0	0	0	0	1		M. PARSONS	1972
CH-AZ-124	Small Hamlet	Upr Piedmont-Rugged	0.3	10	0	0	0	0	0	0	0	0	0	1	AM-AZ-59	M. PARSONS	1972
CH-AZ-125	Small Hamlet	Upr Piedmont-Rugged	0.6	10	0	0	0	0	0	0	0	0	0	1		M. PARSONS	1972
CH-AZ-126	Hamlet	Upr Piedmont-Rugged	6.7	70	0	0	0	0	0	0	0	0	0	1	AM-AZ-41	M. PARSONS	1972

Early Aztec and Late Aztec occupations are tabulated on a presence-absence basis.

CHALCO-XOCHIMILCO REGION - ENVIRONMENTAL DATA
Aztec Sites

Site Number	Environmental Zone	UTM Coordinates East	North	Elev (in m)	Rainfall (in mm)	Modern Soil Depth	Modern Erosion	Modern Land use
CH-AZ-127	Upr Piedmont-Rugged	511.00	2118.81	2530	780	Medium	Moderate	Grazing & Agri
CH-AZ-128	Low Piedmont-Rugged	511.07	2119.66	2490	775	Medium	Moderate	None
CH-AZ-129	Upr Piedmont-Rugged	510.55	2119.48	2530	775	Medium	Moderate	Grazing & Agri
CH-AZ-130	Low Piedmont-Rugged	512.20	2120.01	2385	750	Shallow-Med	Slight-Moderate	Grazing
CH-AZ-131	Low Piedmont-Rugged	512.50	2119.21	2420	760	Medium	Moderate	None
CH-AZ-132	Low Piedmont-Rugged	512.32	2117.96	2490	790	Shallow-Med	Moderate	Grazing & Agri
CH-AZ-133	Low Piedmont-Rugged	512.68	2117.51	2450	800	Medium	Moderate	None
CH-AZ-134	Low Piedmont-Rugged	513.28	2117.66	2430	790	Medium	Moderate	Grazing
CH-AZ-135	Low Piedmont-Rugged	513.57	2117.91	2420	790	Medium	Moderate	Grazing
CH-AZ-136	Low Piedmont-Rugged	513.87	2118.31	2380	780	Shallow	Moderate	Grazing & Agri
CH-AZ-137	Low Piedmont-Rugged	514.20	2118.23	2370	780	Shallow	Moderate	Grazing & Agri
CH-AZ-138	Low Piedmont-Rugged	513.15	2118.58	2390	780	Medium	Moderate	Agricultural
CH-AZ-139	Low Piedmont-Rugged	513.95	2119.79	2350	780	Shallow-Med	Moderate	Agricultural
CH-AZ-140	Upr Piedmont-Rugged	511.00	2117.81	2610	800	Medium	Slight-Moderate	Grazing & Agri
CH-AZ-141	Low Piedmont-Rugged	513.03	2120.56	2330	733	Shallow-Med	Moderate	Agricultural
CH-AZ-142	Low Piedmont-Rugged	511.97	2120.73	2360	750	Medium	Moderate	None
CH-AZ-143	Low Piedmont-Rugged	511.28	2120.56	2400	750	Medium	Moderate	Grazing
CH-AZ-144	Low Piedmont-Rugged	510.70	2120.58	2430	750	Medium	Moderate	Grazing
CH-AZ-145	Low Piedmont-Rugged	510.93	2121.23	2375	750	Medium	Moderate	Grazing
CH-AZ-146	Low Piedmont-Rugged	510.63	2121.46	2360	750	Medium	Moderate	Grazing
CH-AZ-147	Low Piedmont-Rugged	510.22	2120.19	2450	766	Medium	Moderate	Grazing
CH-AZ-148	Low Piedmont-Rugged	509.75	2121.08	2440	760	Medium	Moderate	Grazing
CH-AZ-149	Upr Piedmont-Rugged	509.32	2120.73	2520	775	Medium	Moderate	Grazing
CH-AZ-150	Upr Piedmont-Rugged	508.95	2120.79	2550	775	Shallow-Med	Moderate	Grazing
CH-AZ-151	Low Piedmont-Rugged	508.82	2121.69	2450	775	Shallow-Med	Moderate	Grazing
CH-AZ-152	Low Piedmont-Rugged	511.13	2121.61	2350	750	Medium	Moderate	Grazing
CH-AZ-153	Low Piedmont-Rugged	511.68	2121.69	2335	733	Medium	Moderate	Grazing
CH-AZ-154	Low Piedmont-Smooth	513.85	2121.50	2300	730	Medium	Moderate	Grazing & Agri
CH-AZ-155	Low Piedmont-Smooth	513.85	2121.50	2290	730	Deep	Slight	Agricultural
CH-AZ-156	Low Piedmont-Smooth	514.80	2122.28	2300	750	Medium-Deep	Slight-Moderate	Grazing & Agri
CH-AZ-157	Low Piedmont-Smooth	514.40	2122.28	2290	730	Medium-Deep	Slight-Moderate	Agricultural
CH-AZ-158	Low Piedmont-Smooth	514.12	2122.05	2290	720	Deep	Slight	Agricultural
CH-AZ-159	Low Piedmont-Smooth	513.82	2122.50	2290	700	Deep	Slight-Moderate	Agricultural
CH-AZ-160	Low Piedmont-Smooth	513.32	2122.10	2290	700	Deep	Slight	Agricultural
CH-AZ-161	Low Piedmont-Rugged	512.93	2121.86	2270	700	Medium-Deep	Slight-Moderate	Agricultural
CH-AZ-162	Low Piedmont-Rugged	511.80	2122.16	2295	725	Medium	Slight	Grazing & Agri
CH-AZ-163	Lakeshore Plain	511.78	2122.76	2260	700	Deep	None	Agricultural
CH-AZ-164	Lakeshore Plain	511.97	2122.83	2260	700	Deep	Slight	Agricultural
CH-AZ-165	Lakeshore Plain	512.93	2123.21	2260	700	Deep	Slight	Agricultural
CH-AZ-166	Lakeshore Plain	511.32	2123.11	2260	700	Deep	Very Slight	Agricultural
CH-AZ-167	Low Piedmont-Smooth	516.02	2124.85	2310	750	Medium	Moderate	Agricultural
CH-AZ-168	Lakeshore Plain	514.07	2124.82	2270	690	Deep	None	Agricultural

CHALCO-XOCHIMILCO REGION - PREHISPANIC SETTLEMENT DATA
Aztec Sites

SITE NUMBER	CLASSIFICATION	ENVIRONMENTAL ZONE	AREA (in ha)	POP.	EF	MF	LF	TF	EC	LC	ET	LT	EA	LA	TEMPORARY SITE NO.	SUPERVISOR	YEAR
CH-AZ-127	Lg Disp Village	Upr Piedmont-Rugged	65.3	700	0	0	0	0	0	0	0	0	1	1	AM-AZ-39	M. PARSONS	1972
CH-AZ-128	Sm Disp Village	Low Piedmont-Rugged	21.0	200	0	0	0	0	0	0	0	0	1	1	AM-AZ-43	M. PARSONS	1972
CH-AZ-129	Hamlet	Upr Piedmont-Rugged	8.1	100	0	0	0	0	0	0	0	0	0	1	AM-AZ-42	M. PARSONS	1972
CH-AZ-130	Sm Disp Village	Low Piedmont-Rugged	19.7	200	0	0	0	0	0	0	0	0	1	1	AM-AZ-46	M. PARSONS	1972
CH-AZ-131	Sm Disp Village	Low Piedmont-Rugged	13.4	150	0	0	0	0	0	0	0	0	1	1	AM-AZ-37	M. PARSONS	1972
CH-AZ-132	Hamlet	Low Piedmont-Rugged	6.9	100	0	0	0	0	0	0	0	0	1	1	AM-AZ-44	M. PARSONS	1972
CH-AZ-133	Small Hamlet	Low Piedmont-Rugged	0.6	10	0	0	0	0	0	0	0	0	0	1	AM-AZ-36	M. PARSONS	1972
CH-AZ-134	Small Hamlet	Low Piedmont-Rugged	1.3	10	0	0	0	0	0	0	0	0	0	1		M. PARSONS	1972
CH-AZ-135	Small Hamlet	Low Piedmont-Rugged	0.7	10	0	0	0	0	0	0	0	0	0	0		M. PARSONS	1972
CH-AZ-136	Small Hamlet	Low Piedmont-Rugged	0.5	10	0	0	0	0	0	0	0	0	1	1	AM-AZ-9	M. PARSONS	1972
CH-AZ-137	Hamlet	Low Piedmont-Rugged	3.1	30	0	0	0	0	1	0	0	0	0	1	AM-AZ-9	M. PARSONS	1972
CH-AZ-138	Hamlet	Low Piedmont-Rugged	4.1	50	0	0	0	0	0	0	0	0	1	1	AM-AZ-45	M. PARSONS	1972
CH-AZ-139	Hamlet	Low Piedmont-Rugged	4.9	50	0	0	0	0	1	0	0	0	1	1	AM-AZ-1	M. PARSONS	1972
CH-AZ-140	Hamlet	Upr Piedmont-Rugged	11.2	100	0	0	0	0	0	0	0	0	1	1	AM-AZ-38	M. PARSONS	1972
CH-AZ-141	Hamlet	Low Piedmont-Rugged	2.1	30	0	0	0	0	0	0	0	0	0	0	AM-AZ-47	M. PARSONS	1972
CH-AZ-142	Small Hamlet	Low Piedmont-Rugged	0.6	10	0	0	0	0	0	0	0	0	0	1		M. PARSONS	1972
CH-AZ-143	Small Hamlet	Low Piedmont-Rugged	0.6	10	0	0	0	0	0	0	0	0	0	1		M. PARSONS	1972
CH-AZ-144	Hamlet	Low Piedmont-Rugged	6.0	60	0	0	0	0	0	0	0	0	0	0	AM-AZ-53	M. PARSONS	1972
CH-AZ-145	Hamlet	Low Piedmont-Rugged	2.9	30	0	0	0	0	0	0	0	0	0	1	AM-AZ-56	M. PARSONS	1972
CH-AZ-146	Small Hamlet	Low Piedmont-Rugged	0.6	10	0	0	0	0	0	0	0	0	1	1	AM-ET-2	M. PARSONS	1972
CH-AZ-147	Small Hamlet	Low Piedmont-Rugged	0.3	10	0	0	0	0	0	0	0	0	0	0		M. PARSONS	1972
CH-AZ-148	Hamlet	Low Piedmont-Rugged	10.2	100	0	0	0	0	0	0	0	0	0	1	AM-AZ-54	M. PARSONS	1972
CH-AZ-149	Small Hamlet	Upr Piedmont-Rugged	0.8	10	0	0	0	0	0	0	0	0	0	1	AM-AZ-55	M. PARSONS	1972
CH-AZ-150	Small Hamlet	Upr Piedmont-Rugged	0.3	20	0	0	0	0	0	0	0	0	0	0	CH-AZ-28	J. PARSONS	1972
CH-AZ-151	Hamlet	Low Piedmont-Rugged	6.2	50	0	0	0	0	0	0	0	0	0	1		M. PARSONS	1972
CH-AZ-152	Hamlet	Low Piedmont-Rugged	6.9	70	0	0	0	0	0	0	0	0	1	1	AM-AZ-52	M. PARSONS	1972
CH-AZ-153	Hamlet	Low Piedmont-Rugged	3.8	40	0	0	0	0	0	0	0	0	0	0		M. PARSONS	1972
CH-AZ-154	Hamlet	Low Piedmont-Smooth	5.7	50	0	0	0	0	0	0	0	1	0	1	CH-T-40	M. PARSONS	1969
CH-AZ-155	Hamlet	Low Piedmont-Smooth	2.5	25	0	0	1	0	0	0	0	1	0	1	CH-T-39	M. PARSONS	1969
CH-AZ-156	Questionable	Low Piedmont-Smooth	4.7	60	0	0	1	1	0	0	0	0	0	1	CH-A-33	M. PARSONS	1969
CH-AZ-157	Hamlet	Low Piedmont-Smooth	2.4	30	0	1	1	0	0	0	0	0	1	1	CH-A-41	M. PARSONS	1969
CH-AZ-158	Small Hamlet	Low Piedmont-Smooth	1.2	20	0	1	0	0	0	0	0	1	0	1	CH-T-38	M. PARSONS	1969
CH-AZ-159	Questionable	Low Piedmont-Smooth	2.8	30	0	0	0	0	0	0	0	1	1	1	CH-T-36	M. PARSONS	1969
CH-AZ-160	Hamlet	Low Piedmont-Smooth	1.5	30	0	0	0	0	0	0	0	0	0	1	CH-A-32	M. PARSONS	1969
CH-AZ-161	Questionable	Low Piedmont-Rugged	7.0	70	0	0	0	0	0	0	0	1	0	1	AM-AZ-48	M. PARSONS	1972
CH-AZ-162	Sm Disp Village	Low Piedmont-Rugged	17.9	360	0	1	1	0	0	0	0	0	0	1	AM-AZ-49	M. PARSONS	1972
CH-AZ-163	Small Hamlet	Lakeshore Plain	0.5	10	0	1	0	0	0	0	0	0	1	1	AM-MF-1	M. PARSONS	1972
CH-AZ-164	Small Hamlet	Lakeshore Plain	0.2	10	0	1	1	0	0	0	0	0	1	0	AM-AZ-63	M. PARSONS	1972
CH-AZ-165	Small Hamlet	Lakeshore Plain	0.8	10	0	0	0	0	0	0	0	1	0	1	AM-LT-16	M. PARSONS	1972
CH-AZ-166	Small Hamlet	Lakeshore Plain	0.5	10	0	0	0	0	0	0	0	1	1	0	AM-AZ-57	M. PARSONS	1972
CH-AZ-167	Questionable	Low Piedmont-Smooth	1.5	15	0	0	0	0	0	1	0	0	1	1	CH-C-6	J. PARSONS	1969
CH-AZ-168	Hamlet	Lakeshore Plain	2.5	50	0	0	0	0	0	0	0	0	0	1		J. PARSONS	1969

Early Aztec and Late Aztec occupations are tabulated on a presence-absence basis.

CHALCO-XOCHIMILCO REGION - ENVIRONMENTAL DATA
Aztec Sites

Site Number	Environmental Zone	UTM Coordinates East	North	Elev (in m)	Rainfall (in mm)	Modern Soil Depth	Modern Erosion	Modern Land use
CH-AZ-169	Low Piedmont-Hill	514.22	2126.93	2420	690	Very Shallow	Moderate-Deep	Grazing
CH-AZ-170	Lakeshore Plain	512.45	2128.43	2245	685	Deep	None	Agricultural
CH-AZ-171	Lakeshore Plain	512.20	2129.07	2245	685	Deep	None	Agricultural
CH-AZ-172	Lakeshore Plain	510.43	2129.15	2245	670	Deep	None	Grazing & Agri
CH-AZ-173	Lakeshore Plain	511.32	2127.85	2245	680	Deep	None	Agricultural
CH-AZ-174	Lakeshore Plain	511.65	2127.60	2245	680	Deep	None	Agricultural
CH-AZ-175	Lakeshore Plain	509.68	2125.11	2245	700	Deep	None	Agricultural
CH-AZ-176	Low Piedmont-Rugged	509.93	2122.44	2300	725	Medium	Moderate	Grazing
CH-AZ-177	Low Piedmont-Rugged	508.88	2122.36	2350	750	Shallow-Med	Moderate	Grazing
CH-AZ-178	Low Piedmont-Rugged	508.55	2122.63	2340	750	Shallow-Med	Moderate	Grazing
CH-AZ-179	Low Piedmont-Rugged	508.72	2123.31	2280	733	Medium-Deep	Slight	Agricultural
CH-AZ-180	Low Piedmont-Rugged	508.68	2123.63	2270	725	Deep	Slight	Agricultural
CH-AZ-181	Low Piedmont-Rugged	508.53	2123.94	2260	725	Medium	Moderate	None
CH-AZ-182	Low Piedmont-Rugged	508.13	2123.76	2270	725	Deep	Slight	Agricultural
CH-AZ-183	Low Piedmont-Rugged	506.93	2123.01	2310	766	Shallow-Med	Moderate	Grazing & Agri
CH-AZ-184	Lakeshore Plain	505.82	2123.81	2245	725	Deep	None	Agricultural
CH-AZ-185	Lakebed	505.75	2124.36	2240	725	Deep	None	Agricultural
CH-AZ-186	Lakeshore Plain	508.72	2126.58	2243	675	Deep	None	Agricultural
CH-AZ-187	Lakeshore Plain	508.50	2126.85	2245	680	Deep	None	Agricultural
CH-AZ-188	Lakebed	506.97	2127.16	2240	675	Deep	None	Agricultural
CH-AZ-189	Lakebed	508.25	2128.41	2240	675	Deep	None	Agricultural
CH-AZ-190	Lakebed	508.10	2128.63	2240	670	Deep	None	Agricultural
CH-AZ-191	Lakebed	508.68	2128.97	2240	670	Deep	None	Agricultural
CH-AZ-192	Lakebed	507.55	2129.82	2245	660	Deep	Very Slight	Grazing & Agri
CH-AZ-193	Lakebed	507.40	2128.43	2240	675	Deep	None	Agricultural
CH-AZ-194	Lakebed	507.22	2128.03	2240	675	Deep	None	Agricultural
CH-AZ-195	Lakebed	506.60	2127.95	2240	675	Deep	None	Agricultural
CH-AZ-196	Lakebed	506.72	2128.55	2240	670	Deep	None	Grazing
CH-AZ-197	Island-Lakesh Plain	506.30	2128.65	2248	670	Deep	Slight	Grazing
CH-AZ-198	Island-Lakesh Plain	506.57	2129.85	2290	660	Shallow	Moderate	Grazing
CH-AZ-199	Lakebed	506.18	2128.32	2240	670	Deep	None	Agricultural
CH-AZ-200	Lakebed	506.25	2127.85	2240	675	Deep	None	Grazing & Agri
CH-AZ-201	Lakebed	505.47	2126.38	2240	680	Deep	None	Agricultural
CH-AZ-202	Lakebed	504.68	2123.94	2240	700	Deep	None	Agricultural
CH-AZ-203	Low Piedmont-Rugged	502.07	2123.08	2300	800	Shallow-Med	Moderate	Agricultural
CH-AZ-204	Low Piedmont-Rugged	501.85	2123.69	2280	750	Medium	Slight	Agricultural
CH-AZ-205	Lakebed	504.60	2126.48	2240	690	Deep	None	Grazing & Agri
CH-AZ-206	Lakebed	505.05	2127.04	2240	680	Deep	None	Agricultural
CH-AZ-207	Lakebed	504.68	2127.19	2240	690	Deep	None	Agricultural
CH-AZ-208	Lakebed	504.53	2127.61	2240	690	Deep	None	Agricultural
CH-AZ-209	Lakebed	505.15	2127.76	2240	675	Deep	None	Agricultural
CH-AZ-210	Lakebed	504.95	2127.32	2240	675	Deep	None	Agricultural

CHALCO-XOCHIMILCO REGION - PREHISPANIC SETTLEMENT DATA
Aztec Sites

SITE NUMBER	CLASSIFICATION	ENVIRONMENTAL ZONE	AREA (in ha)	POP.	EF	MF	LF	TF	EC	LC	ET	LT	EA	LA	TEMPORARY SITE NO.	SUPERVISOR	YEAR
CH-AZ-169	Ceremonial Ctr	Low Piedmont-Hill	0.1	0	0	0	0	1	0	0	0	0	1	1	CH-F-5	J. PARSONS	1969
CH-AZ-170	Sm Disp Village	Lakeshore Plain	13.2	150	0	0	0	1	0	0	0	0	1	1	CH-A-18	J. PARSONS	1969
CH-AZ-171	Small Hamlet	Lakeshore Plain	0.5	10	0	0	0	0	0	0	0	1	0	1		J. PARSONS	1969
CH-AZ-172	Local Center	Lakeshore Plain	249.5	12500	0	0	0	0	0	0	1	0	1	1	CH-A-16	J. PARSONS	1969
CH-AZ-173	Hamlet	Lakeshore Plain	2.3	40	0	0	0	0	0	0	0	0	0	1	CH-A-19	J. PARSONS	1969
CH-AZ-174	Hamlet	Lakeshore Plain	7.7	80	0	0	0	0	0	0	1	1	1	0	CH-A-17	J. PARSONS	1969
CH-AZ-175	Questionable	Lakeshore Plain	5.5	100	0	0	0	0	0	0	0	0	0	1	CH-AZ-26	M. PARSONS	1972
CH-AZ-176	Small Hamlet	Low Piedmont-Rugged	0.5	10	0	0	0	0	0	0	0	0	0	1		M. PARSONS	1972
CH-AZ-177	Small Hamlet	Low Piedmont-Rugged	0.8	10	0	0	0	0	0	0	0	0	0	1	CH-AZ-27	J. PARSONS	1972
CH-AZ-178	Small Hamlet	Low Piedmont-Rugged	0.2	10	0	0	1	0	0	0	0	0	0	1		M. PARSONS	1972
CH-AZ-179	Questionable	Low Piedmont-Rugged	0.1	0	0	0	0	0	0	0	0	0	0	1		M. PARSONS	1972
CH-AZ-180	Questionable	Low Piedmont-Rugged	0.1	0	0	0	0	0	0	0	0	0	0	1	AM-TF-6	M. PARSONS	1972
CH-AZ-181	Small Hamlet	Low Piedmont-Rugged	0.8	10	0	0	0	0	0	0	0	0	0	1	AM-AZ-58	M. PARSONS	1972
CH-AZ-182	Small Hamlet	Low Piedmont-Rugged	0.9	10	0	0	1	1	0	0	0	0	0	1	AM-AZ-61	M. PARSONS	1972
CH-AZ-183	Small Hamlet	Low Piedmont-Rugged	0.9	10	0	0	0	0	0	0	0	0	0	1	CH-AZ-23	J. PARSONS	1972
CH-AZ-184	Small Hamlet	Lakeshore Plain	0.8	10	0	0	0	0	0	0	0	0	0	1	CH-AZ-22	J. PARSONS	1972
CH-AZ-185	Small Hamlet	Lakebed	1.6	20	0	0	0	0	0	0	0	0	0	1	CH-AZ-16	J. PARSONS	1972
CH-AZ-186	Questionable	Lakeshore Plain	25.4	500	0	0	0	0	0	0	2	0	1	1	CH-AZ-25	J. PARSONS	1972
CH-AZ-187	Questionable	Lakeshore Plain	4.7	50	0	0	0	0	0	0	1	0	0	1	CH-A-14	J. PARSONS	1969
CH-AZ-188	Hamlet	Lakebed	0.2	50	0	0	0	0	0	0	0	0	1	1	CH-A-13	J. PARSONS	1969
CH-AZ-189	Small Hamlet	Lakebed	1.5	20	0	0	0	0	0	0	0	0	1	1		J. PARSONS	1969
CH-AZ-190	Sm Disp Village	Lakebed	7.7	160	0	0	0	0	0	0	0	0	1	1	CH-A-5	J. PARSONS	1969
CH-AZ-191	Hamlet	Lakebed	3.9	80	0	0	0	0	0	0	0	0	1	1	CH-A-4	J. PARSONS	1969
CH-AZ-192	Local Center	Lakebed	62.1	2500	0	0	0	0	0	0	1	1	0	1	CH-A-1	J. PARSONS	1969
CH-AZ-193	Hamlet	Lakebed	0.2	30	0	0	0	0	0	0	0	0	1	0	CH-A-6	J. PARSONS	1969
CH-AZ-194	Hamlet	Lakebed	4.1	100	0	0	0	0	0	0	0	0	1	0	CH-A-12	J. PARSONS	1969
CH-AZ-195	Hamlet	Lakebed	4.4	90	0	0	0	0	0	0	0	0	1	0	CH-A-11	J. PARSONS	1969
CH-AZ-196	Hamlet	Lakebed	0.1	30	0	0	0	0	0	0	0	0	0	1	CH-A-7	J. PARSONS	1969
CH-AZ-197	Hamlet	Island-Lakesh Plain	2.5	50	0	0	0	0	0	0	0	0	0	1	CH-A-8	J. PARSONS	1969
CH-AZ-198	Questionable	Island-Lakesh Plain	0.1	0	0	0	0	0	0	1	0	0	0	1	CH-A-10	J. PARSONS	1969
CH-AZ-199	Small Hamlet	Lakebed	0.1	20	0	0	0	0	0	0	0	0	0	1	CH-A-11	J. PARSONS	1969
CH-AZ-200	Small Hamlet	Lakebed	1.0	20	0	0	0	0	0	0	0	0	0	1	CH-AZ-15	J. PARSONS	1969
CH-AZ-201	Small Hamlet	Lakebed	0.5	10	0	0	0	0	0	0	0	0	0	1	CH-AZ-13	J. PARSONS	1972
CH-AZ-202	Hamlet	Lakebed	2.3	30	0	0	0	0	0	0	0	0	0	1	CH-AZ-12	J. PARSONS	1972
CH-AZ-203	Small Hamlet	Low Piedmont-Rugged	0.4	10	0	0	0	0	0	0	0	0	0	1	CH-AZ-11	J. PARSONS	1972
CH-AZ-204	Hamlet	Low Piedmont-Rugged	3.8	50	0	0	0	1	0	0	0	0	0	1	CH-AZ-14	J. PARSONS	1972
CH-AZ-205	Hamlet	Lakebed	5.8	100	0	0	0	0	0	0	0	0	1	1		J. PARSONS	1972
CH-AZ-206	Small Hamlet	Lakebed	0.1	10	0	0	0	0	0	0	0	0	0	1	CH-AZ-4	R. WENKE	1972
CH-AZ-207	Small Hamlet	Lakebed	0.1	10	0	0	0	0	0	0	0	0	0	1	CH-AZ-6	R. WENKE	1972
CH-AZ-208	Small Hamlet	Lakebed	0.1	10	0	0	0	0	0	0	0	1	1	1	CH-AZ-5	R. WENKE	1972
CH-AZ-209	Small Hamlet	Lakebed	0.5	10	0	0	0	0	0	0	0	1	1	1	CH-AZ-3	R. WENKE	1972
CH-AZ-210	Small Hamlet	Lakebed	0.1	10	0	0	0	0	0	0	0	0	1	0	CH-A-15	J. PARSONS	1969

Early Aztec and Late Aztec occupations are tabulated on a presence-absence basis.

52

CHALCO-XOCHIMILCO REGION - ENVIRONMENTAL DATA
Aztec Sites

Site Number	Environmental Zone	UTM Coordinates East	North	Elev (in m)	Rainfall (in mm)	Modern Soil Depth	Modern Erosion	Modern Land use
CH-AZ-211	Lakebed	505.45	2128.50	2240	670	Deep	None	Grazing
CH-AZ-212	Island-Lakesh Plain	505.30	2128.90	2245	670	Deep	Very Slight	Grazing
CH-AZ-213	Lakebed	504.72	2128.69	2240	675	Deep	None	Agricultural
CH-AZ-214	Lakebed	504.30	2129.26	2240	675	Deep	None	Agricultural
CH-AZ-215	Lakebed	504.00	2129.36	2240	675	Deep	None	Agricultural
CH-AZ-216	Lakebed	504.50	2129.54	2240	675	Deep	None	Agricultural
CH-AZ-217	Lakebed	504.65	2129.58	2240	675	Deep	None	Grazing
CH-AZ-218	Lakebed	504.53	2129.88	2240	675	Deep	None	None
CH-AZ-219	Lakebed	504.35	2129.86	2240	675	Deep	None	Agricultural
CH-AZ-220	Lakebed	504.38	2130.04	2240	675	Deep	None	Agricultural
CH-AZ-221	Lakebed	504.55	2130.08	2240	675	Deep	None	Grazing
CH-AZ-222	Lakebed	505.03	2130.48	2240	666	Deep	None	Grazing
CH-AZ-223	Lakebed	504.70	2130.41	2240	666	Deep	None	Agricultural
CH-AZ-224	Lakebed	504.43	2130.44	2240	666	Deep	None	Agricultural
CH-AZ-225	Lakebed	505.03	2131.11	2240	650	Deep	None	Agricultural
CH-AZ-226	Lakebed	504.38	2131.46	2240	650	Deep	None	Grazing
CH-AZ-227	Lakebed	504.80	2131.98	2240	650	Deep	None	Grazing
CH-AZ-228	Lakebed	502.65	2131.76	2240	660	Deep	None	None
CH-AZ-229	Lakebed	502.50	2133.54	2240	650	Deep	None	Grazing & Agri
CH-AZ-230	Lakebed	500.60	2132.44	2240	675	Deep	None	Grazing
CH-AZ-231	Lakebed	501.50	2131.66	2240	675	Deep	None	Grazing & Agri
CH-AZ-232	Lakebed	500.80	2131.41	2240	675	Deep	None	Agricultural
CH-AZ-233	Lakebed	501.05	2130.63	2240	680	Deep	None	Agricultural
CH-AZ-234	Lakebed	5C1.57	2130.51	2240	680	Deep	None	Grazing
CH-AZ-235	Lakebed	502.32	2130.44	2240	675	Deep	None	Agricultural
CH-AZ-236	Lakebed	502.35	2129.94	2240	680	Deep	None	Agricultural
CH-AZ-237	Lakebed	502.35	2129.79	2240	680	Deep	None	Agricultural
CH-AZ-238	Lakebed	502.80	2129.11	2240	700	Deep	None	Agricultural
CH-AZ-239	Lakebed	503.30	2128.83	2240	675	Deep	None	Agricultural
CH-AZ-240	Lakebed	503.80	2128.56	2240	675	Deep	None	Agricultural
CH-AZ-241	Lakebed	504.00	2127.71	2240	680	Deep	None	Agricultural
CH-AZ-242	Lakebed	504.07	2127.33	2240	680	Deep	None	Agricultural
CH-AZ-243	Lakebed	503.97	2127.19	2240	680	Deep	None	Agricultural
CH-AZ-244	Lakebed	503.82	2126.48	2240	680	Deep	None	Agricultural
CH-AZ-245	Lakebed	503.78	2126.26	2240	690	Deep	None	Agricultural
CH-AZ-246	Lakebed	503.63	2126.54	2240	690	Deep	None	Agricultural
CH-AZ-247	Lakebed	503.65	2127.08	2240	690	Deep	None	Agricultural
CH-AZ-248	Lakebed	503.22	2127.01	2240	690	Deep	None	Agricultural
CH-AZ-249	Lakebed	503.13	2127.51	2240	690	Deep	None	Agricultural
CH-AZ-250	Lakebed	503.60	2128.01	2240	690	Deep	None	Agricultural
CH-AZ-251	Lakebed	503.40	2128.01	2240	685	Deep	None	Agricultural
CH-AZ-252	Lakebed	503.13	2128.36	2240	680	Deep	None	Agricultural

CHALCO-XOCHIMILCO REGION - PREHISPANIC SETTLEMENT DATA
Aztec Sites

SITE NUMBER	CLASSIFICATION	ENVIRONMENTAL ZONE	AREA (in ha)	POP.	EF	MF	LF	TF	EC	LC	ET	LT	EA	LA	TEMPORARY SITE NO.	SUPERVISOR	YEAR
CH-AZ-211	Small Hamlet	Lakebed	0.1	10	0	0	0	0	0	0	0	0	0	1	CH-A-9	J. PARSONS	1969
CH-AZ-212	Small Hamlet	Island-Lakesh Plain	0.5	10	0	0	0	0	0	0	0	1	1	1	CH-A-3	J. PARSONS	1969
CH-AZ-213	Hamlet	Lakebed	1.5	30	0	0	0	0	0	0	0	0	0	1	CH-AZ-1	R. WENKE	1972
CH-AZ-214	Small Hamlet	Lakebed	0.1	10	0	0	0	0	0	0	0	0	0	1	CH-AZ-1	R. WENKE	1972
CH-AZ-215	Small Hamlet	Lakebed	0.1	10	0	0	0	0	0	0	0	0	0	1	CH-AZ-62	R. WENKE	1972
CH-AZ-216	Small Hamlet	Lakebed	0.1	10	0	0	0	0	0	0	0	0	0	1	CH-AZ-60	R. WENKE	1972
CH-AZ-217	Small Hamlet	Lakebed	0.1	20	0	0	0	0	0	0	0	0	0	1	CH-AZ-61	R. WENKE	1972
CH-AZ-218	Small Hamlet	Lakebed	0.1	10	0	0	0	0	0	0	0	0	0	1	CH-AZ-59	R. WENKE	1972
CH-AZ-219	Small Hamlet	Lakebed	0.1	10	0	0	0	0	0	0	0	0	0	1	CH-AZ-58	R. WENKE	1972
CH-AZ-220	Small Hamlet	Lakebed	0.1	10	0	0	0	0	0	0	0	0	0	1	CH-AZ-56	R. WENKE	1972
CH-AZ-221	Small Hamlet	Lakebed	0.1	20	0	0	0	0	0	0	0	0	0	1	CH-AZ-57	R. WENKE	1972
CH-AZ-222	Small Hamlet	Lakebed	0.1	10	0	0	0	0	0	0	0	0	0	1	CH-AZ-66	R. WENKE	1972
CH-AZ-223	Small Hamlet	Lakebed	0.1	10	0	0	0	0	0	0	0	0	0	1	CH-AZ-55	R. WENKE	1972
CH-AZ-224	Small Hamlet	Lakebed	0.1	10	0	0	0	0	0	0	0	0	0	1	CH-AZ-54	R. WENKE	1972
CH-AZ-225	Small Hamlet	Lakebed	0.1	10	0	0	0	0	0	0	0	0	0	1	CH-AZ-65	R. WENKE	1972
CH-AZ-226	Small Hamlet	Lakebed	0.1	15	0	0	0	0	0	0	0	0	0	1	CH-AZ-53	R. WENKE	1972
CH-AZ-227	Small Hamlet	Lakebed	0.1	10	0	0	0	0	0	0	0	0	0	1	CH-AZ-63	R. WENKE	1972
CH-AZ-228	Small Hamlet	Lakebed	0.1	10	0	0	0	0	0	0	0	0	0	1	CH-AZ-64	R. WENKE	1972
CH-AZ-229	Hamlet	Lakebed	3.6	40	0	0	0	0	0	0	0	0	0	1	CH-AZ-49	R. WENKE	1972
CH-AZ-230	Small Hamlet	Lakebed	0.9	10	0	0	0	0	0	0	0	0	0	1	CH-AZ-48	R. WENKE	1972
CH-AZ-231	Hamlet	Lakebed	9.6	100	0	0	0	0	0	0	0	0	1	1	CH-AZ-45	R. WENKE	1972
CH-AZ-232	Questionable	Lakebed	1.2	15	0	0	0	0	0	0	0	1	0	1	CH-AZ-36	R. WENKE	1972
CH-AZ-233	Small Hamlet	Lakebed	0.9	10	0	0	0	0	0	0	0	1	1	1	CH-AZ-38	R. WENKE	1972
CH-AZ-234	Small Hamlet	Lakebed	0.3	10	0	0	0	0	0	0	0	0	0	1	CH-AZ-39	R. WENKE	1972
CH-AZ-235	Small Hamlet	Lakebed	0.1	10	0	0	0	0	0	0	0	0	1	1	CH-AZ-33	R. WENKE	1972
CH-AZ-236	Small Hamlet	Lakebed	0.1	10	0	0	0	0	0	0	0	0	0	1	CH-AZ-34	R. WENKE	1972
CH-AZ-237	Small Hamlet	Lakebed	0.1	10	0	0	0	0	0	0	0	0	1	1	CH-AZ-35	R. WENKE	1972
CH-AZ-238	Small Hamlet	Lakebed	0.4	10	0	0	0	0	0	0	0	0	0	1	CH-AZ-18	R. WENKE	1972
CH-AZ-239	Small Hamlet	Lakebed	0.1	10	0	0	0	0	0	0	0	0	0	1	CH-AZ-13	R. WENKE	1972
CH-AZ-240	Small Hamlet	Lakebed	0.1	10	0	0	0	0	0	0	0	0	0	1	CH-AZ-7	R. WENKE	1972
CH-AZ-241	Small Hamlet	Lakebed	0.1	10	0	0	0	0	0	0	0	0	0	1	CH-AZ-10	R. WENKE	1972
CH-AZ-242	Small Hamlet	Lakebed	0.4	10	0	0	0	0	0	0	0	0	0	1	CH-AZ-11	R. WENKE	1972
CH-AZ-243	Small Hamlet	Lakebed	0.1	10	0	0	0	0	0	0	0	0	0	1	CH-AZ-12	R. WENKE	1972
CH-AZ-244	Small Hamlet	Lakebed	0.4	10	0	0	0	0	0	0	0	0	0	1	CH-AZ-20	J. PARSONS	1972
CH-AZ-245	Small Hamlet	Lakebed	0.4	10	0	0	0	0	0	0	0	0	0	1	CH-AZ-21	J. PARSONS	1972
CH-AZ-246	Small Hamlet	Lakebed	0.4	10	0	0	0	0	0	0	0	0	0	1	CH-AZ-19	J. PARSONS	1972
CH-AZ-247	Questionable	Lakebed	1.3	10	0	0	0	0	0	0	0	1	0	1	CH-AZ-18	J. PARSONS	1972
CH-AZ-248	Small Hamlet	Lakebed	1.7	20	0	0	0	0	0	0	0	0	0	1	CH-AZ-17	J. PARSONS	1972
CH-AZ-249	Sm Disp Village	Lakebed	7.0	160	0	0	0	0	0	0	0	1	1	0	CH-AZ-16	R. WENKE	1972
CH-AZ-250	Small Hamlet	Lakebed	0.4	10	0	0	0	0	0	0	0	0	0	1	CH-AZ-8	R. WENKE	1972
CH-AZ-251	Small Hamlet	Lakebed	0.7	10	0	0	0	0	0	0	0	0	1	0	CH-AZ-15	R. WENKE	1972
CH-AZ-252	Hamlet	Lakebed	0.1	15	0	0	0	0	0	0	0	1	1	0	CH-AZ-14	R. WENKE	1972

Early Aztec and Late Aztec occupations are tabulated on a presence-absence basis.

CHALCO-XOCHIMILCO REGION - ENVIRONMENTAL DATA
Aztec Sites

Site Number	Environmental Zone	UTM Coordinates East	North	Elev (in m)	Rainfall (in mm)	Modern Soil Depth	Modern Erosion	Modern Land use
CH-AZ-253	Lakebed	502.43	2127.88	2240	710	Deep	None	Agricultural
CH-AZ-254	Lakebed	502.22	2128.44	2240	700	Deep	None	Agricultural
CH-AZ-255	Lakebed	502.25	2129.01	2240	680	Deep	None	Agricultural
CH-AZ-256	Lakebed	501.95	2129.23	2240	685	Deep	None	Agricultural
CH-AZ-257	Lakebed	501.72	2129.16	2240	685	Deep	None	Agricultural
CH-AZ-258	Lakebed	501.55	2129.21	2240	680	Deep	None	Agricultural
CH-AZ-259	Lakebed	501.28	2129.48	2240	680	Deep	None	Agricultural
CH-AZ-260	Lakebed	501.43	2129.01	2240	680	Deep	None	Agricultural
CH-AZ-261	Lakebed	501.20	2128.81	2240	680	Deep	None	Agricultural
CH-AZ-262	Lakebed	501.30	2128.66	2240	690	Deep	None	Agricultural
CH-AZ-263	Lakebed	501.53	2128.26	2240	700	Deep	None	Agricultural
CH-AZ-264	Lakebed	501.85	2127.48	2240	700	Deep	None	Agricultural
CH-AZ-265	Lakebed	501.55	2127.86	2240	700	Deep	None	Agricultural
CH-AZ-266	Lakebed	501.97	2126.86	2240	700	Deep	None	Agricultural
CH-AZ-267	Lakebed	502.10	2126.66	2240	700	Deep	None	Agricultural
CH-AZ-268	Lakebed	501.75	2126.38	2240	700	Deep	None	Agricultural
CH-AZ-269	Lakebed	501.60	2126.46	2240	700	Deep	None	Agricultural
CH-AZ-270	Lakebed	501.43	2126.69	2240	700	Deep	None	Agricultural
CH-AZ-271	Lakebed	500.95	2126.94	2240	725	Deep	None	Agricultural
CH-AZ-272	Lakebed	500.72	2127.16	2240	725	Deep	None	Agricultural
CH-AZ-273	Lakebed	500.38	2127.41	2240	700	Deep	None	Agricultural
CH-AZ-274	Lakebed	500.35	2129.13	2240	700	Deep	None	Agricultural
CH-AZ-275	Lakebed	499.78	2129.95	2240	700	Deep	None	Grazing & Agri
CH-AZ-276	Lakebed	500.75	2130.01	2240	700	Deep	None	Agricultural
CH-AZ-277	Lakebed	501.15	2130.16	2240	675	Deep	None	Grazing & Agri
CH-AZ-278	Lakeshore Plain	499.53	2128.58	2245	715	Deep	None	Agricultural
CH-AZ-279	Lakebed	499.73	2128.88	2240	700	Deep	None	Agricultural
CH-AZ-280	Lakebed	500.19	2128.73	2240	730	Deep	None	Agricultural
CH-AZ-281	Lakeshore Plain	499.86	2128.53	2245	700	Deep	None	Agricultural
CH-AZ-282	Low Piedmont-Rugged	499.61	2125.16	2345	750	Shallow-Med	Moderate	Agricultural
CH-AZ-283	Low Piedmont-Rugged	499.69	2123.70	2290	775	Medium	Moderate	Agricultural
CH-AZ-284	Low Piedmont-Rugged	499.21	2123.13	2330	780	Medium	Moderate	Agricultural
CH-AZ-285	Upr Piedmont-Rugged	499.98	2120.56	2540	990	Medium	Moderate	Agricultural
CH-AZ-286	Upr Piedmont-Rugged	499.58	2120.06	2630	990	Medium	Moderate	Agricultural
CH-AZ-287	Upr Piedmont-Rugged	499.23	2119.43	2700	1120	Medium	Moderate	Agricultural
XO-AZ-1	Lakebed	497.81	2132.03	2240	690	Deep	None	Agricultural
XO-AZ-2	Lakebed	497.69	2131.50	2240	690	Deep	None	Agricultural
XO-AZ-3	Lakebed	497.26	2131.08	2240	700	Deep	None	Agricultural
XO-AZ-4	Lakebed	498.98	2130.28	2240	695	Deep	None	Agricultural
XO-AZ-5	Lakebed	498.44	2130.00	2240	695	Deep	None	Agricultural
XO-AZ-6	Lakebed	497.26	2130.48	2240	700	Deep	None	Agricultural
XO-AZ-7	Lakebed	496.78	2130.78	2240	700	Deep	None	Agricultural

CHALCO-XOCHIMILCO REGION – PREHISPANIC SETTLEMENT DATA
Aztec Sites

SITE NUMBER	CLASSIFICATION	ENVIRONMENTAL ZONE	AREA (in ha)	POP.	OTHER OCCUPATIONS										SURVEY RECORDS		
					EF	MF	LF	TF	EC	LC	ET	LT	EA	LA	TEMPORARY SITE NO.	SUPERVISOR	YEAR
CH-AZ-253	Small Hamlet	Lakebed	0.1	10	0	0	0	0	0	0	0	0	1	1	CH-AZ-21	R. WENKE	1972
CH-AZ-254	Small Hamlet	Lakebed	0.3	10	0	0	0	0	0	0	0	0	0	1	CH-AZ-20	R. WENKE	1972
CH-AZ-255	Small Hamlet	Lakebed	0.1	10	0	0	0	0	0	0	0	0	0	1	CH-AZ-19	R. WENKE	1972
CH-AZ-256	Small Hamlet	Lakebed	0.8	20	0	0	0	0	0	0	0	0	0	1	CH-AZ-24	R. WENKE	1972
CH-AZ-257	Small Hamlet	Lakebed	1.5	20	0	0	0	0	0	0	0	0	0	1	CH-AZ-25	R. WENKE	1972
CH-AZ-258	Small Hamlet	Lakebed	0.1	10	0	0	0	0	0	0	0	0	0	1	CH-AZ-26	R. WENKE	1972
CH-AZ-259	Hamlet	Lakebed	1.7	30	0	0	0	0	0	0	0	0	0	1	CH-AZ-42	R. WENKE	1972
CH-AZ-260	Small Hamlet	Lakebed	1.7	15	0	0	0	0	0	0	0	0	1	1	CH-AZ-27	R. WENKE	1972
CH-AZ-261	Small Hamlet	Lakebed	0.1	10	0	0	0	0	0	0	0	0	0	1	CH-AZ-28	R. WENKE	1972
CH-AZ-262	Small Hamlet	Lakebed	0.4	10	0	0	0	0	0	0	0	0	0	1	CH-AZ-29	R. WENKE	1972
CH-AZ-263	Sm Disp Village	Lakebed	12.1	250	0	0	0	0	0	0	0	0	1	1	CH-AZ-30	R. WENKE	1972
CH-AZ-264	Small Hamlet	Lakebed	0.6	10	0	0	0	0	0	0	0	0	0	1	CH-AZ-22	R. WENKE	1972
CH-AZ-265	Small Hamlet	Lakebed	0.2	10	0	0	0	0	0	0	0	0	0	1	CH-AZ-23	R. WENKE	1972
CH-AZ-266	Small Hamlet	Lakebed	0.1	10	0	0	0	0	0	0	0	0	0	1	CH-AZ-3	J. PARSONS	1972
CH-AZ-267	Hamlet	Lakebed	2.5	50	0	0	0	0	0	0	0	0	0	1	CH-AZ-10	J. PARSONS	1972
CH-AZ-268	Small Hamlet	Lakebed	0.2	10	0	0	0	0	0	0	0	0	0	1	CH-AZ-9	J. PARSONS	1972
CH-AZ-269	Questionable	Lakebed	0.3	10	0	0	0	0	0	0	0	0	0	1	CH-AZ-8	J. PARSONS	1972
CH-AZ-270	Small Hamlet	Lakebed	0.3	20	0	0	0	0	0	0	0	0	0	1	CH-AZ-7	J. PARSONS	1972
CH-AZ-271	Small Hamlet	Lakebed	0.1	10	0	0	0	0	0	0	0	0	0	1	CH-AZ-6	J. PARSONS	1972
CH-AZ-272	Small Hamlet	Lakebed	0.3	20	0	0	0	0	0	0	0	0	0	1	CH-AZ-5	J. PARSONS	1972
CH-AZ-273	Small Hamlet	Lakebed	1.5	15	0	0	0	0	0	0	0	0	1	1	CH-AZ-43	R. WENKE	1972
CH-AZ-274	Small Hamlet	Lakebed	0.2	10	0	0	0	0	0	0	0	0	0	1	CH-AZ-44	R. WENKE	1972
CH-AZ-275	Local Center	Lakebed	90.0	4500	0	0	0	0	0	0	0	0	1	1	CH-AZ-67	R. WENKE	1972
CH-AZ-276	Small Hamlet	Lakebed	0.1	10	0	0	0	0	0	0	0	0	0	1	CH-AZ-41	R. WENKE	1972
CH-AZ-277	Small Hamlet	Lakebed	0.1	10	0	0	0	0	0	0	0	0	0	1	CH-AZ-40	R. WENKE	1972
CH-AZ-278	Hamlet	Lakeshore Plain	2.4	50	0	0	1	1	0	0	0	0	0	1	CH-AZ-29	J. PARSONS	1972
CH-AZ-279	Small Hamlet	Lakebed	0.8	20	0	0	1	1	0	0	0	0	0	1	CH-AZ-31	J. PARSONS	1972
CH-AZ-280	Questionable	Lakebed	2.6	20	0	0	0	0	0	0	0	0	0	1	CH-AZ-32	J. PARSONS	1972
CH-AZ-281	Small Hamlet	Lakeshore Plain	1.8	15	0	0	1	1	0	0	0	0	0	1	CH-AZ-30	J. PARSONS	1972
CH-AZ-282	Local Center	Low Piedmont-Rugged	99.0	2000	0	0	1	1	0	1	1	0	1	1	CH-AZ-1	J. PARSONS	1972
CH-AZ-283	Small Hamlet	Low Piedmont-Rugged	1.0	10	0	0	0	0	0	0	0	0	0	1	CH-AZ-36	J. PARSONS	1972
CH-AZ-284	Small Hamlet	Low Piedmont-Rugged	2.2	20	0	0	0	0	0	0	0	0	0	1	CH-AZ-34	J. PARSONS	1972
CH-AZ-285	Small Hamlet	Upr Piedmont-Rugged	0.4	10	0	0	0	0	0	0	0	0	0	1		J. PARSONS	1972
CH-AZ-286	Small Hamlet	Upr Piedmont-Rugged	0.5	10	0	0	0	0	0	0	0	0	0	1		J. PARSONS	1972
CH-AZ-287	Hamlet	Lakebed	3.0	30	0	0	0	0	0	0	0	0	1	1		M. PARSONS	1972
XO-AZ-1	Small Hamlet	Lakebed	0.6	10	0	0	0	0	0	0	0	0	0	1	XE-LF-1	M. PARSONS	1972
XO-AZ-2	Hamlet	Lakebed	2.2	30	0	0	0	0	0	0	0	0	1	1	XE-AZ-1	M. PARSONS	1972
XO-AZ-3	Hamlet	Lakebed	4.0	50	0	0	0	0	0	0	0	0	1	1	XE-AZ-1	M. PARSONS	1972
XO-AZ-4	Questionable	Lakebed	1.8	40	0	0	0	0	0	0	0	0	0	1	XE-AZ-7	M. PARSONS	1972
XO-AZ-5	Sm Disp Village	Lakebed	7.0	150	0	0	0	0	0	0	0	1	0	1	XE-AZ-1	M. PARSONS	1972
XO-AZ-6	Hamlet	Lakebed	4.5	50	0	0	0	0	0	0	0	0	1	1	XE-AZ-1	M. PARSONS	1972
XO-AZ-7	Hamlet	Lakebed	2.7	30	0	0	0	0	0	0	0	0	1	1	XE-AZ-1	M. PARSONS	1972

Early Aztec and Late Aztec occupations are tabulated on a presence-absence basis.

CHALCO-XOCHIMILCO REGION - ENVIRONMENTAL DATA
Aztec Sites

Site Number	Environmental Zone	UTM Coordinates East	North	Elev (in m)	Rainfall (in mm)	Modern Soil Depth	Modern Erosion	Modern Land use
XO-AZ-8	Lakebed	496.23	2131.95	2240	690	Deep	None	Agricultural
XO-AZ-9	Lakebed	495.91	2132.16	2240	680	Deep	None	Agricultural
XO-AZ-10	Lakebed	496.66	2131.13	2240	700	Deep	None	Agricultural
XO-AZ-11	Lakebed	496.71	2131.88	2240	690	Deep	None	Agricultural
XO-AZ-12	Lakebed	494.98	2131.53	2240	690	Deep	None	Agricultural
XO-AZ-13	Lakebed	495.51	2130.60	2240	700	Deep	None	Agricultural
XO-AZ-14	Lakebed	495.06	2130.35	2240	700	Deep	None	Agricultural
XO-AZ-15	Lakebed	495.03	2130.18	2240	700	Deep	None	Agricultural
XO-AZ-16	Lakebed	495.23	2130.06	2240	700	Deep	None	Agricultural
XO-AZ-17	Lakebed	494.91	2129.93	2240	700	Deep	None	Agricultural
XO-AZ-18	Lakebed	494.46	2130.13	2240	695	Deep	None	Agricultural
XO-AZ-19	Lakebed	494.38	2131.00	2240	680	Deep	None	Agricultural
XO-AZ-20	Lakeshore Plain	495.38	2129.06	2245	720	Deep	None	Agricultural
XO-AZ-21	Upr Piedmont-Rugged	497.61	2126.48	2500	800	Medium	Moderate	Agricultural
XO-AZ-22	Low Piedmont-Rugged	498.46	2125.06	2490	800	Shallow-Med	Slight-Moderate	Agricultural
XO-AZ-23	Low Piedmont-Rugged	496.61	2123.43	2450	775	Medium	Moderate	Agricultural
XO-AZ-24	Low Piedmont-Rugged	497.03	2123.41	2380	780	Medium	Slight-Moderate	Agricultural
XO-AZ-25	Low Piedmont-Rugged	498.94	2123.48	2350	775	Medium	Moderate	Agricultural
XO-AZ-26	Low Piedmont-Rugged	496.96	2122.75	2380	810	Shallow-Med	Moderate	Agricultural
XO-AZ-27	Upr Piedmont-Rugged	497.01	2120.95	2525	840	Shallow-Med	Moderate	Agricultural
XO-AZ-28	Upr Piedmont-Rugged	494.46	2123.50	2520	945	Medium	Moderate	Grazing & Agri
XO-AZ-29	Upr Piedmont-Rugged	492.16	2124.41	2570	920	Medium	Moderate	Grazing
XO-AZ-30	Lakeshore Plain	494.58	2128.20	2260	750	Deep	None	Agricultural
XO-AZ-31	Low Piedmont-Rugged	492.58	2127.31	2280	780	Shallow-Med	Moderate	Agricultural
XO-AZ-32	Lakeshore Plain	491.06	2127.58	2245	775	Deep	None	Agricultural
XO-AZ-33	Low Piedmont-Rugged	490.53	2127.41	2270	780	Medium	Moderate	Agricultural
XO-AZ-34	Low Piedmont-Rugged	489.53	2127.31	2280	790	Medium	Slight-Moderate	Agricultural
XO-AZ-35	Low Piedmont-Rugged	488.28	2126.88	2320	790	Medium	Moderate	Agricultural
XO-AZ-36	Low Piedmont-Rugged	488.58	2126.81	2350	790	Medium	Slight-Moderate	None
XO-AZ-37	Lakeshore Plain	491.16	2128.03	2245	750	Deep	None	Agricultural
XO-AZ-38	Lakeshore Plain	491.19	2128.23	2245	740	Deep	None	Agricultural
XO-AZ-39	Lakebed	491.73	2128.53	2240	750	Deep	None	Agricultural
XO-AZ-40	Lakeshore Plain	491.61	2128.23	2245	800	Deep	None	Agricultural
XO-AZ-41	Lakeshore Plain	491.91	2128.31	2245	750	Deep	None	Agricultural
XO-AZ-42	Lakebed	493.44	2130.70	2240	690	Deep	None	Agricultural
XO-AZ-43	Lakebed	494.16	2131.28	2240	685	Deep	None	Agricultural
XO-AZ-44	Lakebed	493.41	2131.38	2240	680	Deep	None	Agricultural
XO-AZ-45	Lakebed	493.06	2132.28	2240	675	Deep	None	Agricultural
XO-AZ-46	Lakebed	492.78	2131.70	2240	680	Deep	None	Agricultural
XO-AZ-47	Lakebed	492.61	2131.88	2240	680	Deep	None	Agricultural
XO-AZ-48	Lakebed	491.96	2131.85	2240	680	Deep	None	Agricultural
XO-AZ-49	Lakebed	491.91	2132.45	2240	675	Deep	None	Agricultural

CHALCO-XOCHIMILCO REGION - PREHISPANIC SETTLEMENT DATA
Aztec Sites

SITE NUMBER	CLASSIFICATION	ENVIRONMENTAL ZONE	AREA (in ha)	POP.	EF	MF	LF	TF	EC	LC	ET	LT	EA	LA	TEMPORARY SITE NO.	SURVEY RECORDS SUPERVISOR	YEAR
XO-AZ-8	Small Hamlet	Lakebed	0.3	15	0	0	0	0	0	0	0	0	0	1	XE-AZ-2	M. PARSONS	1972
XO-AZ-9	Small Hamlet	Lakebed	0.3	10	0	0	0	0	0	0	0	0	0	1	XE-AZ-3	M. PARSONS	1972
XO-AZ-10	Small Hamlet	Lakebed	0.3	10	0	0	0	0	0	0	0	0	0	1	XE-AZ-5	M. PARSONS	1972
XO-AZ-11	Small Hamlet	Lakebed	0.3	10	0	0	0	0	0	0	0	0	0	1	XE-AZ-4	M. PARSONS	1972
XO-AZ-12	Small Hamlet	Lakebed	0.3	10	0	0	0	0	0	0	0	0	1	1	XE-AZ-6	M. PARSONS	1972
XO-AZ-13	Small Hamlet	Lakebed	0.8	15	0	0	0	0	0	0	0	0	0	1	XE-AZ-9	M. PARSONS	1972
XO-AZ-14	Small Hamlet	Lakebed	1.5	20	0	0	0	0	0	0	0	0	0	1	XE-AZ-8	M. PARSONS	1972
XO-AZ-15	Small Hamlet	Lakebed	0.1	10	0	0	0	0	0	0	0	0	0	1	XE-AZ-10	M. PARSONS	1972
XO-AZ-16	Small Hamlet	Lakebed	0.1	10	0	0	0	0	0	0	0	0	0	1	XE-AZ-11	M. PARSONS	1972
XO-AZ-17	Small Hamlet	Lakebed	0.1	10	0	0	0	0	0	0	0	0	0	1	XE-AZ-12	M. PARSONS	1972
XO-AZ-18	Small Hamlet	Lakebed	0.1	10	0	0	0	0	0	0	0	0	0	1	XE-AZ-28	M. PARSONS	1972
XO-AZ-19	Small Hamlet	Lakebed	0.1	10	0	0	0	0	0	0	0	0	0	1	XE-AZ-27	M. PARSONS	1972
XO-AZ-20	Small Hamlet	Lakeshore Plain	0.5	10	0	0	0	0	0	0	1	0	0	1	XE-ET-1	M. PARSONS	1972
XO-AZ-21	Sm Disp Village	Upr Piedmont-Rugged	12.1	150	0	0	0	0	0	0	0	0	1	1	XE-ET-29	M. PARSONS	1972
XO-AZ-22	Hamlet	Low Piedmont-Rugged	1.6	30	0	0	0	0	0	0	0	0	0	1	CH-AZ-2	J. PARSONS	1972
XO-AZ-23	Hamlet	Low Piedmont-Rugged	3.5	30	0	0	0	0	0	0	0	0	0	1	CH-AZ-73	R. WENKE	1972
XO-AZ-24	Small Hamlet	Low Piedmont-Rugged	1.4	15	0	0	0	0	0	0	0	0	0	1	CH-AZ-74	R. WENKE	1972
XO-AZ-25	Small Hamlet	Low Piedmont-Rugged	0.9	10	0	0	0	0	0	0	0	0	0	1	CH-AZ-35	J. PARSONS	1972
XO-AZ-26	Hamlet	Low Piedmont-Rugged	4.0	40	0	0	0	0	0	0	0	0	0	1	CH-AZ-71	R. WENKE	1972
XO-AZ-27	Hamlet	Upr Piedmont-Rugged	2.8	30	0	0	0	0	0	0	0	0	0	1	CH-AZ-72	R. WENKE	1972
XO-AZ-28	Small Hamlet	Upr Piedmont-Rugged	1.7	20	0	0	0	0	0	0	0	0	0	1	XE-AZ-37	M. PARSONS	1972
XO-AZ-29	Ceremonial Ctr	Upr Piedmont-Rugged	0.1	0	0	0	0	0	0	0	0	0	0	1	XE-AZ-36	M. PARSONS	1972
XO-AZ-30	Questionable	Lakeshore Plain	0.8	10	0	0	0	0	0	0	1	0	0	1	XE-ET-4	M. PARSONS	1972
XO-AZ-31	Ceremonial Ctr	Low Piedmont-Rugged	2.0	0	0	0	0	0	0	0	0	0	0	1	XE-AZ-35	M. PARSONS	1972
XO-AZ-32	Small Hamlet	Lakeshore Plain	0.7	10	0	0	0	1	1	0	0	0	0	1	XW-AZ-36	J. PARSONS	1972
XO-AZ-33	Questionable	Low Piedmont-Rugged	5.4	50	0	0	0	1	1	0	0	1	0	1	XW-AZ-35	J. PARSONS	1972
XO-AZ-34	Sm Disp Village	Low Piedmont-Rugged	6.6	130	0	0	0	1	1	0	0	1	0	1	XW-AZ-42	J. PARSONS	1972
XO-AZ-35	Small Hamlet	Low Piedmont-Rugged	0.8	10	0	0	0	0	0	0	0	0	0	1	XW-AZ-38	J. PARSONS	1972
XO-AZ-36	Ceremonial Ctr	Low Piedmont-Rugged	0.1	0	0	0	0	0	0	0	0	0	0	1	XW-AZ-37	J. PARSONS	1972
XO-AZ-37	Hamlet	Lakeshore Plain	4.0	50	0	0	0	0	0	0	0	0	0	1	XE-AZ-33	M. PARSONS	1972
XO-AZ-38	Small Hamlet	Lakeshore Plain	0.9	20	0	0	0	0	0	0	0	0	1	1	XE-AZ-34	M. PARSONS	1972
XO-AZ-39	Small Hamlet	Lakebed	0.1	10	0	0	0	0	0	0	0	0	0	1	XE-AZ-32	M. PARSONS	1972
XO-AZ-40	Small Hamlet	Lakeshore Plain	0.1	10	0	0	0	0	0	0	0	0	0	1	XE-AZ-31	M. PARSONS	1972
XO-AZ-41	Small Hamlet	Lakeshore Plain	0.7	15	0	0	0	0	0	0	0	0	0	1	XE-AZ-30	M. PARSONS	1972
XO-AZ-42	Small Hamlet	Lakebed	0.1	10	0	0	0	0	0	0	0	0	0	1	XE-AZ-25	M. PARSONS	1972
XO-AZ-43	Small Hamlet	Lakebed	2.1	20	0	0	0	0	0	0	0	0	0	1	XE-AZ-24	M. PARSONS	1972
XO-AZ-44	Small Hamlet	Lakebed	0.1	15	0	0	0	0	0	0	0	0	0	1	XE-AZ-26	M. PARSONS	1972
XO-AZ-45	Small Hamlet	Lakebed	0.1	20	0	0	0	0	0	0	0	0	0	1	XE-AZ-22	M. PARSONS	1972
XO-AZ-46	Hamlet	Lakebed	2.8	40	0	0	0	0	0	0	0	0	0	1	XE-AZ-23	M. PARSONS	1972
XO-AZ-47	Hamlet	Lakebed	8.8	60	0	0	0	0	0	0	0	0	0	1	XE-AZ-20	M. PARSONS	1972
XO-AZ-48	Small Hamlet	Lakebed	0.1	10	0	0	0	0	0	0	0	0	0	1	XE-AZ-21	M. PARSONS	1972
XO-AZ-49	Hamlet	Lakebed	5.0	50	0	0	0	0	0	0	0	0	0	1	XE-AZ-19	M. PARSONS	1972

Early Aztec and Late Aztec occupations are tabulated on a presence-absence basis.

CHALCO-XOCHIMILCO REGION - ENVIRONMENTAL DATA
Aztec Sites

Site Number	Environmental Zone	UTM Coordinates East	North	Elev (in m)	Rainfall (in mm)	Modern Soil Depth	Modern Erosion	Modern Land use
XO-AZ-50	Lakebed	491.73	2132.75	2240	675	Deep	None	Agricultural
XO-AZ-51	Lakebed	491.28	2132.16	2240	680	Deep	None	Agricultural
XO-AZ-52	Lakebed	491.36	2132.28	2240	680	Deep	None	Agricultural
XO-AZ-53	Lakebed	490.48	2132.60	2240	850	Deep	None	Agricultural
XO-AZ-54	Lakebed	489.78	2132.66	2240	685	Deep	None	Agricultural
XO-AZ-55	Lakebed	490.76	2133.73	2240	675	Deep	None	Agricultural
XO-AZ-56	Lakebed	490.98	2133.81	2240	670	Deep	None	Agricultural
XO-AZ-57	Lakebed	491.53	2133.91	2240	670	Deep	None	Agricultural
XO-AZ-58	Lakebed	491.71	2133.88	2240	670	Deep	None	Agricultural
XO-AZ-59	Lakeshore Plain	492.01	2134.95	2245	655	Deep	None	Agricultural
XO-AZ-60	Lakebed	490.61	2134.28	2240	670	Deep	None	Agricultural
XO-AZ-61	Lakebed	490.38	2134.25	2240	670	Deep	None	Agricultural
XO-AZ-62	Lakebed	489.53	2133.98	2240	665	Deep	None	Agricultural
XO-AZ-63	Lakebed	490.36	2134.68	2240	660	Deep	None	Agricultural
XO-AZ-64	Lakebed	490.16	2134.73	2240	660	Deep	None	Agricultural
XO-AZ-65	Lakebed	489.76	2134.85	2240	660	Deep	None	Agricultural
XO-AZ-66	Lakeshore Plain	489.86	2136.03	2245	655	Deep	None	Agricultural
XO-AZ-67	Lakeshore Plain	489.21	2136.06	2245	655	Deep	None	Grazing & Agri
XO-AZ-68	Lakeshore Plain	488.48	2136.68	2245	650	Deep	None	Agricultural
XO-AZ-69	Lakeshore Plain	488.21	2136.98	2245	650	Deep	None	Settlement
XO-AZ-70	Lakeshore Plain	486.57	2138.06	2245	620	Deep	None	None
XO-AZ-71	Lakebed	487.03	2136.68	2240	655	Deep	None	Agricultural
XO-AZ-72	Lakebed	488.71	2132.28	2240	685	Deep	None	Agricultural
XO-AZ-73	Lakebed	488.28	2132.33	2240	680	Deep	None	Agricultural
XO-AZ-74	Lakebed	488.01	2132.28	2240	680	Deep	None	Agricultural
XO-AZ-75	Lakebed	488.38	2131.81	2240	685	Deep	None	Agricultural
XO-AZ-76	Lakebed	487.63	2131.25	2240	690	Deep	None	Agricultural
XO-AZ-77	Lakebed	487.48	2131.06	2240	690	Deep	None	Agricultural
XO-AZ-78	Low Piedmont-Rugged	486.19	2129.06	2270	750	Deep	Slight	Agricultural
XO-AZ-79	Low Piedmont-Rugged	484.84	2131.68	2270	795	Medium	Slight	Agricultural
XO-AZ-80	Low Piedmont-Rugged	484.04	2131.31	2270	810	Medium-Deep	Slight	Agricultural
XO-AZ-81	Low Piedmont-Rugged	484.52	2130.95	2300	795	Medium	Moderate	Agricultural
XO-AZ-82	Low Piedmont-Rugged	484.02	2130.45	2320	800	Medium	Moderate	Grazing & Agri
XO-AZ-83	Low Piedmont-Hill	485.32	2129.20	2450	790	Shallow	Deep	Grazing
XO-AZ-84	Low Piedmont-Hill	485.17	2128.53	2500	795	Shallow	Deep	Grazing
XO-AZ-85	Low Piedmont-Hill	484.19	2128.41	2470	850	Shallow	Deep	Grazing
XO-AZ-86	Low Piedmont-Rugged	483.97	2127.83	2460	900	Medium	Moderate	Agricultural
XO-AZ-87	Lakeshore Plain	488.23	2128.31	2245	1050	Deep	None	Agricultural
XO-AZ-88	Low Piedmont-Rugged	487.19	2124.78	2410	1300	Shallow-Med	Moderate	Grazing & Agri
XO-AZ-89	Upr Piedmont-Rugged	485.82	2124.48	2650	950	Medium	Moderate	Agricultural
XO-AZ-90	Upr Piedmont-Rugged	485.67	2123.75	2650	1000	Medium	Moderate	Agricultural
XO-AZ-91	Low Piedmont-Hill	479.32	2134.50	2360	850	Medium	Slight	None

CHALCO-XOCHIMILCO REGION - PREHISPANIC SETTLEMENT DATA
Aztec Sites

SITE NUMBER	CLASSIFICATION	ENVIRONMENTAL ZONE	AREA (in ha)	POP.	EF	MF	LF	TF	EC	LC	ET	LT	EA	LA	SURVEY RECORDS TEMPORARY SITE NO.	SUPERVISOR	YEAR
XO-AZ-50	Small Hamlet	Lakebed	0.1	10	0	0	0	0	0	0	0	0	0	1	XE-AZ-18	M. PARSONS	1972
XO-AZ-51	Small Hamlet	Lakebed	0.1	10	0	0	0	0	0	0	0	0	0	1	XE-AZ-17	M. PARSONS	1972
XO-AZ-52	Small Hamlet	Lakebed	0.1	10	0	0	0	0	0	0	0	0	0	1	XE-AZ-15	M. PARSONS	1972
XO-AZ-53	Small Hamlet	Lakebed	0.1	10	0	0	0	0	0	0	0	0	0	1	XE-AZ-14	M. PARSONS	1972
XO-AZ-54	Hamlet	Lakebed	5.0	80	0	0	0	0	0	0	0	0	0	1	XE-AZ-13	M. PARSONS	1972
XO-AZ-55	Small Hamlet	Lakebed	1.2	20	0	0	0	0	0	0	0	0	0	1	XW-AZ-25	J. PARSONS	1972
XO-AZ-56	Small Hamlet	Lakebed	0.3	10	0	0	0	0	0	0	0	0	0	1	XW-AZ-26	J. PARSONS	1972
XO-AZ-57	Small Hamlet	Lakebed	0.1	10	0	0	0	0	0	0	0	0	0	1	XE-AZ-38	M. PARSONS	1972
XO-AZ-58	Small Hamlet	Lakebed	1.0	20	0	0	0	0	0	0	0	0	0	1	XW-AZ-27	J. PARSONS	1972
XO-AZ-59	Small Hamlet	Lakeshore Plain	1.5	20	0	0	0	0	0	0	0	0	0	1	XW-AZ-28	J. PARSONS	1972
XO-AZ-60	Small Hamlet	Lakebed	1.2	20	0	0	0	0	0	0	0	0	0	1	XW-AZ-24	J. PARSONS	1972
XO-AZ-61	Small Hamlet	Lakebed	0.5	10	0	0	0	0	0	0	0	0	0	1	XW-AZ-23	J. PARSONS	1972
XO-AZ-62	Small Hamlet	Lakebed	0.6	10	0	0	0	0	0	0	0	0	1	1	XW-AZ-22	J. PARSONS	1972
XO-AZ-63	Small Hamlet	Lakebed	0.4	10	0	0	0	0	0	0	0	0	0	1	XW-AZ-21	J. PARSONS	1972
XO-AZ-64	Small Hamlet	Lakebed	0.4	10	0	0	0	0	0	0	0	0	0	1	XW-AZ-20	J. PARSONS	1972
XO-AZ-65	Small Hamlet	Lakebed	0.1	10	0	0	0	0	0	0	0	0	0	1	XW-AZ-19	J. PARSONS	1972
XO-AZ-66	Questionable	Lakeshore Plain	0.6	10	0	0	0	0	0	0	0	0	0	1	XW-AZ-18	J. PARSONS	1972
XO-AZ-67	Small Hamlet	Lakeshore Plain	0.6	15	0	0	0	0	0	0	0	0	0	1	XW-AZ-17	J. PARSONS	1972
XO-AZ-68	Hamlet	Lakeshore Plain	1.5	30	0	0	0	0	0	0	0	0	1	1	XW-AZ-14	J. PARSONS	1972
XO-AZ-69	Sm Disp Village	Lakeshore Plain	7.7	160	0	0	0	0	0	0	0	0	1	1	XW-AZ-16	J. PARSONS	1972
XO-AZ-70	Questionable	Lakeshore Plain	1.2	10	0	0	0	0	0	0	0	0	1	1	XW-AZ-13	J. PARSONS	1972
XO-AZ-71	Questionable	Lakebed	3.8	50	0	0	0	0	0	0	0	0	1	0	XW-AZ-15	J. PARSONS	1972
XO-AZ-72	Hamlet	Lakebed	5.6	50	0	0	0	0	0	0	0	0	0	1	XW-AZ-1	J. PARSONS	1972
XO-AZ-73	Hamlet	Lakebed	1.8	40	0	0	0	0	0	0	0	0	0	1	XW-AZ-3	J. PARSONS	1972
XO-AZ-74	Small Hamlet	Lakebed	1.6	15	0	0	0	0	0	0	0	0	0	1	XW-AZ-4	J. PARSONS	1972
XO-AZ-75	Hamlet	Lakebed	3.6	30	0	0	0	0	0	0	0	0	0	1	XW-AZ-2	J. PARSONS	1972
XO-AZ-76	Small Hamlet	Lakebed	0.9	10	0	0	0	0	0	0	0	0	0	1	XW-AZ-5	J. PARSONS	1972
XO-AZ-77	Hamlet	Lakebed	1.8	40	0	0	0	0	0	0	0	0	0	1	XW-AZ-6	J. PARSONS	1972
XO-AZ-78	Questionable	Low Piedmont-Rugged	0.8	10	0	0	0	0	0	1	0	0	0	1	XW-AZ-32	J. PARSONS	1972
XO-AZ-79	Hamlet	Low Piedmont-Rugged	2.7	30	0	0	0	1	0	1	1	0	0	1	XW-AZ-9	J. PARSONS	1972
XO-AZ-80	Hamlet	Low Piedmont-Rugged	1.6	30	0	0	0	0	0	0	0	0	0	1	XW-AZ-11	J. PARSONS	1972
XO-AZ-81	Small Hamlet	Low Piedmont-Rugged	1.3	20	0	0	0	0	0	0	0	0	0	1	XW-AZ-8	J. PARSONS	1972
XO-AZ-82	Small Hamlet	Low Piedmont-Rugged	0.6	10	0	0	0	0	0	0	0	0	0	1	XW-AZ-10	J. PARSONS	1972
XO-AZ-83	Ceremonial Ctr	Low Piedmont-Hill	0.3	0	0	0	0	0	0	0	0	0	0	1	XW-AZ-33	J. PARSONS	1972
XO-AZ-84	Ceremonial Ctr	Low Piedmont-Hill	0.5	0	0	0	0	0	0	0	0	0	0	1	XW-AZ-31	J. PARSONS	1972
XO-AZ-85	Ceremonial Ctr	Low Piedmont-Hill	0.7	0	0	0	0	0	0	0	0	0	0	1	XW-AZ-30	J. PARSONS	1972
XO-AZ-86	Hamlet	Low Piedmont-Rugged	3.1	30	0	0	0	0	0	0	0	0	0	1	XW-AZ-29	J. PARSONS	1972
XO-AZ-87	Hamlet	Lakeshore Plain	1.9	40	0	0	0	0	0	0	0	1	0	1	XW-AZ-34	J. PARSONS	1972
XO-AZ-88	Questionable	Low Piedmont-Rugged	0.1	0	0	0	0	0	0	0	0	0	0	1	XW-AZ-41	J. PARSONS	1972
XO-AZ-89	Small Hamlet	Upr Piedmont-Rugged	0.4	10	0	0	0	0	0	0	0	0	0	1	XW-AZ-40	J. PARSONS	1972
XO-AZ-90	Small Hamlet	Upr Piedmont-Rugged	0.3	10	0	0	0	0	0	0	0	0	1	1	XW-AZ-39	J. PARSONS	1972
XO-AZ-91	Ceremonial Ctr	Low Piedmont-Hill	2.7	0	0	0	0	0	0	0	0	0	1	1	XW-AZ-12	J. PARSONS	1972

Early Aztec and Late Aztec occupations are tabulated on a presence-absence basis.

Site Number	Environmental Zone	UTM Coordinates		Elev (in m)	Rainfall (in mm)	Modern Soil Depth	Modern Erosion	Modern Land use
		East	North					
IX-EF-1	Lakeshore Plain	509.65	2133.65	2240	660	Deep	None	Grazing
IX-EF-2	Lakeshore Plain	500.88	2133.60	2240	690	Deep	Very Slight	Agricultural
IX-EF-3	Lakeshore Plain	497.75	2138.63	2240	630	Deep	Very Slight	Agricultural

IXTAPALAPA REGION - ENVIRONMENTAL DATA
Early Formative Sites

IXTAPALAPA REGION - PREHISPANIC SETTLEMENT DATA
Early Formative Sites

| SITE NUMBER | CLASSIFICATION | ENVIRONMENTAL ZONE | AREA (in ha) | POP. | OTHER OCCUPATIONS | | | | | | | | | | TEMPORARY SITE NO. | SURVEY RECORDS | |
					EF	MF	LF	TF	EC	LC	ET	LT	EA	LA		SUPERVISOR	YEAR
IX-EF-1	Sm Disp Village	Lakeshore Plain	9.0	225	0	1	1	1	0	1	0	0	0	0		R. BLANTON	1969
IX-EF-2	Hamlet	Lakeshore Plain	3.0	75	0	1	1	0	1	1	1	1	0	1		R. BLANTON	1969
IX-EF-3	Hamlet	Lakeshore Plain	4.0	100	0	1	1	1	1	1	1	1	0	0		R. BLANTON	1969

IXTAPALAPA REGION - ENVIRONMENTAL DATA
Middle Formative Sites

Site Number	Environmental Zone	UTM Coordinates East	North	Elev (in m)	Rainfall (in mm)	Modern Soil Depth	Modern Erosion	Modern Land use
IX-MF-1	Lakeshore Plain	509.65	2133.65	2240	660	Deep	None	Grazing
IX-MF-2	Lakeshore Plain	500.88	2133.60	2240	690	Deep	Very Slight	Agricultural
IX-MF-3	Lakeshore Plain	497.75	2138.63	2240	630	Deep	Very Slight	Agricultural
IX-MF-4	Lakeshore Plain	497.93	2133.88	2240	680	Deep	None	Agricultural

IXTAPALAPA REGION - PREHISPANIC SETTLEMENT DATA
Middle Formative Sites

SITE NUMBER	CLASSIFICATION	ENVIRONMENTAL ZONE	AREA (in ha)	POP.	OTHER OCCUPATIONS										SURVEY RECORDS		
					EF	MF	LF	TF	EC	LC	ET	LT	EA	LA	TEMPORARY SITE NO.	SUPERVISOR	YEAR
IX-MF-1	Sm Disp Village	Lakeshore Plain	9.0	225	1	1	0	0	0	0	0	0	0	0		R. BLANTON	1969
IX-MF-2	Hamlet	Lakeshore Plain	3.0	75	1	1	1	0	1	1	1	1	0	1		R. BLANTON	1969
IX-MF-3	Hamlet	Lakeshore Plain	4.0	100	1	1	0	1	1	1	1	1	0	0		R. BLANTON	1969
IX-MF-4	Sm Disp Village	Lakeshore Plain	12.5	313	0	0	0	0	1	0	0	1	0	0		R. BLANTON	1969

IXTAPALAPA REGION - ENVIRONMENTAL DATA
Late Formative Sites

Site Number	Environmental Zone	UTM Coordinates East	North	Elev (in m)	Rainfall (in mm)	Modern Soil Depth	Modern Erosion	Modern Land use
IX-LF-1	Upr Piedmont-Rugged	518.63	2141.00	2500	720	Very Shallow	Deep	None
IX-LF-2	Lakeshore Plain	509.45	2134.10	2245	650	Deep	None	Agricultural
IX-LF-3	Lakeshore Plain	504.38	2136.15	2240	650	Medium	Very Slight	None
IX-LF-4	Lakebed	503.55	2135.05	2240	660	Medium	None	None
IX-LF-5	Lakeshore Plain	500.88	2133.60	2240	680	Deep	Very Slight	Agricultural
IX-LF-6	Lakeshore Plain	497.93	2133.88	2240	680	Deep	Very Slight	Settlement
IX-LF-7	Low Piedmont-Rugged	498.07	2136.97	2350	650	Medium	Very Slight	Agricultural
IX-LF-8	Lakeshore Plain	497.75	2138.63	2240	630	Deep	Very Slight	Agricultural
IX-LF-9	Low Piedmont-Rugged	497.50	2138.20	2270	630	Deep	None	Agricultural
IX-LF-10	Lakeshore Plain	497.13	2138.03	2240	630	Deep	Very Slight	Agricultural
IX-LF-11	Lakeshore Plain	496.95	2138.25	2240	630	Deep	Very Slight	None
IX-LF-12	Low Piedmont-Smooth	488.95	2137.95	2260	640	Deep	Slight	Grazing
IX-LF-13	Low Piedmont-Rugged	501.35	2135.85	2410	660	Deep	None	Agricultural

IXTAPALAPA REGION - PREHISPANIC SETTLEMENT DATA
Late Formative Sites

SITE NUMBER	CLASSIFICATION	ENVIRONMENTAL ZONE	AREA (in ha)	POP.	OTHER OCCUPATIONS										TEMPORARY SITE NO.	SURVEY RECORDS	
					EF	MF	LF	TF	EC	LC	ET	LT	EA	LA		SUPERVISOR	YEAR
IX-LF-1	Hamlet	Upr Piedmont-Rugged	2.2	55	0	0	0	0	0	0	0	1	0	0		R. BLANTON	1969
IX-LF-2	Local Center	Lakeshore Plain	37.0	1850	1	1	0	1	0	0	0	0	0	0		R. BLANTON	1969
IX-LF-3	Lg Nucl Village	Lakeshore Plain	20.0	1000	0	0	0	0	1	0	0	0	0	0		R. BLANTON	1969
IX-LF-4	Hamlet	Lakebed	2.5	100	0	0	0	0	0	0	0	0	0	0		R. BLANTON	1969
IX-LF-5	Hamlet	Lakeshore Plain	3.0	75	1	1	0	0	1	1	1	1	0	1		R. BLANTON	1969
IX-LF-6	Local Center	Lakeshore Plain	65.0	3250	0	1	0	0	1	1	1	1	0	1		R. BLANTON	1969
IX-LF-7	Lg Nucl Village	Low Piedmont-Rugged	30.0	1200	0	0	0	1	0	0	0	0	0	0		R. BLANTON	1969
IX-LF-8	Sm Disp Village	Lakeshore Plain	7.0	175	1	1	0	1	1	1	1	1	0	0		R. BLANTON	1969
IX-LF-9	Small Hamlet	Low Piedmont-Rugged	0.1	25	0	0	0	0	0	0	0	1	0	0		R. BLANTON	1969
IX-LF-10	Small Hamlet	Lakeshore Plain	0.1	25	0	0	0	0	0	0	0	0	0	0		R. BLANTON	1969
IX-LF-11	Hamlet	Lakeshore Plain	2.6	65	0	0	0	0	1	0	0	0	0	0		R. BLANTON	1969
IX-LF-12	Sm Nucl Village	Low Piedmont-Smooth	15.0	375	0	0	0	0	0	0	1	0	0	0		R. BLANTON	1969
IX-LF-13	Small Hamlet	Low Piedmont-Rugged	0.1	25	0	0	0	0	0	0	0	0	0	0		R. BLANTON	1969

IXTAPALAPA REGION - ENVIRONMENTAL DATA
Terminal Formative Sites

Site Number	Environmental Zone	UTM Coordinates East	North	Elev (in m)	Rainfall (in mm)	Modern Soil Depth	Modern Erosion	Modern Land use
IX-TF-1	Low Piedmont-Smooth	507.30	2136.93	2310	640	Deep	Deep	Grazing & Agri
IX-TF-2	Low Piedmont-Smooth	509.07	2135.10	2250	650	Medium	Moderate	None
IX-TF-3	Low Piedmont-Smooth	508.43	2135.43	2270	650	Deep	Moderate	Agricultural
IX-TF-4	Lakeshore Plain	509.47	2134.07	2245	660	Deep	None	Settlement
IX-TF-5	Low Piedmont-Rugged	501.70	2138.35	2350	630	Medium	Slight-Moderate	Agricultural
IX-TF-6	Upr Piedmont-Smooth	512.30	2141.93	2500	660	Medium	Slight-Moderate	Grazing
IX-TF-7	Lakeshore Plain	502.88	2139.60	2260	620	Deep	None	None
IX-TF-8	Upr Piedmont-Rugged	500.82	2136.68	2570	650	Medium	Very Slight	Agricultural
IX-TF-9	Low Piedmont-Rugged	498.43	2134.20	2270	680	Deep	None	Agricultural
IX-TF-10	Low Piedmont-Rugged	498.68	2137.20	2360	640	Deep	None	Agricultural
IX-TF-11	Lakeshore Plain	497.53	2138.50	2240	630	Deep	Very Slight	Agricultural
IX-TF-12	Lakeshore Plain	497.78	2140.07	2240	610	Deep	None	Settlement
IX-TF-13	Low Piedmont-Smooth	490.57	2138.50	2385	630	Medium	Slight-Moderate	None

IXTAPALAPA REGION - PREHISPANIC SETTLEMENT DATA
Terminal Formative Sites

| SITE NUMBER | CLASSIFICATION | ENVIRONMENTAL ZONE | AREA (in ha) | POP. | OTHER OCCUPATIONS | | | | | | | | | | TEMPORARY SITE NO. | SURVEY RECORDS | |
					EF	MF	LF	TF	EC	LC	ET	LT	EA	LA		SUPERVISOR	YEAR
IX-TF-1	Small Hamlet	Low Piedmont-Smooth	0.1	10	0	0	0	0	0	0	0	0	0	0		R. BLANTON	1969
IX-TF-2	Sm Disp Village	Low Piedmont-Smooth	16.0	400	0	0	0	0	0	0	0	1	0	0		R. BLANTON	1969
IX-TF-3	Lg Disp Village	Low Piedmont-Smooth	20.0	500	0	0	0	0	0	0	0	0	0	0		R. BLANTON	1969
IX-TF-4	Local Center	Lakeshore Plain	37.0	1850	1	1	1	0	0	0	0	0	0	0		R. BLANTON	1969
IX-TF-5	Local Center	Low Piedmont-Rugged	32.0	1600	0	0	0	0	0	0	0	0	0	0		R. BLANTON	1969
IX-TF-6	Hamlet	Upr Piedmont-Smooth	4.0	100	0	0	0	0	0	0	0	0	0	0		R. BLANTON	1969
IX-TF-7	Hamlet	Lakeshore Plain	0.5	50	0	0	0	0	0	0	0	0	0	0		R. BLANTON	1969
IX-TF-8	Hamlet	Upr Piedmont-Rugged	2.0	50	0	0	0	0	0	0	0	0	0	0		R. BLANTON	1969
IX-TF-9	Hamlet	Low Piedmont-Rugged	2.0	50	0	0	0	0	0	0	0	0	0	0		R. BLANTON	1969
IX-TF-10	Lg Disp Village	Low Piedmont-Rugged	32.0	1600	0	0	0	0	1	1	1	0	0	0		R. BLANTON	1969
IX-TF-11	Sm Disp Village	Lakeshore Plain	6.0	150	1	1	1	0	1	1	1	0	0	0		R. BLANTON	1969
IX-TF-12	Small Hamlet	Lakeshore Plain	0.1	20	0	0	0	0	0	0	0	0	0	0		R. BLANTON	1969
IX-TF-13	Lg Disp Village	Low Piedmont-Smooth	41.0	1025	0	0	0	0	1	1	0	0	0	1		R. BLANTON	1969

IXTAPALAPA REGION - ENVIRONMENTAL DATA
Early Classic Sites

Site Number	Environmental Zone	UTM Coordinates East	North	Elev (in m)	Rainfall (in mm)	Modern Soil Depth	Modern Erosion	Modern Land use
IX-EC-1	Low Piedmont-Smooth	517.00	2138.63	2360	690	Deep	Very Slight	Agricultural
IX-EC-2	Lakeshore Plain	515.38	2137.68	2260	680	Deep	None	Agricultural
IX-EC-3	Upr Piedmont-Smooth	520.00	2140.90	2560	760	Deep	Moderate	Agricultural
IX-EC-4	Upr Piedmont-Smooth	519.38	2140.70	2540	740	Fully Eroded	Deep	Agricultural
IX-EC-5	Low Piedmont-Smooth	517.55	2139.97	2400	690	Fully Eroded	Deep	Grazing & Agri
IX-EC-6	Low Piedmont-Smooth	517.22	2139.40	2350	690	Fully Eroded	Deep	Grazing
IX-EC-7	Low Piedmont-Smooth	513.90	2141.20	2350	670	Shallow-Med	Slight-Moderate	Agricultural
IX-EC-8	Low Piedmont-Smooth	513.20	2142.00	2420	660	Medium	Slight-Moderate	Agricultural
IX-EC-9	Low Piedmont-Smooth	510.00	2141.38	2410	640	Deep	None	Agricultural
IX-EC-10	Low Piedmont-Smooth	509.13	2142.55	2400	630	Medium	Slight	Agricultural
IX-EC-11	Low Piedmont-Smooth	511.90	2138.60	2400	660	Deep	None	Agricultural
IX-EC-12	Lakeshore Plain	511.80	2136.63	2250	670	Deep	None	Agricultural
IX-EC-13	Low Piedmont-Smooth	510.25	2136.18	2300	660	Medium	Slight	Agricultural
IX-EC-14	Low Piedmont-Smooth	508.68	2135.13	2250	650	Medium	Slight	Settlement
IX-EC-15	Low Piedmont-Smooth	507.55	2135.60	2250	650	Medium	Slight	Agricultural
IX-EC-16	Lakeshore Plain	505.95	2136.53	2240	640	Deep	None	Agricultural
IX-EC-17	Lakeshore Plain	504.78	2137.38	2245	640	Deep	None	Settlement
IX-EC-18	Lakeshore Plain	503.18	2139.93	2240	620	Deep	None	Agricultural
IX-EC-19	Lakeshore Plain	503.82	2135.78	2240	650	Deep	None	Settlement
IX-EC-20	Low Piedmont-Smooth	504.88	2139.93	2250	620	Medium	Slight-Moderate	Agricultural
IX-EC-21	Lakeshore Plain	502.38	2134.15	2240	670	Deep	None	Agricultural
IX-EC-22	Low Piedmont-Rugged	501.50	2133.75	2250	680	Medium	Slight	Agricultural
IX-EC-23	Low Piedmont-Rugged	500.88	2133.60	2240	690	Deep	None	Agricultural
IX-EC-24	Low Piedmont-Rugged	500.43	2133.78	2250	680	Medium	None	Agricultural
IX-EC-25	Lakeshore Plain	500.03	2140.10	2240	610	Deep	Slight-Moderate	Settlement
IX-EC-26	Lakeshore Plain	496.88	2138.32	2240	630	Deep	None	Agricultural
IX-EC-27	Low Piedmont-Rugged	498.30	2138.32	2280	620	Deep	None	Agricultural
IX-EC-28	Low Piedmont-Rugged	499.32	2138.85	2290	620	Medium	Slight	Agricultural
IX-EC-29	Low Piedmont-Rugged	498.22	2139.07	2270	620	Medium	Slight	Agricultural
IX-EC-30	Lakeshore Plain	497.78	2138.65	2250	620	Deep	None	Agricultural
IX-EC-31	Lakeshore Plain	497.78	2139.90	2250	610	Medium	Deep	Settlement
IX-EC-32	Lakeshore Plain	498.13	2133.45	2240	680	Deep	None	Settlement
IX-EC-33	Lakeshore Plain	496.70	2133.93	2250	670	Deep	None	Agricultural
IX-EC-34	Lakeshore Plain	494.68	2134.28	2250	670	Deep	None	Settlement
IX-EC-35	Low Piedmont-Smooth	490.55	2138.00	2350	640	Medium	Deep	Agricultural
IX-EC-36	Lakeshore Plain	492.30	2139.20	2240	630	Deep	None	Settlement
IX-EC-37	Low Piedmont-Smooth	490.07	2139.57	2295	630	Medium	Moderate	Agricultural

69

IXTAPALAPA REGION – PREHISPANIC SETTLEMENT DATA
Early Classic Sites

SITE NUMBER	CLASSIFICATION	ENVIRONMENTAL ZONE	AREA (in ha)	POP.	EF	MF	LF	TF	EC	LC	ET	LT	EA	LA	TEMPORARY SITE NO.	SUPERVISOR	YEAR
IX-EC-1	Hamlet	Low Piedmont-Smooth	8.0	80	0	0	0	0	0	0	0	0	1	0		R. BLANTON	1969
IX-EC-2	Hamlet	Lakeshore Plain	8.0	80	0	0	0	0	0	0	0	0	0	0		R. BLANTON	1969
IX-EC-3	Small Hamlet	Upr Piedmont-Smooth	2.2	22	0	0	0	0	0	0	0	0	0	0		R. BLANTON	1969
IX-EC-4	Small Hamlet	Upr Piedmont-Smooth	0.9	10	0	0	0	0	0	0	0	0	0	0		R. BLANTON	1969
IX-EC-5	Small Hamlet	Low Piedmont-Smooth	0.1	10	0	0	0	0	0	0	0	0	0	0		R. BLANTON	1969
IX-EC-6	Hamlet	Low Piedmont-Smooth	10.0	100	0	0	0	0	0	0	1	1	0	0		R. BLANTON	1969
IX-EC-7	Local Center	Low Piedmont-Smooth	36.0	900	0	0	0	0	0	1	1	1	1	0		R. BLANTON	1969
IX-EC-8	Hamlet	Low Piedmont-Smooth	7.0	70	0	0	0	0	0	0	0	1	0	0		R. BLANTON	1969
IX-EC-9	Small Hamlet	Low Piedmont-Smooth	0.1	10	0	0	0	0	0	0	0	0	0	0		R. BLANTON	1969
IX-EC-10	Small Hamlet	Low Piedmont-Smooth	0.1	10	0	0	0	0	0	1	1	0	0	0		R. BLANTON	1969
IX-EC-11	Sm Disp Village	Low Piedmont-Smooth	11.0	275	0	0	0	0	0	0	0	0	0	0		R. BLANTON	1969
IX-EC-12	Hamlet	Lakeshore Plain	3.0	30	0	0	0	0	0	0	0	0	0	0		R. BLANTON	1969
IX-EC-13	Sm Disp Village	Low Piedmont-Smooth	17.0	170	0	0	0	0	1	0	0	0	0	0		R. BLANTON	1969
IX-EC-14	Hamlet	Low Piedmont-Smooth	2.5	25	0	0	1	1	0	0	0	0	0	0		R. BLANTON	1969
IX-EC-15	Ceremonial Ctr	Low Piedmont-Smooth	0.1	0	0	0	0	0	0	0	0	0	0	0		R. BLANTON	1969
IX-EC-16	Small Hamlet	Lakeshore Plain	0.1	10	0	0	0	0	0	1	1	1	0	1		R. BLANTON	1969
IX-EC-17	Sm Disp Village	Lakeshore Plain	15.0	150	1	1	1	1	0	0	1	1	0	1		R. BLANTON	1969
IX-EC-18	Lg Disp Village	Lakeshore Plain	22.0	550	0	0	0	0	0	1	1	1	0	1		R. BLANTON	1969
IX-EC-19	Sm Disp Village	Lakeshore Plain	33.0	330	0	0	1	0	0	0	0	0	0	1		R. BLANTON	1969
IX-EC-20	Hamlet	Low Piedmont-Smooth	5.0	50	0	0	0	0	0	1	1	1	0	1		R. BLANTON	1969
IX-EC-21	Small Hamlet	Lakeshore Plain	1.0	10	0	0	0	0	0	0	0	0	0	1		R. BLANTON	1969
IX-EC-22	Small Hamlet	Low Piedmont-Rugged	0.1	10	0	0	0	0	0	0	1	1	0	0		R. BLANTON	1969
IX-EC-23	Hamlet	Lakeshore Plain	3.0	30	1	1	1	0	0	1	1	1	0	0		R. BLANTON	1969
IX-EC-24	Small Hamlet	Low Piedmont-Rugged	1.0	10	0	0	0	0	0	0	1	1	0	0		R. BLANTON	1969
IX-EC-25	Hamlet	Lakeshore Plain	3.5	35	0	0	0	0	0	0	0	0	0	1		R. BLANTON	1969
IX-EC-26	Hamlet	Lakeshore Plain	10.0	100	0	0	1	0	0	1	1	1	0	0		R. BLANTON	1969
IX-EC-27	Hamlet	Low Piedmont-Rugged	3.0	30	0	0	0	0	0	1	1	1	0	1		R. BLANTON	1969
IX-EC-28	Small Hamlet	Low Piedmont-Rugged	2.0	20	0	0	0	0	0	0	0	0	0	0		R. BLANTON	1969
IX-EC-29	Hamlet	Low Piedmont-Rugged	4.5	45	0	0	0	0	0	0	0	0	0	0		R. BLANTON	1969
IX-EC-30	Hamlet	Lakeshore Plain	8.0	80	1	1	1	1	0	1	1	1	0	0		R. BLANTON	1969
IX-EC-31	Small Hamlet	Lakeshore Plain	0.1	10	0	0	0	0	0	1	1	1	0	1		R. BLANTON	1969
IX-EC-32	Hamlet	Lakeshore Plain	2.5	25	0	1	1	0	0	0	0	0	0	0		R. BLANTON	1969
IX-EC-33	Hamlet	Lakeshore Plain	10.0	100	0	0	0	0	0	0	1	0	0	0		R. BLANTON	1969
IX-EC-34	Sm Disp Village	Lakeshore Plain	12.0	120	0	0	0	1	0	1	1	1	0	1		R. BLANTON	1969
IX-EC-35	Small Hamlet	Low Piedmont-Smooth	1.0	10	0	0	0	1	0	0	0	0	0	0		R. BLANTON	1969
IX-EC-36	Sm Disp Village	Lakeshore Plain	33.0	330	0	0	0	0	0	1	1	1	0	0		R. BLANTON	1969
IX-EC-37	Local Center	Low Piedmont-Smooth	76.0	760	0	0	0	0	0	1	1	1	0	1		R. BLANTON	1969

IXTAPALAPA REGION - ENVIRONMENTAL DATA
Late Classic Sites

Site Number	Environmental Zone	UTM Coordinates East	North	Elev (in m)	Rainfall (in mm)	Modern Soil Depth	Modern Erosion	Modern Land use
IX-LC-1	Low Piedmont-Smooth	513.90	2141.20	2350	670	Shallow-Med	Slight-Moderate	Agricultural
IX-LC-2	Low Piedmont-Smooth	510.25	2136.18	2300	660	Deep	None	Agricultural
IX-LC-3	Lakeshore Plain	503.18	2139.93	2240	620	Deep	None	Agricultural
IX-LC-4	Lakeshore Plain	500.88	2133.60	2240	690	Deep	None	Agricultural
IX-LC-5	Low Piedmont-Rugged	498.30	2138.32	2280	620	Deep	None	Agricultural
IX-LC-6	Lakeshore Plain	497.78	2138.65	2250	620	Deep	None	Agricultural
IX-LC-7	Lakeshore Plain	494.68	2134.28	2250	670	Deep	None	Agricultural
IX-LC-8	Low Piedmont-Smooth	490.07	2139.57	2295	630	Medium	Moderate	Agricultural

71

IXTAPALAPA REGION - PREHISPANIC SETTLEMENT DATA
Late Classic Sites

SITE NUMBER	CLASSIFICATION	ENVIRONMENTAL ZONE	AREA (in ha)	POP.	OTHER OCCUPATIONS										TEMPORARY SITE NO.	SURVEY RECORDS	
					EF	MF	LF	TF	EC	LC	ET	LT	EA	LA		SUPERVISOR	YEAR
IX-LC-1	Local Center	Low Piedmont-Smooth	36.0	900	0	0	0	0	1	0	1	1	1	1		R. BLANTON	1969
IX-LC-2	Sm Disp Village	Low Piedmont-Smooth	17.0	170	0	0	0	0	1	0	0	0	0	0		R. BLANTON	1969
IX-LC-3	Lg Disp Village	Lakeshore Plain	22.0	550	0	0	0	0	1	0	1	1	0	1		R. BLANTON	1969
IX-LC-4	Hamlet	Lakeshore Plain	3.0	30	1	1	1	0	1	0	1	1	0	1		R. BLANTON	1969
IX-LC-5	Hamlet	Low Piedmont-Rugged	3.0	30	0	1	0	0	1	0	1	1	0	1		R. BLANTON	1969
IX-LC-6	Hamlet	Lakeshore Plain	8.0	80	1	1	1	1	1	1	1	1	0	0		R. BLANTON	1969
IX-LC-7	Sm Disp Village	Lakeshore Plain	12.0	120	0	0	0	0	1	0	1	1	0	1		R. BLANTON	1969
IX-LC-8	Local Center	Low Piedmont-Smooth	76.0	760	0	0	0	0	1	0	1	1	0	1		R. BLANTON	1969

IXTAPALAPA REGION - ENVIRONMENTAL DATA
Early Toltec Sites

Site Number	Environmental Zone	UTM Coordinates East	North	Elev (in m)	Rainfall (in mm)	Modern Soil Depth	Modern Erosion	Modern Land use
IX-ET-1	Low Piedmont-Smooth	514.00	2141.43	2350	670	Medium	Moderate	Grazing & Agri
IX-ET-2	Low Piedmont-Smooth	509.72	2142.97	2420	630	Deep	None	Agricultural
IX-ET-3	Low Piedmont-Smooth	509.05	2142.53	2410	630	Medium	Slight	Agricultural
IX-ET-4	Low Piedmont-Smooth	504.97	2139.97	2250	610	Medium	Moderate	Grazing & Agri
IX-ET-5	Lakeshore Plain	503.03	2139.75	2240	610	Deep	None	Agricultural
IX-ET-6	Low Piedmont-Rugged	500.55	2133.78	2250	690	Medium	None	Agricultural
IX-ET-7	Lakeshore Plain	501.75	2140.03	2250	610	Deep	Slight	Settlement
IX-ET-8	Lakeshore Plain	496.80	2138.43	2240	630	Deep	Very Slight	Agricultural
IX-ET-9	Lakeshore Plain	497.63	2138.57	2250	630	Deep	Very Slight	Agricultural
IX-ET-10	Lakeshore Plain	497.80	2140.75	2240	600	Deep	Very Slight	Settlement
IX-ET-11	Low Piedmont-Rugged	497.78	2134.28	2250	670	Medium	None	Agricultural
IX-ET-12	Lakeshore Plain	494.65	2134.28	2250	670	Deep	None	Agricultural
IX-ET-13	Low Piedmont-Smooth	489.95	2139.38	2295	630	Deep	Slight	Agricultural
IX-ET-14	Lakeshore Plain	494.25	2139.32	2240	630	Deep	None	Settlement
IX-ET-15	Lakeshore Plain	500.88	2133.63	2240	690	Deep	None	Agricultural
IX-ET-16	Low Piedmont-Smooth	505.38	2140.53	2250	610	Fully Eroded	Slight	Agricultural
IX-ET-17	Lakeshore Plain	506.05	2136.45	2240	640	Deep	None	Agricultural
IX-ET-18	Lakeshore Plain	500.28	2140.05	2250	610	Deep	Slight	Agricultural
IX-ET-19	Low Piedmont-Rugged	498.30	2138.40	2270	630	Deep	None	Agricultural
IX-ET-20	Low Piedmont-Rugged	498.97	2139.72	2260	620	Deep	None	Agricultural
IX-ET-21	Lakeshore Plain	499.95	2140.45	2250	610	Deep	None	Settlement

IXTAPALAPA REGION - PREHISPANIC SETTLEMENT DATA
Early Toltec Sites

SITE NUMBER	CLASSIFICATION	ENVIRONMENTAL ZONE	AREA (in ha)	POP.	OTHER OCCUPATIONS										TEMPORARY SITE NO.	SURVEY RECORDS	
					EF	MF	LF	TF	EC	LC	ET	LT	EA	LA		SUPERVISOR	YEAR
IX-ET-1	Hamlet	Low Piedmont-Smooth	3.0	75	0	0	0	0	1	1	0	1	1	1		R. BLANTON	1969
IX-ET-2	Small Hamlet	Low Piedmont-Smooth	0.1	10	0	0	0	0	0	0	0	0	0	0		R. BLANTON	1969
IX-ET-3	Small Hamlet	Low Piedmont-Smooth	0.1	10	0	0	0	0	1	0	0	0	0	0		R. BLANTON	1969
IX-ET-4	Hamlet	Low Piedmont-Smooth	3.5	88	0	0	0	0	0	1	0	1	0	1		R. BLANTON	1969
IX-ET-5	Lg Disp Village	Lakeshore Plain	28.0	700	0	0	0	0	1	1	0	1	1	1		R. BLANTON	1969
IX-ET-6	Small Hamlet	Low Piedmont-Rugged	2.0	20	0	0	0	0	1	0	0	1	0	0		R. BLANTON	1969
IX-ET-7	Sm Disp Village	Lakeshore Plain	5.0	125	0	0	0	0	0	0	0	1	1	1		R. BLANTON	1969
IX-ET-8	Sm Disp Village	Lakeshore Plain	5.0	125	0	0	0	0	1	0	0	0	0	0		R. BLANTON	1969
IX-ET-9	Hamlet	Lakeshore Plain	4.0	40	1	1	1	1	1	1	0	1	0	0		R. BLANTON	1969
IX-ET-10	Small Hamlet	Lakeshore Plain	0.1	10	0	0	0	0	0	0	0	1	0	1		R. BLANTON	1969
IX-ET-11	Sm Disp Village	Low Piedmont-Rugged	5.0	125	0	0	1	0	1	0	0	0	0	0		R. BLANTON	1969
IX-ET-12	Hamlet	Lakeshore Plain	5.0	50	0	0	0	0	1	1	0	1	0	1		R. BLANTON	1969
IX-ET-13	Regional Center	Low Piedmont-Smooth	169.0	4225	0	0	0	0	1	1	0	1	0	1		R. BLANTON	1969
IX-ET-14	Lg Nucl Village	Lakeshore Plain	22.0	550	1	1	1	1	1	1	0	1	0	1		R. BLANTON	1969
IX-ET-15	Small Hamlet	Lakeshore Plain	2.0	20	0	0	0	0	1	1	0	1	0	1		R. BLANTON	1969
IX-ET-16	Small Hamlet	Low Piedmont-Smooth	2.0	20	0	0	0	0	0	0	0	1	0	1		R. BLANTON	1969
IX-ET-17	Small Hamlet	Lakeshore Plain	0.1	10	0	0	0	0	0	0	0	1	0	1		R. BLANTON	1969
IX-ET-18	Hamlet	Lakeshore Plain	3.0	30	0	0	0	0	1	0	1	0	0	1		R. BLANTON	1969
IX-ET-19	Hamlet	Low Piedmont-Rugged	3.0	30	0	0	0	0	1	1	0	1	0	0		R. BLANTON	1969
IX-ET-20	Small Hamlet	Low Piedmont-Rugged	0.9	10	0	0	0	0	0	0	0	1	0	1		R. BLANTON	1969
IX-ET-21	Small Hamlet	Lakeshore Plain	0.1	10	0	0	0	0	0	0	0	0	0	1		R. BLANTON	1969

IXTAPALAPA REGION – ENVIRONMENTAL DATA
Late Toltec Sites

Site Number	Environmental Zone	UTM Coordinates East	North	Elev (in m)	Rainfall (in mm)	Modern Soil Depth	Modern Erosion	Modern Land use
IX-LT-1	Upr Piedmont-Smooth	518.50	2141.05	2500	710	Fully Eroded	Deep	None
IX-LT-2	Low Piedmont-Smooth	517.75	2140.07	2400	700	Fully Eroded	Deep	Agricultural
IX-LT-3	Low Piedmont-Smooth	516.50	2140.03	2360	690	Deep	None	Agricultural
IX-LT-4	Low Piedmont-Smooth	517.13	2139.28	2350	690	Shallow	Deep	None
IX-LT-5	Low Piedmont-Smooth	518.07	2138.95	2400	700	Fully Eroded	Deep	None
IX-LT-6	Lakeshore Plain	515.28	2137.25	2270	680	Deep	None	Agricultural
IX-LT-7	Low Piedmont-Smooth	516.82	2138.63	2350	690	Deep	Slight	Agricultural
IX-LT-8	Low Piedmont-Smooth	513.00	2139.53	2300	660	Deep	Slight	Agricultural
IX-LT-9	Low Piedmont-Smooth	513.13	2140.20	2300	660	Deep	None	Agricultural
IX-LT-10	Low Piedmont-Smooth	514.00	2141.43	2300	670	Medium	Moderate	Agricultural
IX-LT-11	Low Piedmont-Smooth	513.15	2142.07	2420	660	Medium	Slight	Agricultural
IX-LT-12	Lakeshore Plain	513.38	2138.00	2260	670	Very Shallow	None	Agricultural
IX-LT-13	Low Piedmont-Smooth	511.95	2138.50	2400	660	Deep	Slight	Agricultural
IX-LT-14	Lakeshore Plain	511.95	2136.70	2260	660	Deep	None	Agricultural
IX-LT-15	Lakeshore Plain	510.25	2135.50	2250	650	Deep	None	Agricultural
IX-LT-16	Lakeshore Plain	508.93	2135.35	2250	650	Deep	None	Agricultural
IX-LT-17	Lakeshore Plain	508.60	2135.18	2250	650	Deep	None	Agricultural
IX-LT-18	Lakeshore Plain	506.93	2136.10	2250	640	Deep	None	Agricultural
IX-LT-19	Lakeshore Plain	505.95	2136.57	2240	640	Deep	None	Agricultural
IX-LT-20	Lakeshore Plain	504.70	2137.50	2250	640	Deep	None	Agricultural
IX-LT-21	Lakeshore Plain	505.13	2140.43	2250	610	Deep	None	Agricultural
IX-LT-22	Lakeshore Plain	503.03	2139.75	2240	620	Deep	None	Settlement
IX-LT-23	Lakeshore Plain	502.38	2139.30	2260	620	Deep	None	Settlement
IX-LT-24	Lakeshore Plain	501.45	2140.05	2250	620	Deep	Slight	Settlement
IX-LT-25	Lakeshore Plain	501.10	2141.25	2240	600	Deep	Slight	None
IX-LT-26	Low Piedmont-Rugged	501.50	2139.13	2280	620	Deep	Slight	Agricultural
IX-LT-27	Low Piedmont-Rugged	501.45	2133.70	2250	680	Medium	None	Agricultural
IX-LT-28	Low Piedmont-Rugged	500.40	2133.80	2250	680	Medium	None	Agricultural
IX-LT-29	Low Piedmont-Rugged	499.18	2133.68	2250	680	Medium	Slight	Agricultural
IX-LT-30	Low Piedmont-Rugged	503.53	2136.82	2270	650	Medium	None	Agricultural
IX-LT-31	Low Piedmont-Rugged	497.68	2137.63	2280	640	Deep	None	Agricultural
IX-LT-32	Low Piedmont-Rugged	498.30	2138.40	2280	630	Deep	None	Agricultural
IX-LT-33	Lakeshore Plain	497.63	2138.57	2250	630	Deep	None	Agricultural
IX-LT-34	Low Piedmont-Rugged	499.10	2139.32	2260	620	Deep	None	Agricultural
IX-LT-35	Lakeshore Plain	498.07	2140.18	2250	610	Deep	None	Agricultural
IX-LT-36	Lakeshore Plain	497.80	2140.75	2240	600	Deep	Slight	Settlement
IX-LT-37	Lakeshore Plain	497.82	2139.97	2250	610	Medium	Moderate	Settlement
IX-LT-38	Low Piedmont-Rugged	498.30	2133.90	2250	680	Medium	None	Grazing
IX-LT-39	Low Piedmont-Rugged	497.13	2134.57	2250	670	Deep	None	Settlement
IX-LT-40	Lakeshore Plain	494.95	2135.07	2250	670	Deep	None	None
IX-LT-41	Lakeshore Plain	494.78	2134.80	2250	670	Deep	None	None
IX-LT-42	Lakeshore Plain	495.90	2137.30	2250	640	Deep	None	None

IXTAPALAPA REGION - PREHISPANIC SETTLEMENT DATA
Late Toltec Sites

SITE NUMBER	CLASSIFICATION	ENVIRONMENTAL ZONE	AREA (in ha)	POP.	EF	MF	LF	TF	EC	LC	ET	LT	EA	LA	TEMPORARY SITE NO.	SUPERVISOR	YEAR
IX-LT-1	Small Hamlet	Upr Piedmont-Smooth	1.0	20	0	0	1	0	0	0	0	0	0	0		R. BLANTON	1969
IX-LT-2	Hamlet	Low Piedmont-Smooth	2.5	25	0	0	0	0	0	0	0	0	1	1		R. BLANTON	1969
IX-LT-3	Small Hamlet	Low Piedmont-Smooth	0.9	10	0	0	0	0	0	0	0	0	0	1		R. BLANTON	1969
IX-LT-4	Hamlet	Low Piedmont-Smooth	6.5	65	0	0	0	0	1	0	0	0	0	0		R. BLANTON	1969
IX-LT-5	Small Hamlet	Low Piedmont-Smooth	0.1	10	0	0	0	0	0	0	0	0	0	0		R. BLANTON	1969
IX-LT-6	Hamlet	Lakeshore Plain	14.0	80	0	0	0	0	1	0	0	0	0	0		R. BLANTON	1969
IX-LT-7	Hamlet	Low Piedmont-Smooth	14.0	100	0	0	0	1	0	0	0	0	0	0		R. BLANTON	1969
IX-LT-8	Hamlet	Low Piedmont-Smooth	11.0	150	0	0	0	0	0	0	0	0	0	0		R. BLANTON	1969
IX-LT-9	Sm Disp Village	Low Piedmont-Smooth	29.0	150	0	0	0	0	0	0	0	0	0	1		R. BLANTON	1969
IX-LT-10	Hamlet	Low Piedmont-Smooth	2.5	30	0	0	0	0	1	1	1	0	1	0		R. BLANTON	1969
IX-LT-11	Small Hamlet	Low Piedmont-Smooth	2.0	20	0	0	0	0	1	0	0	0	0	0		R. BLANTON	1969
IX-LT-12	Hamlet	Lakeshore Plain	3.5	30	0	0	0	0	0	0	0	0	0	0		R. BLANTON	1969
IX-LT-13	Small Hamlet	Low Piedmont-Smooth	0.1	10	0	0	0	0	0	0	0	0	0	0		R. BLANTON	1969
IX-LT-14	Hamlet	Lakeshore Plain	2.5	25	0	0	0	0	1	0	0	0	0	0		R. BLANTON	1969
IX-LT-15	Hamlet	Lakeshore Plain	4.5	40	0	0	0	0	0	0	0	0	0	0		R. BLANTON	1969
IX-LT-16	Small Hamlet	Lakeshore Plain	0.9	10	0	0	0	0	0	0	0	0	0	0		R. BLANTON	1969
IX-LT-17	Hamlet	Lakeshore Plain	4.0	40	0	0	0	1	1	1	0	0	0	0		R. BLANTON	1969
IX-LT-18	Small Hamlet	Lakeshore Plain	0.1	10	0	0	0	0	0	0	0	0	0	0		R. BLANTON	1969
IX-LT-19	Hamlet	Lakeshore Plain	3.0	30	0	0	0	0	1	0	1	0	0	1		R. BLANTON	1969
IX-LT-20	Sm Disp Village	Lakeshore Plain	18.0	180	0	0	0	0	1	0	0	0	0	0		R. BLANTON	1969
IX-LT-21	Hamlet	Lakeshore Plain	4.0	40	0	0	0	0	0	0	1	0	0	1		R. BLANTON	1969
IX-LT-22	Hamlet	Lakeshore Plain	9.0	90	0	0	0	0	1	1	1	0	0	0		R. BLANTON	1969
IX-LT-23	Small Hamlet	Lakeshore Plain	0.9	10	0	0	0	0	0	0	0	0	0	0		R. BLANTON	1969
IX-LT-24	Small Hamlet	Lakeshore Plain	1.5	20	0	0	0	0	0	0	0	1	1	1		R. BLANTON	1969
IX-LT-25	Small Hamlet	Lakeshore Plain	0.1	10	0	0	0	0	0	0	0	0	0	0		R. BLANTON	1969
IX-LT-26	Small Hamlet	Low Piedmont-Rugged	0.1	10	0	0	0	0	0	0	0	0	0	0		R. BLANTON	1969
IX-LT-27	Small Hamlet	Low Piedmont-Rugged	0.1	10	0	0	0	0	1	0	0	0	0	0		R. BLANTON	1969
IX-LT-28	Small Hamlet	Low Piedmont-Rugged	1.0	15	0	0	0	0	0	0	1	0	0	0		R. BLANTON	1969
IX-LT-29	Small Hamlet	Low Piedmont-Rugged	2.0	20	0	1	0	0	0	0	0	0	0	0		R. BLANTON	1969
IX-LT-30	Small Hamlet	Low Piedmont-Rugged	0.1	10	0	0	0	0	0	0	0	0	0	1		R. BLANTON	1969
IX-LT-31	Hamlet	Low Piedmont-Rugged	5.0	50	0	0	1	0	0	0	1	0	0	0		R. BLANTON	1969
IX-LT-32	Small Hamlet	Low Piedmont-Rugged	0.1	10	0	0	1	0	0	0	1	0	0	1		R. BLANTON	1969
IX-LT-33	Hamlet	Lakeshore Plain	6.0	60	1	0	1	0	0	0	1	0	0	0		R. BLANTON	1969
IX-LT-34	Hamlet	Low Piedmont-Rugged	6.0	60	0	0	0	0	0	0	0	0	0	1		R. BLANTON	1969
IX-LT-35	Small Hamlet	Lakeshore Plain	1.1	15	0	0	0	0	0	0	1	0	0	0		R. BLANTON	1969
IX-LT-36	Small Hamlet	Lakeshore Plain	0.1	10	0	0	0	0	1	0	1	0	0	1		R. BLANTON	1969
IX-LT-37	Small Hamlet	Lakeshore Plain	0.1	10	0	0	0	0	0	0	0	0	0	0		R. BLANTON	1969
IX-LT-38	Hamlet	Low Piedmont-Rugged	4.5	45	0	1	0	0	0	0	0	0	0	0		R. BLANTON	1969
IX-LT-39	Hamlet	Low Piedmont-Rugged	5.0	50	0	0	0	0	0	0	0	0	0	0		R. BLANTON	1969
IX-LT-40	Small Hamlet	Lakeshore Plain	1.5	15	0	0	0	0	0	0	1	0	0	0		R. BLANTON	1969
IX-LT-41	Hamlet	Lakeshore Plain	6.0	60	0	0	0	0	0	1	1	1	0	0		R. BLANTON	1969
IX-LT-42	Hamlet	Lakeshore Plain	4.5	45	0	0	0	0	0	0	0	0	0	0		R. BLANTON	1969

IXTAPALAPA REGION - ENVIRONMENTAL DATA
Late Toltec Sites

Site Number	Environmental Zone	UTM Coordinates East	North	Elev (in m)	Rainfall (in mm)	Modern Soil Depth	Modern Erosion	Modern Land use
IX-LT-43	Lakeshore Plain	492.47	2139.47	2240	620	Deep	None	Settlement
IX-LT-44	Low Piedmont-Smooth	489.95	2139.38	2260	630	Deep	Slight-Moderate	Grazing
IX-LT-45	Lakeshore Plain	500.88	2133.63	2240	680	Deep	None	None
IX-LT-46	Upr Piedmont-Smooth	510.45	2139.63	2700	650	Medium	Moderate	None
IX-LT-47	Lakeshore Plain	494.47	2134.25	2240	670	Deep	None	None
IX-LT-48	Low Piedmont-Rugged	501.35	2134.03	2260	680	Medium	None	None

IXTAPALAPA REGION - PREHISPANIC SETTLEMENT DATA
Late Toltec Sites

SITE NUMBER	CLASSIFICATION	ENVIRONMENTAL ZONE	AREA (in ha)	POP.	OTHER OCCUPATIONS										SURVEY RECORDS		
					EF	MF	LF	TF	EC	LC	ET	LT	EA	LA	TEMPORARY SITE NO.	SUPERVISOR	YEAR
IX-LT-43	Hamlet	Lakeshore Plain	2.5	25	0	0	0	0	1	0	0	0	0	1		R. BLANTON	1969
IX-LT-44	Sm Disp Village	Low Piedmont-Smooth	11.5	120	0	0	0	0	1	1	1	0	0	1		R. BLANTON	1969
IX-LT-45	Small Hamlet	Lakeshore Plain	2.0	20	1	1	1	0	1	1	1	0	0	1		R. BLANTON	1969
IX-LT-46	Ceremonial Ctr	Upr Piedmont-Smooth	0.1	0	0	0	0	0	0	0	0	0	0	1		R. BLANTON	1969
IX-LT-47	Small Hamlet	Lakeshore Plain	2.0	20	0	0	0	0	0	1	0	0	0	1		R. BLANTON	1969
IX-LT-48	Small Hamlet	Low Piedmont-Rugged	0.1	10	0	0	0	0	0	0	0	0	0	0		R. BLANTON	1969

IXTAPALAPA REGION - ENVIRONMENTAL DATA
Aztec Sites

Site Number	Environmental Zone	UTM Coordinates East	UTM Coordinates North	Elev (in m)	Rainfall (in mm)	Modern Soil Depth	Modern Erosion	Modern Land use
IX-A-1	Low Piedmont-Hill	516.90	2140.75	2460	680	Very Shallow	Moderate	Agricultural
IX-A-2	Low Piedmont-Smooth	517.85	2140.13	2400	690	Very Shallow	Deep	Agricultural
IX-A-3	Upr Piedmont-Smooth	519.35	2140.68	2530	730	Shallow-Med	Slight-Moderate	Grazing & Agri
IX-A-4	Low Piedmont-Smooth	518.38	2139.75	2450	700	Medium	Moderate	Agricultural
IX-A-5	Low Piedmont-Smooth	518.45	2138.72	2450	700	Shallow-Med	Moderate	Grazing
IX-A-6	Low Piedmont-Smooth	518.82	2138.55	2450	720	Shallow	Moderate-Deep	None
IX-A-7	Low Piedmont-Smooth	518.00	2138.18	2400	700	Medium	Deep	Grazing
IX-A-8	Upr Piedmont-Smooth	519.57	2137.78	2550	760	Deep	Slight	Agricultural
IX-A-9	Low Piedmont-Smooth	517.88	2137.07	2425	710	Deep	None	Agricultural
IX-A-10	Low Piedmont-Smooth	516.57	2139.95	2360	680	Deep	Slight	Agricultural
IX-A-11	Low Piedmont-Smooth	513.95	2141.15	2350	660	Medium	Deep	Grazing & Agri
IX-A-12	Low Piedmont-Smooth	513.18	2140.32	2300	660	Deep	Slight-Moderate	Agricultural
IX-A-13	Upr Piedmont-Smooth	510.47	2139.65	2718	640	Medium	Moderate	None
IX-A-14	Upr Piedmont-Smooth	510.68	2139.05	2600	650	Deep	Slight	Agricultural
IX-A-15	Upr Piedmont-Smooth	509.78	2139.15	2560	640	Shallow-Med	Slight	None
IX-A-16	Low Piedmont-Smooth	508.70	2142.07	2400	620	Deep	Slight	Agricultural
IX-A-17	Upr Piedmont-Smooth	508.38	2138.88	2700	630	Shallow	Moderate	None
IX-A-18	Upr Piedmont-Smooth	510.15	2138.47	2510	650	Deep	Slight	Grazing & Agri
IX-A-19	Upr Piedmont-Smooth	509.40	2138.75	2560	640	Deep	Slight	Agricultural
IX-A-20	Low Piedmont-Smooth	510.28	2141.07	2440	640	Medium	Moderate	None
IX-A-21	Upr Piedmont-Smooth	508.38	2138.03	2550	640	Medium	Deep	Agricultural
IX-A-22	Low Piedmont-Smooth	508.32	2137.72	2470	640	Fully Eroded	Deep	Agricultural
IX-A-23	Low Piedmont-Smooth	508.38	2137.35	2440	640	Very Shallow	Deep	Agricultural
IX-A-24	Low Piedmont-Smooth	507.25	2136.65	2280	650	Very Shallow	Deep	Agricultural
IX-A-25	Low Piedmont-Hill	509.05	2136.65	2390	650	Fully Eroded	Deep	Agricultural
IX-A-26	Low Piedmont-Smooth	511.78	2137.50	2375	660	Medium	Moderate	Grazing & Agri
IX-A-27	Low Piedmont-Smooth	512.68	2138.63	2360	660	Deep	Slight	Agricultural
IX-A-28	Low Piedmont-Smooth	513.20	2138.35	2310	660	Medium	Slight-Moderate	Grazing
IX-A-29	Lakeshore Plain	511.97	2136.57	2270	670	Deep	None	Agricultural
IX-A-30	Low Piedmont-Smooth	511.30	2137.90	2460	660	Deep	Slight-Moderate	Grazing & Agri
IX-A-31	Low Piedmont-Hill	509.22	2133.35	2400	660	Medium	Very Slight	Agricultural
IX-A-32	Low Piedmont-Smooth	506.80	2136.38	2450	650	Medium	Moderate	Agricultural
IX-A-33	Low Piedmont-Smooth	507.15	2137.10	2300	650	Medium	Deep	Agricultural
IX-A-34	Lakeshore Plain	506.00	2136.45	2240	640	Deep	None	Agricultural
IX-A-35	Low Piedmont-Smooth	505.72	2137.70	2260	630	Medium	Moderate	Agricultural
IX-A-36	Low Piedmont-Rugged	504.40	2137.40	2250	640	Deep	Slight	Agricultural
IX-A-37	Low Piedmont-Rugged	505.18	2140.20	2250	610	Medium	Slight	Agricultural
IX-A-38	Lakeshore Plain	503.20	2139.72	2250	620	Medium	None	Settlement
IX-A-39	Low Piedmont-Rugged	502.50	2138.63	2300	630	Medium	None	Agricultural
IX-A-40	Low Piedmont-Rugged	502.15	2138.57	2300	630	Medium	None	Agricultural
IX-A-41	Lakeshore Plain	501.60	2140.00	2250	620	Deep	Very Slight	Settlement
IX-A-42	Lakeshore Plain	500.65	2140.22	2240	610	Deep	None	Settlement

IXTAPALAPA REGION – PREHISPANIC SETTLEMENT DATA
Aztec Sites

SITE NUMBER	CLASSIFICATION	ENVIRONMENTAL ZONE	AREA (in ha)	POP.	EF	MF	LF	TF	EC	LC	ET	LT	EA	LA	TEMPORARY SITE NO.	SUPERVISOR	YEAR
IX-A-1	Questionable	Low Piedmont-Hill	0.1	0	0	0	0	0	0	0	0	0	0	1		R. BLANTON	1969
IX-A-2	Hamlet	Low Piedmont-Smooth	8.0	80	0	0	0	0	1	0	0	1	0	1		R. BLANTON	1969
IX-A-3	Small Hamlet	Upr Piedmont-Smooth	2.2	20	0	0	0	0	0	0	0	0	1	1		R. BLANTON	1969
IX-A-4	Sm Disp Village	Low Piedmont-Smooth	18.0	180	0	0	0	0	0	0	0	0	0	1		R. BLANTON	1969
IX-A-5	Small Hamlet	Low Piedmont-Smooth	0.2	10	0	0	0	0	0	0	0	0	0	1		R. BLANTON	1969
IX-A-6	Small Hamlet	Low Piedmont-Smooth	0.1	10	0	0	0	0	0	0	0	0	1	1		R. BLANTON	1969
IX-A-7	Small Hamlet	Low Piedmont-Smooth	0.9	20	0	0	0	0	0	0	0	0	0	1		R. BLANTON	1969
IX-A-8	Sm Disp Village	Upr Piedmont-Smooth	13.0	130	0	0	0	0	0	0	0	0	0	1		R. BLANTON	1969
IX-A-9	Sm Disp Village	Low Piedmont-Smooth	11.0	110	0	0	0	0	0	0	0	0	1	1		R. BLANTON	1969
IX-A-10	Small Hamlet	Low Piedmont-Smooth	0.1	10	0	0	0	0	0	0	0	1	0	1		R. BLANTON	1969
IX-A-11	Hamlet	Low Piedmont-Smooth	10.0	100	0	0	0	0	1	1	1	1	1	1		R. BLANTON	1969
IX-A-12	Hamlet	Low Piedmont-Smooth	5.6	56	0	0	0	0	0	0	0	1	0	1		R. BLANTON	1969
IX-A-13	Ceremonial Ctr	Upr Piedmont-Smooth	0.1	0	0	0	0	0	0	0	0	1	0	1		R. BLANTON	1969
IX-A-14	Ceremonial Ctr	Upr Piedmont-Smooth	0.1	0	0	0	0	0	0	0	0	0	0	1		R. BLANTON	1969
IX-A-15	Ceremonial Ctr	Upr Piedmont-Smooth	0.1	0	0	0	0	0	0	0	0	0	0	1		R. BLANTON	1969
IX-A-16	Small Hamlet	Low Piedmont-Smooth	0.1	10	0	0	0	0	0	0	0	0	0	1		R. BLANTON	1969
IX-A-17	Ceremonial Ctr	Low Piedmont-Smooth	0.1	0	0	0	0	0	0	0	0	0	0	1		R. BLANTON	1969
IX-A-18	Small Hamlet	Upr Piedmont-Smooth	0.1	10	0	0	0	0	0	0	0	0	1	1		R. BLANTON	1969
IX-A-19	Small Hamlet	Upr Piedmont-Smooth	0.1	10	0	0	0	0	0	0	0	0	0	1		R. BLANTON	1969
IX-A-20	Ceremonial Ctr	Low Piedmont-Smooth	0.1	0	0	0	0	0	0	0	0	0	1	1		R. BLANTON	1969
IX-A-21	Small Hamlet	Upr Piedmont-Smooth	0.9	20	0	0	0	0	0	0	0	0	1	1		R. BLANTON	1969
IX-A-22	Small Hamlet	Low Piedmont-Smooth	0.1	10	0	0	0	0	0	0	0	0	0	1		R. BLANTON	1969
IX-A-23	Small Hamlet	Low Piedmont-Smooth	0.1	10	0	0	0	0	0	0	0	0	0	1		R. BLANTON	1969
IX-A-24	Small Hamlet	Low Piedmont-Smooth	0.1	10	0	0	0	0	0	0	0	0	0	1		R. BLANTON	1969
IX-A-25	Small Hamlet	Low Piedmont-Smooth	0.1	10	0	0	0	0	0	0	0	0	0	1		R. BLANTON	1969
IX-A-26	Local Center	Low Piedmont-Hill	90.0	1630	0	0	0	0	0	0	0	0	1	1		R. BLANTON	1969
IX-A-27	Hamlet	Low Piedmont-Smooth	3.0	30	0	0	0	0	0	0	0	0	1	1		R. BLANTON	1969
IX-A-28	Small Hamlet	Low Piedmont-Smooth	0.1	10	0	0	0	0	0	0	0	0	0	1		R. BLANTON	1969
IX-A-29	Small Hamlet	Lakeshore Plain	2.5	20	0	0	0	0	0	1	0	1	0	1		R. BLANTON	1969
IX-A-30	Ceremonial Ctr	Low Piedmont-Smooth	0.1	0	0	0	0	0	0	0	0	1	1	0		R. BLANTON	1969
IX-A-31	Small Hamlet	Low Piedmont-Hill	0.1	10	0	0	0	0	0	0	0	0	0	1		R. BLANTON	1969
IX-A-32	Small Hamlet	Low Piedmont-Smooth	1.0	20	0	0	0	0	0	0	0	0	1	1		R. BLANTON	1969
IX-A-33	Small Hamlet	Low Piedmont-Smooth	0.1	10	0	0	0	0	0	0	0	0	1	1		R. BLANTON	1969
IX-A-34	Hamlet	Lakeshore Plain	4.0	40	0	0	0	0	1	0	1	1	0	1		R. BLANTON	1969
IX-A-35	Ceremonial Ctr	Low Piedmont-Smooth	0.1	0	0	0	0	0	0	0	0	0	1	1		R. BLANTON	1969
IX-A-36	Hamlet	Low Piedmont-Rugged	10.0	100	0	0	0	0	0	0	0	1	0	1		R. BLANTON	1969
IX-A-37	Sm Disp Village	Low Piedmont-Rugged	24.0	480	0	0	0	0	1	1	2	1	0	1		R. BLANTON	1969
IX-A-38	Small Hamlet	Lakeshore Plain	2.0	20	0	0	0	0	1	1	1	1	0	0		R. BLANTON	1969
IX-A-39	Small Hamlet	Low Piedmont-Rugged	0.1	10	0	0	0	0	0	0	0	0	0	0		R. BLANTON	1969
IX-A-40	Small Hamlet	Low Piedmont-Rugged	0.1	10	0	0	0	0	0	0	0	0	1	1		R. BLANTON	1969
IX-A-41	Sm Disp Village	Lakeshore Plain	18.0	450	0	0	0	0	0	0	0	1	1	1		R. BLANTON	1969
IX-A-42	Sm Disp Village	Lakeshore Plain	4.6	115	0	0	0	0	0	0	0	0	0	1		R. BLANTON	1969

Early Aztec and Late Aztec occupations are tabulated on a presence-absence basis.

IXTAPALAPA REGION - ENVIRONMENTAL DATA
Aztec Sites

Site Number	Environmental Zone	UTM Coordinates East	North	Elev (in m)	Rainfall (in mm)	Modern Soil Depth	Modern Erosion	Modern Land use
IX-A-43	Lakeshore Plain	500.22	2140.22	2240	610	Deep	None	Settlement
IX-A-44	Low Piedmont-Rugged	501.18	2139.28	2280	620	Deep	None	Agricultural
IX-A-45	Low Piedmont-Rugged	500.15	2138.00	2380	630	Medium	None	Agricultural
IX-A-46	Low Piedmont-Rugged	501.28	2137.65	2420	640	Medium	None	None
IX-A-47	Low Piedmont-Rugged	502.35	2137.32	2350	640	Medium	Slight	Agricultural
IX-A-48	Low Piedmont-Rugged	501.22	2136.78	2490	650	Very Shallow	Moderate	Agricultural
IX-A-49	Low Piedmont-Rugged	503.60	2136.57	2270	650	Medium	None	Agricultural
IX-A-50	Low Piedmont-Rugged	501.68	2136.30	2400	650	Medium	Moderate	Agricultural
IX-A-51	Low Piedmont-Rugged	501.93	2135.93	2350	660	Medium	None	Agricultural
IX-A-52	Low Piedmont-Rugged	503.03	2135.75	2280	660	Medium	None	Agricultural
IX-A-53	Lakeshore Plain	503.85	2136.05	2250	650	Deep	None	Agricultural
IX-A-54	Low Piedmont-Rugged	503.38	2135.45	2260	660	Medium	None	Agricultural
IX-A-55	Low Piedmont-Rugged	502.38	2135.18	2270	670	Medium	Slight	Agricultural
IX-A-56	Lakeshore Plain	502.28	2133.95	2240	680	Medium	None	Agricultural
IX-A-57	Lakeshore Plain	501.75	2133.57	2240	690	Deep	None	Agricultural
IX-A-58	Low Piedmont-Rugged	498.22	2138.40	2270	630	Deep	None	Agricultural
IX-A-59	Low Piedmont-Rugged	498.90	2139.60	2250	620	Deep	None	Agricultural
IX-A-60	Lakeshore Plain	497.35	2139.35	2240	620	Deep	None	Settlement
IX-A-61	Lakeshore Plain	497.55	2139.65	2240	620	Medium	Deep	Settlement
IX-A-62	Lakeshore Plain	497.70	2140.05	2240	610	Deep	None	Settlement
IX-A-63	Lakeshore Plain	497.85	2140.47	2240	610	Deep	None	Settlement
IX-A-64	Lakeshore Plain	498.32	2140.80	2240	610	Deep	None	Agricultural
IX-A-65	Lakeshore Plain	494.28	2135.75	2240	670	Deep	None	Agricultural
IX-A-66	Lakeshore Plain	492.47	2137.95	2240	640	Deep	None	Agricultural
IX-A-67	Lakeshore Plain	492.78	2139.38	2240	630	Deep	None	Settlement
IX-A-68	Lakebed	491.68	2140.03	2240	620	Deep	None	Settlement
IX-A-69	Lakeshore Plain	489.32	2139.88	2245	630	Deep	None	Settlement
IX-A-70	Lakeshore Plain	487.70	2139.40	2240	630	Deep	None	Settlement
IX-A-71	Lakebed	488.38	2138.72	2240	640	Deep	None	Settlement
IX-A-72	Lakebed	488.25	2137.43	2240	650	Deep	None	Settlement
IX-A-73	Low Piedmont-Rugged	500.97	2139.03	2290	620	Deep	None	Agricultural
IX-A-74	Low Piedmont-Hill	490.57	2138.55	2450	630	Deep	Moderate-Deep	None
IX-A-75	Lakeshore Plain	488.50	2138.50	2245	640	Deep	None	Settlement

IXTAPALAPA REGION - PREHISPANIC SETTLEMENT DATA
Aztec Sites

SITE NUMBER	CLASSIFICATION	ENVIRONMENTAL ZONE	AREA (in ha)	POP.	EF	MF	LF	TF	EC	LC	ET	LT	EA	LA	TEMPORARY SITE NO.	SUPERVISOR	YEAR
IX-A-43	Small Hamlet	Lakeshore Plain	0.1	10	0	0	0	0	0	1	0	1	0	1		R. BLANTON	1969
IX-A-44	Hamlet	Low Piedmont-Rugged	3.6	50	0	0	0	0	0	0	0	0	1	1		R. BLANTON	1969
IX-A-45	Small Hamlet	Low Piedmont-Rugged	0.1	10	0	0	0	0	0	0	0	0	0	1		R. BLANTON	1969
IX-A-46	Small Hamlet	Low Piedmont-Rugged	0.1	10	0	0	0	0	0	0	0	0	0	1		R. BLANTON	1969
IX-A-47	Small Hamlet	Low Piedmont-Rugged	0.1	10	0	0	0	0	0	0	0	0	0	1		R. BLANTON	1969
IX-A-48	Small Hamlet	Low Piedmont-Rugged	0.1	10	0	0	0	0	0	0	0	0	0	1		R. BLANTON	1969
IX-A-49	Small Hamlet	Low Piedmont-Rugged	0.1	10	0	0	0	0	0	0	0	1	0	1		R. BLANTON	1969
IX-A-50	Small Hamlet	Low Piedmont-Rugged	2.0	20	0	0	0	0	0	0	0	0	0	1		R. BLANTON	1969
IX-A-51	Small Hamlet	Low Piedmont-Rugged	0.1	10	0	0	0	0	0	0	0	0	1	1		R. BLANTON	1969
IX-A-52	Small Hamlet	Low Piedmont-Rugged	0.1	10	0	0	0	0	0	0	0	0	0	1		R. BLANTON	1969
IX-A-53	Lg Disp Village	Lakeshore Plain	29.0	725	0	0	1	0	1	0	0	0	0	1		R. BLANTON	1969
IX-A-54	Small Hamlet	Low Piedmont-Rugged	0.1	10	0	0	0	0	0	0	0	0	0	1		R. BLANTON	1969
IX-A-55	Small Hamlet	Low Piedmont-Rugged	0.1	10	0	0	0	0	0	0	0	0	0	1		R. BLANTON	1969
IX-A-56	Small Hamlet	Lakeshore Plain	0.9	15	0	1	0	0	0	1	0	0	0	1		R. BLANTON	1969
IX-A-57	Hamlet	Lakeshore Plain	3.0	30	1	1	1	0	1	1	1	1	0	1		R. BLANTON	1969
IX-A-58	Small Hamlet	Low Piedmont-Rugged	0.1	10	0	0	0	0	1	0	1	0	0	1		R. BLANTON	1969
IX-A-59	Small Hamlet	Low Piedmont-Rugged	0.9	20	0	0	0	0	0	0	1	1	0	1		R. BLANTON	1969
IX-A-60	Sm Disp Village	Lakeshore Plain	4.4	110	0	0	0	0	0	0	0	0	0	1		R. BLANTON	1969
IX-A-61	Hamlet	Lakeshore Plain	1.0	25	0	0	0	0	0	0	0	1	0	1		R. BLANTON	1969
IX-A-62	Hamlet	Lakeshore Plain	1.2	25	0	0	0	0	0	0	1	1	0	1		R. BLANTON	1969
IX-A-63	Small Hamlet	Lakeshore Plain	0.1	15	0	0	0	0	0	0	0	0	0	1		R. BLANTON	1969
IX-A-64	Sm Disp Village	Lakeshore Plain	6.8	150	0	0	0	0	0	0	0	0	0	1		R. BLANTON	1969
IX-A-65	Hamlet	Lakeshore Plain	2.0	45	0	0	0	0	1	1	0	1	0	1		R. BLANTON	1969
IX-A-66	Small Hamlet	Lakeshore Plain	0.1	10	0	0	0	0	0	0	0	0	0	1		R. BLANTON	1969
IX-A-67	Lg Disp Village	Lakeshore Plain	38.0	963	0	0	0	0	1	0	1	1	0	1		R. BLANTON	1969
IX-A-68	Hamlet	Lakebed	1.7	30	0	0	0	0	0	0	0	0	0	1		R. BLANTON	1969
IX-A-69	Local Center	Lakeshore Plain	30.0	2800	0	0	0	0	0	0	1	0	0	1		R. BLANTON	1969
IX-A-70	Local Center	Lakeshore Plain	0.0	1100	0	0	0	0	0	0	0	0	0	1		R. BLANTON	1969
IX-A-71	Small Hamlet	Lakebed	0.1	20	0	0	0	0	0	0	0	0	0	1		R. BLANTON	1969
IX-A-72	Regional Center	Lakebed	65.0	3250	0	0	0	0	0	0	0	0	1	1		R. BLANTON	1969
IX-A-73	Small Hamlet	Low Piedmont-Rugged	0.1	10	0	0	0	0	0	0	0	0	0	1		R. BLANTON	1969
IX-A-74	Ceremonial Ctr	Low Piedmont-Hill	0.1	0	0	0	0	1	0	0	0	0	0	1		R. BLANTON	1969
IX-A-75	Hamlet	Lakeshore Plain	3.0	75	0	0	0	0	0	1	0	0	1	1		R. BLANTON	1969

Early Aztec and Late Aztec occupations are tabulated on a presence-absence basis.

TEXCOCO REGION – ENVIRONMENTAL DATA
Middle Formative Sites

Site Number	Environmental Zone	UTM Coordinates East	UTM Coordinates North	Elev (in m)	Rainfall (in mm)	Modern Soil Depth	Modern Erosion	Modern Land use
TX-MF-1	Lower Piedmont	514.90	2163.10	2290	610	Deep	None	Agricultural
TX-MF-2	Lower Piedmont	517.00	2162.80	2330	650	Shallow	Moderate	Grazing
TX-MF-3	Lower Piedmont	519.40	2162.60	2335	670	Shallow	Moderate-Deep	Grazing & Agri
TX-MF-4	Lower Piedmont	517.80	2160.00	2310	660	Deep	Very Slight	Settlement
TX-MF-5	Lower Piedmont	518.90	2158.00	2335	680	Deep	Moderate	Grazing
TX-MF-6	Lower Piedmont	517.50	2157.80	2335	670	Shallow	Moderate	Agricultural
TX-MF-7	Lower Piedmont	518.60	2157.70	2350	680	Shallow	Moderate	Grazing
TX-MF-8	Lower Piedmont	518.10	2157.30	2335	680	Shallow	Deep	Grazing
TX-MF-9	Lower Piedmont	518.70	2155.70	2375	680	Deep	Slight-Moderate	Grazing
TX-MF-10	Lower Piedmont	517.50	2159.90	2405	680	Very Shallow	Deep	Grazing
TX-MF-11	Lower Piedmont	518.50	2160.00	2425	690	Shallow	Moderate	Grazing
TX-MF-12	Lower Piedmont	515.50	2150.60	2390	700	Fully Eroded	Deep	Grazing
TX-MF-13	Lakeshore Plain	506.60	2146.00	2240	600	Deep	Slight	Agricultural
TX-MF-14	Lakeshore Plain	506.30	2142.80	2270	600	Shallow	Slight-Moderate	Grazing & Agri
TX-MF-15	Lower Piedmont	514.40	2142.90	2345	670	Deep	Moderate	Agricultural
TX-MF-16	Lower Piedmont	516.70	2142.80	2430	700	Deep	Slight-Moderate	Agricultural
TX-MF-17	Lower Piedmont	516.40	2143.10	2450	720	Medium	Slight	Agricultural
TX-MF-18	Upper Piedmont	518.30	2141.40	2500	730	Shallow	Moderate-Deep	Grazing & Agri
TX-MF-19	Upper Piedmont	518.80	2143.80	2560	760	Fully Eroded	Deep	Grazing

TEXCOCO REGION - PREHISPANIC SETTLEMENT DATA
Middle Formative Sites

SITE NUMBER	CLASSIFICATION	ENVIRONMENTAL ZONE	AREA (in ha)	POP.	OTHER OCCUPATIONS										SURVEY RECORDS		
					EF	MF	LF	TF	EC	LC	ET	LT	EA	LA	TEMPORARY SITE NO.	SUPERVISOR	YEAR
TX-MF-1	Small Hamlet	Lower Piedmont	0.9	20	0	0	0	0	0	0	1	1	0	1	TX-F-1	M. PARSONS	1967
TX-MF-2	Small Hamlet	Lower Piedmont	0.9	20	0	0	1	1	0	0	0	0	0	0	TX-F-3	M. PARSONS	1967
TX-MF-3	Hamlet	Lower Piedmont	5.0	50	0	0	1	1	0	0	0	0	0	0	TX-F-7	M. PARSONS	1967
TX-MF-4	Small Hamlet	Lower Piedmont	0.9	20	0	0	1	0	0	0	0	0	0	0	TX-F-10	J. PARSONS	1967
TX-MF-5	Hamlet	Lower Piedmont	4.0	80	0	0	0	1	0	1	0	0	0	0	TX-F-11	J. PARSONS	1967
TX-MF-6	Small Hamlet	Lower Piedmont	1.0	20	0	0	0	1	0	1	1	0	0	0	TX-F-4	J. PARSONS	1967
TX-MF-7	Hamlet	Lower Piedmont	4.0	80	0	0	0	1	0	0	0	0	0	0	TX-F-4	J. PARSONS	1967
TX-MF-8	Hamlet	Lower Piedmont	2.0	40	0	0	1	1	0	0	0	0	0	0	TX-F-5	J. PARSONS	1967
TX-MF-9	Small Hamlet	Lower Piedmont	0.9	20	0	0	1	0	0	0	0	0	0	0	TX-F-7	J. PARSONS	1967
TX-MF-10	Small Hamlet	Lower Piedmont	1.0	20	0	0	0	1	0	0	0	0	0	0		J. PARSONS	1967
TX-MF-11	Small Hamlet	Lower Piedmont	1.0	20	0	0	1	0	1	0	0	0	0	0		J. PARSONS	1967
TX-MF-12	Small Hamlet	Lower Piedmont	0.9	20	0	0	1	1	0	0	0	0	0	0		J. PARSONS	1967
TX-MF-13	Lg Nucl Village	Lakeshore Plain	45.0	1200	0	0	1	1	0	0	0	0	0	1	TX-F-5	R. HIRNING	1967
TX-MF-14	Small Hamlet	Lakeshore Plain	0.9	20	0	0	0	0	0	0	0	0	0	0	TX-F-6	R. HIRNING	1967
TX-MF-15	Small Hamlet	Lower Piedmont	0.9	20	0	0	1	1	0	0	0	0	0	0	TX-F-7	R. HIRNING	1967
TX-MF-16	Small Hamlet	Lower Piedmont	1.0	20	0	0	1	1	0	0	0	0	1	1	TX-F-8	R. HIRNING	1967
TX-MF-17	Small Hamlet	Lower Piedmont	1.0	20	0	0	0	1	0	0	0	0	0	0	TX-F-8	R. HIRNING	1967
TX-MF-18	Small Hamlet	Upper Piedmont	1.0	20	0	0	1	1	0	0	0	0	0	0	TX-F-11	R. HIRNING	1967
TX-MF-19	Small Hamlet	Upper Piedmont	0.9	20	0	0	1	1	0	0	0	0	0	0	TX-F-9	R. HIRNING	1967

TEXCOCO REGION - ENVIRONMENTAL DATA
Late Formative Sites

Site Number	Environmental Zone	UTM Coordinates East	North	Elev (in m)	Rainfall (in mm)	Modern Soil Depth	Modern Erosion	Modern Land use
TX-LF-1	Lower Piedmont	513.00	2164.60	2430	600	Shallow	Moderate-Deep	Grazing
TX-LF-2	Lower Piedmont	513.50	2165.00	2350	610	Deep	Slight	Grazing
TX-LF-3	Lower Piedmont	514.60	2165.20	2310	610	Shallow	Moderate-Deep	Grazing & Agri
TX-LF-4	Lower Piedmont	524.40	2165.20	2290	600	Deep	Slight	Agricultural
TX-LF-5	Lower Piedmont	516.40	2163.20	2330	640	Shallow	Moderate	Grazing
TX-LF-6	Lower Piedmont	516.90	2163.00	2310	650	Shallow-Med	Moderate-Deep	Grazing
TX-LF-7	Lower Piedmont	518.40	2162.20	2320	660	Shallow	Moderate-Deep	Grazing & Agri
TX-LF-8	Lower Piedmont	519.40	2162.70	2320	670	Very Shallow	Deep	Grazing & Agri
TX-LF-9	Lower Piedmont	518.20	2159.90	2330	660	Medium-Deep	Very Slight	Agricultural
TX-LF-10	Lower Piedmont	518.20	2157.50	2350	670	Shallow	Moderate-Deep	Grazing & Agri
TX-LF-11	Lower Piedmont	518.30	2157.00	2335	670	Shallow	Moderate-Deep	Grazing
TX-LF-12	Lower Piedmont	519.20	2154.80	2430	700	Medium	Slight-Moderate	Agricultural
TX-LF-13	Lakeshore Plain	506.30	2155.90	2240	600	Deep	None	Grazing
TX-LF-14	Lakeshore Plain	506.50	2154.70	2240	600	Deep	None	Grazing
TX-LF-15	Lakeshore Plain	509.60	2153.60	2240	600	Deep	None	Grazing
TX-LF-16	Lower Piedmont	518.30	2151.60	2480	730	Shallow	Deep	Grazing
TX-LF-17	Lower Piedmont	517.70	2151.00	2400	720	Shallow	Deep	Grazing & Agri
TX-LF-18	Lower Piedmont	517.00	2150.40	2393	710	Shallow	Deep	Grazing & Agri
TX-LF-19	Lower Piedmont	514.90	2146.60	2395	680	Shallow	Deep	Grazing
TX-LF-20	Lower Piedmont	506.40	2144.20	2405	700	Fully Eroded	Deep	None
TX-LF-21	Upper Piedmont	518.70	2143.80	2570	760	Shallow	Slight	Grazing
TX-LF-22	Lower Piedmont	516.90	2142.70	2455	750	Medium	Slight-Moderate	Settlement
TX-LF-23	Upper Piedmont	518.60	2141.20	2505	740	Shallow	Moderate-Deep	Grazing
TX-LF-24	Lower Piedmont	517.60	2141.50	2450	710	Shallow	Moderate	Grazing & Agri
TX-LF-25	Lower Piedmont	514.40	2143.00	2345	670	Medium	Slight	Agricultural
TX-LF-26	Lakeshore Plain	506.60	2141.70	2240	600	Deep	None	Agricultural
TX-LF-27	Lakeshore Plain	506.20	2141.40	2240	600	Deep	None	Grazing & Agri
TX-LF-28	Lakeshore Plain	505.60	2141.30	2250	600	Medium	Slight-Moderate	Agricultural
TX-LF-29	Lakeshore Plain	506.60	2140.70	2240	600	Deep	None	Agricultural

TEXCOCO REGION - PREHISPANIC SETTLEMENT DATA
Late Formative Sites

SITE NUMBER	CLASSIFICATION	ENVIRONMENTAL ZONE	AREA (in ha)	POP.	EF	MF	LF	TF	EC	LC	ET	LT	EA	LA	TEMPORARY SITE NO.	SUPERVISOR	YEAR
TX-LF-1	Ceremonial Ctr	Lower Piedmont	0.3	0	0	0	0	0	1	0	1	0	0	0	TX-T-7	M. PARSONS	1967
TX-LF-2	Small Hamlet	Lower Piedmont	0.9	20	0	0	0	0	0	0	0	0	1	1	TX-F-2	M. PARSONS	1967
TX-LF-3	Small Hamlet	Lower Piedmont	0.9	20	0	0	0	0	0	0	0	0	1	0	TX-F-2	M. PARSONS	1967
TX-LF-4	Small Hamlet	Lower Piedmont	0.9	20	1	0	0	0	0	0	1	1	0	0	TX-F-1	M. PARSONS	1967
TX-LF-5	Small Hamlet	Lower Piedmont	0.9	20	1	0	0	1	0	0	1	0	0	0	TX-F-3	M. PARSONS	1967
TX-LF-6	Small Hamlet	Lower Piedmont	0.9	20	0	0	0	1	1	1	1	1	1	1	TX-F-3	M. PARSONS	1967
TX-LF-7	Hamlet	Lower Piedmont	2.0	40	0	0	0	0	0	0	1	1	0	0	TX-F-7	M. PARSONS	1967
TX-LF-8	Sm Disp Village	Lower Piedmont	20.0	500	1	1	0	0	0	0	0	0	0	1	TX-F-7	M. PARSONS	1967
TX-LF-9	Lg Nucl Village	Lower Piedmont	33.0	1300	1	1	0	0	0	0	0	0	1	0	TX-F-10	J. PARSONS	1967
TX-LF-10	Small Hamlet	Lower Piedmont	1.0	20	0	1	0	1	0	0	0	0	0	0	TX-F-4	J. PARSONS	1967
TX-LF-11	Small Hamlet	Lower Piedmont	1.0	20	1	1	1	1	0	0	0	0	0	0	TX-F-4	J. PARSONS	1967
TX-LF-12	Local Center	Lower Piedmont	86.0	3500	3	3	3	3	0	0	0	0	0	0	TX-F-5	J. PARSONS	1967
TX-LF-13	Small Hamlet	Lakeshore Plain	0.9	20	0	0	0	0	0	0	1	0	0	0	TX-F-2	J. PARSONS	1967
TX-LF-14	Sm Disp Village	Lakeshore Plain	4.5	160	0	0	0	0	0	0	0	0	0	0	TX-F-1	J. PARSONS	1967
TX-LF-15	Hamlet	Lakeshore Plain	2.0	40	0	0	0	1	0	0	0	1	0	0	TX-F-3	J. PARSONS	1967
TX-LF-16	Hamlet	Lower Piedmont	6.0	60	0	0	0	0	1	0	0	0	0	0		J. PARSONS	1967
TX-LF-17	Sm Disp Village	Lower Piedmont	8.0	200	0	0	0	1	0	0	0	0	0	0		J. PARSONS	1967
TX-LF-18	Sm Disp Village	Lower Piedmont	9.0	200	1	0	0	1	0	0	0	0	0	0		J. PARSONS	1967
TX-LF-19	Hamlet	Lower Piedmont	2.0	40	0	0	0	0	0	0	0	0	0	0		J. PARSONS	1967
TX-LF-20	Small Hamlet	Lower Piedmont	0.9	20	0	0	0	1	0	0	0	0	0	0		R. HIRNING	1967
TX-LF-21	Small Hamlet	Upper Piedmont	0.9	20	1	0	0	1	0	0	0	0	0	0	TX-F-9	R. HIRNING	1967
TX-LF-22	Lg Nucl Village	Lower Piedmont	40.0	1800	0	0	0	0	0	0	0	0	1	1	TX-F-8	R. HIRNING	1967
TX-LF-23	Sm Disp Village	Upper Piedmont	6.0	120	1	0	1	0	0	0	0	0	0	0	TX-F-11	R. HIRNING	1967
TX-LF-24	Hamlet	Lower Piedmont	3.0	60	0	0	0	0	0	0	0	0	0	0	TX-F-10	R. HIRNING	1967
TX-LF-25	Hamlet	Lower Piedmont	3.0	60	1	0	0	1	1	0	0	0	0	1	TX-F-7	R. HIRNING	1967
TX-LF-26	Small Hamlet	Lakeshore Plain	1.0	20	0	0	0	0	0	0	0	0	0	0	TX-F-5	R. HIRNING	1967
TX-LF-27	Small Hamlet	Lakeshore Plain	1.0	20	0	0	0	0	0	0	0	0	1	1	TX-F-5	R. HIRNING	1967
TX-LF-28	Small Hamlet	Lakeshore Plain	0.9	20	0	0	0	1	0	0	0	1	0	0	TX-F-5	R. HIRNING	1967
TX-LF-29	Sm Disp Village	Lakeshore Plain	12.0	250	0	1	0	1	0	0	0	0	0	1	TX-F-5	R. HIRNING	1967

The column groups are: SURVEY RECORDS spanning (TEMPORARY SITE NO., SUPERVISOR, YEAR); OTHER OCCUPATIONS spanning (EF, MF, LF, TF, EC, LC, ET, LT, EA, LA).

86

TEXCOCO REGION - ENVIRONMENTAL DATA
Terminal Formative Sites

Site Number	Environmental Zone	UTM Coordinates East	North	Elev (in m)	Rainfall (in mm)	Modern Soil Depth	Modern Erosion	Modern Land use
TX-TF-1	Lower Piedmont	514.00	2164.10	2320	600	Shallow	Deep	Grazing
TX-TF-2	Lower Piedmont	514.80	2165.20	2490	620	Shallow	Moderate-Deep	Grazing & Agri
TX-TF-3	Upper Piedmont	514.00	2165.90	2620	630	Shallow	Moderate	Grazing & Agri
TX-TF-4	Lower Piedmont	517.10	2165.90	2420	640	Shallow	Moderate	Grazing & Agri
TX-TF-5	Lower Piedmont	519.40	2166.70	2340	650	Shallow	Deep	Grazing & Agri
TX-TF-6	Lower Piedmont	520.10	2166.00	2420	660	Shallow	Moderate	Grazing & Agri
TX-TF-7	Lower Piedmont	521.20	2166.20	2380	670	Very Shallow	Deep	Grazing & Agri
TX-TF-8	Lower Piedmont	521.30	2165.10	2330	670	Shallow-Med	Moderate	Agricultural
TX-TF-9	Lower Piedmont	520.70	2164.60	2330	670	Medium	Slight-Moderate	Grazing & Agri
TX-TF-10	Lower Piedmont	516.60	2162.40	2320	640	Shallow-Med	Moderate-Deep	Grazing & Agri
TX-TF-11	Lower Piedmont	519.00	2162.50	2335	660	Shallow	Deep	Grazing & Agri
TX-TF-12	Lower Piedmont	520.70	2162.80	2390	670	Shallow-Med	Moderate	Agricultural
TX-TF-13	Upper Piedmont	524.20	2161.70	2565	730	Very Shallow	Deep	Grazing & Agri
TX-TF-14	Lower Piedmont	518.90	2159.40	2485	670	Shallow-Med	Slight-Moderate	Grazing & Agri
TX-TF-15	Lower Piedmont	518.20	2167.80	2415	670	Shallow	Moderate-Deep	Grazing & Agri
TX-TF-16	Upper Piedmont	521.20	2158.40	2505	720	Shallow	Moderate-Deep	Grazing & Agri
TX-TF-17	Lower Piedmont	518.60	2156.80	2345	680	Shallow	Moderate	Grazing & Agri
TX-TF-18	Lower Piedmont	516.10	2156.10	2305	650	Shallow	Moderate-Deep	Grazing & Agri
TX-TF-19	Lower Piedmont	516.30	2155.70	2340	660	Shallow	Moderate-Deep	Grazing & Agri
TX-TF-20	Lower Piedmont	519.10	2155.00	2430	700	Medium	Slight	Agricultural
TX-TF-21	Lower Piedmont	518.40	2154.30	2410	700	Shallow	Moderate-Deep	Grazing & Agri
TX-TF-22	Upper Piedmont	519.80	2155.10	2575	700	Shallow	Moderate	Grazing & Agri
TX-TF-23	Lower Piedmont	519.70	2153.70	2480	740	Shallow	Deep	Grazing
TX-TF-24	Lower Piedmont	520.10	2152.90	2480	750	Medium	Deep	Grazing & Agri
TX-TF-25	Lower Piedmont	518.70	2152.20	2485	740	Very Shallow	Deep	Grazing & Agri
TX-TF-26	Lower Piedmont	517.10	2152.80	2400	690	Shallow	Deep	Grazing & Agri
TX-TF-27	Lower Piedmont	513.70	2152.50	2290	650	Medium	Slight-Moderate	Agricultural
TX-TF-28	Lakeshore Plain	509.50	2153.60	2240	600	Deep	None	Grazing
TX-TF-29	Lakeshore Plain	506.50	2155.00	2240	600	Deep	None	Agricultural
TX-TF-30	Lower Piedmont	518.90	2150.80	2495	760	Very Shallow	Deep	Grazing
TX-TF-31	Lower Piedmont	517.40	2150.50	2430	720	Very Shallow	Deep	Grazing
TX-TF-32	Lower Piedmont	516.50	2150.60	2390	700	Shallow	Deep	Grazing
TX-TF-33	Lower Piedmont	518.00	2149.90	2465	750	Very Shallow	Deep	Grazing
TX-TF-34	Lower Piedmont	517.50	2149.30	2415	740	Fully Eroded	Deep	Grazing
TX-TF-35	Lower Piedmont	516.50	2149.70	2400	710	Shallow	Deep	Grazing
TX-TF-36	Lower Piedmont	514.90	2148.20	2425	680	Shallow-Med	Moderate	Grazing & Agri
TX-TF-37	Lower Piedmont	516.10	2145.10	2440	700	Shallow	Slight-Moderate	Grazing & Agri
TX-TF-38	Lower Piedmont	516.10	2144.20	2415	700	Fully Eroded	Deep	None
TX-TF-39	Upper Piedmont	508.70	2143.60	2540	750	Very Shallow	Slight-Moderate	Grazing
TX-TF-40	Lower Piedmont	516.60	2153.50	2435	700	Medium	Slight-Moderate	Agricultural
TX-TF-41	Lower Piedmont	516.70	2142.60	2430	700	Medium	Slight	Agricultural
TX-TF-42	Lower Piedmont	518.20	2141.70	2480	730	Shallow	Moderate	Grazing & Agri

TEXCOCO REGION - PREHISPANIC SETTLEMENT DATA
Terminal Formative Sites

SITE NUMBER	CLASSIFICATION	ENVIRONMENTAL ZONE	AREA (in ha)	POP.	EF	MF	LF	TF	EC	LC	ET	LT	EA	LA	TEMPORARY SITE NO.	SUPERVISOR	YEAR
TX-TF-1	Local Center	Lower Piedmont	74.0	2500	0	0	0	0	0	0	1	0	1	1	TX-F-2	M. PARSONS	1967
TX-TF-2	Sm Elite Dist	Lower Piedmont	8.0	150	0	0	0	0	0	0	0	0	0	0	TX-F-14	M. PARSONS	1967
TX-TF-3	Ceremonial Ctr	Upper Piedmont	1.0	0	0	0	0	0	0	1	1	1	1	0	T-A-35	M. PARSONS	1967
TX-TF-4	Lg Elite Dist	Lower Piedmont	17.0	600	0	0	0	0	0	0	0	0	0	0	TX-TF-4	M. PARSONS	1967
TX-TF-5	Small Hamlet	Lower Piedmont	0.9	20	0	0	0	0	0	0	0	1	1	1	TX-A-22	M. PARSONS	1967
TX-TF-6	Sm Elite Dist	Lower Piedmont	2.0	100	0	0	0	0	0	0	0	0	0	0	TX-F-8	M. PARSONS	1967
TX-TF-7	Sm Nucl Village	Lower Piedmont	6.0	150	0	0	0	0	0	0	0	1	1	1	TX-F-10	M. PARSONS	1967
TX-TF-8	Small Hamlet	Lower Piedmont	0.9	20	0	0	0	0	0	0	0	0	0	0	TX-F-11	M. PARSONS	1967
TX-TF-9	Small Hamlet	Lower Piedmont	0.9	20	0	0	0	0	0	0	0	0	0	0	TX-F-11	M. PARSONS	1967
TX-TF-10	Sm Elite Dist	Lower Piedmont	0.9	20	0	0	0	0	0	0	0	0	0	0	TX-F-3	M. PARSONS	1967
TX-TF-11	Lg Nucl Village	Lower Piedmont	25.0	800	0	0	1	0	0	1	0	0	0	0	TX-F-7	M. PARSONS	1967
TX-TF-12	Small Hamlet	Lower Piedmont	0.9	20	0	0	0	0	0	0	0	1	1	1	TX-F-12	M. PARSONS	1967
TX-TF-13	Sm Nucl Village	Upper Piedmont	10.0	300	0	0	0	0	0	0	0	0	0	0	TX-F-9	M. PARSONS	1967
TX-TF-14	Lg Elite Dist	Lower Piedmont	18.0	500	0	0	0	0	0	0	0	0	0	0	TX-F-9	M. PARSONS	1967
TX-TF-15	Ceremonial Ctr	Lower Piedmont	5.0		0	0	0	0	0	0	0	0	1	1	TX-F-12	M. PARSONS	1967
TX-TF-16	Sm Nucl Village	Upper Piedmont	6.0	150	0	0	0	0	0	0	0	0	0	0	TX-F-8	M. PARSONS	1967
TX-TF-17	Local Center	Lower Piedmont	118.0	3500	0	3	2	0	2	1	0	0	1	1	TX-F-4	J. PARSONS	1967
TX-TF-18	Small Hamlet	Lower Piedmont	0.9	20	0	0	0	0	0	0	0	0	1	1	TX-A-13	J. PARSONS	1967
TX-TF-19	Sm Disp Village	Lower Piedmont	11.0	150	0	0	0	0	1	0	0	0	1	1	TX-F-6	J. PARSONS	1967
TX-TF-20	Sm Disp Village	Lower Piedmont	24.0	350	0	0	1	0	0	0	0	0	1	1	TX-F-5	J. PARSONS	1967
TX-TF-21	Sm Disp Village	Lower Piedmont	40.0	200	0	0	0	0	0	0	0	0	1	1	TX-F-7	J. PARSONS	1967
TX-TF-22	Small Hamlet	Upper Piedmont	4.0	20	0	0	0	0	0	0	1	0	1	1	TX-A-16	J. PARSONS	1967
TX-TF-23	Hamlet	Lower Piedmont	0.9	40	0	0	1	0	0	0	0	0	1	1	TX-F-7	J. PARSONS	1967
TX-TF-24	Small Hamlet	Lower Piedmont	0.9	20	0	0	0	0	0	0	0	0	1	1	TX-A-20	J. PARSONS	1967
TX-TF-25	Lg Disp Village	Lower Piedmont	50.0	750	0	0	1	0	0	0	0	0	1	1	TX-A-19	J. PARSONS	1967
TX-TF-26	Small Hamlet	Lower Piedmont	1.0	20	0	0	0	0	1	0	0	0	1	1	TX-A-10	J. PARSONS	1967
TX-TF-27	Small Hamlet	Lower Piedmont	0.9	20	0	0	0	0	0	0	0	0	1	1	TX-A-10	J. PARSONS	1967
TX-TF-28	Small Hamlet	Lakeshore Plain	1.0	20	0	0	1	0	0	0	1	1	1	0	TX-F-3	J. PARSONS	1967
TX-TF-29	Small Hamlet	Lakeshore Plain	1.0	20	0	0	1	0	0	0	0	0	1	1	TX-F-2	J. PARSONS	1967
TX-TF-30	Local Center	Lower Piedmont	50.0	2000	0	0	0	0	0	0	0	0	0	1		J. PARSONS	1967
TX-TF-31	Sm Disp Village	Lower Piedmont	19.0	400	0	0	0	0	1	0	0	0	0	0		J. PARSONS	1967
TX-TF-32	Sm Disp Village	Lower Piedmont	12.0	200	0	1	1	0	0	0	0	0	0	0		J. PARSONS	1967
TX-TF-33	Sm Nucl Village	Lower Piedmont	15.0	500	0	0	0	0	1	0	0	0	0	1		J. PARSONS	1967
TX-TF-34	Sm Nucl Village	Lower Piedmont	9.0	300	0	0	0	0	0	0	0	0	0	0		J. PARSONS	1967
TX-TF-35	Sm Disp Village	Lower Piedmont	16.0	200	0	0	0	0	0	0	0	0	0	0		J. PARSONS	1967
TX-TF-36	Lg Elite Dist	Lower Piedmont	35.0	1200	0	0	0	0	0	0	0	0	0	0		J. PARSONS	1967
TX-TF-37	Sm Disp Village	Lower Piedmont	10.0	100	0	0	0	0	1	0	0	0	0	1		J. PARSONS	1967
TX-TF-38	Hamlet	Lower Piedmont	4.0	80	0	0	0	0	0	0	0	0	0	0		J. PARSONS	1967
TX-TF-39	Hamlet	Upper Piedmont	10.0	100	0	0	0	0	0	0	0	0	0	0		J. PARSONS	1967
TX-TF-40	Hamlet	Lower Piedmont	4.0	80	0	1	1	0	0	0	0	0	0	0	TX-F-9	R. HIRNING	1967
TX-TF-41	Small Hamlet	Lower Piedmont	1.0	20	0	0	1	0	0	0	0	0	0	0	TX-F-8	R. HIRNING	1967
TX-TF-42	Small Hamlet	Lower Piedmont	1.0	20	0	1	1	0	0	0	0	0	0	0	TX-F-11	R. HIRNING	1967

Note: Columns EF, MF, LF, TF, EC, LC, ET, LT, EA, LA are grouped under "OTHER OCCUPATIONS"; SUPERVISOR and YEAR are grouped under "SURVEY RECORDS".

TEXCOCO REGION - ENVIRONMENTAL DATA
Terminal Formative Sites

Site Number	Environmental Zone	UTM Coordinates East	North	Elev (in m)	Rainfall (in mm)	Modern Soil Depth	Modern Erosion	Modern Land use
TX-TF-43	Lower Piedmont	514.40	2142.80	2350	670	Medium	Slight	Agricultural
TX-TF-44	Lakeshore Plain	514.00	2148.30	2240	600	Deep	None	Agricultural
TX-TF-45	Lakeshore Plain	514.30	2146.40	2240	600	Deep	None	Grazing
TX-TF-46	Lakebed	505.80	2148.60	2240	600	Deep	None	Grazing
TX-TF-47	Lakeshore Plain	502.70	2145.20	2250	600	Medium	Slight	Agricultural
TX-TF-48	Upper Piedmont	504.60	2144.40	2520	600	Shallow-Med	Slight	Grazing & Agri
TX-TF-49	Lakeshore Plain	505.70	2146.40	2250	600	Shallow-Med	Slight	Agricultural
TX-TF-50	Lakeshore Plain	506.60	2146.00	2240	600	Deep	Very Slight	Agricultural
TX-TF-51	Lower Piedmont	506.80	2142.20	2310	610	Shallow-Med	Slight-Moderate	Grazing
TX-TF-52	Lower Piedmont	513.70	2155.80	2310	635	Shallow-Med	Moderate	Agricultural

TEXCOCO REGION - PREHISPANIC SETTLEMENT DATA
Terminal Formative Sites

| SITE NUMBER | CLASSIFICATION | ENVIRONMENTAL ZONE | AREA (in ha) | POP. | OTHER OCCUPATIONS | | | | | | | | | | TEMPORARY SITE NO. | SURVEY RECORDS | |
					EF	MF	LF	TF	EC	LC	ET	LT	EA	LA		SUPERVISOR	YEAR
TX-TF-43	Small Hamlet	Lower Piedmont	1.0	20	0	1	1	0	0	0	0	0	0	1	TX-F-7	R. HIRNING	1967
TX-TF-44	Sm Nucl Village	Lakeshore Plain	11.0	300	0	0	0	0	0	0	0	0	1	1	TX-F-3	R. HIRNING	1967
TX-TF-45	Small Hamlet	Lakeshore Plain	1.0	20	0	0	0	0	0	0	0	0	1	1	TX-A-1	R. HIRNING	1967
TX-TF-46	Lg Nucl Village	Lakebed	19.0	800	0	0	0	0	0	0	0	0	0	0	TX-F-2	R. HIRNING	1967
TX-TF-47	Questionable	Lakeshore Plain	5.0	0	0	0	0	0	0	0	1	0	0	0	TX-T-3	R. HIRNING	1967
TX-TF-48	Ceremonial Ctr	Upper Piedmont	0.1	0	0	0	0	0	0	0	0	1	1	1	TX-A-4	R. HIRNING	1967
TX-TF-49	Small Hamlet	Lakeshore Plain	0.9	20	0	0	1	0	0	0	0	1	0	0	TX-T-2	R. HIRNING	1967
TX-TF-50	Local Center	Lakeshore Plain	52.0	1500	0	1	1	0	0	0	0	0	0	1	TX-F-5	R. HIRNING	1967
TX-TF-51	Lg Elite Dist	Lower Piedmont	40.0	1200	0	0	0	0	1	0	0	0	0	0	TX-F-6	R. HIRNING	1967
TX-TF-52	Small Hamlet	Lower Piedmont	0.9	10	0	0	0	0	1	0	0	0	0	0		J. PARSONS	1967

TEXCOCO REGION - ENVIRONMENTAL DATA
Early Classic Sites

Site Number	Environmental Zone	UTM Coordinates East	North	Elev (in m)	Rainfall (in mm)	Modern Soil Depth	Modern Erosion	Modern Land use
TX-EC-1	Lakeshore Plain	508.90	2163.60	2250	600	Deep	None	Grazing
TX-EC-2	Lower Piedmont	509.00	2164.10	2430	600	Shallow	Moderate-Deep	Grazing
TX-EC-3	Lower Piedmont	514.80	2163.80	2295	600	Deep	Very Slight	Agricultural
TX-EC-4	Lower Piedmont	518.10	2165.40	2320	650	Shallow	Deep	Grazing
TX-EC-5	Lower Piedmont	508.20	2162.40	2330	660	Shallow-Med	Moderate	Grazing & Agri
TX-EC-6	Lower Piedmont	516.90	2162.50	2320	650	Medium	Slight	Agricultural
TX-EC-7	Lower Piedmont	515.10	2161.50	2290	610	Deep	Very Slight	Agricultural
TX-EC-8	Lower Piedmont	521.20	2153.50	2465	720	Shallow-Med	Slight-Moderate	Grazing & Agri
TX-EC-9	Lower Piedmont	518.60	2157.60	2340	680	Shallow	Moderate	Grazing & Agri
TX-EC-10	Lower Piedmont	519.00	2157.00	2370	670	Shallow	Moderate-Deep	Grazing
TX-EC-11	Lower Piedmont	517.80	2156.90	2340	670	Shallow	Moderate-Deep	Grazing
TX-EC-12	Lower Piedmont	517.20	2157.80	2340	660	Shallow	Moderate	Grazing & Agri
TX-EC-13	Lower Piedmont	518.00	2156.90	2315	660	Shallow	Moderate-Deep	Grazing
TX-EC-14	Lower Piedmont	515.80	2156.70	2310	650	Medium	Slight	Agricultural
TX-EC-15	Lower Piedmont	515.90	2155.60	2320	660	Medium	Slight-Moderate	Agricultural
TX-EC-16	Lower Piedmont	516.40	2154.20	2360	670	Shallow-Med	Moderate	Agricultural
TX-EC-17	Lower Piedmont	514.90	2154.60	2310	650	Shallow-Med	Moderate	Agricultural
TX-EC-18	Lower Piedmont	515.10	2153.10	2315	660	Shallow-Med	Moderate	Grazing & Agri
TX-EC-19	Lower Piedmont	514.80	2152.50	2310	660	Shallow-Med	Slight-Moderate	Grazing
TX-EC-20	Lower Piedmont	513.90	2152.40	2290	650	Shallow-Med	Slight-Moderate	Agricultural
TX-EC-21	Lower Piedmont	517.40	2150.60	2435	770	Very Shallow	Deep	Grazing
TX-EC-22	Lower Piedmont	518.10	2150.00	2490	750	Very Shallow	Deep	Grazing
TX-EC-23	Upper Piedmont	518.80	2145.40	2600	770	Very Shallow	Deep	Grazing
TX-EC-24	Lower Piedmont	516.90	2145.10	2490	730	Shallow	Slight	Grazing
TX-EC-25	Lower Piedmont	513.00	2146.10	2260	650	Shallow	Slight-Moderate	Grazing
TX-EC-26	Upper Piedmont	518.50	2142.90	2525	750	Shallow-Med	Moderate-Deep	Grazing & Agri
TX-EC-27	Upper Piedmont	518.90	2142.20	2530	750	Very Shallow	Deep	Grazing
TX-EC-28	Lower Piedmont	514.50	2143.00	2340	670	Shallow	Slight	Agricultural
TX-EC-29	Lower Piedmont	514.30	2144.20	2310	670	Deep	Slight	Agricultural
TX-EC-30	Lower Piedmont	514.00	2143.30	2420	660	Very Shallow	Moderate-Deep	Grazing
TX-EC-31	Lower Piedmont	513.50	2142.90	2300	650	Medium	Slight-Moderate	Agricultural
TX-EC-32	Lower Piedmont	510.10	2144.30	2275	630	Medium	Slight-Moderate	Grazing & Agri
TX-EC-33	Lakeshore Plain	509.90	2147.90	2240	600	Deep	None	Agricultural
TX-EC-34	Lakeshore Plain	505.90	2146.80	2240	600	Medium-Deep	Slight	Settlement
TX-EC-35	Lakeshore Plain	504.50	2143.40	2240	600	Shallow	Moderate-Deep	Grazing & Agri
TX-EC-36	Lakeshore Plain	505.10	2143.20	2240	600	Shallow	Moderate-Deep	Grazing
TX-EC-37	Lakeshore Plain	505.80	2141.20	2270	600	Shallow	Moderate-Deep	Grazing & Agri

TEXCOCO REGION - PREHISPANIC SETTLEMENT DATA
Early Classic Sites

SITE NUMBER	CLASSIFICATION	ENVIRONMENTAL ZONE	AREA (in ha)	POP.	EF	MF	LF	TF	EC	LC	ET	LT	EA	LA	TEMPORARY SITE NO.	SUPERVISOR	YEAR
TX-EC-1	Small Hamlet	Lakeshore Plain	0.7	10	0	0	0	0	0	0	1	0	1	1	TX-C-1	M. PARSONS	1967
TX-EC-2	Ceremonial Ctr	Lower Piedmont	0.2	0	0	0	1	0	0	0	1	1	0	0	TX-T-7	M. PARSONS	1967
TX-EC-3	Hamlet	Lower Piedmont	10.0	100	0	0	0	0	1	1	1	1	0	0	TX-C-3	M. PARSONS	1967
TX-EC-4	Small Hamlet	Lower Piedmont	1.0	20	0	0	0	1	0	0	0	1	1	1	TX-T-8	M. PARSONS	1967
TX-EC-5	Small Hamlet	Lower Piedmont	0.9	20	0	0	1	1	0	0	1	1	1	0	TX-F-7	M. PARSONS	1967
TX-EC-6	Small Hamlet	Lower Piedmont	0.9	20	0	0	1	1	1	0	1	1	0	0	TX-C-4	M. PARSONS	1967
TX-EC-7	Hamlet	Lower Piedmont	4.0	40	0	0	0	0	0	0	0	1	1	1	TX-C-2	M. PARSONS	1967
TX-EC-8	Hamlet	Lower Piedmont	2.5	50	0	0	0	0	1	0	0	0	0	0	TX-C-11	J. PARSONS	1967
TX-EC-9	Hamlet	Lower Piedmont	1.0	50	0	0	0	1	0	0	0	0	1	1	TX-C-9	J. PARSONS	1967
TX-EC-10	Hamlet	Lower Piedmont	4.0	80	0	0	0	0	1	0	0	0	1	1	TX-C-8	J. PARSONS	1967
TX-EC-11	Small Hamlet	Lower Piedmont	0.9	10	0	0	0	1	0	0	0	1	0	1	TX-A-14	J. PARSONS	1967
TX-EC-12	Hamlet	Lower Piedmont	5.0	100	0	1	0	1	1	0	1	0	1	0	TX-C-7	J. PARSONS	1967
TX-EC-13	Hamlet	Lower Piedmont	6.0	100	0	0	0	0	1	0	0	1	0	1	TX-C-6	J. PARSONS	1967
TX-EC-14	Sm Nucl Village	Lower Piedmont	6.0	240	0	0	0	0	0	0	0	0	1	0	TX-C-5	J. PARSONS	1967
TX-EC-15	Small Hamlet	Lower Piedmont	0.9	10	0	0	0	1	0	0	0	0	0	1	TX-C-4	J. PARSONS	1967
TX-EC-16	Small Hamlet	Lower Piedmont	0.9	10	0	0	0	0	1	0	0	0	0	0	TX-C-10	J. PARSONS	1967
TX-EC-17	Small Hamlet	Lower Piedmont	0.9	20	0	0	0	1	1	0	0	0	0	0	TX-C-3	J. PARSONS	1967
TX-EC-18	Sm Disp Village	Lower Piedmont	25.0	500	0	0	0	0	1	0	0	0	0	1	TX-C-2	J. PARSONS	1967
TX-EC-19	Sm Nucl Village	Lower Piedmont	6.0	200	0	0	0	0	0	0	0	0	1	1	TX-C-1	J. PARSONS	1967
TX-EC-20	Small Hamlet	Lower Piedmont	0.9	10	0	0	0	1	0	0	0	0	1	1	TX-A-10	J. PARSONS	1967
TX-EC-21	Hamlet	Lower Piedmont	5.0	100	0	0	0	1	1	0	0	0	0	0		J. PARSONS	1967
TX-EC-22	Hamlet	Lower Piedmont	2.0	40	0	0	0	1	0	0	0	0	1	1		J. PARSONS	1967
TX-EC-23	Small Hamlet	Upper Piedmont	0.9	10	0	0	0	0	0	0	0	0	0	0		J. PARSONS	1967
TX-EC-24	Sm Disp Village	Lower Piedmont	13.0	250	0	0	0	1	0	0	0	0	0	0		J. PARSONS	1967
TX-EC-25	Small Hamlet	Lower Piedmont	0.9	10	0	0	0	0	0	0	0	0	0	0		J. PARSONS	1967
TX-EC-26	Hamlet	Upper Piedmont	4.0	80	0	1	1	0	0	0	0	0	1	0	TX-C-8	R. HIRNING	1967
TX-EC-27	Hamlet	Upper Piedmont	3.0	60	0	0	1	0	0	0	0	0	0	0	TX-C-8	R. HIRNING	1967
TX-EC-28	Small Hamlet	Lower Piedmont	1.0	10	0	0	0	0	0	0	1	0	1	0	TX-C-7	R. HIRNING	1967
TX-EC-29	Small Hamlet	Lower Piedmont	0.9	20	0	0	0	0	0	0	0	1	0	0	TX-T-7	R. HIRNING	1967
TX-EC-30	Ceremonial Ctr	Lower Piedmont	0.9	0	0	0	0	0	0	0	0	0	0	1	TX-C-6	R. HIRNING	1967
TX-EC-31	Hamlet	Lower Piedmont	5.0	50	0	0	0	0	0	1	1	1	0	0	TX-C-5	R. HIRNING	1967
TX-EC-32	Local Center	Lower Piedmont	60.0	900	0	0	0	0	0	1	1	1	1	0	TX-C-4	R. HIRNING	1967
TX-EC-33	Small Hamlet	Lakeshore Plain	1.0	20	0	0	0	0	1	0	0	0	0	1	TX-F-4	R. HIRNING	1967
TX-EC-34	Hamlet	Lakeshore Plain	3.0	30	0	0	0	0	1	1	1	1	1	1	TX-C-1	R. HIRNING	1967
TX-EC-35	Hamlet	Lakeshore Plain	4.0	80	0	0	0	0	1	0	0	0	0	0	TX-C-2	R. HIRNING	1967
TX-EC-36	Hamlet	Lakeshore Plain	3.0	60	0	0	0	0	1	0	1	0	0	0	TX-C-2	R. HIRNING	1967
TX-EC-37	Small Hamlet	Lakeshore Plain	1.0	10	0	0	0	0	0	1	1	0	0	0	TX-C-3	R. HIRNING	1967

92

TEXCOCO REGION - ENVIRONMENTAL DATA
Late Classic Sites

Site Number	Environmental Zone	UTM Coordinates East	North	Elev (in m)	Rainfall (in mm)	Modern Soil Depth	Modern Erosion	Modern Land use
TX-LC-1	Lakeshore Plain	508.90	2163.60	2250	600	Deep	None	Agricultural
TX-LC-2	Lower Piedmont	515.40	2163.50	2295	600	Deep	None	Agricultural
TX-LC-3	Lower Piedmont	514.40	2166.30	2340	620	Medium	Moderate	Agricultural
TX-LC-4	Lower Piedmont	517.00	2165.60	2330	640	Shallow	Moderate-Deep	Agricultural
TX-LC-5	Lower Piedmont	517.40	2162.50	2320	650	Medium	Slight	Agricultural
TX-LC-6	Lower Piedmont	518.00	2162.00	2330	600	Shallow-Med	Moderate	Grazing & Agri
TX-LC-7	Lower Piedmont	515.10	2161.50	2290	610	Deep	None	Agricultural
TX-LC-8	Lower Piedmont	521.20	2153.50	2465	720	Shallow-Med	Slight-Moderate	Agricultural
TX-LC-9	Lower Piedmont	519.10	2157.90	2340	690	Shallow	Moderate-Deep	Grazing & Agri
TX-LC-10	Lower Piedmont	519.00	2156.80	2370	680	Shallow	Moderate-Deep	Grazing
TX-LC-11	Lower Piedmont	517.80	2156.90	2340	670	Shallow	Moderate	Grazing & Agri
TX-LC-12	Lower Piedmont	518.00	2156.90	2315	660	Shallow	Moderate-Deep	Agricultural
TX-LC-13	Lower Piedmont	515.80	2156.70	2310	650	Medium	Slight	Agricultural
TX-LC-14	Lower Piedmont	516.40	2154.20	2360	670	Shallow-Med	Moderate	Agricultural
TX-LC-15	Lower Piedmont	515.10	2154.70	2310	610	Shallow-Med	Moderate	Agricultural
TX-LC-16	Lower Piedmont	515.20	2153.00	2315	620	Shallow-Med	Moderate	Agricultural
TX-LC-17	Lower Piedmont	514.00	2143.30	2300	650	Medium	Slight-Moderate	Agricultural
TX-LC-18	Lower Piedmont	510.10	2144.30	2275	630	Medium	Slight-Moderate	Agricultural
TX-LC-19	Lakeshore Plain	509.90	2147.90	2240	650	Deep	None	Agricultural
TX-LC-20	Lakeshore Plain	505.40	2147.10	2240	600	Medium-Deep	Very Slight	Agricultural
TX-LC-21	Lakeshore Plain	504.50	2143.40	2240	600	Shallow	Moderate-Deep	Grazing
TX-LC-22	Lakeshore Plain	505.10	2143.20	2240	600	Shallow	Moderate-Deep	Grazing
TX-LC-23	Lakeshore Plain	505.80	2141.20	2270	600	Shallow	Moderate-Deep	Grazing & Agri

TEXCOCO REGION - PREHISPANIC SETTLEMENT DATA
Late Classic Sites

SITE NUMBER	CLASSIFICATION	ENVIRONMENTAL ZONE	AREA (in ha)	POP.	OTHER OCCUPATIONS EF	MF	LF	TF	EC	LC	ET	LT	EA	LA	SURVEY RECORDS TEMPORARY SITE NO.	SUPERVISOR	YEAR
TX-LC-1	Small Hamlet	Lakeshore Plain	0.7	10	0	0	0	0	1	0	1	0	0	1	TX-C-1	M. PARSONS	1967
TX-LC-2	Hamlet	Lower Piedmont	10.0	100	0	0	0	0	1	0	1	1	0	0	TX-C-3	M. PARSONS	1967
TX-LC-3	Small Hamlet	Lower Piedmont	0.9	10	0	0	0	0	0	0	0	0	1	1	TX-A-20	M. PARSONS	1967
TX-LC-4	Hamlet	Lower Piedmont	3.0	30	0	0	0	0	0	1	0	0	0	0	TX-C-5	M. PARSONS	1967
TX-LC-5	Small Hamlet	Lower Piedmont	0.9	10	0	0	1	1	1	1	1	0	0	0	TX-C-4	M. PARSONS	1967
TX-LC-6	Small Hamlet	Lower Piedmont	0.9	10	0	0	1	1	0	1	1	0	0	0	TX-F-7	M. PARSONS	1967
TX-LC-7	Small Hamlet	Lower Piedmont	4.0	20	0	0	0	0	1	0	1	1	1	1	TX-C-2	M. PARSONS	1967
TX-LC-8	Small Hamlet	Lower Piedmont	2.0	20	0	0	0	0	1	0	0	0	0	0	TX-C-11	J. PARSONS	1967
TX-LC-9	Sm Disp Village	Lower Piedmont	9.0	175	0	0	1	0	1	0	0	0	1	1	TX-C-9	J. PARSONS	1967
TX-LC-10	Small Hamlet	Lower Piedmont	2.0	20	0	0	0	0	1	0	0	1	1	1	TX-C-8	J. PARSONS	1967
TX-LC-11	Hamlet	Lower Piedmont	5.0	100	0	1	0	1	0	1	0	0	0	0	TX-C-7	J. PARSONS	1967
TX-LC-12	Hamlet	Lower Piedmont	3.0	30	0	0	0	0	1	0	0	0	0	0	TX-C-6	J. PARSONS	1967
TX-LC-13	Sm Nucl Village	Lower Piedmont	6.0	150	0	0	0	0	1	0	1	0	0	0	TX-C-5	J. PARSONS	1967
TX-LC-14	Small Hamlet	Lower Piedmont	0.9	10	0	0	0	0	1	0	0	0	0	0	TX-C-10	J. PARSONS	1967
TX-LC-15	Small Hamlet	Lower Piedmont	0.9	10	0	0	0	1	1	0	0	0	0	0	TX-C-3	J. PARSONS	1967
TX-LC-16	Hamlet	Lower Piedmont	4.0	40	0	0	0	0	1	0	0	0	1	1	TX-C-2	J. PARSONS	1967
TX-LC-17	Hamlet	Lower Piedmont	4.0	40	0	0	0	0	1	0	0	0	0	0	TX-C-5	R. HIRNING	1967
TX-LC-18	Regional Center	Lower Piedmont	80.0	1200	0	0	0	0	1	0	1	1	0	1	TX-C-4	R. HIRNING	1967
TX-LC-19	Small Hamlet	Lakeshore Plain	0.9	10	0	0	0	0	1	0	0	0	0	0	TX-F-4	R. HIRNING	1967
TX-LC-20	Small Hamlet	Lakeshore Plain	1.0	10	0	0	0	0	1	0	1	1	1	1	TX-C-1	R. HIRNING	1967
TX-LC-21	Small Hamlet	Lakeshore Plain	2.0	20	0	0	0	0	1	0	0	0	0	0	TX-C-2	R. HIRNING	1967
TX-LC-22	Small Hamlet	Lakeshore Plain	1.0	10	0	0	0	0	1	0	0	0	0	0	TX-C-2	R. HIRNING	1967
TX-LC-23	Small Hamlet	Lakeshore Plain	0.9	10	0	0	0	0	1	0	1	0	0	0	TX-C-3	R. HIRNING	1967

94

TEXCOCO REGION - ENVIRONMENTAL DATA
Early Toltec Sites

Site Number	Environmental Zone	UTM Coordinates East	UTM Coordinates North	Elev (in m)	Rainfall (in mm)	Modern Soil Depth	Modern Erosion	Modern Land use
TX-ET-1	Lakeshore Plain	508.00	2161.20	2250	600	Deep	None	Agricultural
TX-ET-2	Lower Piedmont	508.70	2165.50	2335	600	Shallow	Deep	Grazing & Agri
TX-ET-3	Lower Piedmont	512.80	2163.70	2310	600	Shallow-Med	Moderate-Deep	Grazing & Agri
TX-ET-4	Lower Piedmont	514.20	2164.00	2320	600	Medium	Moderate	Grazing & Agri
TX-ET-5	Lower Piedmont	513.00	2164.20	2430	600	Shallow	Moderate-Deep	Grazing
TX-ET-6	Upper Piedmont	523.60	2165.80	2620	620	Shallow	Moderate	Grazing & Agri
TX-ET-7	Lower Piedmont	517.20	2165.10	2325	640	Medium	Moderate	Agricultural
TX-ET-8	Lower Piedmont	518.60	2166.00	2315	650	Shallow	Deep	Grazing
TX-ET-9	Lower Piedmont	520.90	2165.80	2380	660	Shallow	Deep	Grazing & Agri
TX-ET-10	Lower Piedmont	520.10	2164.70	2300	660	Medium	Slight-Moderate	Agricultural
TX-ET-11	Lower Piedmont	521.70	2163.00	2420	670	Medium	Slight	Grazing & Agri
TX-ET-12	Lower Piedmont	520.00	2163.30	2345	670	Shallow	Deep	Grazing & Agri
TX-ET-13	Lower Piedmont	517.80	2162.50	2315	650	Shallow-Med	Moderate-Deep	Grazing & Agri
TX-ET-14	Lower Piedmont	514.90	2161.60	2290	610	Deep	None	Agricultural
TX-ET-15	Lower Piedmont	514.40	2156.50	2285	640	Medium	Slight	Settlement
TX-ET-16	Lakebed	505.10	2154.20	2240	600	Deep	None	None
TX-ET-17	Lower Piedmont	508.80	2144.20	2320	650	Medium	Slight	Agricultural
TX-ET-18	Lower Piedmont	511.60	2144.00	2275	640	Medium	Slight-Moderate	Grazing & Agri
TX-ET-19	Lakeshore Plain	505.30	2146.90	2250	600	Shallow-Med	Moderate-Deep	Grazing & Agri
TX-ET-20	Lakeshore Plain	506.30	2145.10	2260	600	Shallow	Moderate	Grazing & Agri
TX-ET-21	Lakeshore Plain	502.80	2145.20	2245	600	Medium	Very Slight	Settlement
TX-ET-22	Lakeshore Plain	505.80	2142.50	2250	600	Deep	Slight	Agricultural
TX-ET-23	Lower Piedmont	505.60	2141.20	2260	600	Medium	Moderate-Deep	Grazing & Agri
TX-ET-24	Lower Piedmont	508.50	2142.60	2420	650	Shallow	Moderate-Deep	Grazing

TEXCOCO REGION - PREHISPANIC SETTLEMENT DATA
Early Toltec Sites

SITE NUMBER	CLASSIFICATION	ENVIRONMENTAL ZONE	AREA (in ha)	POP.	EF	MF	LF	TF	EC	LC	ET	LT	EA	LA	TEMPORARY SITE NO.	SUPERVISOR	YEAR
TX-ET-1	Small Hamlet	Lakeshore Plain	2.0	20	0	0	0	0	0	0	0	1	1	1	TX-T-16	M. PARSONS	1967
TX-ET-2	Hamlet	Lower Piedmont	3.0	60	0	0	0	0	0	0	0	0	1	1	TX-T-12	M. PARSONS	1967
TX-ET-3	Hamlet	Lower Piedmont	2.0	40	0	0	0	0	0	0	0	0	0	0	TX-T-10	M. PARSONS	1967
TX-ET-4	Regional Center	Lower Piedmont	180.0	7200	0	0	0	1	1	1	0	1	1	1	TX-T-5	M. PARSONS	1967
TX-ET-5	Ceremonial Ctr	Lower Piedmont	2.0	0	0	0	1	0	1	0	0	0	0	0	TX-T-7	M. PARSONS	1967
TX-ET-6	Ceremonial Ctr	Upper Piedmont	1.0	0	0	0	1	1	0	0	0	0	1	1	T-A-35	M. PARSONS	1967
TX-ET-7	Regional Center	Lower Piedmont	200.0	8000	0	0	0	1	1	0	0	1	1	1	TX-T-8	M. PARSONS	1967
TX-ET-8	Sm Disp Village	Lower Piedmont	19.0	300	0	0	0	0	0	0	0	0	0	0	TX-T-26	M. PARSONS	1967
TX-ET-9	Small Hamlet	Lower Piedmont	0.9	10	0	0	0	1	0	0	0	0	1	1	TX-F-10	M. PARSONS	1967
TX-ET-10	Hamlet	Lower Piedmont	9.0	90	0	0	0	0	0	0	0	0	1	1	TX-T-27	M. PARSONS	1967
TX-ET-11	Hamlet	Lower Piedmont	2.0	40	0	0	0	0	0	0	0	0	0	0	TX-T-30	M. PARSONS	1967
TX-ET-12	Hamlet	Lower Piedmont	3.0	30	0	0	0	0	0	0	0	0	1	0	TX-T-28	M. PARSONS	1967
TX-ET-13	Lg Disp Village	Lower Piedmont	80.0	1600	0	0	0	1	0	0	0	3	1	1	TX-T-18	M. PARSONS	1967
TX-ET-14	Small Hamlet	Lower Piedmont	1.0	10	0	0	0	0	0	1	1	1	1	1	TX-T-11	M. PARSONS	1967
TX-ET-15	Sm Disp Village	Lower Piedmont	23.0	300	0	0	0	0	0	0	0	0	0	1	TX-T-5	J. PARSONS	1967
TX-ET-16	Questionable	Lakebed	0.9	0	0	0	0	0	0	0	0	1	0	1	TX-T-6	J. PARSONS	1967
TX-ET-17	Lg Disp Village	Lower Piedmont	35.0	700	0	0	0	0	1	1	0	0	0	0	TX-T-8	R. HIRNING	1967
TX-ET-18	Regional Center	Lower Piedmont	400.0	12000	0	0	0	0	1	1	1	1	1	0	TX-T-6	R. HIRNING	1967
TX-ET-19	Lg Disp Village	Lakeshore Plain	30.0	600	0	0	0	0	1	1	0	1	1	1	TX-T-2	R. HIRNING	1967
TX-ET-20	Small Hamlet	Lakeshore Plain	1.0	10	0	0	0	0	0	0	0	0	0	0	TX-T-1	R. HIRNING	1967
TX-ET-21	Sm Disp Village	Lakeshore Plain	20.0	200	0	0	0	1	0	0	0	1	1	1	TX-T-3	R. HIRNING	1967
TX-ET-22	Sm Disp Village	Lakeshore Plain	8.0	160	0	0	0	0	0	0	0	0	0	0	TX-T-4	R. HIRNING	1967
TX-ET-23	Sm Disp Village	Lower Piedmont	35.0	400	0	0	0	0	1	1	1	1	0	0	TX-T-5	R. HIRNING	1967
TX-ET-24	Ceremonial Ctr	Lower Piedmont	0.9	0	0	0	0	0	0	0	0	0	0	1		R. HIRNING	1967

TEXCOCO REGION - ENVIRONMENTAL DATA
Late Toltec Sites

Site Number	Environmental Zone	UTM Coordinates East	North	Elev (in m)	Rainfall (in mm)	Modern Soil Depth	Modern Erosion	Modern Land use
TX-LT-1	Lakeshore Plain	504.20	2160.50	2250	600	Shallow	Moderate-Deep	Grazing
TX-LT-2	Lakeshore Plain	504.80	2160.90	2240	600	Deep	None	Grazing
TX-LT-3	Lakeshore Plain	505.50	2162.60	2250	600	Deep	None	Agricultural
TX-LT-4	Lakeshore Plain	507.70	2161.20	2250	600	Deep	None	Agricultural
TX-LT-5	Lakeshore Plain	508.90	2164.10	2250	610	Deep	None	Grazing
TX-LT-6	Lakeshore Plain	510.20	2163.60	2260	600	Deep	None	Agricultural
TX-LT-7	Lakeshore Plain	510.20	2162.40	2260	600	Deep	None	Agricultural
TX-LT-8	Lower Piedmont	511.40	2163.30	2270	600	Deep	None	Agricultural
TX-LT-9	Lower Piedmont	511.70	2162.20	2270	600	Deep	None	Agricultural
TX-LT-10	Lower Piedmont	513.40	2162.00	2280	600	Deep	None	Agricultural
TX-LT-11	Lower Piedmont	514.80	2161.80	2290	610	Deep	None	Agricultural
TX-LT-12	Lower Piedmont	514.50	2163.90	2290	600	Deep	Very Slight	Agricultural
TX-LT-13	Lower Piedmont	512.70	2163.80	2280	600	Shallow-Med	Moderate	Grazing & Agri
TX-LT-14	Upper Piedmont	513.60	2165.80	2620	620	Shallow	Moderate	Grazing & Agri
TX-LT-15	Lower Piedmont	513.50	2164.70	2315	600	Shallow	Deep	Grazing & Agri
TX-LT-16	Lower Piedmont	515.40	2164.70	2300	620	Deep	Slight	Agricultural
TX-LT-17	Lower Piedmont	515.20	2165.80	2310	620	Shallow-Med	Moderate-Deep	Grazing & Agri
TX-LT-18	Lower Piedmont	517.20	2167.30	2450	630	Shallow	Deep	Grazing & Agri
TX-LT-19	Lower Piedmont	517.40	2167.70	2410	630	Shallow	Deep	Grazing
TX-LT-20	Lower Piedmont	517.90	2166.50	2330	640	Shallow	Deep	Grazing
TX-LT-21	Lower Piedmont	518.40	2164.60	2330	650	Shallow	Moderate	Grazing & Agri
TX-LT-22	Lower Piedmont	517.60	2165.20	2325	640	Shallow	Moderate	Grazing & Agri
TX-LT-23	Lower Piedmont	516.40	2165.10	2330	620	Deep	Slight	Agricultural
TX-LT-24	Lower Piedmont	516.60	2164.10	2290	630	Deep	Slight	Grazing & Agri
TX-LT-25	Lower Piedmont	516.00	2162.60	2320	630	Shallow	Moderate-Deep	None
TX-LT-26	Lower Piedmont	516.70	2161.90	2300	650	Medium	Slight	Agricultural
TX-LT-27	Lower Piedmont	516.90	2162.70	2310	650	Deep	Slight	Agricultural
TX-LT-28	Lower Piedmont	518.00	2163.00	2315	650	Shallow-Med	Moderate	Agricultural
TX-LT-29	Lower Piedmont	519.80	2164.30	2310	670	Deep	Slight	Agricultural
TX-LT-30	Lower Piedmont	520.70	2164.30	2320	670	Medium	Moderate	Grazing & Agri
TX-LT-31	Lakeshore Plain	523.10	2164.80	2400	680	Shallow	Deep	Grazing
TX-LT-32	Lakeshore Plain	507.80	2157.10	2245	600	Deep	None	Grazing
TX-LT-33	Lakeshore Plain	508.50	2156.20	2240	600	Deep	None	Agricultural
TX-LT-34	Lakeshore Plain	509.10	2155.50	2240	600	Deep	None	Agricultural
TX-LT-35	Lakeshore Plain	506.60	2156.10	2240	600	Deep	None	Agricultural
TX-LT-36	Lakeshore Plain	506.90	2155.00	2240	600	Deep	None	Grazing
TX-LT-37	Lakebed	505.10	2154.30	2240	600	Deep	None	None
TX-LT-38	Lakeshore Plain	509.40	2153.90	2250	600	Deep	None	Grazing
TX-LT-39	Lower Piedmont	511.50	2157.90	2270	610	Deep	None	Agricultural
TX-LT-40	Lakeshore Plain	511.90	2156.90	2245	610	Deep	None	Agricultural
TX-LT-41	Lower Piedmont	514.20	2157.50	2285	640	Deep	None	Agricultural
TX-LT-42	Lower Piedmont	515.90	2156.80	2310	650	Medium	Slight	Agricultural

TEXCOCO REGION – PREHISPANIC SETTLEMENT DATA
Late Toltec Sites

SITE NUMBER	CLASSIFICATION	ENVIRONMENTAL ZONE	AREA (in ha)	POP.	EF	MF	LF	TF	EC	LC	ET	LT	EA	LA	TEMPORARY SITE NO.	SUPERVISOR	YEAR
TX-LT-1	Hamlet	Lakeshore Plain	3.0	60	0	0	0	0	0	0	0	0	1	1	TX-T-1	M. PARSONS	1967
TX-LT-2	Hamlet	Lakeshore Plain	1.0	30	0	0	0	0	0	0	0	0	0	1	TX-T-2	M. PARSONS	1967
TX-LT-3	Small Hamlet	Lakeshore Plain	0.1	10	0	0	0	0	0	0	0	0	0	1	TX-T-9	M. PARSONS	1967
TX-LT-4	Small Hamlet	Lakeshore Plain	2.0	20	0	0	0	0	0	0	1	0	1	1	TX-A-16	M. PARSONS	1967
TX-LT-5	Small Hamlet	Lakeshore Plain	0.7	10	0	0	0	0	1	1	0	0	0	1	TX-C-1	M. PARSONS	1967
TX-LT-6	Hamlet	Lakeshore Plain	5.0	50	0	0	0	0	0	0	0	0	1	1	TX-T-4	M. PARSONS	1967
TX-LT-7	Hamlet	Lakeshore Plain	7.0	100	0	0	0	0	0	0	0	0	0	0	TX-T-13	M. PARSONS	1967
TX-LT-8	Small Hamlet	Lower Piedmont	2.0	20	0	0	0	0	0	0	0	0	0	0	TX-T-6	M. PARSONS	1967
TX-LT-9	Small Hamlet	Lower Piedmont	1.0	20	0	0	0	0	0	0	0	0	0	0	TX-T-17	M. PARSONS	1967
TX-LT-10	Hamlet	Lower Piedmont	6.0	60	0	0	0	0	0	0	0	0	0	1	TX-T-15	M. PARSONS	1967
TX-LT-11	Small Hamlet	Lower Piedmont	2.0	20	0	0	0	0	2	1	1	0	1	1	TX-T-11	M. PARSONS	1967
TX-LT-12	Lg Disp Village	Lower Piedmont	50.0	750	0	0	0	0	2	1	1	0	1	1	TX-T-5	M. PARSONS	1967
TX-LT-13	Small Hamlet	Lower Piedmont	0.1	15	0	0	0	0	0	0	0	0	0	0	TX-T-10	M. PARSONS	1967
TX-LT-14	Ceremonial Ctr	Upper Piedmont	1.0	0	0	0	0	1	0	0	1	0	1	1	T-A-35	M. PARSONS	1967
TX-LT-15	Small Hamlet	Lower Piedmont	1.0	10	0	0	0	1	0	0	1	0	1	1	TX-T-14	M. PARSONS	1967
TX-LT-16	Small Hamlet	Lower Piedmont	0.9	10	0	0	0	0	0	0	0	0	0	1	TX-T-21	M. PARSONS	1967
TX-LT-17	Small Hamlet	Lower Piedmont	0.9	20	0	0	0	0	0	0	0	0	1	1	TX-T-20	M. PARSONS	1967
TX-LT-18	Hamlet	Lower Piedmont	2.0	40	0	0	0	0	0	0	0	0	0	0	TX-T-29	M. PARSONS	1967
TX-LT-19	Small Hamlet	Lower Piedmont	0.9	10	0	0	0	0	0	0	0	0	1	1	TX-A-22	M. PARSONS	1967
TX-LT-20	Small Hamlet	Lower Piedmont	0.9	10	0	0	0	0	0	0	1	0	1	1	TX-A-22	M. PARSONS	1967
TX-LT-21	Small Hamlet	Lower Piedmont	0.1	20	0	0	0	0	0	0	0	0	0	0	TX-T-8	M. PARSONS	1967
TX-LT-22	Small Hamlet	Lower Piedmont	2.0	20	0	0	0	0	0	0	1	0	1	1	TX-T-8	M. PARSONS	1967
TX-LT-23	Small Hamlet	Lower Piedmont	0.9	10	0	0	0	0	0	0	1	0	1	1	TX-T-23	M. PARSONS	1967
TX-LT-24	Hamlet	Lower Piedmont	3.0	30	0	0	0	0	0	0	0	0	1	1	TX-T-24	M. PARSONS	1967
TX-LT-25	Questionable	Lower Piedmont	0.1	0	0	0	0	0	1	1	0	0	0	0	TX-T-24	M. PARSONS	1967
TX-LT-26	Hamlet	Lower Piedmont	3.0	30	0	0	0	0	0	0	1	0	1	1	TX-T-31	M. PARSONS	1967
TX-LT-27	Small Hamlet	Lower Piedmont	0.9	10	0	0	0	0	1	1	1	0	1	1	TX-F-3	M. PARSONS	1967
TX-LT-28	Sm Disp Village	Lower Piedmont	14.0	150	0	0	0	1	0	0	1	0	0	0	TX-T-18	M. PARSONS	1967
TX-LT-29	Hamlet	Lower Piedmont	4.0	40	0	0	0	0	0	0	0	0	0	0	TX-T-27	M. PARSONS	1967
TX-LT-30	Small Hamlet	Lower Piedmont	2.0	20	0	0	0	0	0	0	0	0	1	1	TX-T-27	M. PARSONS	1967
TX-LT-31	Hamlet	Lower Piedmont	2.0	40	0	0	0	0	0	0	0	0	1	1	TX-T-25	M. PARSONS	1967
TX-LT-32	Hamlet	Lakeshore Plain	4.0	80	0	0	0	0	0	0	0	0	0	1	TX-T-3	J. PARSONS	1967
TX-LT-33	Hamlet	Lakeshore Plain	5.0	60	0	0	0	0	0	0	0	0	0	0	TX-T-2	J. PARSONS	1967
TX-LT-34	Sm Disp Village	Lakeshore Plain	12.0	120	0	0	0	0	0	0	0	0	0	0	TX-T-2	J. PARSONS	1967
TX-LT-35	Sm Disp Village	Lakeshore Plain	20.0	300	0	0	0	0	0	0	0	0	0	0	TX-T-1	J. PARSONS	1967
TX-LT-36	Hamlet	Lakeshore Plain	2.0	40	0	0	1	1	0	0	0	0	1	1	TX-A-1	J. PARSONS	1967
TX-LT-37	Questionable	Lakebed	0.9	0	0	0	0	0	0	0	0	0	0	0	TX-T-6	J. PARSONS	1967
TX-LT-38	Hamlet	Lakeshore Plain	3.0	100	0	0	1	1	0	0	0	0	0	0	TX-F-3	J. PARSONS	1967
TX-LT-39	Hamlet	Lower Piedmont	3.0	30	0	0	0	0	0	0	0	0	0	1	TX-T-4	J. PARSONS	1967
TX-LT-40	Questionable	Lakeshore Plain	0.9	0	0	0	0	0	0	0	0	0	0	0	TX-A-11	J. PARSONS	1967
TX-LT-41	Small Hamlet	Lower Piedmont	0.9	10	0	0	0	0	0	0	0	0	0	0		J. PARSONS	1967
TX-LT-42	Small Hamlet	Lower Piedmont	1.0	10	0	0	0	0	1	1	0	0	0	0	TX-C-5	J. PARSONS	1967

TEXCOCO REGION - ENVIRONMENTAL DATA
Late Toltec Sites

Site Number	Environmental Zone	UTM Coordinates East	North	Elev (in m)	Rainfall (in mm)	Modern Soil Depth	Modern Erosion	Modern Land Use
TX-LT-43	Lower Piedmont	517.50	2157.70	2340	670	Shallow	Moderate	Grazing & Agri
TX-LT-44	Upper Piedmont	520.10	2155.20	2575	700	Shallow	Moderate	Grazing & Agri
TX-LT-45	Upper Piedmont	521.60	2155.00	2560	760	Very Shallow	Deep	None
TX-LT-46	Upper Piedmont	519.90	2154.50	2520	730	Fully Eroded	Deep	Grazing
TX-LT-47	Upper Piedmont	520.80	2154.80	2510	770	Very Shallow	Deep	Grazing
TX-LT-48	Upper Piedmont	520.20	2154.50	2560	750	Very Shallow	Deep	Grazing
TX-LT-49	Lower Piedmont	513.20	2152.90	2275	640	Medium	Moderate	Agricultural
TX-LT-50	Lower Piedmont	517.80	2151.50	2450	730	Very Shallow	Deep	Grazing
TX-LT-51	Lower Piedmont	514.20	2144.30	2305	670	Medium	Slight-Moderate	Agricultural
TX-LT-52	Lower Piedmont	513.40	2143.80	2290	660	Deep	Slight	Agricultural
TX-LT-53	Lower Piedmont	511.10	2144.30	2265	640	Medium	Slight-Moderate	Agricultural
TX-LT-54	Lakeshore Plain	505.70	2146.60	2250	600	Shallow-Med	Moderate-Deep	Grazing & Agri
TX-LT-55	Upper Piedmont	504.70	2144.50	2520	600	Shallow-Med	Moderate	Grazing & Agri
TX-LT-56	Lakeshore Plain	503.00	2144.50	2245	600	Deep	Very Slight	Grazing
TX-LT-57	Lakeshore Plain	505.00	2142.80	2240	600	Deep	None	Agricultural
TX-LT-58	Lakeshore Plain	506.00	2142.40	2250	600	Deep	None	Settlement
TX-LT-59	Lower Piedmont	505.50	2141.50	2265	600	Shallow	Moderate-Deep	Grazing & Agri

TEXCOCO REGION - PREHISPANIC SETTLEMENT DATA
Late Toltec Sites

SITE NUMBER	CLASSIFICATION	ENVIRONMENTAL ZONE	AREA (in ha)	POP.	EF	MF	LF	TF	EC	LC	ET	LT	EA	LA	TEMPORARY SITE NO.	SUPERVISOR	YEAR
TX-LT-43	Small Hamlet	Lower Piedmont	1.0	20	0	1	0	1	1	1	0	0	0	0	TX-C-7	J. PARSONS	1967
TX-LT-44	Small Hamlet	Upper Piedmont	1.0	10	0	0	1	1	0	0	0	0	0	1	TX-A-16	J. PARSONS	1967
TX-LT-45	Small Hamlet	Upper Piedmont	1.0	10	0	0	0	0	0	0	0	1	1	1	TX-A-25	J. PARSONS	1967
TX-LT-46	Small Hamlet	Upper Piedmont	1.0	10	0	0	0	0	0	0	0	1	1	1	TX-A-22	J. PARSONS	1967
TX-LT-47	Small Hamlet	Upper Piedmont	1.0	10	0	0	0	0	0	0	0	1	1	1	TX-A-20	J. PARSONS	1967
TX-LT-48	Small Hamlet	Upper Piedmont	1.0	10	0	0	0	0	0	0	0	0	1	1	TX-A-19	J. PARSONS	1967
TX-LT-49	Small Hamlet	Lower Piedmont	1.0	10	0	0	0	0	0	0	0	1	1	1	TX-A-10	J. PARSONS	1967
TX-LT-50	Small Hamlet	Lower Piedmont	0.2	20	0	0	0	0	0	0	0	0	0	0		J. PARSONS	1967
TX-LT-51	Small Hamlet	Lower Piedmont	1.0	10	0	0	0	0	1	0	0	0	0	0	TX-T-7	R. HIRNING	1967
TX-LT-52	Hamlet	Lower Piedmont	4.0	80	0	0	0	0	0	0	0	0	0	0	TX-T-9	R. HIRNING	1967
TX-LT-53	Local Center	Lower Piedmont	125.0	1500	0	0	0	0	1	1	1	0	0	1	TX-T-6	R. HIRNING	1967
TX-LT-54	Sm Disp Village	Lakeshore Plain	25.0	250	0	0	0	0	1	1	1	0	0	1	TX-T-2	R. HIRNING	1967
TX-LT-55	Ceremonial Ctr	Upper Piedmont	0.1	0	0	0	0	1	0	0	0	0	1	1	TX-A-4	R. HIRNING	1967
TX-LT-56	Sm Disp Village	Lakeshore Plain	40.0	400	0	0	0	1	0	0	1	0	1	1	TX-T-3	R. HIRNING	1967
TX-LT-57	Sm Disp Village	Lakeshore Plain	30.0	300	0	0	0	0	0	0	1	0	1	1	TX-T-4	R. HIRNING	1967
TX-LT-58	Sm Disp Village	Lakeshore Plain	17.0	200	0	0	0	0	0	1	0	0	0	0	TX-T-5	R. HIRNING	1967
TX-LT-59	Sm Disp Village	Lower Piedmont	15.0	150	0	0	0	0	1	0	1	0	0	0	TX-T-5	R. HIRNING	1967

TEXCOCO REGION - ENVIRONMENTAL DATA
Aztec Sites

Site Number	Environmental Zone	UTM Coordinates East	North	Elev (in m)	Rainfall (in mm)	Modern Soil Depth	Modern Erosion	Modern Land use
TX-A-1	Lakeshore Plain	504.30	2160.60	2250	600	Shallow	Slight-Moderate	Grazing
TX-A-2	Lakeshore Plain	504.80	2161.00	2240	600	Deep	None	Grazing
TX-A-3	Lakeshore Plain	504.70	2161.50	2255	600	Shallow	Slight-Moderate	Grazing & Agri
TX-A-4	Lakeshore Plain	505.60	2162.70	2250	600	Deep	None	Agricultural
TX-A-5	Lakeshore Plain	505.40	2164.50	2260	600	Deep	None	Agricultural
TX-A-6	Lakeshore Plain	507.80	2161.30	2260	600		Slight	Settlement
TX-A-7	Lakeshore Plain	508.70	2160.80	2250	600	Deep	None	Agricultural
TX-A-8	Lakeshore Plain	508.40	2162.20	2250	600	Deep	None	Agricultural
TX-A-9	Lakeshore Plain	508.90	2163.70	2250	610	Deep	None	None
TX-A-10	Lakeshore Plain	510.20	2163.50	2260	600	Deep	None	Agricultural
TX-A-11	Lakeshore Plain	510.10	2162.20	2260	600	Deep	None	Agricultural
TX-A-12	Lower Piedmont	511.80	2162.00	2270	600	Deep	None	Settlement
TX-A-13	Lower Piedmont	513.20	2162.20	2280	600	Deep	None	Agricultural
TX-A-14	Lower Piedmont	514.60	2161.90	2290	600	Deep	None	Agricultural
TX-A-15	Lower Piedmont	514.70	2160.40	2290	620	Deep	None	Agricultural
TX-A-16	Lower Piedmont	515.60	2164.80	2290	620	Deep	None	Agricultural
TX-A-17	Lower Piedmont	514.30	2164.00	2325	600	Medium	Slight	Grazing & Agri
TX-A-18	Lower Piedmont	512.90	2165.30	2335	620	Shallow	Deep	Grazing
TX-A-19	Lower Piedmont	513.10	2164.50	2470	620	Shallow	Slight-Moderate	Grazing
TX-A-20	Upper Piedmont	513.70	2165.80	2620	620	Shallow	Moderate	Grazing & Agri
TX-A-21	Lower Piedmont	514.70	2165.90	2360	620	Shallow	Deep	Grazing
TX-A-22	Lower Piedmont	515.60	2164.70	2290	620	Deep	Very Slight	Settlement
TX-A-23	Lower Piedmont	515.60	2167.20	2360	620	Shallow-Med	Moderate	Grazing & Agri
TX-A-24	Lower Piedmont	518.50	2166.20	2400	650	Very Shallow	Deep	Grazing & Agri
TX-A-25	Lower Piedmont	520.90	2165.40	2345	670	Shallow-Med	Deep	Grazing & Agri
TX-A-26	Lower Piedmont	522.60	2165.60	2445	680	Very Shallow	Deep	Grazing & Agri
TX-A-27	Lower Piedmont	522.70	2164.40	2395	680	Shallow	Deep	Grazing & Agri
TX-A-28	Upper Piedmont	524.20	2165.00	2540	690	Shallow	Deep	Grazing & Agri
TX-A-29	Upper Piedmont	523.70	2164.20	2610	690	Shallow	Moderate-Deep	Grazing & Agri
TX-A-30	Upper Piedmont	524.80	2163.30	2555	720	Very Shallow	Deep	Grazing & Agri
TX-A-31	Upper Piedmont	524.60	2161.80	2580	730	Very Shallow	Deep	Grazing & Agri
TX-A-32	Lower Piedmont	523.40	2162.10	2420	700	Very Shallow	Deep	Grazing
TX-A-33	Lower Piedmont	523.60	2162.70	2400	700	Shallow	Moderate	Grazing
TX-A-34	Lower Piedmont	523.60	2163.70	2410	690	Shallow	Moderate-Deep	Grazing & Agri
TX-A-35	Lower Piedmont	521.70	2163.60	2390	690	Medium	Slight-Moderate	Agricultural
TX-A-36	Lower Piedmont	522.90	2163.00	2400	690	Medium	Slight	Agricultural
TX-A-37	Lower Piedmont	521.50	2163.10	2410	670	Medium	Slight	Agricultural
TX-A-38	Lower Piedmont	520.40	2162.50	2345	670	Shallow	Deep	Grazing
TX-A-39	Lower Piedmont	524.80	2163.40	2345	670	Shallow	Deep	None
TX-A-40	Lower Piedmont	517.60	2162.40	2315	650	Shallow-Med	Moderate	Agricultural
TX-A-41	Lower Piedmont	516.80	2163.40	2290	650	Medium	Moderate	Grazing
TX-A-42	Lakebed	504.10	2156.10	2240	600	Deep	None	None

TEXCOCO REGION - PREHISPANIC SETTLEMENT DATA
Aztec Sites

SITE NUMBER	CLASSIFICATION	ENVIRONMENTAL ZONE	AREA (in ha)	POP.	EF	MF	LF	TF	EC	LC	ET	LT	EA	LA	TEMPORARY SITE NO.	SUPERVISOR	YEAR
TX-A-1	Hamlet	Lakeshore Plain	4.0	80	0	0	0	0	0	0	0	1	1	1	TX-A-1	M. PARSONS	1967
TX-A-2	Small Hamlet	Lakeshore Plain	1.0	20	0	0	0	0	0	0	0	1	0	1	TX-A-2	M. PARSONS	1967
TX-A-3	Hamlet	Lakeshore Plain	8.0	100	0	0	0	0	0	0	0	0	1	1	TX-A-3	M. PARSONS	1967
TX-A-4	Small Hamlet	Lakeshore Plain	0.1	10	0	0	0	0	0	0	0	0	0	1	TX-A-5	M. PARSONS	1967
TX-A-5	Questionable	Lakeshore Plain	0.1	0	0	0	0	0	0	0	0	0	0	1	TX-A-4	M. PARSONS	1967
TX-A-6	Ceremonial Ctr	Lakeshore Plain	30.0	0	0	0	0	0	0	0	1	0	1	1	TX-A-16	M. PARSONS	1967
TX-A-7	Hamlet	Lakeshore Plain	2.0	60	0	0	0	0	0	0	0	0	1	1	TX-A-19	M. PARSONS	1967
TX-A-8	Small Hamlet	Lakeshore Plain	0.9	20	0	0	0	0	0	1	0	0	0	0	TX-A-6	M. PARSONS	1967
TX-A-9	Small Hamlet	Lakeshore Plain	1.0	20	0	0	0	0	0	0	0	0	0	0	TX-A-7	M. PARSONS	1967
TX-A-10	Sm Disp Village	Lakeshore Plain	36.0	300	0	0	0	0	0	0	0	1	1	1	TX-A-8	M. PARSONS	1967
TX-A-11	Sm Disp Village	Lakeshore Plain	24.0	250	0	0	0	0	0	0	0	1	0	1	TX-A-13	M. PARSONS	1967
TX-A-12	Sm Disp Village	Lower Piedmont	12.0	150	0	0	0	0	0	0	0	1	0	1	TX-A-17	M. PARSONS	1967
TX-A-13	Hamlet	Lower Piedmont	5.0	50	0	0	0	0	0	0	0	1	0	1	TX-A-15	M. PARSONS	1967
TX-A-14	Sm Disp Village	Lower Piedmont	15.0	150	0	0	0	0	1	1	1	1	1	1	TX-A-10	M. PARSONS	1967
TX-A-15	Hamlet	Lower Piedmont	2.0	40	0	0	0	0	0	0	0	0	0	1	TX-A-14	M. PARSONS	1967
TX-A-16	Sm Disp Village	Lower Piedmont	6.0	200	0	0	0	0	0	0	0	0	1	0	TX-A-21	M. PARSONS	1967
TX-A-17	Lg Disp Village	Lower Piedmont	115.0	600	0	1	0	1	1	1	1	2	1	1	TX-A-18	M. PARSONS	1967
TX-A-18	Hamlet	Lower Piedmont	3.0	50	0	0	0	0	0	0	1	0	1	1	TX-A-11	M. PARSONS	1967
TX-A-19	Ceremonial Ctr	Lower Piedmont	0.2	0	0	0	0	0	0	0	0	0	0	0	TX-A-9	M. PARSONS	1967
TX-A-20	Ceremonial Ctr	Upper Piedmont	1.0	0	0	0	1	0	0	0	1	1	1	1	TX-A-35	M. PARSONS	1967
TX-A-21	Sm Disp Village	Lower Piedmont	55.0	500	0	0	0	0	0	0	0	0	1	1	TX-A-20	M. PARSONS	1967
TX-A-22	Questionable	Lower Piedmont	13.0	150	0	0	0	0	0	0	0	0	0	1	TX-A-26	M. PARSONS	1967
TX-A-23	Sm Disp Village	Lower Piedmont	18.0	150	0	0	0	0	0	0	0	0	1	1	TX-A-28	M. PARSONS	1967
TX-A-24	Regional Center	Lower Piedmont	450.0	13500	0	0	1	0	2	0	2	4	1	1	TX-A-22	M. PARSONS	1967
TX-A-25	Lg Disp Village	Lower Piedmont	115.0	1200	0	0	0	0	0	0	0	0	1	1	TX-A-32	M. PARSONS	1967
TX-A-26	Sm Disp Village	Lower Piedmont	10.0	150	0	0	0	0	0	0	0	0	1	1	TX-A-29	M. PARSONS	1967
TX-A-27	Sm Disp Village	Lower Piedmont	17.0	300	0	0	0	0	0	0	0	1	1	1	TX-A-30	M. PARSONS	1967
TX-A-28	Lg D.sp Village	Upper Piedmont	75.0	1200	0	0	0	0	0	0	0	0	0	1	TX-A-31	M. PARSONS	1967
TX-A-29	Ceremonial Ctr	Upper Piedmont	0.1	0	0	0	0	0	0	0	0	0	0	0	TX-A-40	M. PARSONS	1967
TX-A-30	Lg Disp Village	Upper Piedmont	100.0	1500	0	0	0	0	0	0	0	0	0	1	TX-A-37	M. PARSONS	1967
TX-A-31	Lg Disp Village	Upper Piedmont	50.0	700	0	0	0	0	0	0	0	0	1	1	TX-A-36	M. PARSONS	1967
TX-A-32	Hamlet	Lower Piedmont	4.0	80	0	0	0	0	0	0	0	0	1	1	TX-A-35	M. PARSONS	1967
TX-A-33	Small Hamlet	Lower Piedmont	0.9	15	0	0	0	0	0	0	0	0	0	1	TX-A-37	M. PARSONS	1967
TX-A-34	Hamlet	Lower Piedmont	6.0	60	0	0	0	0	0	0	0	1	0	0	TX-A-38	M. PARSONS	1967
TX-A-35	Sm Disp Village	Lower Piedmont	30.0	400	0	0	1	0	0	0	0	0	1	1	TX-A-34	M. PARSONS	1967
TX-A-36	Small Hamlet	Lower Piedmont	1.0	10	0	0	0	0	0	0	0	0	1	1	TX-A-34	M. PARSONS	1967
TX-A-37	Hamlet	Lower Piedmont	5.0	50	0	0	0	0	0	0	1	0	0	1	TX-A-34	M. PARSONS	1967
TX-A-38	Lg Disp Village	Lower Piedmont	65.0	650	0	0	1	0	0	0	0	1	1	1	TX-A-33	M. PARSONS	1967
TX-A-39	Sm Disp Village	Lower Piedmont	10.0	150	0	0	0	0	0	0	1	0	1	1	TX-A-33	M. PARSONS	1967
TX-A-40	Lg Disp Village	Lower Piedmont	100.0	1500	0	0	0	0	0	0	1	2	1	1	TX-A-24	M. PARSONS	1967
TX-A-41	Hamlet	Lower Piedmont	3.0	60	0	0	0	0	0	0	0	1	1	1	TX-A-23	M. PARSONS	1967
TX-A-42	Questionable	Lakebed	2.0	0	0	0	0	0	0	0	0	0	0	1	TX-A-54	J. PARSONS	1967

Early Aztec and Late Aztec occupations are tabulated on a presence-absence basis.

TEXCOCO REGION - ENVIRONMENTAL DATA
Aztec Sites

Site Number	Environmental Zone	UTM Coordinates East	North	Elev (in m)	Rainfall (in mm)	Modern Soil Depth	Modern Erosion	Modern Land use
TX-A-43	Lakebed	505.10	2154.10	2240	600	Deep	None	None
TX-A-44	Lakeshore Plain	506.80	2155.10	2240	600	Deep	None	Grazing
TX-A-45	Lakeshore Plain	507.50	2155.60	2240	600	Deep	None	Agricultural
TX-A-46	Lakeshore Plain	508.70	2155.40	2240	600	Deep	None	Agricultural
TX-A-47	Lakeshore Plain	507.90	2157.00	2240	600	Deep	None	Grazing
TX-A-48	Lakeshore Plain	508.00	2157.90	2250	600	Deep	None	Agricultural
TX-A-49	Lakeshore Plain	509.60	2157.50	2250	600	Deep	None	Agricultural
TX-A-50	Lakeshore Plain	509.80	2156.30	2240	600	Deep	None	Agricultural
TX-A-51	Lakeshore Plain	509.80	2155.30	2240	600	Deep	None	None
TX-A-52	Lakeshore Plain	510.30	2153.70	2240	600	Deep	None	Agricultural
TX-A-53	Lakeshore Plain	511.10	2152.80	2245	600	Deep	None	Agricultural
TX-A-54	Lakeshore Plain	511.60	2154.60	2250	610	Deep	None	Settlement
TX-A-55	Lakeshore Plain	511.20	2155.70	2245	600	Deep	None	Agricultural
TX-A-56	Lakeshore Plain	513.00	2157.10	2275	620	Deep	Very Slight	Settlement
TX-A-57	Lower Piedmont	516.00	2155.60	2335	660	Shallow-Med	Moderate-Deep	Agricultural
TX-A-58	Lower Piedmont	517.90	2154.60	2385	696	Shallow	Deep	Grazing
TX-A-59	Lower Piedmont	520.10	2154.20	2495	740	Very Shallow	Deep	Agricultural
TX-A-60	Upper Piedmont	520.90	2155.20	2505	750	Shallow	Moderate-Deep	Grazing
TX-A-61	Upper Piedmont	519.70	2155.20	2575	700	Shallow	Moderate	Grazing
TX-A-62	Upper Piedmont	519.30	2155.40	2590	690	Shallow	Slight-Moderate	Grazing
TX-A-63	Lower Piedmont	520.20	2155.90	2440	690	Shallow-Med	Slight-Moderate	Grazing
TX-A-64	Lower Piedmont	516.90	2156.90	2340	660	Shallow	Moderate	Grazing
TX-A-65	Lower Piedmont	518.00	2157.10	2335	670	Shallow	Moderate-Deep	Grazing & Agri
TX-A-66	Lower Piedmont	519.30	2157.10	2360	680	Shallow	Moderate	Agricultural
TX-A-67	Lower Piedmont	518.30	2158.60	2415	670	Shallow	Moderate	Grazing & Agri
TX-A-68	Lower Piedmont	518.40	2159.40	2335	670	Shallow	Moderate-Deep	Grazing & Agri
TX-A-69	Lower Piedmont	520.30	2158.50	2455	690	Very Shallow	Deep	Grazing & Agri
TX-A-70	Upper Piedmont	521.30	2158.40	2510	730	Very Shallow	Deep	Grazing
TX-A-71	Upper Piedmont	521.40	2158.10	2515	730	Shallow	Deep	Grazing
TX-A-72	Upper Piedmont	521.70	2159.70	2560	700	Very Shallow	Deep	None
TX-A-73	Upper Piedmont	523.90	2160.10	2570	740	Very Shallow	Deep	Grazing
TX-A-74	Upper Piedmont	523.90	2157.90	2635	800	Very Shallow	Deep	Grazing
TX-A-75	Upper Piedmont	523.80	2155.40	2665	840	Shallow	Deep	Settlement
TX-A-76	Upper Piedmont	521.90	2157.40	2585	750	Fully Eroded	Deep	Grazing
TX-A-77	Upper Piedmont	522.00	2156.60	2535	750	Shallow-Med	Deep	Grazing
TX-A-78	Upper Piedmont	522.60	2155.50	2565	780	Very Shallow	Deep	None
TX-A-79	Upper Piedmont	523.00	2154.30	2595	810	Fully Eroded	Deep	None
TX-A-80	Upper Piedmont	521.50	2155.00	2595	750	Fully Eroded	Deep	Grazing
TX-A-81	Upper Piedmont	521.10	2156.20	2505	730	Fully Eroded	Deep	Grazing
TX-A-82	Upper Piedmont	521.10	2154.20	2570	770	Very Shallow	Deep	Grazing
TX-A-83	Upper Piedmont	522.60	2153.70	2600	840	Shallow	Deep	Grazing
TX-A-84	Upper Piedmont	517.20	2153.00	2600	850	Very Shallow	Deep	Grazing

TEXCOCO REGION - PREHISPANIC SETTLEMENT DATA
Aztec Sites

SITE NUMBER	CLASSIFICATION	ENVIRONMENTAL ZONE	AREA (in ha)	POP.	EF	MF	LF	TF	EC	LC	ET	LT	EA	LA	TEMPORARY SITE NO.	SUPERVISOR	YEAR
TX-A-43	Questionable	Lakebed	3.0	0	0	0	0	0	0	0	0	1	0	1	TX-A-55	J. PARSONS	1967
TX-A-44	Hamlet	Lakeshore Plain	2.0	40	0	0	1	1	0	0	0	1	1	1	TX-A-1	J. PARSONS	1967
TX-A-45	Hamlet	Lakeshore Plain	5.0	100	0	0	1	0	0	0	0	1	0	1	TX-A-2	J. PARSONS	1967
TX-A-46	Sm Disp Village	Lakeshore Plain	20.0	200	0	0	0	0	0	0	0	1	1	1	TX-A-3	J. PARSONS	1967
TX-A-47	Hamlet	Lakeshore Plain	5.0	100	0	0	0	0	0	0	0	1	0	1	TX-A-51	J. PARSONS	1967
TX-A-48	Small Hamlet	Lakeshore Plain	0.1	15	0	0	0	0	0	0	0	0	0	1	TX-A-53	J. PARSONS	1967
TX-A-49	Sm Disp Village	Lakeshore Plain	25.0	300	0	0	0	0	0	0	0	0	1	1	TX-A-52	J. PARSONS	1967
TX-A-50	Hamlet	Lakeshore Plain	3.0	60	0	0	0	0	0	0	0	0	0	1	TX-A-6	J. PARSONS	1967
TX-A-51	Small Hamlet	Lakeshore Plain	0.2	20	0	0	0	0	0	0	0	0	0	1	TX-A-5	J. PARSONS	1967
TX-A-52	Hamlet	Lakeshore Plain	3.0	60	0	0	0	0	0	0	0	0	1	1	TX-A-4	J. PARSONS	1967
TX-A-53	Sm Disp Village	Lakeshore Plain	25.0	500	0	0	0	0	0	0	0	0	1	1	TX-A-9	J. PARSONS	1967
TX-A-54	Hamlet	Lakeshore Plain	5.0	60	0	0	0	0	0	0	0	0	0	1	TX-A-7	J. PARSONS	1967
TX-A-55	Small Hamlet	Lakeshore Plain	0.9	15	0	0	0	0	0	0	0	0	1	1	TX-A-8	J. PARSONS	1967
TX-A-56	Regional Center	Lakeshore Plain	450.0	25000	0	0	0	0	0	0	1	2	0	1	TX-A-11	J. PARSONS	1967
TX-A-57	Sm Disp Village	Lower Piedmont	50.0	400	0	0	0	0	1	0	0	0	1	1	TX-A-17	J. PARSONS	1967
TX-A-58	Sm Disp Village	Lower Piedmont	100.0	500	0	0	1	1	0	0	0	0	0	1	TX-A-23	J. PARSONS	1967
TX-A-59	Lg Disp Village	Lower Piedmont	75.0	750	0	0	0	1	0	0	0	0	0	1	TX-A-22	J. PARSONS	1967
TX-A-60	Sm Disp Village	Upper Piedmont	20.0	200	0	0	0	0	0	0	0	0	0	1	TX-A-21	J. PARSONS	1967
TX-A-61	Ceremonial Ctr	Upper Piedmont	5.0	0	0	0	0	0	0	0	0	1	0	1	TX-A-16	J. PARSONS	1967
TX-A-62	Ceremonial Ctr	Upper Piedmont	15.0	0	0	0	0	1	0	0	0	0	0	1	TX-A-31	J. PARSONS	1967
TX-A-63	Small Hamlet	Lower Piedmont	0.9	15	0	0	0	0	0	0	0	0	0	1	TX-A-44	J. PARSONS	1967
TX-A-64	Sm Disp Village	Lower Piedmont	35.0	400	0	0	0	0	0	1	0	0	0	1	TX-A-13	J. PARSONS	1967
TX-A-65	Sm Disp Village	Lower Piedmont	25.0	300	0	1	2	1	0	2	0	0	0	1	TX-A-14	J. PARSONS	1967
TX-A-66	Sm Disp Village	Lower Piedmont	50.0	400	0	0	0	1	0	2	0	0	0	1	TX-A-15	J. PARSONS	1967
TX-A-67	Ceremonial Ctr	Lower Piedmont	5.0	0	0	0	0	1	0	0	0	0	0	1	TX-A-56	J. PARSONS	1967
TX-A-68	Small Hamlet	Lower Piedmont	5.0	50	0	0	0	0	0	0	0	0	0	0	TX-A-58	J. PARSONS	1967
TX-A-69	Sm Disp Village	Lower Piedmont	30.0	400	0	0	0	0	0	0	0	0	0	1	TX-A-39	J. PARSONS	1967
TX-A-70	Hamlet	Upper Piedmont	7.0	60	0	0	0	0	0	0	0	0	0	1	TX-A-40	J. PARSONS	1967
TX-A-71	Hamlet	Upper Piedmont	9.0	90	0	0	0	0	0	0	0	0	0	1	TX-A-43	J. PARSONS	1967
TX-A-72	Lg Disp Village	Upper Piedmont	400.0	8000	0	0	0	0	0	0	0	0	0	1	TX-A-42	J. PARSONS	1967
TX-A-73	Questionable	Upper Piedmont	30.0	350	0	0	0	0	0	0	0	0	0	1	TX-A-49	J. PARSONS	1967
TX-A-74	Questionable	Upper Piedmont	3.0	40	0	0	0	0	0	0	0	0	0	0		J. PARSONS	1967
TX-A-75	Hamlet	Upper Piedmont	4.0	40	0	0	0	0	0	0	0	0	0	1		J. PARSONS	1967
TX-A-76	Sm Disp Village	Upper Piedmont	15.0	250	0	0	0	0	0	0	0	0	0	0	TX-A-38	J. PARSONS	1967
TX-A-77	Hamlet	Upper Piedmont	7.0	70	0	0	0	0	0	0	0	0	0	1	TX-A-32	J. PARSONS	1967
TX-A-78	Lg Disp Village	Upper Piedmont	100.0	1500	0	0	0	0	0	0	0	0	0	1	TX-A-35	J. PARSONS	1967
TX-A-79	Hamlet	Upper Piedmont	11.0	100	0	0	0	0	0	0	0	0	0	1	TX-A-33	J. PARSONS	1967
TX-A-80	Sm Disp Village	Upper Piedmont	30.0	150	0	0	0	0	0	0	0	0	0	1	TX-A-28	J. PARSONS	1967
TX-A-81	Sm Disp Village	Upper Piedmont	30.0	300	0	0	0	0	0	0	0	0	0	1	TX-A-25	J. PARSONS	1967
TX-A-82	Ceremonial Ctr	Upper Piedmont	0.1	0	0	0	0	0	0	0	0	0	0	1	TX-A-36	J. PARSONS	1967
TX-A-83	Small Hamlet	Upper Piedmont	0.9	15	0	0	0	0	0	0	0	0	0	1	TX-A-30	J. PARSONS	1967
TX-A-84	Small Hamlet	Upper Piedmont	0.9	15	0	0	0	0	0	0	0	0	1	1	TX-A-27	J. PARSONS	1967

Early Aztec and Late Aztec occupations are tabulated on a presence-absence basis.

TEXCOCO REGION - ENVIRONMENTAL DATA
Aztec Sites

Site Number	Environmental Zone	UTM Coordinates East	North	Elev (in m)	Rainfall (in mm)	Modern Soil Depth	Modern Erosion	Modern Land use
TX-A-85	Upper Piedmont	520.80	2153.90	2525	760	Shallow	Deep	Grazing
TX-A-86	Upper Piedmont	520.10	2154.20	2520	730	Fully Eroded	Deep	Grazing
TX-A-87	Lower Piedmont	514.60	2153.10	2430	660	Shallow-Med	Moderate	Grazing & Agri
TX-A-88	Lower Piedmont	514.20	2150.70	2320	670	Shallow-Med	Slight-Moderate	Agricultural
TX-A-89	Lower Piedmont	518.30	2151.20	2475	740	Shallow	Deep	Grazing
TX-A-90	Lower Piedmont	518.40	2150.30	2475	750	Shallow	Deep	Grazing
TX-A-91	Lower Piedmont	518.30	2149.70	2495	750	Shallow	Slight-Moderate	Grazing
TX-A-92	Upper Piedmont	519.00	2149.50	2540	770	Shallow	Deep	Grazing
TX-A-93	Upper Piedmont	519.70	2148.60	2600	790	Shallow	Moderate	Grazing
TX-A-94	Lower Piedmont	514.50	2147.60	2345	680	Shallow	Moderate	Grazing & Agri
TX-A-95	Lower Piedmont	514.30	2146.40	2340	680	Shallow	Moderate	Grazing & Agri
TX-A-96	Lower Piedmont	516.20	2144.90	2400	700	Shallow	Moderate	Grazing & Agri
TX-A-97	Lower Piedmont	516.30	2144.20	2400	700	Shallow	Moderate	Grazing & Agri
TX-A-98	Lower Piedmont	517.30	2144.60	2540	730	Shallow	Deep	Grazing
TX-A-99	Lower Piedmont	516.60	2142.90	2420	700	Shallow-Med	Slight-Moderate	Settlement
TX-A-100	Lower Piedmont	514.90	2142.60	2335	670	Medium	Slight	Agricultural
TX-A-101	Lower Piedmont	513.90	2143.40	2420	670	Shallow	Moderate-Deep	Grazing
TX-A-102	Lower Piedmont	512.50	2143.20	2290	650	Medium	Slight-Moderate	Grazing & Agri
TX-A-103	Lakeshore Plain	510.20	2144.60	2255	630	Medium	Slight-Moderate	Grazing & Agri
TX-A-104	Lakeshore Plain	507.90	2144.30	2250	600	Deep	None	Agricultural
TX-A-105	Lower Piedmont	506.90	2142.00	2310	610	Shallow-Med	Slight-Moderate	Grazing
TX-A-106	Lakeshore Plain	504.50	2143.40	2240	600	Deep	None	Agricultural
TX-A-107	Lakeshore Plain	502.80	2144.20	2240	600	Deep	None	Grazing
TX-A-108	Upper Piedmont	504.60	2144.60	2520	600	Shallow-Med	Slight	Grazing
TX-A-109	Lakeshore Plain	506.60	2146.20	2245	600	Deep	None	Settlement
TX-A-110	Lakeshore Plain	504.50	2147.80	2240	600	Deep	None	Grazing

TEXCOCO REGION - PREHISPANIC SETTLEMENT DATA
Aztec Sites

SITE NUMBER	CLASSIFICATION	ENVIRONMENTAL ZONE	AREA (in ha)	POP.	OTHER OCCUPATIONS										TEMPORARY SITE NO.	SURVEY RECORDS	
					EF	MF	LF	TF	EC	LC	ET	LT	EA	LA		SUPERVISOR	YEAR
TX-A-85	Small Hamlet	Upper Piedmont	0.9	15	0	0	0	0	0	0	0	0	1	0	TX-A-26	J. PARSONS	1967
TX-A-86	Sm Disp Village	Upper Piedmont	20.0	300	0	0	0	1	0	0	0	0	0	1	TX-A-20	J. PARSONS	1967
TX-A-87	Local Center	Lower Piedmont	840.0	23000	0	0	0	0	0	0	0	0	1	1	TX-A-10	J. PARSONS	1967
TX-A-88	Local Center	Lower Piedmont	210.0	11000	0	0	0	0	0	0	0	0	1	1		J. PARSONS	1967
TX-A-89	Hamlet	Lower Piedmont	4.0	50	0	0	0	0	0	0	0	0	0	1		J. PARSONS	1967
TX-A-90	Hamlet	Lower Piedmont	4.0	50	0	0	0	0	0	0	0	0	0	1		J. PARSONS	1967
TX-A-91	Hamlet	Lower Piedmont	15.0	100	0	0	0	0	0	0	0	0	0	1		J. PARSONS	1967
TX-A-92	Hamlet	Upper Piedmont	7.0	50	0	0	0	0	0	0	0	0	0	1		J. PARSONS	1967
TX-A-93	Hamlet	Upper Piedmont	2.0	40	0	0	0	0	0	0	0	0	0	1		J. PARSONS	1967
TX-A-94	Hamlet	Lower Piedmont	7.0	50	0	0	0	0	0	0	0	0	0	1		J. PARSONS	1967
TX-A-95	Hamlet	Lower Piedmont	10.0	100	0	0	0	0	0	0	0	0	0	1		J. PARSONS	1967
TX-A-96	Hamlet	Lower Piedmont	4.0	50	0	0	0	0	0	0	0	0	0	1		J. PARSONS	1967
TX-A-97	Hamlet	Lower Piedmont	4.0	50	0	0	0	0	0	0	0	0	0	1		J. PARSONS	1967
TX-A-98	Hamlet	Lower Piedmont	4.0	50	0	0	0	0	0	0	0	0	0	1		J. PARSONS	1967
TX-A-99	Local Center	Lower Piedmont	85.0	2500	0	0	0	0	0	0	0	0	1	1	TX-A-11	R. HIRNING	1967
TX-A-100	Ceremonial Ctr	Lower Piedmont	5.0	0	0	0	0	0	0	0	0	0	0	0	TX-A-10	R. HIRNING	1967
TX-A-101	Ceremonial Ctr	Lower Piedmont	1.0	0	0	0	0	0	1	1	1	0	0	0	TX-A-9	R. HIRNING	1967
TX-A-102	Hamlet	Lower Piedmont	12.0	100	0	0	0	0	1	1	1	0	0	0	TX-T-4	R. HIRNING	1967
TX-A-103	Sm Disp Village	Lakeshore Plain	45.0	450	0	0	0	0	1	1	1	1	0	1	TX-T-4	R. HIRNING	1967
TX-A-104	Hamlet	Lakeshore Plain	5.0	50	0	0	0	0	0	0	0	0	0	1		R. HIRNING	1967
TX-A-105	Hamlet	Lower Piedmont	3.0	50	0	0	0	1	0	0	0	0	0	1	TX-A-8	R. HIRNING	1967
TX-A-106	Questionable	Lakeshore Plain	1.0	50	0	0	0	0	0	0	0	1	1	1	TX-A-7	R. HIRNING	1967
TX-A-107	Questionable	Lakeshore Plain	32.0	400	0	0	0	0	0	0	0	1	1	1	TX-A-6	R. HIRNING	1967
TX-A-108	Ceremonial Ctr	Upper Piedmont	0.1	0	0	0	0	1	0	0	0	1	1	1	TX-A-4	R. HIRNING	1967
TX-A-109	Local Center	Lakeshore Plain	260.0	12000	0	0	0	0	0	0	0	0	1	1	TX-A-3	R. HIRNING	1967
TX-A-110	Sm Disp Village	Lakeshore Plain	17.0	250	0	0	0	0	0	0	0	0	1	1	TX-A-1	R. HIRNING	1967

Early Aztec and Late Aztec occupations are tabulated on a presence-absence basis.

ZUMPANGO REGION - ENVIRONMENTAL DATA
Late Formative Sites

Site Number	Environmental Zone	UTM Coordinates East	North	Elev (in m)	Rainfall (in mm)	Modern Soil Depth	Modern Erosion	Modern Land use
ZU-LF-1	Lower Piedmont	493.70	2206.20	2340	600	Medium	None	Agricultural

ZUMPANGO REGION - PREHISPANIC SETTLEMENT DATA
Late Formative Sites

SITE NUMBER	CLASSIFICATION	ENVIRONMENTAL ZONE	AREA (in ha)	POP.	OTHER OCCUPATIONS										TEMPORARY SITE NO.	SURVEY RECORDS	
					EF	MF	LF	TF	EC	LC	ET	LT	EA	LA		SUPERVISOR	YEAR
ZU-LF-1	Hamlet	Lower Piedmont	3.0	30	O	O	O	O	O	O	O	O	O	O	ZU-LF-1	J. PARSONS	1973

ZUMPANGO REGION - ENVIRONMENTAL DATA
Terminal Formative Sites

Site Number	Environmental Zone	UTM Coordinates East	North	Elev (in m)	Rainfall (in mm)	Modern Soil Depth	Modern Erosion	Modern Land use
ZU-TF-1	Lower Piedmont	489.18	2205.53	2310	600	Shallow	Deep	Agricultural
ZU-TF-2	Lakeshore Plain	484.30	2206.03	2255	600	Medium	None	Agricultural
ZU-TF-3	Lower Piedmont	489.00	2202.38	2315	600	Shallow	Moderate-Deep	Agricultural
ZU-TF-4	Lower Piedmont	488.28	2198.55	2300	670	Shallow-Med	None	Agricultural
ZU-TF-5	Lower Piedmont	478.82	2187.53	2360	660	Medium	Moderate-Deep	Agricultural
ZU-TF-6	Lower Piedmont	492.88	2191.93	2325	670	Shallow	Deep	Agricultural
ZU-TF-7	Lower Piedmont	494.03	2191.25	2300	670	Medium	Moderate	Agricultural
ZU-TF-8	Lakeshore Plain	493.07	2190.13	2290	680	Medium	None	Agricultural
ZU-TF-9	Lakeshore Plain	492.47	2189.38	2290	690	Medium	None	Agricultural
ZU-TF-10	Lower Piedmont	482.22	2190.68	2295	700	Medium	None	Agricultural
ZU-TF-11	Lower Piedmont	478.82	2187.43	2290	670	Shallow	Deep	Grazing & Agri
ZU-TF-12	Lower Piedmont	497.93	2188.32	2280	630	Shallow	None	Agricultural
ZU-TF-13	Lakeshore Plain	492.88	2187.75	2270	690	Deep	None	Agricultural
ZU-TF-14	Lakeshore Plain	491.80	2187.53	2260	700	Deep	None	Agricultural
ZU-TF-15	Lakeshore Plain	491.57	2187.30	2255	700	Deep	None	Agricultural
ZU-TF-16	Lakeshore Plain	491.55	2187.05	2250	700	Deep	None	Agricultural
ZU-TF-17	Lakeshore Plain	492.60	2187.40	2260	690	Deep	None	Agricultural
ZU-TF-18	Lakeshore Plain	492.60	2186.97	2255	690	Medium	None	Agricultural
ZU-TF-19	Lakeshore Plain	492.70	2186.65	2250	680	Medium	None	Agricultural
ZU-TF-20	Lakeshore Plain	492.47	2186.35	2245	700	Deep	None	Agricultural
ZU-TF-21	Lakeshore Plain	495.00	2186.65	2247	650	Medium	None	Agricultural
ZU-TF-22	Lakeshore Plain	494.03	2185.57	2245	650	Deep	None	Agricultural
ZU-TF-23	Lakeshore Plain	493.47	2185.50	2245	650	Medium	None	Agricultural
ZU-TF-24	Lakeshore Plain	493.35	2185.28	2245	650	Medium	None	Agricultural
ZU-TF-25	Lakeshore Plain	492.63	2184.90	2245	650	Deep	None	Agricultural
ZU-TF-26	Lakeshore Plain	492.97	2184.00	2245	630	Deep	None	Agricultural

ZUMPANGO REGION - PREHISPANIC SETTLEMENT DATA
Terminal Formative Sites

SITE NUMBER	CLASSIFICATION	ENVIRONMENTAL ZONE	AREA (in ha)	POP.	OTHER OCCUPATIONS										TEMPORARY SITE NO.	SURVEY RECORDS	
					EF	MF	LF	TF	EC	LC	ET	LT	EA	LA		SUPERVISOR	YEAR
ZU-TF-1	Small Hamlet	Lower Piedmont	0.1	5	0	0	0	0	1	1	0	0	0	0	ZU-CL-16	M. PARSONS	1973
ZU-TF-2	Small Hamlet	Lakeshore Plain	0.5	5	0	0	0	0	1	0	0	0	0	0	ZU-CL-5	M. PARSONS	1973
ZU-TF-3	Hamlet	Lower Piedmont	2.9	40	0	0	0	0	1	0	0	0	0	0	ZU-TF-17	J. PARSONS	1973
ZU-TF-4	Small Hamlet	Lower Piedmont	0.5	10	0	0	0	0	1	1	0	0	0	0	ZU-CL-14	J. PARSONS	1973
ZU-TF-5	Hamlet	Lower Piedmont	3.5	70	0	0	0	0	1	1	0	0	0	1	ZU-TF-2	J. PARSONS	1973
ZU-TF-6	Small Hamlet	Lower Piedmont	2.3	30	0	0	0	0	1	0	0	0	0	0	ZU-CL-25	J. PARSONS	1973
ZU-TF-7	Hamlet	Lower Piedmont	7.8	100	0	0	0	0	0	0	0	0	0	3	ZU-TF-1	J. PARSONS	1973
ZU-TF-8	Hamlet	Lakeshore Plain	4.2	40	0	0	0	0	0	0	0	0	0	0	ZU-TF-3	J. PARSONS	1973
ZU-TF-9	Small Hamlet	Lakeshore Plain	0.7	10	0	0	0	0	0	0	0	0	0	0	ZU-TF-4	J. PARSONS	1973
ZU-TF-10	Small Hamlet	Lower Piedmont	0.1	5	0	0	0	0	1	0	0	0	0	0	ZU-CL-36	M. PARSONS	1973
ZU-TF-11	Hamlet	Lower Piedmont	2.4	60	0	0	0	0	1	1	0	0	0	1	ZU-TF-2	M. PARSONS	1973
ZU-TF-12	Small Hamlet	Lower Piedmont	0.8	10	0	0	0	0	1	1	0	0	0	0	ZU-CL-35	J. PARSONS	1973
ZU-TF-13	Small Hamlet	Lakeshore Plain	1.3	15	0	0	0	0	0	0	0	0	0	0	ZU-TF-8	J. PARSONS	1973
ZU-TF-14	Small Hamlet	Lakeshore Plain	1.3	15	0	0	0	0	0	0	0	0	0	1	ZU-TF-7	J. PARSONS	1973
ZU-TF-15	Small Hamlet	Lakeshore Plain	1.1	10	0	0	0	0	0	0	0	0	0	0	ZU-TF-12	J. PARSONS	1973
ZU-TF-16	Small Hamlet	Lakeshore Plain	1.8	20	0	0	0	0	0	0	0	0	0	1	ZU-TF-6	J. PARSONS	1973
ZU-TF-17	Hamlet	Lakeshore Plain	3.5	40	0	0	0	0	0	0	0	0	0	0	ZU-TF-9	J. PARSONS	1973
ZU-TF-18	Small Hamlet	Lakeshore Plain	1.0	10	0	0	0	0	0	0	0	0	0	0	ZU-TF-10	J. PARSONS	1973
ZU-TF-19	Small Hamlet	Lakeshore Plain	0.8	10	0	0	0	0	0	0	0	0	0	0	ZU-TF-11	J. PARSONS	1973
ZU-TF-20	Hamlet	Lakeshore Plain	3.0	60	0	0	0	0	0	0	0	0	0	0	ZU-TF-5	J. PARSONS	1973
ZU-TF-21	Small Hamlet	Lakeshore Plain	0.8	10	0	0	0	0	1	1	1	0	1	0	ZU-CL-37	J. PARSONS	1973
ZU-TF-22	Hamlet	Lakeshore Plain	1.2	30	0	0	0	0	0	0	0	0	0	0	ZU-TF-16	J. PARSONS	1973
ZU-TF-23	Small Hamlet	Lakeshore Plain	0.9	10	0	0	0	0	0	0	0	1	0	0	ZU-TF-15	J. PARSONS	1973
ZU-TF-24	Small Hamlet	Lakeshore Plain	1.4	20	0	0	0	0	0	0	0	1	0	0	ZU-TF-14	J. PARSONS	1973
ZU-TF-25	Hamlet	Lakeshore Plain	4.0	100	0	0	0	0	1	1	0	0	0	0	ZU-TF-13	J. PARSONS	1973
ZU-TF-26	Small Hamlet	Lakeshore Plain	0.5	5	0	0	0	0	0	1	0	0	0	0	ZU-CL-40	J. PARSONS	1973

ZUMPANGO REGION - ENVIRONMENTAL DATA
Early Classic Sites

Site Number	Environmental Zone	UTM Coordinates East	North	Elev (in m)	Rainfall (in mm)	Modern Soil Depth	Modern Erosion	Modern Land use
ZU-EC-1	Lower Piedmont	495.85	2206.15	2348	600	Medium	None	Agricultural
ZU-EC-2	Lower Piedmont	495.25	2206.18	2340	600	Medium	Slight	Agricultural
ZU-EC-3	Lower Piedmont	494.00	2205.35	2345	600	Medium	None	Agricultural
ZU-EC-4	Lower Piedmont	497.78	2203.32	2340	600	Medium	None	Agricultural
ZU-EC-5	Lower Piedmont	497.50	2203.10	2330	600	Medium	None	Agricultural
ZU-EC-6	Lower Piedmont	492.60	2204.85	2345	600	Medium	None	Agricultural
ZU-EC-7	Lower Piedmont	492.32	2203.65	2345	600	Deep	None	Agricultural
ZU-EC-8	Lower Piedmont	489.25	2205.60	2315	600	Shallow	Deep	Agricultural
ZU-EC-9	Lower Piedmont	488.95	2205.70	2315	600	Shallow	None	Agricultural
ZU-EC-10	Lower Piedmont	486.47	2208.38	2288	600	Shallow	None	Agricultural
ZU-EC-11	Lower Piedmont	485.50	2209.35	2270	600	Medium	None	Agricultural
ZU-EC-12	Lower Piedmont	484.38	2209.40	2243	600	Shallow	Moderate	Grazing
ZU-EC-13	Lower Piedmont	484.30	2209.05	2243	600	Shallow	Moderate	Grazing
ZU-EC-14	Lower Piedmont	481.63	2207.13	2175	600	Deep	None	Agricultural
ZU-EC-15	Lower Piedmont	482.80	2207.13	2200	600	Shallow	None	Agricultural
ZU-EC-16	Lower Piedmont	485.50	2206.57	2275	600	Shallow	Deep	Agricultural
ZU-EC-17	Lower Piedmont	484.30	2206.03	2255	600	Medium	None	Agricultural
ZU-EC-18	Lower Piedmont	483.70	2206.07	2240	600	Medium	None	Agricultural
ZU-EC-19	Lower Piedmont	485.00	2205.57	2252	600	Medium	None	Agricultural
ZU-EC-20	Lower Piedmont	484.25	2204.88	2225	600	Medium	None	Agricultural
ZU-EC-21	Lower Piedmont	484.03	2204.53	2225	600	Medium	None	Agricultural
ZU-EC-22	Lower Piedmont	482.28	2204.15	2190	620	Deep	None	Agricultural
ZU-EC-23	Lower Piedmont	481.75	2204.50	2190	620	Deep	None	Agricultural
ZU-EC-24	Lower Piedmont	483.10	2203.07	2195	630	Medium	None	Agricultural
ZU-EC-25	Lower Piedmont	484.35	2202.70	2210	630	Medium	None	Agricultural
ZU-EC-26	Lower Piedmont	485.15	2204.25	2230	600	Medium	None	Agricultural
ZU-EC-27	Lower Piedmont	485.55	2204.35	2245	600	Medium	None	Agricultural
ZU-EC-28	Lower Piedmont	485.20	2203.82	2225	600	Medium	None	Agricultural
ZU-EC-29	Lower Piedmont	486.15	2203.45	2228	600	Deep	None	Agricultural
ZU-EC-30	Lower Piedmont	488.72	2204.25	2258	600	Deep	None	Agricultural
ZU-EC-31	Lower Piedmont	489.05	2202.38	2320	600	Shallow	Moderate-Deep	Agricultural
ZU-EC-32	Lower Piedmont	489.05	2201.75	2330	610	Shallow	Moderate	Agricultural
ZU-EC-33	Lower Piedmont	493.22	2201.10	2290	600	Shallow	Deep	Grazing
ZU-EC-34	Lower Piedmont	492.50	2200.25	2305	600	Shallow	Deep	Grazing & Agri
ZU-EC-35	Lower Piedmont	495.10	2200.93	2325	600	Shallow	Moderate	Agricultural
ZU-EC-36	Lower Piedmont	495.38	2201.55	2325	600	Shallow	Slight	Agricultural
ZU-EC-37	Lower Piedmont	495.30	2201.72	2325	600	Shallow	Slight	Grazing & Agri
ZU-EC-38	Lower Piedmont	494.93	2194.57	2347	610	Shallow	Moderate	Grazing & Agri
ZU-EC-39	Lower Piedmont	494.97	2194.82	2315	630	Medium	None	Agricultural
ZU-EC-40	Lower Piedmont	494.65	2194.63	2310	640	Medium	None	Agricultural
ZU-EC-41	Lower Piedmont	494.57	2193.50	2315	650	Medium	None	Agricultural
ZU-EC-42	Lower Piedmont	493.70	2194.63	2340	640	Shallow	Deep	Grazing

ZUMPANGO REGION – PREHISPANIC SETTLEMENT DATA
Early Classic Sites

SITE NUMBER	CLASSIFICATION	ENVIRONMENTAL ZONE	AREA (in ha)	POP.	EF	MF	LF	TF	EC	LC	ET	LT	EA	LA	TEMPORARY SITE NO.	SUPERVISOR	YEAR
ZU-EC-1	Sm Nucl Village	Lower Piedmont	5.1	200	0	0	0	0	1	0	0	0	0	0	ZU-CL-5	J. PARSONS	1973
ZU-EC-2	Hamlet	Lower Piedmont	1.7	60	0	0	0	0	1	0	0	0	0	0	ZU-CL-3	J. PARSONS	1973
ZU-EC-3	Hamlet	Lower Piedmont	3.0	30	0	0	0	0	1	0	0	0	0	0	ZU-CL-2	J. PARSONS	1973
ZU-EC-4	Hamlet	Lower Piedmont	3.5	80	0	0	0	0	1	0	0	0	0	0	ZU-CL-7	J. PARSONS	1973
ZU-EC-5	Small Hamlet	Lower Piedmont	0.5	10	0	0	0	0	1	0	0	0	0	1	ZU-CL-6	J. PARSONS	1973
ZU-EC-6	Small Hamlet	Lower Piedmont	1.8	20	0	0	0	0	1	0	0	0	0	0	ZU-CL-9	J. PARSONS	1973
ZU-EC-7	Hamlet	Lower Piedmont	3.0	70	0	0	0	0	1	0	1	0	0	0	ZU-CL-10	J. PARSONS	1973
ZU-EC-8	Hamlet	Lower Piedmont	2.4	50	0	0	0	1	1	0	0	0	0	1	ZU-CL-16	M. PARSONS	1973
ZU-EC-9	Small Hamlet	Lower Piedmont	0.4	5	0	0	0	0	1	0	0	0	0	0	ZU-CL-15	M. PARSONS	1973
ZU-EC-10	Hamlet	Lower Piedmont	2.1	40	0	0	0	0	1	0	0	0	0	0	ZU-CL-8	M. PARSONS	1973
ZU-EC-11	Small Hamlet	Lower Piedmont	1.2	10	0	0	0	0	1	0	0	0	0	0	ZU-CL-20	M. PARSONS	1973
ZU-EC-12	Hamlet	Lower Piedmont	2.4	40	0	0	0	0	1	0	1	0	0	0	ZU-CL-19	M. PARSONS	1973
ZU-EC-13	Hamlet	Lower Piedmont	1.6	30	0	0	0	0	1	0	1	0	0	1	ZU-CL-18	M. PARSONS	1973
ZU-EC-14	Hamlet	Lower Piedmont	1.1	20	0	0	0	0	1	0	1	0	0	0	ZU-CL-17	M. PARSONS	1973
ZU-EC-15	Small Hamlet	Lower Piedmont	0.7	10	0	0	0	0	1	0	0	0	0	0	ZU-CL-7	M. PARSONS	1973
ZU-EC-16	Small Hamlet	Lower Piedmont	1.0	10	0	0	0	0	1	0	0	0	0	0	ZU-CL-9	M. PARSONS	1973
ZU-EC-17	Small Hamlet	Lower Piedmont	0.5	5	0	0	0	0	0	1	0	0	0	0	ZU-CL-5	M. PARSONS	1973
ZU-EC-18	Hamlet	Lower Piedmont	4.5	100	0	0	0	0	1	0	1	0	0	0	ZU-CL-6	M. PARSONS	1973
ZU-EC-19	Small Hamlet	Lower Piedmont	0.7	20	0	0	0	0	1	0	0	0	0	0	ZU-CL-10	M. PARSONS	1973
ZU-EC-20	Small Hamlet	Lower Piedmont	0.7	10	0	0	0	0	1	0	1	0	0	0	ZU-CL-4	M. PARSONS	1973
ZU-EC-21	Small Hamlet	Lower Piedmont	0.9	10	0	0	0	0	1	0	0	0	0	0	ZU-CL-3	M. PARSONS	1973
ZU-EC-22	Small Hamlet	Lower Piedmont	0.4	10	0	0	0	0	1	0	0	0	0	0	ZU-CL-2	M. PARSONS	1973
ZU-EC-23	Hamlet	Lower Piedmont	4.4	40	0	0	0	0	1	0	0	0	0	0	ZU-CL-1	M. PARSONS	1973
ZU-EC-24	Hamlet	Lower Piedmont	1.4	30	0	0	0	0	1	0	0	0	0	0	ZU-CL-31	M. PARSONS	1973
ZU-EC-25	Small Hamlet	Lower Piedmont	0.4	5	0	0	0	0	1	0	0	0	0	0	ZU-CL-32	M. PARSONS	1973
ZU-EC-26	Small Hamlet	Lower Piedmont	0.2	5	0	0	0	0	1	0	0	0	0	0	ZU-CL-11	M. PARSONS	1973
ZU-EC-27	Small Hamlet	Lower Piedmont	1.5	10	0	0	0	0	1	0	0	0	0	0	ZU-CL-25	M. PARSONS	1973
ZU-EC-28	Hamlet	Lower Piedmont	2.4	50	0	0	0	0	1	0	1	0	0	1	ZU-CL-12	M. PARSONS	1973
ZU-EC-29	Hamlet	Lower Piedmont	3.9	80	0	0	0	0	1	0	1	0	0	0	ZU-CL-13	M. PARSONS	1973
ZU-EC-30	Hamlet	Lower Piedmont	3.8	80	0	0	0	0	1	0	1	0	0	1	ZU-CL-14	M. PARSONS	1973
ZU-EC-31	Hamlet	Lower Piedmont	3.5	70	0	0	0	1	1	0	0	0	0	1	ZU-CL-43	J. PARSONS	1973
ZU-EC-32	Hamlet	Lower Piedmont	1.7	40	0	0	0	0	1	0	1	0	0	0	ZU-CL-42	J. PARSONS	1973
ZU-EC-33	Hamlet	Lower Piedmont	2.1	50	0	0	0	0	1	0	1	0	0	1	ZU-CL-11	J. PARSONS	1973
ZU-EC-34	Hamlet	Lower Piedmont	5.3	100	0	0	0	0	1	0	0	0	0	0	ZU-CL-12	J. PARSONS	1973
ZU-EC-35	Small Hamlet	Lower Piedmont	0.6	10	0	0	0	0	1	0	0	0	0	1	ZU-CL-15	J. PARSONS	1973
ZU-EC-36	Hamlet	Lower Piedmont	2.8	60	0	0	0	0	1	0	1	0	0	0	ZU-CL-16	J. PARSONS	1973
ZU-EC-37	Small Hamlet	Lower Piedmont	0.6	20	0	0	0	0	1	0	0	0	0	0	ZU-CL-17	J. PARSONS	1973
ZU-EC-38	Lg Nucl Village	Lower Piedmont	16.4	600	0	0	0	0	1	0	0	0	0	0	ZU-CL-18	J. PARSONS	1973
ZU-EC-39	Hamlet	Lower Piedmont	1.5	30	0	0	0	0	1	0	0	0	0	0	ZU-CL-21	J. PARSONS	1973
ZU-EC-40	Small Hamlet	Lower Piedmont	0.3	5	0	0	0	0	0	1	0	0	0	0	ZU-CL-20	J. PARSONS	1973
ZU-EC-41	Small Hamlet	Lower Piedmont	0.4	10	0	0	0	0	1	0	0	0	0	0	ZU-CL-22	J. PARSONS	1973
ZU-EC-42	Hamlet	Lower Piedmont	3.9	80	0	0	0	0	1	0	1	0	0	1	ZU-CL-19	J. PARSONS	1973

ZUMPANGO REGION - ENVIRONMENTAL DATA
Early Classic Sites

Site Number	Environmental Zone	UTM Coordinates East	UTM Coordinates North	Elev (in m)	Rainfall (in mm)	Modern Soil Depth	Modern Erosion	Modern Land use
ZU-EC-43	Lower Piedmont	492.18	2194.15	2351	660	Medium	Deep	Grazing
ZU-EC-44	Lakeshore Plain	489.25	2194.13	2285	690	Medium	None	Agricultural
ZU-EC-45	Lower Piedmont	487.18	2194.50	2325	700	Shallow	Moderate	Agricultural
ZU-EC-46	Lower Piedmont	487.22	2194.78	2325	700	Shallow	Moderate	Agricultural
ZU-EC-47	Lower Piedmont	487.07	2194.97	2330	700	Shallow	Moderate	Agricultural
ZU-EC-48	Lower Piedmont	488.22	2198.05	2325	670	Medium	None	Grazing & Agri
ZU-EC-49	Lower Piedmont	487.90	2200.53	2280	630	Medium	None	Agricultural
ZU-EC-50	Lower Piedmont	486.90	2200.03	2270	650	Medium	None	Agricultural
ZU-EC-51	Lower Piedmont	486.07	2199.63	2297	670	Medium	None	Agricultural
ZU-EC-52	Lower Piedmont	484.15	2200.18	2230	680	Medium	None	Agricultural
ZU-EC-53	Lower Piedmont	483.95	2199.63	2255	690	Shallow	Deep	None
ZU-EC-54	Lower Piedmont	483.75	2198.80	2255	700	Shallow	Deep	Agricultural
ZU-EC-55	Lower Piedmont	483.57	2199.72	2270	690	Shallow	None	Agricultural
ZU-EC-56	Lower Piedmont	482.78	2196.00	2323	700	Medium-Deep	None	Agricultural
ZU-EC-57	Lower Piedmont	479.15	2195.05	2270	690	Deep	Moderate	Agricultural
ZU-EC-58	Lower Piedmont	478.95	2195.43	2260	690	Medium	Moderate	Agricultural
ZU-EC-59	Lower Piedmont	478.35	2194.88	2260	690	Medium	Moderate	Agricultural
ZU-EC-60	Lower Piedmont	481.00	2208.45	2275	690	Deep	Moderate	Agricultural
ZU-EC-61	Lower Piedmont	482.15	2208.20	2297	700	Medium	None	Agricultural
ZU-EC-62	Lower Piedmont	483.50	2190.47	2304	700	Medium	None	Agricultural
ZU-EC-63	Lakeshore Plain	486.97	2190.80	2260	700	Medium	None	Agricultural
ZU-EC-64	Lakeshore Plain	488.13	2191.18	2275	700	Medium	None	Agricultural
ZU-EC-65	Lakeshore Plain	490.82	2190.55	2260	700	Medium	None	Agricultural
ZU-EC-66	Lower Piedmont	492.88	2191.82	2320	670	Shallow	Deep	Grazing & Agri
ZU-EC-67	Lower Piedmont	495.00	2191.78	2295	640	Shallow	Deep	Grazing & Agri
ZU-EC-68	Lower Piedmont	495.63	2188.68	2303	660	Shallow	Moderate	Grazing & Agri
ZU-EC-69	Lakeshore Plain	497.57	2188.38	2260	630	Shallow	None	Agricultural
ZU-EC-70	Lower Piedmont	497.85	2188.35	2280	630	Shallow	None	Agricultural
ZU-EC-71	Lakeshore Plain	494.97	2186.57	2245	650	Medium	None	Agricultural
ZU-EC-72	Lakeshore Plain	492.80	2188.03	2275	690	Deep	None	Agricultural
ZU-EC-73	Lakeshore Plain	491.63	2188.88	2270	700	Deep	None	Agricultural
ZU-EC-74	Lakeshore Plain	492.43	2184.93	2245	650	Deep	None	Agricultural
ZU-EC-75	Lakeshore Plain	493.63	2184.70	2245	630	Deep	None	Agricultural
ZU-EC-76	Lakeshore Plain	492.82	2183.95	2245	630	Deep	None	Agricultural
ZU-EC-77	Lakeshore Plain	489.20	2184.88	2245	650	Medium	None	Agricultural
ZU-EC-78	Lakeshore Plain	480.78	2189.20	2263	680	Deep	Slight	Agricultural
ZU-EC-79	Lower Piedmont	476.65	2189.88	2300	670	Shallow	None	Agricultural
ZU-EC-80	Lower Piedmont	475.45	2191.72	2275	670	Medium	None	Agricultural
ZU-EC-81	Lower Piedmont	478.85	2187.55	2288	670	Shallow	Deep	Grazing & Agri
ZU-EC-82	Lower Piedmont	479.28	2185.32	2275	660	Shallow	Moderate-Deep	Agricultural
ZU-EC-83	Lower Piedmont	479.68	2182.70	2270	650	Medium	Moderate	Agricultural
ZU-EC-84	Lower Piedmont	486.80	2178.60	2313	620	Shallow	Moderate	Agricultural
ZU-EC-85	Lakeshore Plain	488.00	2174.05	2245	610	Deep	None	Grazing & Agri

ZUMPANGO REGION – PREHISPANIC SETTLEMENT DATA
Early Classic Sites

SITE NUMBER	CLASSIFICATION	ENVIRONMENTAL ZONE	AREA (in ha)	POP.	EF	MF	LF	TF	EC	LC	ET	LT	EA	LA	TEMPORARY SITE NO.	SUPERVISOR	YEAR
ZU-EC-43	Hamlet	Lower Piedmont	2.7	60	0	0	0	1	0	0	0	0	0	0	ZU-CL-24	J. PARSONS	1973
ZU-EC-44	Hamlet	Lakeshore Plain	2.9	30	0	0	0	0	0	1	0	0	0	1	ZU-CL-26	J. PARSONS	1973
ZU-EC-45	Small Hamlet	Lower Piedmont	0.3	10	0	0	0	0	1	0	0	0	0	0	ZU-CL-29	M. PARSONS	1973
ZU-EC-46	Small Hamlet	Lower Piedmont	0.4	5	0	0	0	0	1	1	0	0	0	0	ZU-CL-28	M. PARSONS	1973
ZU-EC-47	Small Hamlet	Lower Piedmont	0.6	5	0	0	0	0	1	0	0	0	0	1	ZU-CL-27	M. PARSONS	1973
ZU-EC-48	Sm Disp Village	Lower Piedmont	11.8	320	0	0	1	1	1	1	0	0	0	0	ZU-CL-14	J. PARSONS	1973
ZU-EC-49	Sm Disp Village	Lower Piedmont	8.2	240	0	0	0	0	1	1	0	0	0	1	ZU-CL-13	J. PARSONS	1973
ZU-EC-50	Hamlet	Lower Piedmont	3.1	30	0	0	0	0	1	0	1	0	0	1	ZU-CL-26	M. PARSONS	1973
ZU-EC-51	Hamlet	Lower Piedmont	3.4	70	0	0	0	0	1	0	0	0	0	0	ZU-CL-30	M. PARSONS	1973
ZU-EC-52	Small Hamlet	Lower Piedmont	0.2	5	0	0	0	0	1	1	0	0	0	0	ZU-CL-24	M. PARSONS	1973
ZU-EC-53	Small Hamlet	Lower Piedmont	0.1	5	0	0	0	0	1	0	1	0	0	0	ZU-CL-23	M. PARSONS	1973
ZU-EC-54	Small Hamlet	Lower Piedmont	0.5	10	0	0	0	0	1	0	0	0	0	0	ZU-CL-22	M. PARSONS	1973
ZU-EC-55	Hamlet	Lower Piedmont	1.4	40	0	0	0	0	1	1	1	0	0	0	ZU-CL-21	M. PARSONS	1973
ZU-EC-56	Local Center	Lower Piedmont	19.5	1000	0	0	0	0	1	0	0	0	0	0	ZU-CL-33	M. PARSONS	1973
ZU-EC-57	Sm Nucl Village	Lower Piedmont	5.9	200	0	0	0	0	1	0	0	0	0	0	ZU-CL-40	M. PARSONS	1973
ZU-EC-58	Hamlet	Lower Piedmont	2.3	50	0	0	0	0	1	0	0	0	0	0	ZU-CL-39	M. PARSONS	1973
ZU-EC-59	Sm Nucl Village	Lower Piedmont	3.9	150	0	0	0	0	1	1	0	0	0	0	ZU-CL-38	M. PARSONS	1973
ZU-EC-60	Hamlet	Lower Piedmont	2.7	50	0	0	0	0	1	0	1	0	0	0	ZU-CL-44	M. PARSONS	1973
ZU-EC-61	Hamlet	Lower Piedmont	2.5	50	0	0	1	0	0	1	0	0	0	0	ZU-CL-36	M. PARSONS	1973
ZU-EC-62	Hamlet	Lower Piedmont	3.6	70	0	0	0	0	1	0	1	0	0	1	ZU-CL-37	M. PARSONS	1973
ZU-EC-63	Hamlet	Lakeshore Plain	1.7	40	0	0	0	0	1	0	0	0	0	0	ZU-CL-35	M. PARSONS	1973
ZU-EC-64	Small Hamlet	Lakeshore Plain	1.3	10	0	0	0	0	1	1	0	0	0	0	ZU-CL-29	J. PARSONS	1973
ZU-EC-65	Sm Disp Village	Lakeshore Plain	5.6	120	0	0	0	0	1	0	0	0	0	0	ZU-CL-30	J. PARSONS	1973
ZU-EC-66	Hamlet	Lower Piedmont	3.1	30	0	0	1	0	0	0	0	0	0	1	ZU-CL-25	J. PARSONS	1973
ZU-EC-67	Hamlet	Lower Piedmont	2.4	50	0	0	0	0	1	1	0	0	0	0	ZU-CL-23	J. PARSONS	1973
ZU-EC-68	Sm Disp Village	Lower Piedmont	6.5	120	0	0	0	0	1	1	0	0	0	0	ZU-CL-33	J. PARSONS	1973
ZU-EC-69	Small Hamlet	Lakeshore Plain	0.8	10	0	0	0	0	1	0	0	0	0	0	ZU-CL-34	J. PARSONS	1973
ZU-EC-70	Small Hamlet	Lower Piedmont	1.9	20	0	0	1	0	1	1	0	0	0	0	ZU-CL-35	J. PARSONS	1973
ZU-EC-71	Sm Disp Village	Lakeshore Plain	6.3	120	0	0	0	0	1	0	1	0	0	0	ZU-CL-37	J. PARSONS	1973
ZU-EC-72	Sm Disp Village	Lakeshore Plain	5.5	120	0	0	0	0	1	0	0	0	0	0	ZU-CL-32	J. PARSONS	1973
ZU-EC-73	Small Hamlet	Lakeshore Plain	0.7	10	0	0	0	0	1	0	0	0	0	0	ZU-CL-31	J. PARSONS	1973
ZU-EC-74	Small Hamlet	Lakeshore Plain	2.2	20	0	0	0	0	1	1	0	0	0	0	ZU-CL-39	J. PARSONS	1973
ZU-EC-75	Hamlet	Lakeshore Plain	3.3	60	0	0	1	0	1	1	0	0	0	0	ZU-CL-38	J. PARSONS	1973
ZU-EC-76	Hamlet	Lower Piedmont	2.9	60	0	0	0	0	1	0	0	0	0	0	ZU-CL-40	J. PARSONS	1973
ZU-EC-77	Sm Nucl Village	Lakeshore Plain	5.3	160	0	0	0	0	1	1	1	0	0	0	ZU-CL-36	J. PARSONS	1973
ZU-EC-78	Sm Nucl Village	Lakeshore Plain	10.1	300	0	0	0	0	1	1	0	0	0	2	ZU-CL-45	M. PARSONS	1973
ZU-EC-79	Hamlet	Lower Piedmont	2.0	40	0	0	0	0	1	0	0	0	0	1	ZU-CL-43	M. PARSONS	1973
ZU-EC-80	Hamlet	Lower Piedmont	2.1	40	0	0	1	0	1	0	0	0	0	1	ZU-CL-42	M. PARSONS	1973
ZU-EC-81	Hamlet	Lower Piedmont	2.3	60	0	0	0	0	1	0	0	0	0	0	ZU-CL-46	M. PARSONS	1973
ZU-EC-82	Hamlet	Lower Piedmont	2.0	30	0	0	0	0	1	1	0	0	0	1	ZU-CL-47	J. PARSONS	1973
ZU-EC-83	Small Hamlet	Lower Piedmont	0.7	5	0	0	0	0	1	0	0	0	0	0	ZU-CL-48	M. PARSONS	1973
ZU-EC-84	Local Center	Lower Piedmont	21.0	800	0	0	0	0	1	1	0	0	0	1	ZU-CL-27	J. PARSONS	1973
ZU-EC-85	Sm Disp Village	Lakeshore Plain	7.6	200	0	0	0	0	1	0	0	0	0	1	ZU-CL-28	J. PARSONS	1973

ZUMPANGO REGION - ENVIRONMENTAL DATA
Late Classic Sites

Site Number	Environmental Zone	UTM Coordinates East	UTM Coordinates North	Elev (in m)	Rainfall (in mm)	Modern Soil Depth	Modern Erosion	Modern Land use
ZU-LC-1	Lower Piedmont	497.05	2210.47	2396	600	Medium	None	Agricultural
ZU-LC-2	Lower Piedmont	496.03	2207.00	2360	600	Medium	None	Agricultural
ZU-LC-3	Lower Piedmont	495.85	2206.15	2348	600	Medium	None	Agricultural
ZU-LC-4	Lower Piedmont	494.00	2205.35	2345	600	Medium	None	Agricultural
ZU-LC-5	Lower Piedmont	493.65	2205.82	2340	600	Medium	None	Agricultural
ZU-LC-6	Lower Piedmont	497.78	2203.32	2340	600	Medium	None	Agricultural
ZU-LC-7	Lower Piedmont	497.50	2203.10	2330	600	Medium	None	Agricultural
ZU-LC-8	Lower Piedmont	492.60	2204.85	2345	600	Medium	None	Agricultural
ZU-LC-9	Lower Piedmont	492.32	2203.65	2345	600	Deep	None	Agricultural
ZU-LC-10	Lower Piedmont	489.25	2205.60	2315	600	Shallow	Deep	Agricultural
ZU-LC-11	Lower Piedmont	488.95	2205.70	2315	600	Shallow	None	Agricultural
ZU-LC-12	Lower Piedmont	486.47	2208.38	2288	600	Shallow	None	Agricultural
ZU-LC-13	Lower Piedmont	485.50	2209.35	2270	600	Medium	None	Agricultural
ZU-LC-14	Lower Piedmont	484.38	2209.40	2243	600	Shallow	Moderate	Grazing
ZU-LC-15	Lower Piedmont	484.30	2209.05	2243	600	Shallow	Moderate	Grazing
ZU-LC-16	Lower Piedmont	481.63	2207.13	2175	600	Deep	None	Agricultural
ZU-LC-17	Lower Piedmont	482.80	2207.13	2200	600	Shallow	None	Agricultural
ZU-LC-18	Lower Piedmont	485.50	2206.57	2275	600	Shallow	Deep	Agricultural
ZU-LC-19	Lower Piedmont	483.70	2206.07	2240	600	Medium	None	Agricultural
ZU-LC-20	Lower Piedmont	485.00	2205.57	2252	600	Medium	None	Agricultural
ZU-LC-21	Lower Piedmont	484.25	2204.88	2225	600	Medium	None	Agricultural
ZU-LC-22	Lower Piedmont	484.03	2204.53	2225	600	Medium	None	Agricultural
ZU-LC-23	Lower Piedmont	482.28	2204.15	2190	620	Deep	None	Agricultural
ZU-LC-24	Lower Piedmont	481.75	2204.50	2190	620	Deep	None	Agricultural
ZU-LC-25	Lower Piedmont	483.10	2203.07	2195	620	Medium	None	Agricultural
ZU-LC-26	Lower Piedmont	484.35	2202.70	2210	630	Medium	None	Agricultural
ZU-LC-27	Lower Piedmont	485.15	2204.25	2230	600	Medium	None	Agricultural
ZU-LC-28	Lower Piedmont	485.55	2204.35	2245	600	Medium	None	Agricultural
ZU-LC-29	Lower Piedmont	485.20	2203.82	2225	600	Medium	None	Agricultural
ZU-LC-30	Lower Piedmont	486.15	2203.45	2228	600	Deep	None	Agricultural
ZU-LC-31	Lower Piedmont	488.72	2204.25	2259	600	Deep	None	Agricultural
ZU-LC-32	Lower Piedmont	489.05	2202.38	2320	600	Shallow	Moderate	Agricultural
ZU-LC-33	Lower Piedmont	489.05	2201.75	2330	610	Shallow	Moderate	Agricultural
ZU-LC-34	Lower Piedmont	490.75	2202.03	2302	600	Shallow	Moderate-Deep	Agricultural
ZU-LC-35	Lower Piedmont	493.22	2201.10	2290	600	Shallow	Deep	Grazing
ZU-LC-36	Lower Piedmont	492.50	2200.25	2305	600	Shallow	Deep	Grazing & Agri
ZU-LC-37	Lower Piedmont	495.10	2200.93	2325	600	Shallow	Moderate	Agricultural
ZU-LC-38	Lower Piedmont	495.38	2202.55	2325	600	Shallow	Slight	Agricultural
ZU-LC-39	Lower Piedmont	495.30	2201.72	2325	600	Shallow	Slight	Agricultural
ZU-LC-40	Lower Piedmont	494.93	2196.57	2347	610	Shallow	Moderate	Grazing & Agri
ZU-LC-41	Lower Piedmont	494.65	2194.63	2310	640	Medium	None	Agricultural
ZU-LC-42	Lower Piedmont	493.70	2194.63	2340	640	Shallow	Deep	Grazing

ZUMPANGO REGION - PREHISPANIC SETTLEMENT DATA
Late Classic Sites

SITE NUMBER	CLASSIFICATION	ENVIRONMENTAL ZONE	AREA (in ha)	POP.	EF	MF	LF	TF	EC	LC	ET	LT	EA	LA	TEMPORARY SITE NO.	SUPERVISOR	YEAR
ZU-LC-1	Sm Disp Village	Lower Piedmont	5.7	110	0	0	0	0	0	0	0	0	0	0	ZU-CL-8	J. PARSONS	1973
ZU-LC-2	Sm Nucl Village	Lower Piedmont	8.2	260	0	0	0	0	0	0	0	0	0	0	ZU-CL-4	J. PARSONS	1973
ZU-LC-3	Sm Nucl Village	Lower Piedmont	5.1	150	0	0	0	0	1	0	0	0	0	0	ZU-CL-5	J. PARSONS	1973
ZU-LC-4	Hamlet	Lower Piedmont	3.0	30	0	0	0	0	1	0	0	0	0	0	ZU-CL-2	J. PARSONS	1973
ZU-LC-5	Sm Nucl Village	Lower Piedmont	4.4	140	0	0	0	0	0	0	1	0	0	0	ZU-CL-1	J. PARSONS	1973
ZU-LC-6	Hamlet	Lower Piedmont	3.5	80	0	0	0	0	0	0	0	1	0	1	ZU-CL-7	J. PARSONS	1973
ZU-LC-7	Small Hamlet	Lower Piedmont	0.5	10	0	0	0	0	1	0	0	0	0	1	ZU-CL-6	J. PARSONS	1973
ZU-LC-8	Small Hamlet	Lower Piedmont	1.8	20	0	0	0	0	1	0	0	1	0	0	ZU-CL-9	J. PARSONS	1973
ZU-LC-9	Hamlet	Lower Piedmont	3.0	70	0	0	0	0	1	0	0	0	0	0	ZU-CL-10	J. PARSONS	1973
ZU-LC-10	Hamlet	Lower Piedmont	2.4	40	0	0	0	0	1	0	1	0	0	1	ZU-CL-16	J. PARSONS	1973
ZU-LC-11	Small Hamlet	Lower Piedmont	0.4	5	0	0	0	1	1	0	0	0	0	0	ZU-CL-15	M. PARSONS	1973
ZU-LC-12	Hamlet	Lower Piedmont	2.1	30	0	0	0	0	1	0	0	0	0	0	ZU-CL-8	M. PARSONS	1973
ZU-LC-13	Small Hamlet	Lower Piedmont	1.2	10	0	0	0	0	1	0	0	0	0	0	ZU-CL-20	M. PARSONS	1973
ZU-LC-14	Small Hamlet	Lower Piedmont	2.4	20	0	0	0	0	1	0	1	0	0	0	ZU-CL-19	M. PARSONS	1973
ZU-LC-15	Hamlet	Lower Piedmont	1.6	30	0	0	0	0	1	0	0	0	0	0	ZU-CL-18	M. PARSONS	1973
ZU-LC-16	Hamlet	Lower Piedmont	1.1	30	0	0	0	0	1	0	1	0	0	1	ZU-CL-17	M. PARSONS	1973
ZU-LC-17	Small Hamlet	Lower Piedmont	0.7	10	0	0	0	0	0	0	0	0	0	0	ZU-CL-7	M. PARSONS	1973
ZU-LC-18	Small Hamlet	Lower Piedmont	1.0	10	0	0	0	0	0	0	0	0	0	0	ZU-CL-9	M. PARSONS	1973
ZU-LC-19	Hamlet	Lower Piedmont	4.5	80	0	0	0	0	1	0	1	0	0	0	ZU-CL-6	M. PARSONS	1973
ZU-LC-20	Small Hamlet	Lower Piedmont	0.7	20	0	0	0	0	1	0	0	0	0	0	ZU-CL-10	M. PARSONS	1973
ZU-LC-21	Small Hamlet	Lower Piedmont	0.7	10	0	0	0	0	1	0	1	0	0	0	ZU-CL-4	M. PARSONS	1973
ZU-LC-22	Small Hamlet	Lower Piedmont	0.9	10	0	0	0	0	0	0	0	0	0	0	ZU-CL-3	M. PARSONS	1973
ZU-LC-23	Small Hamlet	Lower Piedmont	0.4	10	0	0	0	0	0	0	0	0	0	0	ZU-CL-2	M. PARSONS	1973
ZU-LC-24	Hamlet	Lower Piedmont	4.4	40	0	0	0	0	0	0	0	0	0	0	ZU-CL-1	M. PARSONS	1973
ZU-LC-25	Hamlet	Lower Piedmont	1.4	30	0	0	0	0	0	0	0	0	0	0	ZU-CL-31	M. PARSONS	1973
ZU-LC-26	Small Hamlet	Lower Piedmont	0.4	5	0	0	0	0	0	0	0	0	0	0	ZU-CL-32	M. PARSONS	1973
ZU-LC-27	Small Hamlet	Lower Piedmont	0.2	5	0	0	0	0	1	0	0	0	0	0	ZU-CL-11	M. PARSONS	1973
ZU-LC-28	Small Hamlet	Lower Piedmont	1.5	10	0	0	0	0	0	0	0	0	0	0	ZU-CL-25	M. PARSONS	1973
ZU-LC-29	Hamlet	Lower Piedmont	2.4	50	0	0	0	0	1	0	1	0	0	0	ZU-CL-12	M. PARSONS	1973
ZU-LC-30	Hamlet	Lower Piedmont	3.9	70	0	0	0	0	0	0	0	0	0	1	ZU-CL-13	M. PARSONS	1973
ZU-LC-31	Hamlet	Lower Piedmont	3.8	80	0	0	0	0	1	0	1	0	0	1	ZU-CL-14	M. PARSONS	1973
ZU-LC-32	Hamlet	Lower Piedmont	3.5	70	0	0	0	1	1	0	0	0	0	1	ZU-CL-43	J. PARSONS	1973
ZU-LC-33	Hamlet	Lower Piedmont	1.7	40	0	0	0	0	0	0	0	0	0	0	ZU-CL-42	J. PARSONS	1973
ZU-LC-34	Hamlet	Lower Piedmont	4.0	80	0	0	0	0	1	0	1	0	0	1	ZU-CL-41	J. PARSONS	1973
ZU-LC-35	Hamlet	Lower Piedmont	2.1	50	0	0	0	0	0	0	0	0	0	0	ZU-CL-11	J. PARSONS	1973
ZU-LC-36	Hamlet	Lower Piedmont	5.3	100	0	0	0	0	1	0	1	0	0	0	ZU-CL-12	J. PARSONS	1973
ZU-LC-37	Small Hamlet	Lower Piedmont	0.6	10	0	0	0	0	1	0	1	0	0	1	ZU-CL-15	J. PARSONS	1973
ZU-LC-38	Lg Disp Village	Lower Piedmont	17.2	600	0	0	0	0	0	0	2	0	0	0	ZU-CL-16	J. PARSONS	1973
ZU-LC-39	Small Hamlet	Lower Piedmont	0.6	10	0	0	0	0	1	0	0	0	0	0	ZU-CL-17	J. PARSONS	1973
ZU-LC-40	Lg Nucl Village	Lower Piedmont	16.4	600	0	0	0	0	1	0	0	0	0	0	ZU-CL-18	J. PARSONS	1973
ZU-LC-41	Small Hamlet	Lower Piedmont	0.3	5	0	0	0	0	0	0	0	0	0	0	ZU-CL-20	J. PARSONS	1973
ZU-LC-42	Hamlet	Lower Piedmont	3.9	80	0	0	0	0	0	0	1	0	0	1	ZU-CL-19	J. PARSONS	1973

ZUMPANGO REGION - ENVIRONMENTAL DATA
Late Classic Sites

Site Number	Environmental Zone	UTM Coordinates East	North	Elev (in m)	Rainfall (in mm)	Modern Soil Depth	Modern Erosion	Modern Land use
ZU-LC-43	Lakeshore Plain	489.25	2194.13	2285	690	Medium	None	Agricultural
ZU-LC-44	Lower Piedmont	487.18	2194.50	2325	700	Shallow	Moderate	Agricultural
ZU-LC-45	Lower Piedmont	487.22	2194.78	2325	700	Shallow	Moderate	Agricultural
ZU-LC-46	Lower Piedmont	487.07	2194.97	2330	700	Shallow	Moderate	Agricultural
ZU-LC-47	Lower Piedmont	488.22	2198.05	2325	670	Medium	None	Agricultural
ZU-LC-48	Lakeshore Plain	487.90	2200.53	2280	630	Medium	None	Agricultural
ZU-LC-49	Lower Piedmont	486.90	2200.03	2270	650	Medium	None	Agricultural
ZU-LC-50	Lower Piedmont	486.07	2199.63	2297	670	Medium	None	Agricultural
ZU-LC-51	Lower Piedmont	484.15	2200.18	2230	680	Medium	None	Agricultural
ZU-LC-52	Lower Piedmont	483.95	2199.63	2255	690	Shallow	Deep	None
ZU-LC-53	Lower Piedmont	483.75	2198.80	2255	700	Medium	Deep	Agricultural
ZU-LC-54	Lower Piedmont	483.57	2199.72	2270	690	Shallow	None	Agricultural
ZU-LC-55	Lower Piedmont	482.78	2196.00	2323	700	Medium-Deep	None	Agricultural
ZU-LC-56	Lower Piedmont	479.15	2195.05	2270	690	Deep	Moderate	Agricultural
ZU-LC-57	Lower Piedmont	478.95	2195.43	2270	690	Medium	Moderate	Agricultural
ZU-LC-58	Lower Piedmont	478.35	2194.88	2260	690	Medium	Moderate	Agricultural
ZU-LC-59	Lower Piedmont	481.00	2208.45	2275	690	Deep	Moderate	Agricultural
ZU-LC-60	Lower Piedmont	483.50	2190.47	2304	700	Medium	None	Agricultural
ZU-LC-61	Upper Piedmont	484.55	2193.18	2505	700	Medium	None	Agricultural
ZU-LC-62	Lakeshore Plain	486.97	2190.80	2260	700	Medium	None	Agricultural
ZU-LC-63	Lakeshore Plain	488.13	2191.18	2275	700	Medium	None	Agricultural
ZU-LC-64	Lakeshore Plain	490.82	2190.55	2260	700	Medium	None	Grazing & Agri
ZU-LC-65	Lower Piedmont	495.00	2191.78	2295	640	Shallow	Deep	Grazing & Agri
ZU-LC-66	Lower Piedmont	495.63	2188.68	2303	660	Shallow	Moderate	Grazing & Agri
ZU-LC-67	Lakeshore Plain	497.57	2188.38	2260	630	Shallow	None	Agricultural
ZU-LC-68	Lower Piedmont	497.85	2188.35	2280	630	Shallow	None	Agricultural
ZU-LC-69	Lakeshore Plain	494.97	2186.57	2245	650	Medium	None	Agricultural
ZU-LC-70	Lakeshore Plain	492.80	2188.03	2275	690	Deep	None	Agricultural
ZU-LC-71	Lakeshore Plain	491.63	2188.88	2245	700	Deep	None	Agricultural
ZU-LC-72	Lakeshore Plain	492.43	2184.93	2245	650	Deep	None	Agricultural
ZU-LC-73	Lakeshore Plain	493.63	2184.70	2245	630	Deep	None	Agricultural
ZU-LC-74	Lakeshore Plain	489.20	2184.88	2245	650	Medium	None	Agricultural
ZU-LC-75	Lakeshore Plain	480.78	2189.20	2263	680	Deep	None	Agricultural
ZU-LC-76	Lower Piedmont	476.65	2189.88	2300	670	Shallow	None	Agricultural
ZU-LC-77	Lower Piedmont	478.85	2187.55	2288	670	Shallow	Deep	Grazing & Agri
ZU-LC-78	Lower Piedmont	479.28	2185.32	2275	660	Shallow	Moderate-Deep	Agricultural
ZU-LC-79	Lower Piedmont	479.68	2182.70	2270	650	Medium	Moderate	Agricultural
ZU-LC-80	Lower Piedmont	486.80	2178.60	2313	620	Shallow	Moderate	Agricultural
ZU-LC-81	Lakeshore Plain	488.00	2174.05	2245	610	Deep	None	Grazing & Agri

ZUMPANGO REGION – PREHISPANIC SETTLEMENT DATA
Late Classic Sites

SITE NUMBER	CLASSIFICATION	ENVIRONMENTAL ZONE	AREA (in ha)	POP.	EF	MF	LF	TF	EC	LC	ET	LT	EA	LA	TEMPORARY SITE NO.	SUPERVISOR	YEAR
ZU-LC-43	Hamlet	Lakeshore Plain	3.6	40	0	0	0	0	1	0	1	0	0	0	ZU-CL-26	J. PARSONS	1973
ZU-LC-44	Small Hamlet	Lower Piedmont	0.3	10	0	0	0	0	0	0	0	0	0	0	ZU-CL-29	M. PARSONS	1973
ZU-LC-45	Small Hamlet	Lower Piedmont	0.4	5	0	0	0	0	1	0	0	1	0	0	ZU-CL-28	M. PARSONS	1973
ZU-LC-46	Small Hamlet	Lower Piedmont	0.6	5	0	0	0	0	1	0	0	0	0	1	ZU-CL-27	M. PARSONS	1973
ZU-LC-47	Sm Nucl Village	Lower Piedmont	9.1	200	0	0	0	1	1	0	1	0	0	0	ZU-CL-14	J. PARSONS	1973
ZU-LC-48	Sm Nucl Village	Lakeshore Plain	10.8	300	0	0	0	0	1	0	1	0	0	0	ZU-CL-13	J. PARSONS	1973
ZU-LC-49	Hamlet	Lower Piedmont	3.1	30	0	0	0	0	1	0	0	0	0	1	ZU-CL-26	M. PARSONS	1973
ZU-LC-50	Hamlet	Lower Piedmont	3.4	70	0	0	0	0	1	0	0	0	0	0	ZU-CL-30	M. PARSONS	1973
ZU-LC-51	Small Hamlet	Lower Piedmont	0.2	5	0	0	0	0	1	0	0	0	0	0	ZU-CL-24	M. PARSONS	1973
ZU-LC-52	Small Hamlet	Lower Piedmont	0.1	5	0	0	0	0	1	0	0	0	0	0	ZU-CL-23	M. PARSONS	1973
ZU-LC-53	Small Hamlet	Lower Piedmont	0.5	10	0	0	0	0	1	0	1	0	0	0	ZU-CL-22	M. PARSONS	1973
ZU-LC-54	Hamlet	Lower Piedmont	1.4	40	0	0	0	0	1	0	0	0	0	0	ZU-CL-21	M. PARSONS	1973
ZU-LC-55	Local Center	Lower Piedmont	16.9	900	0	0	0	0	1	0	1	0	0	1	ZU-CL-33	M. PARSONS	1973
ZU-LC-56	Sm Nucl Village	Lower Piedmont	5.9	200	0	0	0	0	1	0	0	0	0	0	ZU-CL-40	M. PARSONS	1973
ZU-LC-57	Hamlet	Lower Piedmont	2.3	50	0	0	0	0	1	0	0	0	0	0	ZU-CL-39	M. PARSONS	1973
ZU-LC-58	Sm Nucl Village	Lower Piedmont	3.9	120	0	0	0	0	1	0	0	0	0	0	ZU-CL-38	M. PARSONS	1973
ZU-LC-59	Hamlet	Lower Piedmont	2.7	40	0	0	0	0	1	0	1	0	0	0	ZU-CL-44	M. PARSONS	1973
ZU-LC-60	Hamlet	Lower Piedmont	3.6	70	0	0	0	0	1	0	0	0	0	1	ZU-CL-37	M. PARSONS	1973
ZU-LC-61	Small Hamlet	Upper Piedmont	1.1	20	0	0	0	0	0	0	0	0	0	0	ZU-CL-34	M. PARSONS	1973
ZU-LC-62	Hamlet	Lakeshore Plain	3.2	60	0	0	0	0	1	0	0	0	0	0	ZU-CL-35	M. PARSONS	1973
ZU-LC-63	Small Hamlet	Lakeshore Plain	1.3	10	0	0	0	0	1	0	1	0	0	1	ZU-CL-29	J. PARSONS	1973
ZU-LC-64	Sm Disp Village	Lakeshore Plain	5.6	120	0	0	0	0	1	0	0	0	0	0	ZU-CL-30	J. PARSONS	1973
ZU-LC-65	Hamlet	Lower Piedmont	2.4	50	0	0	0	0	1	0	0	0	0	0	ZU-CL-23	J. PARSONS	1973
ZU-LC-66	Sm Disp Village	Lower Piedmont	6.5	120	0	0	0	0	1	0	1	0	0	0	ZU-CL-33	J. PARSONS	1973
ZU-LC-67	Small Hamlet	Lakeshore Plain	0.8	10	0	0	0	0	1	0	0	0	0	0	ZU-CL-34	J. PARSONS	1973
ZU-LC-68	Small Hamlet	Lower Piedmont	1.9	20	0	0	0	1	1	0	0	0	0	0	ZU-CL-35	J. PARSONS	1973
ZU-LC-69	Sm Disp Village	Lakeshore Plain	6.3	120	0	0	0	1	1	0	1	0	0	0	ZU-CL-37	J. PARSONS	1973
ZU-LC-70	Sm Nucl Village	Lakeshore Plain	5.5	150	0	0	0	0	1	0	0	0	0	0	ZU-CL-32	J. PARSONS	1973
ZU-LC-71	Small Hamlet	Lakeshore Plain	0.7	10	0	0	0	0	1	0	0	0	0	0	ZU-CL-31	J. PARSONS	1973
ZU-LC-72	Small Hamlet	Lakeshore Plain	2.2	20	0	0	0	1	1	0	1	0	0	0	ZU-CL-39	J. PARSONS	1973
ZU-LC-73	Hamlet	Lakeshore Plain	3.3	50	0	0	0	0	1	0	1	0	0	0	ZU-CL-38	J. PARSONS	1973
ZU-LC-74	Sm Nucl Village	Lakeshore Plain	5.3	160	0	0	0	0	1	0	0	0	0	0	ZU-CL-36	J. PARSONS	1973
ZU-LC-75	Sm Nucl Village	Lakeshore Plain	10.1	300	0	0	0	0	1	0	1	0	0	1	ZU-CL-45	M. PARSONS	1973
ZU-LC-76	Hamlet	Lower Piedmont	2.0	50	0	0	0	0	1	0	0	0	0	0	ZU-CL-43	M. PARSONS	1973
ZU-LC-77	Hamlet	Lower Piedmont	2.3	60	0	0	0	1	1	0	0	0	0	1	ZU-CL-46	M. PARSONS	1973
ZU-LC-78	Hamlet	Lower Piedmont	2.0	30	0	0	0	0	1	0	0	0	0	0	ZU-CL-47	M. PARSONS	1973
ZU-LC-79	Small Hamlet	Lower Piedmont	0.7	5	0	0	0	0	1	0	0	0	0	1	ZU-CL-48	M. PARSONS	1973
ZU-LC-80	Local Center	Lower Piedmont	22.8	800	0	0	0	0	1	0	1	0	0	0	ZU-CL-27	J. PARSONS	1973
ZU-LC-81	Sm Disp Village	Lakeshore Plain	7.6	200	0	0	0	0	1	0	0	0	0	1	ZU-CL-28	J. PARSONS	1973

ZUMPANGO REGION - ENVIRONMENTAL DATA
Early Toltec Sites

Site Number	Environmental Zone	UTM Coordinates East	North	Elev (in m)	Rainfall (in mm)	Modern Soil Depth	Modern Erosion	Modern Land use
ZU-ET-1	Lower Piedmont	496.72	2207.25	2388	600	Medium	None	Agricultural
ZU-ET-2	Lower Piedmont	493.53	2205.75	2340	600	Medium	None	Agricultural
ZU-ET-3	Lower Piedmont	492.28	2203.63	2345	600	Deep	None	Agricultural
ZU-ET-4	Lower Piedmont	488.60	2204.50	2260	600	Deep	None	Agricultural
ZU-ET-5	Lower Piedmont	484.35	2209.28	2243	600	Shallow	Moderate	Grazing
ZU-ET-6	Lower Piedmont	481.50	2209.22	2175	600	Deep	None	Agricultural
ZU-ET-7	Lower Piedmont	483.70	2206.20	2240	600	Medium	None	Agricultural
ZU-ET-8	Lower Piedmont	486.18	2205.75	2250	600	Medium	None	None
ZU-ET-9	Lower Piedmont	486.25	2203.63	2228	600	Deep	None	Agricultural
ZU-ET-10	Lower Piedmont	485.18	2203.88	2225	600	Medium	None	Agricultural
ZU-ET-11	Lower Piedmont	484.28	2204.85	2225	600	Medium	None	Agricultural
ZU-ET-12	Lower Piedmont	480.47	2201.18	2483	690	Deep	None	Grazing
ZU-ET-13	Lower Piedmont	483.50	2199.93	2270	680	Shallow	None	Agricultural
ZU-ET-14	Lower Piedmont	487.85	2200.85	2278	630	Medium	None	Agricultural
ZU-ET-15	Lower Piedmont	493.22	2201.32	2290	600	Shallow	Deep	Grazing
ZU-ET-16	Lower Piedmont	495.40	2200.18	2325	600	Shallow	Slight	Agricultural
ZU-ET-17	Lower Piedmont	489.05	2198.18	2328	670	Medium	None	Agricultural
ZU-ET-18	Lakeshore Plain	489.30	2194.50	2285	690	Medium	None	Agricultural
ZU-ET-19	Lower Piedmont	482.90	2196.03	2323	700	Medium-Deep	None	Agricultural
ZU-ET-20	Lower Piedmont	480.97	2194.57	2290	700	Medium	Moderate	Agricultural
ZU-ET-21	Lower Piedmont	481.32	2190.95	2275	690	Deep	Moderate	Agricultural
ZU-ET-22	Lower Piedmont	475.32	2189.45	2280	690	Medium	None	Agricultural
ZU-ET-23	Lakeshore Plain	481.03	2189.18	2255	680	Deep	Slight	Agricultural
ZU-ET-24	Lower Piedmont	483.75	2190.47	2299	700	Medium	None	Agricultural
ZU-ET-25	Upper Piedmont	484.68	2193.50	2505	700	Medium	None	Agricultural
ZU-ET-26	Lakeshore Plain	492.93	2188.07	2275	690	Deep	None	Agricultural
ZU-ET-27	Lower Piedmont	495.75	2188.82	2303	660	Shallow	Moderate	Grazing & Agri
ZU-ET-28	Lakeshore Plain	493.60	2184.75	2245	640	Deep	None	Agricultural
ZU-ET-29	Lakeshore Plain	485.30	2176.82	2268	630	Medium-Deep	Slight	Agricultural
ZU-ET-30	Lakeshore Plain	487.43	2174.22	2245	610	Deep	None	Grazing & Agri

ZUMPANGO REGION – PREHISPANIC SETTLEMENT DATA
Early Toltec Sites

SITE NUMBER	CLASSIFICATION	ENVIRONMENTAL ZONE	AREA (in ha)	POP.	EF	MF	LF	TF	EC	LC	ET	LT	EA	LA	TEMPORARY SITE NO.	SUPERVISOR	YEAR
ZU-ET-1	Sm Nucl Village	Lower Piedmont	10.0	300	0	0	0	0	0	0	0	0	0	1	ZU-ET-1	J. PARSONS	1973
ZU-ET-2	Sm Nucl Village	Lower Piedmont	4.4	130	0	0	0	0	0	1	0	0	0	0	ZU-CL-1	J. PARSONS	1973
ZU-ET-3	Hamlet	Lower Piedmont	3.0	90	0	0	0	0	1	1	0	0	0	0	ZU-CL-10	J. PARSONS	1973
ZU-ET-4	Small Hamlet	Lower Piedmont	0.5	20	0	0	0	0	1	1	0	0	0	0	ZU-CL-14	M. PARSONS	1973
ZU-ET-5	Hamlet	Lower Piedmont	2.4	50	0	0	0	0	1	1	0	0	0	0	ZU-CL-19	M. PARSONS	1973
ZU-ET-6	Small Hamlet	Lower Piedmont	1.1	20	0	0	0	0	1	1	0	0	0	1	ZU-CL-17	M. PARSONS	1973
ZU-ET-7	Sm Nucl Village	Lower Piedmont	4.5	150	0	0	0	0	1	1	0	0	0	0	ZU-CL-6	M. PARSONS	1973
ZU-ET-8	Small Hamlet	Lower Piedmont	0.3	5	0	0	0	0	0	0	0	0	0	0		M. PARSONS	1973
ZU-ET-9	Hamlet	Lower Piedmont	3.9	80	0	0	0	0	1	1	0	0	0	1	ZU-CL-13	M. PARSONS	1973
ZU-ET-10	Hamlet	Lower Piedmont	2.4	50	0	0	0	0	1	1	0	0	0	0	ZU-CL-12	M. PARSONS	1973
ZU-ET-11	Small Hamlet	Lower Piedmont	0.7	10	0	0	0	0	1	1	0	0	0	0	ZU-CL-4	M. PARSONS	1973
ZU-ET-12	Local Center	Lower Piedmont	28.6	1500	0	0	0	0	0	0	0	0	0	0	ZU-ET-1	M. PARSONS	1973
ZU-ET-13	Hamlet	Lower Piedmont	1.4	40	0	0	0	0	1	1	0	0	0	0	ZU-CL-21	M. PARSONS	1973
ZU-ET-14	Sm Disp Village	Lower Piedmont	6.5	150	0	0	0	0	1	1	0	0	0	1	ZU-CL-13	J. PARSONS	1973
ZU-ET-15	Hamlet	Lower Piedmont	2.1	40	0	0	0	0	1	1	1	0	0	0	ZU-CL-11	J. PARSONS	1973
ZU-ET-16	Sm Disp Village	Lower Piedmont	13.4	300	0	0	0	0	1	1	1	0	0	0	ZU-CL-16	J. PARSONS	1973
ZU-ET-17	Hamlet	Lower Piedmont	3.3	70	0	0	0	0	1	1	0	0	0	0	ZU-CL-14	J. PARSONS	1973
ZU-ET-18	Hamlet	Lakeshore Plain	3.6	40	0	0	0	0	1	1	0	0	0	0	ZU-CL-26	J. PARSONS	1973
ZU-ET-19	Lg Nucl Village	Lower Piedmont	19.5	800	0	0	0	0	1	1	0	0	0	1	ZU-CL-33	M. PARSONS	1973
ZU-ET-20	Hamlet	Lower Piedmont	3.4	70	0	0	0	0	0	0	0	0	0	0	ZU-CL-43	M. PARSONS	1973
ZU-ET-21	Small Hamlet	Lower Piedmont	0.8	20	0	0	0	0	1	1	0	0	0	0	ZU-CL-44	M. PARSONS	1973
ZU-ET-22	Hamlet	Lower Piedmont	1.0	30	0	0	0	0	0	0	1	0	0	1	ZU-LT-80	M. PARSONS	1973
ZU-ET-23	Hamlet	Lakeshore Plain	3.8	80	0	0	0	0	1	1	1	0	0	2	ZU-ET-2	M. PARSONS	1973
ZU-ET-24	Hamlet	Lower Piedmont	1.8	40	0	0	0	0	1	1	0	0	0	1	ZU-CL-37	M. PARSONS	1973
ZU-ET-25	Small Hamlet	Upper Piedmont	1.1	20	0	0	0	0	0	0	0	0	0	0	ZU-CL-34	M. PARSONS	1973
ZU-ET-26	Sm Disp Village	Lakeshore Plain	5.5	120	0	0	0	0	1	1	0	0	0	0	ZU-CL-32	J. PARSONS	1973
ZU-ET-27	Sm Disp Village	Lower Piedmont	6.5	130	0	0	0	0	1	1	0	0	0	0	ZU-CL-33	J. PARSONS	1973
ZU-ET-28	Hamlet	Lakeshore Plain	3.3	70	0	0	0	0	1	1	1	0	0	0	ZU-CL-38	J. PARSONS	1973
ZU-ET-29	Sm Disp Village	Lakeshore Plain	7.2	150	0	0	0	0	0	0	0	1	0	0	ZU-LT-70	M. PARSONS	1973
ZU-ET-30	Sm Nucl Village	Lakeshore Plain	10.4	300	0	0	0	0	1	1	0	0	0	1	ZU-CL-28	J. PARSONS	1973

OTHER OCCUPATIONS: EF MF LF TF EC LC ET LT EA LA
SURVEY RECORDS: TEMPORARY SITE NO., SUPERVISOR, YEAR

ZUMPANGO REGION - ENVIRONMENTAL DATA
Late Toltec Sites

Site Number	Environmental Zone	UTM Coordinates East	North	Elev (in m)	Rainfall (in mm)	Modern Soil Depth	Modern Erosion	Modern Land use
ZU-LT-1	Lower Piedmont	497.63	2210.50	2395	600	Deep	None	Agricultural
ZU-LT-2	Lower Piedmont	495.45	2210.10	2495	600	Medium	Moderate	Agricultural
ZU-LT-3	Lower Piedmont	496.22	2209.70	2425	600	Shallow-Med	Moderate	Agricultural
ZU-LT-4	Lower Piedmont	496.35	2209.30	2400	600	Shallow	Moderate	Agricultural
ZU-LT-5	Lower Piedmont	496.35	2208.90	2375	600	Shallow	Moderate	Agricultural
ZU-LT-6	Lower Piedmont	493.38	2208.82	2405	600	Medium	None	Agricultural
ZU-LT-7	Lower Piedmont	494.28	2207.93	2360	600	Deep	None	Agricultural
ZU-LT-8	Lower Piedmont	493.05	2207.93	2400	600	Deep	Moderate	Agricultural
ZU-LT-9	Lower Piedmont	498.00	2206.90	2425	600	Shallow	Moderate	Grazing
ZU-LT-10	Lower Piedmont	495.90	2206.38	2350	600	Deep	None	Agricultural
ZU-LT-11	Lower Piedmont	494.63	2206.55	2345	600	Deep	Slight	Agricultural
ZU-LT-12	Lower Piedmont	490.40	2207.82	2365	600	Shallow	Deep	Agricultural
ZU-LT-13	Lower Piedmont	490.38	2207.28	2365	600	Shallow	Deep	Agricultural
ZU-LT-14	Lower Piedmont	488.53	2208.53	2250	600	Medium	None	Agricultural
ZU-LT-15	Lower Piedmont	487.53	2208.55	2300	600	Medium	None	Agricultural
ZU-LT-16	Lower Piedmont	487.78	2208.30	2305	600	Medium	None	Agricultural
ZU-LT-17	Lower Piedmont	485.50	2207.47	2250	600	Medium	None	Agricultural
ZU-LT-18	Lower Piedmont	486.03	2207.28	2260	600	Medium	None	Agricultural
ZU-LT-19	Lower Piedmont	485.97	2206.88	2280	600	Medium	None	Agricultural
ZU-LT-20	Lower Piedmont	486.85	2206.90	2280	600	Medium	None	Agricultural
ZU-LT-21	Lower Piedmont	488.38	2206.38	2365	600	Medium	Slight	None
ZU-LT-22	Lower Piedmont	488.70	2204.95	2300	600	Medium	None	Agricultural
ZU-LT-23	Lower Piedmont	489.03	2205.18	2305	600	Medium	None	Agricultural
ZU-LT-24	Lower Piedmont	489.00	2205.78	2320	600	Medium	None	Agricultural
ZU-LT-25	Lower Piedmont	489.72	2205.38	2308	600	Shallow	Deep	Agricultural
ZU-LT-26	Lower Piedmont	490.07	2205.32	2310	600	Shallow	Deep	Agricultural
ZU-LT-27	Lower Piedmont	490.30	2205.47	2320	600	Shallow	Deep	Grazing
ZU-LT-28	Lower Piedmont	490.55	2205.63	2325	600	Shallow	Deep	Grazing
ZU-LT-29	Lower Piedmont	490.40	2204.68	2295	600	Shallow	Deep	Grazing
ZU-LT-30	Lower Piedmont	492.38	2204.63	2360	600	Medium	None	Agricultural
ZU-LT-31	Lower Piedmont	495.03	2205.18	2320	600	Medium	Moderate	Agricultural
ZU-LT-32	Lower Piedmont	496.05	2205.55	2340	600	Medium	None	Agricultural
ZU-LT-33	Lower Piedmont	495.90	2205.00	2338	600	Shallow	Moderate	Agricultural
ZU-LT-34	Lower Piedmont	497.18	2205.15	2348	600	Shallow	Deep	Grazing
ZU-LT-35	Lower Piedmont	497.50	2204.80	2350	600	Shallow	Deep	Grazing
ZU-LT-36	Lower Piedmont	498.28	2203.95	2350	600	Shallow	None	Agricultural
ZU-LT-37	Lower Piedmont	498.78	2203.25	2350	600	Medium	None	Agricultural
ZU-LT-38	Lower Piedmont	498.22	2203.10	2340	600	Medium	None	Agricultural
ZU-LT-39	Lower Piedmont	498.53	2202.63	2340	600	Medium	None	Agricultural
ZU-LT-40	Lower Piedmont	499.22	2202.07	2340	600	Medium	None	Agricultural
ZU-LT-41	Lower Piedmont	495.90	2203.35	2315	600	Deep	None	Agricultural
ZU-LT-42	Lower Piedmont	495.50	2202.88	2310	600	Shallow-Med	Moderate	Agricultural

ZUMPANGO REGION - PREHISPANIC SETTLEMENT DATA
Late Toltec Sites

SITE NUMBER	CLASSIFICATION	ENVIRONMENTAL ZONE	AREA (in ha)	POP.	EF	MF	LF	TF	EC	LC	ET	LT	EA	LA	TEMPORARY SITE NO.	SUPERVISOR	YEAR
ZU-LT-1	Sm Disp Village	Lower Piedmont	6.4	130	0	0	0	0	0	0	1	0	0	0	ZU-LT-20	J. PARSONS	1973
ZU-LT-2	Small Hamlet	Lower Piedmont	0.7	10	0	0	0	0	0	0	0	0	0	1	ZU-LT-21	J. PARSONS	1973
ZU-LT-3	Sm Disp Village	Lower Piedmont	7.9	160	0	0	0	0	0	0	0	0	0	1	ZU-LT-19	J. PARSONS	1973
ZU-LT-4	Small Hamlet	Lower Piedmont	1.4	10	0	0	0	0	0	0	0	0	0	1	ZU-LT-18	J. PARSONS	1973
ZU-LT-5	Small Hamlet	Lower Piedmont	0.8	20	0	0	0	0	0	0	0	0	0	0	ZU-LT-17	J. PARSONS	1973
ZU-LT-6	Small Hamlet	Lower Piedmont	0.6	10	0	0	0	0	0	0	0	0	0	0	ZU-LT-24	J. PARSONS	1973
ZU-LT-7	Small Hamlet	Lower Piedmont	0.5	20	0	0	0	0	0	0	0	0	0	1	ZU-LT-22	J. PARSONS	1973
ZU-LT-8	Hamlet	Lower Piedmont	2.0	40	0	0	0	0	0	0	0	0	0	0	ZU-LT-23	J. PARSONS	1973
ZU-LT-9	Hamlet	Lower Piedmont	1.3	30	0	0	0	0	0	0	0	0	0	0	ZU-LT-16	J. PARSONS	1973
ZU-LT-10	Hamlet	Lower Piedmont	1.4	30	0	0	0	0	0	0	0	0	0	0	ZU-LT-2	J. PARSONS	1973
ZU-LT-11	Small Hamlet	Lower Piedmont	0.4	10	0	0	0	0	0	0	0	0	0	0	ZU-LT-1	J. PARSONS	1973
ZU-LT-12	Small Hamlet	Lower Piedmont	0.4	10	0	0	0	0	0	0	0	0	0	0	ZU-LT-32	J. PARSONS	1973
ZU-LT-13	Small Hamlet	Lower Piedmont	0.1	5	0	0	0	0	0	0	0	0	0	0	ZU-LT-31	M. PARSONS	1973
ZU-LT-14	Small Hamlet	Lower Piedmont	0.4	5	0	0	0	0	0	0	0	0	0	0	ZU-LT-33	M. PARSONS	1973
ZU-LT-15	Small Hamlet	Lower Piedmont	0.9	20	0	0	0	0	0	0	0	0	0	0	ZU-LT-30	M. PARSONS	1973
ZU-LT-16	Hamlet	Lower Piedmont	1.5	40	0	0	0	0	0	0	0	0	0	0	ZU-LT-31	M. PARSONS	1973
ZU-LT-17	Sm Disp Village	Lower Piedmont	5.4	160	0	0	0	0	0	0	0	0	0	0	ZU-LT-14	M. PARSONS	1973
ZU-LT-18	Hamlet	Lower Piedmont	2.5	50	0	0	0	0	0	0	0	0	0	0	ZU-LT-16	M. PARSONS	1973
ZU-LT-19	Hamlet	Lower Piedmont	1.6	30	0	0	0	0	0	0	0	0	0	0	ZU-LT-15	M. PARSONS	1973
ZU-LT-20	Hamlet	Lower Piedmont	1.9	60	0	0	0	0	0	0	0	0	0	0	ZU-LT-17	M. PARSONS	1973
ZU-LT-21	Small Hamlet	Lower Piedmont	0.6	10	0	0	0	0	0	0	0	0	0	0	ZU-LT-32	M. PARSONS	1973
ZU-LT-22	Small Hamlet	Lower Piedmont	0.5	10	0	0	0	0	0	0	0	0	0	0	ZU-LT-25	M. PARSONS	1973
ZU-LT-23	Small Hamlet	Lower Piedmont	0.8	20	0	0	0	0	0	0	0	0	0	0	ZU-LT-26	M. PARSONS	1973
ZU-LT-24	Small Hamlet	Lower Piedmont	0.3	10	0	0	0	0	0	0	0	0	0	0	ZU-LT-34	M. PARSONS	1973
ZU-LT-25	Small Hamlet	Lower Piedmont	1.0	20	0	0	0	0	1	1	0	0	0	1	ZU-LT-27	M. PARSONS	1973
ZU-LT-26	Small Hamlet	Lower Piedmont	0.3	10	0	0	0	0	0	0	0	0	0	0	ZU-LT-28	M. PARSONS	1973
ZU-LT-27	Small Hamlet	Lower Piedmont	0.6	10	0	0	0	0	0	0	0	0	0	0	ZU-LT-30	J. PARSONS	1973
ZU-LT-28	Small Hamlet	Lower Piedmont	0.1	5	0	0	0	0	0	0	0	0	0	0	ZU-LT-29	J. PARSONS	1973
ZU-LT-29	Hamlet	Lower Piedmont	2.0	60	0	0	0	0	0	0	0	0	0	0	ZU-LT-28	J. PARSONS	1973
ZU-LT-30	Lg Nucl Village	Lower Piedmont	16.8	680	0	0	0	0	0	0	0	0	0	1	ZU-LT-27	J. PARSONS	1973
ZU-LT-31	Hamlet	Lower Piedmont	1.4	50	0	0	0	0	0	0	0	0	0	0	ZU-LT-5	J. PARSONS	1973
ZU-LT-32	Small Hamlet	Lower Piedmont	1.1	20	0	0	0	0	0	0	0	0	0	0	ZU-LT-3	J. PARSONS	1973
ZU-LT-33	Sm Disp Village	Lower Piedmont	10.7	250	0	0	0	0	0	0	0	0	0	2	ZU-LT-4	J. PARSONS	1973
ZU-LT-34	Sm Disp Village	Lower Piedmont	6.8	200	0	0	0	0	0	0	0	0	0	0	ZU-LT-15	J. PARSONS	1973
ZU-LT-35	Hamlet	Lower Piedmont	2.6	50	0	0	0	0	0	0	0	0	0	0	ZU-LT-13	J. PARSONS	1973
ZU-LT-36	Hamlet	Lower Piedmont	1.3	30	0	0	0	0	0	0	0	0	0	1	ZU-LT-12	J. PARSONS	1973
ZU-LT-37	Hamlet	Lower Piedmont	2.3	50	0	0	0	0	0	0	0	0	0	1	ZU-LT-14	J. PARSONS	1973
ZU-LT-38	Lg Nucl Village	Lower Piedmont	15.7	500	0	0	0	0	0	0	0	0	0	0	ZU-LT-10	J. PARSONS	1973
ZU-LT-39	Sm Disp Village	Lower Piedmont	7.0	150	0	0	0	0	0	0	0	0	0	0	ZU-LT-9	J. PARSONS	1973
ZU-LT-40	Hamlet	Lower Piedmont	4.4	90	0	0	0	0	0	0	0	0	0	0	ZU-LT-8	J. PARSONS	1973
ZU-LT-41	Sm Nucl Village	Lower Piedmont	10.8	400	0	0	0	0	0	0	0	0	0	0	ZU-LT-7	J. PARSONS	1973
ZU-LT-42	Sm Nucl Village	Lower Piedmont	5.7	170	0	0	0	0	0	0	0	0	0	1	ZU-LT-6	J. PARSONS	1973

ZUMPANGO REGION – ENVIRONMENTAL DATA
Late Toltec Sites

Site Number	Environmental Zone	UTM Coordinates East	North	Elev (in m)	Rainfall (in mm)	Modern Soil Depth	Modern Erosion	Modern Land use
ZU-LT-43	Lower Piedmont	496.57	2201.43	2308	600	Medium	Slight	Agricultural
ZU-LT-44	Lower Piedmont	496.05	2201.10	2320	600	Deep	None	Agricultural
ZU-LT-45	Lower Piedmont	495.60	2201.20	2310	600	Shallow	Deep	None
ZU-LT-46	Lower Piedmont	496.22	2200.68	2335	600	Deep	None	Agricultural
ZU-LT-47	Lower Piedmont	495.70	2200.70	2328	600	Medium	Moderate	Agricultural
ZU-LT-48	Lower Piedmont	496.07	2199.82	2335	600	Shallow	Slight	Agricultural
ZU-LT-49	Lower Piedmont	495.70	2200.13	2330	600	Shallow	Slight	Grazing
ZU-LT-50	Lower Piedmont	492.93	2200.25	2310	600	Shallow	Deep	Grazing
ZU-LT-51	Lower Piedmont	493.45	2200.50	2300	600	Shallow	Deep	Grazing
ZU-LT-52	Lower Piedmont	493.70	2200.95	2310	600	Shallow	Deep	Agricultural
ZU-LT-53	Lower Piedmont	493.50	2201.40	2320	600	Shallow	Moderate-Deep	Agricultural
ZU-LT-54	Lower Piedmont	492.70	2202.53	2348	600	Shallow	Deep	Grazing & Agri
ZU-LT-55	Lower Piedmont	492.15	2201.97	2330	600	Shallow	Deep	Agricultural
ZU-LT-56	Lower Piedmont	491.32	2203.30	2333	600	Shallow	Deep	Agricultural
ZU-LT-57	Lower Piedmont	490.30	2202.20	2300	600	Shallow	Deep	Agricultural
ZU-LT-58	Lower Piedmont	489.53	2202.20	2315	600	Shallow	Moderate	Agricultural
ZU-LT-59	Lower Piedmont	489.32	2203.20	2300	600	Medium	Moderate	Agricultural
ZU-LT-60	Lower Piedmont	489.25	2204.50	2258	600	Deep	None	Agricultural
ZU-LT-61	Lower Piedmont	488.25	2203.80	2250	600	Medium	Slight	Settlement
ZU-LT-62	Lower Piedmont	487.72	2203.32	2255	600	Medium	Slight	Agricultural
ZU-LT-63	Lower Piedmont	487.35	2204.75	2275	600	Medium	Slight	Agricultural
ZU-LT-64	Lower Piedmont	487.03	2204.82	2270	600	Medium	None	Agricultural
ZU-LT-65	Lower Piedmont	486.82	2204.28	2260	600	Medium	Slight	Agricultural
ZU-LT-66	Lower Piedmont	486.32	2204.90	2250	600	Medium	Moderate	Agricultural
ZU-LT-67	Lower Piedmont	484.03	2204.35	2215	600	Medium	None	Agricultural
ZU-LT-68	Lower Piedmont	483.40	2204.93	2200	600	Deep	Slight	Agricultural
ZU-LT-69	Lower Piedmont	483.40	2205.75	2218	600	Deep	None	Agricultural
ZU-LT-70	Lower Piedmont	484.05	2206.50	2255	600	Shallow	None	Agricultural
ZU-LT-71	Lower Piedmont	482.85	2206.63	2200	600	Medium	None	Agricultural
ZU-LT-72	Lower Piedmont	481.78	2203.95	2208	630	Medium	Moderate	Agricultural
ZU-LT-73	Lower Piedmont	480.63	2204.40	2220	630	Medium	Slight	Agricultural
ZU-LT-74	Lower Piedmont	480.70	2203.35	2255	650	Medium	None	Agricultural
ZU-LT-75	Lower Piedmont	479.40	2204.60	2243	640	Medium	Slight	Agricultural
ZU-LT-76	Lower Piedmont	479.70	2205.72	2245	620	Medium	Slight	Agricultural
ZU-LT-77	Lower Piedmont	478.15	2204.63	2260	650	Medium	Moderate	Agricultural
ZU-LT-78	Lower Piedmont	477.00	2206.63	2345	610	Medium	Moderate	Agricultural
ZU-LT-79	Lower Piedmont	477.43	2204.32	2285	640	Medium	Moderate	Agricultural
ZU-LT-80	Lower Piedmont	478.18	2204.13	2278	650	Medium	None	Agricultural
ZU-LT-81	Lower Piedmont	477.95	2201.60	2260	700	Shallow	Slight	Grazing
ZU-LT-82	Lower Piedmont	479.65	2202.00	2223	680	Shallow	Moderate	Grazing
ZU-LT-83	Lower Piedmont	482.63	2201.00	2250	680	Shallow	Moderate	Grazing
ZU-LT-84	Lower Piedmont	483.60	2198.72	2280	700	Shallow	Deep	Agricultural

ZUMPANGO REGION – PREHISPANIC SETTLEMENT DATA
Late Toltec Sites

SITE NUMBER	CLASSIFICATION	ENVIRONMENTAL ZONE	AREA (in ha)	POP.	EF	MF	LF	TF	EC	LC	ET	LT	EA	LA	TEMPORARY SITE NO.	SUPERVISOR	YEAR
ZU-LT-43	Sm Disp Village	Lower Piedmont	8.2	160	0	0	0	0	0	0	0	0	0	1	ZU-LT-61	J. PARSONS	1973
ZU-LT-44	Hamlet	Lower Piedmont	1.4	30	0	0	0	0	0	0	0	0	0	0	ZU-LT-59	J. PARSONS	1973
ZU-LT-45	Hamlet	Lower Piedmont	2.9	60	0	0	0	0	0	0	0	0	0	1	ZU-LT-60	J. PARSONS	1973
ZU-LT-46	Sm Disp Village	Lower Piedmont	10.4	210	0	0	0	0	0	0	0	0	0	0	ZU-LT-57	J. PARSONS	1973
ZU-LT-47	Sm Disp Village	Lower Piedmont	8.7	180	0	0	0	0	0	0	0	0	0	2	ZU-LT-58	J. PARSONS	1973
ZU-LT-48	Sm Nucl Village	Lower Piedmont	5.1	200	0	0	0	0	1	0	0	0	0	0	ZU-LT-62	J. PARSONS	1973
ZU-LT-49	Sm Disp Village	Lower Piedmont	5.6	110	0	0	0	0	1	1	0	0	0	0	ZU-LT-63	J. PARSONS	1973
ZU-LT-50	Small Hamlet	Lower Piedmont	0.4	10	0	0	0	0	0	0	0	0	0	1	ZU-LT-38	J. PARSONS	1973
ZU-LT-51	Small Hamlet	Lower Piedmont	1.4	10	0	0	0	0	0	0	0	0	0	1	ZU-LT-34	J. PARSONS	1973
ZU-LT-52	Hamlet	Lower Piedmont	2.2	40	0	0	0	0	1	1	0	0	0	0	ZU-LT-33	J. PARSONS	1973
ZU-LT-53	Hamlet	Lower Piedmont	3.0	60	0	0	0	0	0	0	0	0	0	1	ZU-LT-11	J. PARSONS	1973
ZU-LT-54	Sm Disp Village	Lower Piedmont	5.9	120	0	0	0	0	0	0	0	0	0	1	ZU-LT-25	J. PARSONS	1973
ZU-LT-55	Hamlet	Lower Piedmont	1.4	30	0	0	0	0	0	0	0	0	0	0	ZU-LT-11	J. PARSONS	1973
ZU-LT-56	Hamlet	Lower Piedmont	1.5	30	0	0	0	0	0	0	0	0	0	1	ZU-LT-26	J. PARSONS	1973
ZU-LT-57	Sm Disp Village	Lower Piedmont	6.0	200	0	0	0	0	0	0	0	0	0	0	ZU-LT-11	J. PARSONS	1973
ZU-LT-58	Hamlet	Lower Piedmont	2.3	50	0	0	0	0	0	0	0	0	0	0	ZU-LT-11	J. PARSONS	1973
ZU-LT-59	Small Hamlet	Lower Piedmont	0.8	10	0	0	0	0	1	0	0	0	0	1	ZU-LT-29	M. PARSONS	1973
ZU-LT-60	Hamlet	Lower Piedmont	3.1	60	0	0	0	0	1	1	1	0	0	1	ZU-LT-24	M. PARSONS	1973
ZU-LT-61	Small Hamlet	Lower Piedmont	0.6	10	0	0	0	0	0	0	0	0	0	1	ZU-LT-22	M. PARSONS	1973
ZU-LT-62	Small Hamlet	Lower Piedmont	0.1	5	0	0	0	0	0	0	0	0	0	0	ZU-LT-23	M. PARSONS	1973
ZU-LT-63	Small Hamlet	Lower Piedmont	0.4	10	0	0	0	0	0	0	0	0	0	0	ZU-LT-21	M. PARSONS	1973
ZU-LT-64	Small Hamlet	Lower Piedmont	0.2	5	0	0	0	0	0	0	0	0	0	0	ZU-LT-20	M. PARSONS	1973
ZU-LT-65	Small Hamlet	Lower Piedmont	0.4	10	0	0	0	0	0	0	0	0	0	0	ZU-LT-19	M. PARSONS	1973
ZU-LT-66	Small Hamlet	Lower Piedmont	0.9	10	0	0	0	0	0	0	0	0	0	0	ZU-LT-18	M. PARSONS	1973
ZU-LT-67	Small Hamlet	Lower Piedmont	0.1	5	0	0	0	0	0	0	0	0	0	0	ZU-LT-13	M. PARSONS	1973
ZU-LT-68	Small Hamlet	Lower Piedmont	0.4	5	0	0	0	0	0	0	0	0	0	0	ZU-LT-9	M. PARSONS	1973
ZU-LT-69	Sm Disp Village	Lower Piedmont	5.5	120	0	0	0	0	0	0	0	0	0	0	ZU-LT-10	M. PARSONS	1973
ZU-LT-70	Hamlet	Lower Piedmont	0.8	30	0	0	0	0	0	0	0	0	0	1	ZU-LT-12	M. PARSONS	1973
ZU-LT-71	Small Hamlet	Lower Piedmont	0.9	5	0	0	0	0	0	0	0	0	0	0	ZU-LT-11	M. PARSONS	1973
ZU-LT-72	Sm Disp Village	Lower Piedmont	6.1	120	0	0	0	0	0	0	0	0	0	1	ZU-LT-8	M. PARSONS	1973
ZU-LT-73	Small Hamlet	Lower Piedmont	0.7	10	0	0	0	0	0	0	0	0	0	0	ZU-LT-6	M. PARSONS	1973
ZU-LT-74	Hamlet	Lower Piedmont	4.1	80	0	0	0	0	0	0	0	0	0	0	ZU-LT-43	M. PARSONS	1973
ZU-LT-75	Local Center	Lower Piedmont	10.7	400	0	0	0	0	0	0	0	0	0	0	ZU-LT-5	M. PARSONS	1973
ZU-LT-76	Small Hamlet	Lower Piedmont	0.1	10	0	0	0	0	0	0	0	0	0	0	ZU-LT-7	M. PARSONS	1973
ZU-LT-77	Small Hamlet	Lower Piedmont	0.8	20	0	0	0	0	0	0	0	0	0	0	ZU-LT-4	M. PARSONS	1973
ZU-LT-78	Small Hamlet	Lower Piedmont	0.8	10	0	0	0	0	0	0	0	0	0	0	ZU-LT-1	M. PARSONS	1973
ZU-LT-79	Hamlet	Lower Piedmont	2.9	90	0	0	0	0	0	0	0	0	0	0	ZU-LT-2	M. PARSONS	1973
ZU-LT-80	Sm Disp Village	Lower Piedmont	11.5	230	0	0	0	0	0	0	0	0	0	0	ZU-LT-3	M. PARSONS	1973
ZU-LT-81	Hamlet	Lower Piedmont	3.3	70	0	0	0	0	0	0	0	0	0	0	ZU-LT-45	M. PARSONS	1973
ZU-LT-82	Hamlet	Lower Piedmont	4.1	80	0	0	0	0	0	0	0	0	0	0	ZU-LT-44	M. PARSONS	1973
ZU-LT-83	Small Hamlet	Lower Piedmont	0.5	5	0	0	0	0	0	0	0	0	0	0	ZU-LT-42	M. PARSONS	1973
ZU-LT-84	Small Hamlet	Lower Piedmont	1.2	10	0	0	0	0	0	0	0	0	0	0	ZU-LT-39	M. PARSONS	1973

ZUMPANGO REGION - ENVIRONMENTAL DATA
Late Toltec Sites

Site Number	Environmental Zone	UTM Coordinates East	North	Elev (in m)	Rainfall (in mm)	Modern Soil Depth	Modern Erosion	Modern Land use
ZU-LT-85	Lower Piedmont	483.78	2199.57	2280	690	Medium	None	Agricultural
ZU-LT-86	Lower Piedmont	484.25	2199.65	2265	680	Shallow	Deep	Agricultural
ZU-LT-87	Lower Piedmont	484.10	2199.07	2265	700	Shallow	Deep	Agricultural
ZU-LT-88	Lower Piedmont	484.72	2199.72	2245	670	Shallow	Deep	Agricultural
ZU-LT-89	Lower Piedmont	484.68	2200.03	2245	670	Shallow	Deep	Agricultural
ZU-LT-90	Lower Piedmont	487.13	2199.75	2293	650	Medium	None	Agricultural
ZU-LT-91	Lower Piedmont	487.32	2199.97	2265	650	Medium	None	Agricultural
ZU-LT-92	Lower Piedmont	486.65	2202.00	2248	620	Shallow	Moderate	Agricultural
ZU-LT-93	Lower Piedmont	487.78	2201.95	2275	620	Shallow	Moderate	Agricultural
ZU-LT-94	Lower Piedmont	488.15	2201.55	2285	620	Shallow	Moderate	Agricultural
ZU-LT-95	Lower Piedmont	489.10	2201.63	2315	610	Shallow	Slight	Agricultural
ZU-LT-96	Lower Piedmont	488.85	2201.10	2303	630	Shallow	Deep	Agricultural
ZU-LT-97	Lower Piedmont	489.50	2200.60	2350	630	Medium	Slight	Agricultural
ZU-LT-98	Lower Piedmont	489.85	2200.53	2355	630	Medium	Slight	Agricultural
ZU-LT-99	Lower Piedmont	490.90	2200.65	2340	610	Shallow	Deep	Agricultural
ZU-LT-100	Lower Piedmont	490.93	2199.88	2355	640	Shallow	Slight	Grazing
ZU-LT-101	Lower Piedmont	490.47	2199.63	2350	640	Shallow	Deep	Grazing & Agri
ZU-LT-102	Lower Piedmont	490.55	2198.85	2350	630	Shallow	Deep	Grazing & Agri
ZU-LT-103	Lower Piedmont	491.53	2199.53	2330	610	Deep	Moderate	Agricultural
ZU-LT-104	Lower Piedmont	492.20	2199.78	2308	600	Shallow	Deep	Agricultural
ZU-LT-105	Lower Piedmont	492.65	2199.75	2315	600	Shallow	Deep	Agricultural
ZU-LT-106	Lower Piedmont	493.43	2199.47	2335	600	Shallow	Deep	Agricultural
ZU-LT-107	Lower Piedmont	492.47	2199.18	2360	600	Shallow	Deep	Agricultural
ZU-LT-108	Lower Piedmont	492.97	2199.15	2360	600	Shallow	Deep	Grazing & Agri
ZU-LT-109	Lower Piedmont	492.72	2198.88	2353	600	Shallow	Deep	Grazing & Agri
ZU-LT-110	Lower Piedmont	492.97	2198.88	2353	600	Shallow	Deep	Grazing & Agri
ZU-LT-111	Lower Piedmont	493.60	2199.07	2345	600	Shallow	Deep	Grazing
ZU-LT-112	Lower Piedmont	495.45	2198.93	2350	600	Shallow	Moderate	Agricultural
ZU-LT-113	Lower Piedmont	495.97	2198.43	2355	600	Shallow	Moderate	Agricultural
ZU-LT-114	Lower Piedmont	496.22	2198.43	2355	600	Shallow	Moderate	Agricultural
ZU-LT-115	Lower Piedmont	493.57	2197.90	2370	600	Shallow	Deep	Agricultural
ZU-LT-116	Lower Piedmont	493.57	2198.15	2370	610	Shallow	Slight	Agricultural
ZU-LT-117	Lower Piedmont	492.63	2198.03	2375	610	Shallow	Deep	Agricultural
ZU-LT-118	Lower Piedmont	492.82	2197.43	2410	620	Shallow	Deep	Agricultural
ZU-LT-119	Lower Piedmont	492.22	2196.10	2370	640	Shallow	Deep	Agricultural
ZU-LT-120	Lower Piedmont	492.88	2195.30	2395	640	Shallow	Deep	Grazing
ZU-LT-121	Lower Piedmont	492.93	2194.95	2393	650	Shallow	Deep	Grazing
ZU-LT-122	Lower Piedmont	492.57	2194.40	2375	650	Shallow	Moderate	Agricultural
ZU-LT-123	Lower Piedmont	493.75	2194.50	2350	640	Shallow	Deep	Grazing
ZU-LT-124	Lower Piedmont	493.70	2194.35	2350	640	Shallow	Deep	Grazing
ZU-LT-125	Lower Piedmont	493.80	2194.35	2350	640	Shallow	Deep	Grazing
ZU-LT-126	Lower Piedmont	494.47	2193.35	2315	640	Medium	None	Agricultural

ZUMPANGO REGION - PREHISPANIC SETTLEMENT DATA
Late Toltec Sites

SITE NUMBER	CLASSIFICATION	ENVIRONMENTAL ZONE	AREA (in ha)	POP.	EF	MF	LF	TF	EC	LC	ET	LT	EA	LA	TEMPORARY SITE NO.	SUPERVISOR	YEAR
ZU-LT-85	Small Hamlet	Lower Piedmont	0.6	10	0	0	0	0	0	0	0	0	0	0	ZU-LT-35	M. PARSONS	1973
ZU-LT-86	Small Hamlet	Lower Piedmont	0.9	20	0	0	0	0	0	0	0	0	0	0	ZU-LT-36	M. PARSONS	1973
ZU-LT-87	Local Center	Lower Piedmont	10.7	300	0	0	0	0	1	0	0	0	0	1	ZU-LT-37	M. PARSONS	1973
ZU-LT-88	Small Hamlet	Lower Piedmont	1.2	20	0	0	0	0	1	0	0	0	0	0	ZU-LT-40	M. PARSONS	1973
ZU-LT-89	Hamlet	Lower Piedmont	4.0	80	0	0	0	0	0	0	0	0	0	1	ZU-LT-41	M. PARSONS	1973
ZU-LT-90	Hamlet	Lower Piedmont	2.1	40	0	0	0	0	0	0	0	0	0	0	ZU-LT-52	M. PARSONS	1973
ZU-LT-91	Small Hamlet	Lower Piedmont	1.7	20	0	0	0	0	1	0	0	0	0	1	ZU-LT-48	M. PARSONS	1973
ZU-LT-92	Sm Nucl Village	Lower Piedmont	4.4	150	0	0	0	0	0	0	0	0	0	1	ZU-LT-46	M. PARSONS	1973
ZU-LT-93	Hamlet	Lower Piedmont	3.4	70	0	0	0	0	0	0	0	0	0	0	ZU-LT-47	M. PARSONS	1973
ZU-LT-94	Small Hamlet	Lower Piedmont	0.4	10	0	0	0	0	0	0	0	0	0	0	ZU-LT-53	M. PARSONS	1973
ZU-LT-95	Hamlet	Lower Piedmont	1.0	30	0	0	0	0	0	0	0	0	0	1	ZU-LT-56	J. PARSONS	1973
ZU-LT-96	Sm Disp Village	Lower Piedmont	6.4	130	0	0	0	0	0	0	0	0	0	0	ZU-LT-50	J. PARSONS	1973
ZU-LT-97	Small Hamlet	Lower Piedmont	0.6	5	0	0	0	0	0	0	0	0	0	1	ZU-LT-51	J. PARSONS	1973
ZU-LT-98	Small Hamlet	Lower Piedmont	0.9	10	0	0	0	0	0	0	0	0	0	1	ZU-LT-52	J. PARSONS	1973
ZU-LT-99	Hamlet	Lower Piedmont	2.2	40	0	0	0	0	0	0	0	0	0	0	ZU-LT-41	J. PARSONS	1973
ZU-LT-100	Hamlet	Lower Piedmont	1.5	30	0	0	0	0	0	0	0	0	0	1	ZU-LT-53	J. PARSONS	1973
ZU-LT-101	Small Hamlet	Lower Piedmont	0.4	5	0	0	0	0	0	0	0	0	0	1	ZU-LT-40	J. PARSONS	1973
ZU-LT-102	Small Hamlet	Lower Piedmont	0.9	20	0	0	0	0	0	0	0	0	0	1	ZU-LT-49	J. PARSONS	1973
ZU-LT-103	Sm Disp Village	Lower Piedmont	8.6	170	0	0	0	0	0	0	0	0	0	1	ZU-LT-39	J. PARSONS	1973
ZU-LT-104	Sm Disp Village	Lower Piedmont	5.6	120	0	0	0	0	0	0	0	0	0	1	ZU-LT-37	J. PARSONS	1973
ZU-LT-105	Small Hamlet	Lower Piedmont	0.6	10	0	0	0	0	0	0	0	0	0	1	ZU-LT-36	J. PARSONS	1973
ZU-LT-106	Small Hamlet	Lower Piedmont	0.1	5	0	0	0	0	0	0	0	0	0	0	ZU-LT-35	J. PARSONS	1973
ZU-LT-107	Hamlet	Lower Piedmont	2.1	40	0	0	0	0	0	0	0	0	0	1	ZU-LT-47	J. PARSONS	1973
ZU-LT-108	Small Hamlet	Lower Piedmont	0.1	5	0	0	0	0	0	0	0	0	0	0	ZU-LT-48	J. PARSONS	1973
ZU-LT-109	Hamlet	Lower Piedmont	1.0	30	0	0	0	0	0	0	0	0	0	1	ZU-LT-46	J. PARSONS	1973
ZU-LT-110	Hamlet	Lower Piedmont	1.0	30	0	0	0	0	0	0	0	0	0	0	ZU-LT-46	J. PARSONS	1973
ZU-LT-111	Small Hamlet	Lower Piedmont	1.9	20	0	0	0	0	0	0	0	0	0	1	ZU-LT-42	J. PARSONS	1973
ZU-LT-112	Small Hamlet	Lower Piedmont	0.8	10	0	0	0	0	0	0	0	0	0	0	ZU-LT-64	J. PARSONS	1973
ZU-LT-113	Small Hamlet	Lower Piedmont	0.5	10	0	0	0	0	0	0	0	0	0	0	ZU-LT-65	J. PARSONS	1973
ZU-LT-114	Small Hamlet	Lower Piedmont	1.5	20	0	0	0	0	0	0	0	0	0	0	ZU-LT-65	J. PARSONS	1973
ZU-LT-115	Hamlet	Lower Piedmont	1.2	30	0	0	0	0	0	0	0	0	0	0	ZU-LT-43	J. PARSONS	1973
ZU-LT-116	Hamlet	Lower Piedmont	4.0	100	0	0	0	0	0	0	0	0	0	0	ZU-LT-43	J. PARSONS	1973
ZU-LT-117	Hamlet	Lower Piedmont	2.1	40	0	0	0	0	0	0	0	0	0	0	ZU-LT-45	J. PARSONS	1973
ZU-LT-118	Hamlet	Lower Piedmont	4.3	90	0	0	0	0	0	0	0	0	0	1	ZU-LT-44	J. PARSONS	1973
ZU-LT-119	Hamlet	Lower Piedmont	4.3	90	0	0	0	0	0	0	0	0	0	1	ZU-LT-69	J. PARSONS	1973
ZU-LT-120	Small Hamlet	Lower Piedmont	0.2	5	0	0	0	0	0	0	0	0	0	0	ZU-LT-70	J. PARSONS	1973
ZU-LT-121	Hamlet	Lower Piedmont	3.5	70	0	0	0	0	1	0	0	0	0	1	ZU-LT-71	J. PARSONS	1973
ZU-LT-122	Hamlet	Lower Piedmont	1.9	40	0	0	0	0	1	0	0	0	0	0	ZU-LT-72	J. PARSONS	1973
ZU-LT-123	Small Hamlet	Lower Piedmont	0.5	10	0	0	0	0	1	0	0	0	0	1	ZU-LT-66	J. PARSONS	1973
ZU-LT-124	Small Hamlet	Lower Piedmont	0.1	5	0	0	0	0	0	0	0	0	0	0	ZU-LT-67	J. PARSONS	1973
ZU-LT-125	Small Hamlet	Lower Piedmont	0.1	5	0	0	0	0	0	0	0	0	0	0	ZU-LT-67	J. PARSONS	1973
ZU-LT-126	Small Hamlet	Lower Piedmont	0.7	10	0	0	0	0	0	0	0	0	0	0	ZU-LT-68	J. PARSONS	1973

ZUMPANGO REGION - ENVIRONMENTAL DATA
Late Toltec Sites

Site Number	Environmental Zone	UTM Coordinates East	North	Elev (in m)	Rainfall (in mm)	Modern Soil Depth	Modern Erosion	Modern Land use
ZU-LT-127	Lower Piedmont	493.20	2193.20	2345	660	Shallow	Moderate	Grazing & Agri
ZU-LT-128	Lower Piedmont	493.30	2193.40	2345	660	Shallow	Moderate	Grazing & Agri
ZU-LT-129	Lower Piedmont	492.72	2193.75	2360	660	Medium	Deep	Grazing & Agri
ZU-LT-130	Lower Piedmont	490.88	2195.07	2355	670	Shallow	Moderate	Grazing
ZU-LT-131	Lower Piedmont	490.78	2194.97	2355	670	Shallow	Moderate	Grazing
ZU-LT-132	Lower Piedmont	488.97	2198.50	2325	650	Shallow	Deep	Agricultural
ZU-LT-133	Lower Piedmont	488.80	2197.88	2325	660	Medium	None	Agricultural
ZU-LT-134	Lower Piedmont	484.72	2198.28	2258	700	Deep	Slight	Agricultural
ZU-LT-135	Lower Piedmont	479.82	2196.75	2290	700	Medium	Moderate	Grazing & Agri
ZU-LT-136	Lower Piedmont	478.07	2197.60	2270	700	Medium	Moderate	Agricultural
ZU-LT-137	Lower Piedmont	476.82	2197.63	2270	700	Shallow	Deep	Grazing
ZU-LT-138	Lower Piedmont	474.97	2193.82	2305	700	Shallow	Deep	None
ZU-LT-139	Lower Piedmont	474.90	2193.45	2298	700	Shallow	Deep	None
ZU-LT-140	Lower Piedmont	475.35	2193.40	2285	700	Shallow	Deep	None
ZU-LT-141	Lower Piedmont	475.22	2192.68	2270	700	Medium	Deep	Agricultural
ZU-LT-142	Lower Piedmont	475.35	2192.32	2265	700	Medium	Deep	Agricultural
ZU-LT-143	Lower Piedmont	481.00	2193.03	2330	700	Shallow	Deep	Agricultural
ZU-LT-144	Lower Piedmont	482.53	2196.22	2295	700	Medium	None	Agricultural
ZU-LT-145	Lower Piedmont	482.55	2196.00	2295	700	Medium	Slight	Agricultural
ZU-LT-146	Lower Piedmont	481.75	2195.00	2290	700	Medium	Moderate	Agricultural
ZU-LT-147	Lower Piedmont	483.25	2196.22	2315	700	Medium	Slight	Agricultural
ZU-LT-148	Lower Piedmont	482.43	2194.28	2345	700	Medium	None	Agricultural
ZU-LT-149	Lower Piedmont	485.25	2195.28	2400	700	Medium	None	Grazing
ZU-LT-150	Lower Piedmont	485.63	2195.40	2380	700	Medium	None	Agricultural
ZU-LT-151	Lower Piedmont	485.72	2195.03	2390	700	Medium	None	Agricultural
ZU-LT-152	Lower Piedmont	486.55	2195.63	2348	700	Medium	None	Agricultural
ZU-LT-153	Lower Piedmont	484.07	2192.03	2340	700	Medium	None	Grazing
ZU-LT-154	Lower Piedmont	484.55	2191.88	2345	700	Shallow	None	Agricultural
ZU-LT-155	Lower Piedmont	485.80	2192.43	2345	700	Shallow	Moderate	Agricultural
ZU-LT-156	Lower Piedmont	486.47	2193.00	2340	700	Shallow	Deep	Grazing & Agri
ZU-LT-157	Lower Piedmont	486.90	2193.35	2340	700	Medium	None	Agricultural
ZU-LT-158	Lower Piedmont	486.47	2192.38	2320	700	Medium	None	Agricultural
ZU-LT-159	Lower Piedmont	487.05	2192.95	2325	700	Shallow	Moderate	Agricultural
ZU-LT-160	Lower Piedmont	487.50	2192.55	2313	700	Medium	None	Agricultural
ZU-LT-161	Lower Piedmont	487.75	2192.22	2305	700	Medium	Slight	Agricultural
ZU-LT-162	Lower Piedmont	487.78	2194.68	2325	700	Shallow	Deep	Agricultural
ZU-LT-163	Lakeshore Plain	487.80	2191.00	2270	700	Medium	None	Agricultural
ZU-LT-164	Lakeshore Plain	487.97	2191.03	2270	700	Medium	None	Agricultural
ZU-LT-165	Lower Piedmont	491.82	2190.70	2280	690	Deep	None	Agricultural
ZU-LT-166	Lower Piedmont	492.20	2190.65	2280	690	Deep	None	Agricultural
ZU-LT-167	Lower Piedmont	491.88	2190.40	2280	690	Deep	None	Agricultural
ZU-LT-168	Lakeshore Plain	494.10	2188.20	2270	680	Medium	None	Agricultural

ZUMPANGO REGION - PREHISPANIC SETTLEMENT DATA
Late Toltec Sites

SITE NUMBER	CLASSIFICATION	ENVIRONMENTAL ZONE	AREA (in ha)	POP.	EF	MF	LF	TF	EC	LC	ET	LT	EA	LA	TEMPORARY SITE NO.	SUPERVISOR	YEAR
ZU-LT-127	Small Hamlet	Lower Piedmont	1.0	20	0	0	0	0	0	0	0	0	0	0	ZU-LT-75	J. PARSONS	1973
ZU-LT-128	Small Hamlet	Lower Piedmont	0.9	20	0	0	0	0	0	0	0	0	0	0	ZU-LT-74	J. PARSONS	1973
ZU-LT-129	Hamlet	Lower Piedmont	7.3	70	0	0	0	0	0	0	0	0	0	1	ZU-LT-73	J. PARSONS	1973
ZU-LT-130	Small Hamlet	Lower Piedmont	0.1	5	0	0	0	0	0	0	0	0	0	1	ZU-LT-76	J. PARSONS	1973
ZU-LT-131	Small Hamlet	Lower Piedmont	0.1	5	0	0	0	0	0	0	0	0	0	1	ZU-LT-77	J. PARSONS	1973
ZU-LT-132	Small Hamlet	Lower Piedmont	1.1	20	0	0	0	0	0	0	0	0	0	0	ZU-LT-55	J. PARSONS	1973
ZU-LT-133	Sm Disp Village	Lower Piedmont	10.3	210	0	0	0	0	0	1	1	0	0	0	ZU-LT-54	J. PARSONS	1973
ZU-LT-134	Sm Nucl Village	Lower Piedmont	4.1	160	0	0	0	0	1	0	0	0	0	1	ZU-LT-38	M. PARSONS	1973
ZU-LT-135	Local Center	Lower Piedmont	34.5	1200	0	0	0	0	0	0	0	0	0	1	ZU-LT-73	M. PARSONS	1973
ZU-LT-136	Small Hamlet	Lower Piedmont	1.1	20	0	0	0	0	0	0	0	0	0	1	ZU-LT-71	M. PARSONS	1973
ZU-LT-137	Small Hamlet	Lower Piedmont	1.4	20	0	0	0	0	0	0	0	0	0	1	ZU-LT-72	M. PARSONS	1973
ZU-LT-138	Hamlet	Lower Piedmont	1.7	30	0	0	0	0	0	0	0	0	0	0	ZU-LT-75	M. PARSONS	1973
ZU-LT-139	Hamlet	Lower Piedmont	1.5	30	0	0	0	0	0	0	0	0	0	1	ZU-LT-76	M. PARSONS	1973
ZU-LT-140	Hamlet	Lower Piedmont	2.6	50	0	0	0	0	0	0	0	0	0	1	ZU-LT-77	M. PARSONS	1973
ZU-LT-141	Small Hamlet	Lower Piedmont	1.4	20	0	0	0	0	0	0	0	0	0	1	ZU-LT-78	M. PARSONS	1973
ZU-LT-142	Small Hamlet	Lower Piedmont	2.0	20	0	0	0	0	0	0	0	0	0	1	ZU-LT-79	M. PARSONS	1973
ZU-LT-143	Hamlet	Lower Piedmont	1.7	30	0	0	0	0	0	0	0	0	0	0	ZU-LT-74	M. PARSONS	1973
ZU-LT-144	Small Hamlet	Lower Piedmont	0.4	10	0	0	0	0	0	0	0	0	0	0	ZU-LT-58	M. PARSONS	1973
ZU-LT-145	Small Hamlet	Lower Piedmont	1.1	30	0	0	0	0	0	0	0	0	0	0	ZU-LT-57	M. PARSONS	1973
ZU-LT-146	Small Hamlet	Lower Piedmont	1.1	10	0	0	0	0	0	0	0	0	0	0	ZU-LT-86	M. PARSONS	1973
ZU-LT-147	Small Hamlet	Lower Piedmont	0.8	20	0	0	0	0	0	0	0	0	0	0	ZU-LT-56	M. PARSONS	1973
ZU-LT-148	Small Hamlet	Lower Piedmont	0.5	5	0	0	0	0	0	0	0	0	0	0	ZU-LT-59	M. PARSONS	1973
ZU-LT-149	Questionable	Lower Piedmont	0.1	0	0	0	0	0	0	0	0	0	0	0	ZU-LT-55	M. PARSONS	1973
ZU-LT-150	Small Hamlet	Lower Piedmont	0.5	10	0	0	0	0	0	0	0	0	0	2	ZU-LT-54	M. PARSONS	1973
ZU-LT-151	Hamlet	Lower Piedmont	3.6	70	0	0	0	0	0	0	0	0	0	0	ZU-LT-49	M. PARSONS	1973
ZU-LT-152	Hamlet	Lower Piedmont	1.3	40	0	0	0	0	0	0	0	0	0	0	ZU-LT-50	M. PARSONS	1973
ZU-LT-153	Small Hamlet	Lower Piedmont	0.1	5	0	0	0	0	0	0	0	0	0	1	ZU-AZ-80	M. PARSONS	1973
ZU-LT-154	Small Hamlet	Lower Piedmont	0.4	5	0	0	0	0	0	0	0	0	0	0	ZU-LT-60	M. PARSONS	1973
ZU-LT-155	Small Hamlet	Lower Piedmont	0.7	20	0	0	0	0	0	0	0	0	0	0	ZU-LT-64	M. PARSONS	1973
ZU-LT-156	Hamlet	Lower Piedmont	4.1	100	0	0	0	0	0	0	0	0	0	0	ZU-LT-62	M. PARSONS	1973
ZU-LT-157	Hamlet	Lower Piedmont	5.0	100	0	0	0	0	0	0	0	0	0	0	ZU-LT-61	M. PARSONS	1973
ZU-LT-158	Small Hamlet	Lower Piedmont	0.3	5	0	0	0	0	0	0	0	0	0	0	ZU-LT-65	M. PARSONS	1973
ZU-LT-159	Small Hamlet	Lower Piedmont	1.0	10	0	0	0	0	0	0	0	0	0	0	ZU-LT-63	M. PARSONS	1973
ZU-LT-160	Small Hamlet	Lower Piedmont	1.2	10	0	0	0	0	0	0	0	0	0	0	ZU-LT-66	M. PARSONS	1973
ZU-LT-161	Small Hamlet	Lower Piedmont	0.8	5	0	0	0	0	0	0	0	0	0	0	ZU-LT-80	J. PARSONS	1973
ZU-LT-162	Small Hamlet	Lower Piedmont	0.8	20	0	0	0	0	0	0	0	0	0	0	ZU-LT-51	M. PARSONS	1973
ZU-LT-163	Hamlet	Lakeshore Plain	2.3	50	0	0	0	0	0	0	0	0	0	1	ZU-LT-87	J. PARSONS	1973
ZU-LT-164	Small Hamlet	Lakeshore Plain	0.7	10	0	0	0	0	0	0	0	0	0	0	ZU-LT-86	J. PARSONS	1973
ZU-LT-165	Hamlet	Lower Piedmont	2.9	30	0	0	0	0	0	0	0	0	0	0	ZU-LT-88	J. PARSONS	1973
ZU-LT-166	Small Hamlet	Lower Piedmont	1.9	20	0	0	0	0	0	0	0	0	0	1	ZU-LT-89	J. PARSONS	1973
ZU-LT-167	Small Hamlet	Lower Piedmont	1.1	10	0	0	0	0	0	0	0	0	0	1	ZU-LT-90	J. PARSONS	1973
ZU-LT-168	Small Hamlet	Lakeshore Plain	0.8	10	0	0	0	0	0	0	0	0	0	0	ZU-LT-99	J. PARSONS	1973

ZUMPANGO REGION - ENVIRONMENTAL DATA
Late Toltec Sites

Site Number	Environmental Zone	UTM Coordinates East	North	Elev (in m)	Rainfall (in mm)	Modern Soil Depth	Modern Erosion	Modern Land use
ZU-LT-169	Lower Piedmont	494.60	2188.15	2298	670	Medium	None	Agricultural
ZU-LT-170	Lower Piedmont	495.18	2187.47	2275	650	Medium	None	Agricultural
ZU-LT-171	Lower Piedmont	494.60	2187.07	2255	660	Medium	None	Agricultural
ZU-LT-172	Lakeshore Plain	495.68	2186.90	2245	650	Medium	None	Agricultural
ZU-LT-173	Lakeshore Plain	496.28	2187.03	2245	640	Deep	None	Agricultural
ZU-LT-174	Lakeshore Plain	495.32	2186.40	2245	650	Medium	None	Agricultural
ZU-LT-175	Lakeshore Plain	494.63	2185.63	2245	650	Deep	None	Agricultural
ZU-LT-176	Lakeshore Plain	493.40	2185.05	2245	660	Deep	Slight	Agricultural
ZU-LT-177	Lakeshore Plain	492.93	2184.07	2245	650	Deep	None	Agricultural
ZU-LT-178	Lakeshore Plain	492.10	2183.57	2240	640	Deep	None	Agricultural
ZU-LT-179	Lakeshore Plain	491.95	2184.68	2240	680	Deep	None	Agricultural
ZU-LT-180	Lakeshore Plain	492.07	2185.18	2240	680	Deep	None	Agricultural
ZU-LT-181	Lakeshore Plain	491.80	2185.18	2240	680	Deep	None	Agricultural
ZU-LT-182	Lakeshore Plain	492.07	2185.55	2240	680	Deep	None	Agricultural
ZU-LT-183	Lakeshore Plain	491.95	2185.63	2240	680	Deep	None	Agricultural
ZU-LT-184	Lakeshore Plain	492.45	2186.28	2245	700	Medium	None	Agricultural
ZU-LT-185	Lakeshore Plain	492.10	2186.60	2250	700	Medium	None	Agricultural
ZU-LT-186	Lakeshore Plain	492.25	2186.88	2255	700	Medium	None	Agricultural
ZU-LT-187	Lakeshore Plain	492.50	2187.03	2255	700	Medium	None	Agricultural
ZU-LT-188	Lakeshore Plain	492.20	2187.75	2260	700	Medium	None	Agricultural
ZU-LT-189	Lakeshore Plain	491.85	2187.53	2255	700	Medium	None	Agricultural
ZU-LT-190	Lakeshore Plain	491.47	2187.25	2250	700	Medium	None	Agricultural
ZU-LT-191	Lakeshore Plain	490.22	2186.05	2245	700	Deep	None	Agricultural
ZU-LT-192	Lakeshore Plain	489.50	2186.75	2240	700	Medium	None	Agricultural
ZU-LT-193	Lakeshore Plain	487.78	2185.57	2245	680	Deep	None	Agricultural
ZU-LT-194	Lakeshore Plain	488.05	2185.10	2245	680	Deep	None	Agricultural
ZU-LT-195	Lakeshore Plain	482.68	2189.63	2270	700	Deep	None	Agricultural
ZU-LT-196	Lakeshore Plain	482.03	2189.68	2280	700	Deep	None	Agricultural
ZU-LT-197	Lakeshore Plain	481.00	2189.18	2255	690	Deep	None	Agricultural
ZU-LT-198	Lakeshore Plain	479.15	2188.93	2250	690	Deep	None	Agricultural
ZU-LT-199	Lakeshore Plain	478.57	2188.60	2255	690	Deep	None	Agricultural
ZU-LT-200	Lakeshore Plain	478.65	2189.22	2255	690	Deep	None	Agricultural
ZU-LT-201	Lower Piedmont	476.32	2189.28	2300	690	Shallow	Deep	Grazing
ZU-LT-202	Lower Piedmont	475.80	2189.22	2295	690	Shallow	Moderate	Agricultural
ZU-LT-203	Lower Piedmont	475.28	2189.55	2288	690	Medium	None	Agricultural
ZU-LT-204	Lower Piedmont	478.90	2184.25	2290	680	Medium	Moderate	Agricultural
ZU-LT-205	Lower Piedmont	480.25	2185.50	2275	680	Medium	Moderate	Agricultural
ZU-LT-206	Lower Piedmont	479.85	2182.90	2275	670	Medium	Moderate	Agricultural
ZU-LT-207	Lakeshore Plain	484.28	2178.55	2250	630	Deep	None	Agricultural
ZU-LT-208	Lakeshore Plain	484.63	2178.88	2260	630	Deep	None	Agricultural
ZU-LT-209	Lakeshore Plain	486.97	2179.72	2250	620	Deep	None	Agricultural
ZU-LT-210	Lower Piedmont	488.63	2177.80	2305	610	Shallow	Slight	Agricultural

ZUMPANGO REGION - PREHISPANIC SETTLEMENT DATA
Late Toltec Sites

SITE NUMBER	CLASSIFICATION	ENVIRONMENTAL ZONE	AREA (in ha)	POP.	OTHER OCCUPATIONS										SURVEY RECORDS		
					EF	MF	LF	TF	EC	LC	ET	LT	EA	LA	TEMPORARY SITE NO.	SUPERVISOR	YEAR
ZU-LT-169	Sm Disp Village	Lower Piedmont	5.9	120	0	0	0	0	0	0	0	0	0	0	ZU-LT-10	J. PARSONS	1973
ZU-LT-170	Small Hamlet	Lower Piedmont	0.6	5	0	0	0	0	0	0	0	0	0	0	ZU-LT-10	J. PARSONS	1973
ZU-LT-171	Small Hamlet	Lower Piedmont	0.8	10	0	0	0	0	0	0	0	0	0	0	ZU-LT-10	J. PARSONS	1973
ZU-LT-172	Small Hamlet	Lakeshore Plain	1.1	10	0	0	0	0	0	0	0	0	0	0	ZU-LT-10	J. PARSONS	1973
ZU-LT-173	Small Hamlet	Lakeshore Plain	1.3	10	0	0	0	0	0	0	0	0	0	0	ZU-LT-10	J. PARSONS	1973
ZU-LT-174	Sm Disp Village	Lakeshore Plain	8.9	180	0	0	0	1	1	1	0	0	0	0	ZU-LT-10	J. PARSONS	1973
ZU-LT-175	Small Hamlet	Lakeshore Plain	2.1	20	0	0	0	0	0	0	0	0	0	0	ZU-LT-10	J. PARSONS	1973
ZU-LT-176	Sm Disp Village	Lakeshore Plain	16.8	340	0	0	0	2	0	0	0	0	0	0	ZU-LT-10	J. PARSONS	1973
ZU-LT-177	Hamlet	Lakeshore Plain	2.1	40	0	0	0	0	0	0	0	0	0	0	ZU-LT-11	J. PARSONS	1973
ZU-LT-178	Hamlet	Lakeshore Plain	1.4	40	0	0	0	0	0	0	0	0	0	0	ZU-LT-10	J. PARSONS	1973
ZU-LT-179	Small Hamlet	Lakeshore Plain	1.0	20	0	0	0	0	0	0	0	0	0	0	ZU-LT-10	J. PARSONS	1973
ZU-LT-180	Sm Disp Village	Lakeshore Plain	6.5	130	0	0	0	0	0	0	0	0	0	0	ZU-LT-10	J. PARSONS	1973
ZU-LT-181	Hamlet	Lakeshore Plain	3.0	60	0	0	0	0	0	0	0	0	0	0	ZU-LT-10	J. PARSONS	1973
ZU-LT-182	Small Hamlet	Lakeshore Plain	0.3	10	0	0	0	0	0	0	0	0	0	0	ZU-LT-10	J. PARSONS	1973
ZU-LT-183	Small Hamlet	Lakeshore Plain	0.6	10	0	0	0	0	0	0	0	0	0	0	ZU-LT-10	J. PARSONS	1973
ZU-LT-184	Small Hamlet	Lakeshore Plain	0.5	5	0	0	0	0	0	0	0	0	0	0	ZU-LT-96	J. PARSONS	1973
ZU-LT-185	Hamlet	Lakeshore Plain	1.5	30	0	0	0	0	0	0	0	0	0	0	ZU-LT-95	J. PARSONS	1973
ZU-LT-186	Small Hamlet	Lakeshore Plain	0.6	5	0	0	0	0	0	0	0	0	0	0	ZU-LT-94	J. PARSONS	1973
ZU-LT-187	Small Hamlet	Lakeshore Plain	0.9	20	0	0	0	0	0	0	0	0	0	0	ZU-LT-93	J. PARSONS	1973
ZU-LT-188	Small Hamlet	Lakeshore Plain	1.1	20	0	0	0	0	0	0	0	0	0	0	ZU-LT-91	J. PARSONS	1973
ZU-LT-189	Small Hamlet	Lakeshore Plain	1.1	20	0	0	0	0	0	0	0	0	0	0	ZU-LT-92	J. PARSONS	1973
ZU-LT-190	Small Hamlet	Lakeshore Plain	0.6	10	0	0	0	0	0	0	0	0	0	0	ZU-LT-97	J. PARSONS	1973
ZU-LT-191	Sm Disp Village	Lakeshore Plain	8.5	170	0	0	0	0	0	0	0	0	0	0	ZU-LT-98	J. PARSONS	1973
ZU-LT-192	Sm Disp Village	Lakeshore Plain	12.0	240	0	0	0	0	0	0	0	0	0	0	ZU-LT-85	J. PARSONS	1973
ZU-LT-193	Hamlet	Lakeshore Plain	1.6	30	0	0	0	0	0	0	0	0	0	3	ZU-LT-78	J. PARSONS	1973
ZU-LT-194	Small Hamlet	Lakeshore Plain	0.3	10	0	0	0	0	0	0	0	0	0	1	ZU-LT-79	J. PARSONS	1973
ZU-LT-195	Hamlet	Lakeshore Plain	0.8	30	0	0	0	0	0	0	0	0	0	0	ZU-LT-67	M. PARSONS	1973
ZU-LT-196	Hamlet	Lakeshore Plain	1.3	30	0	0	0	0	1	1	0	0	0	0	ZU-LT-87	M. PARSONS	1973
ZU-LT-197	Hamlet	Lakeshore Plain	5.1	100	0	0	0	0	1	1	0	0	0	2	ZU-LT-88	M. PARSONS	1973
ZU-LT-198	Small Hamlet	Lakeshore Plain	1.3	10	0	0	0	0	0	0	0	0	0	1	ZU-LT-84	M. PARSONS	1973
ZU-LT-199	Small Hamlet	Lakeshore Plain	1.1	10	0	0	0	0	0	0	0	0	0	0	ZU-LT-85	M. PARSONS	1973
ZU-LT-200	Small Hamlet	Lakeshore Plain	0.3	5	0	0	0	0	0	0	0	0	0	1	ZU-LT-83	M. PARSONS	1973
ZU-LT-201	Small Hamlet	Lower Piedmont	0.8	10	0	0	0	0	0	0	0	0	0	0	ZU-LT-82	M. PARSONS	1973
ZU-LT-202	Small Hamlet	Lower Piedmont	1.4	10	0	0	0	0	0	0	0	0	0	0	ZU-LT-81	M. PARSONS	1973
ZU-LT-203	Sm Nucl Village	Lower Piedmont	11.5	400	0	0	0	0	0	0	0	0	0	1	ZU-LT-80	M. PARSONS	1973
ZU-LT-204	Small Hamlet	Lower Piedmont	1.2	20	0	0	0	0	0	0	0	0	0	0	ZU-LT-90	M. PARSONS	1973
ZU-LT-205	Hamlet	Lower Piedmont	5.0	50	0	0	0	0	0	0	0	0	0	1	ZU-LT-89	M. PARSONS	1973
ZU-LT-206	Sm Nucl Village	Lower Piedmont	13.5	400	0	0	0	0	0	0	0	0	0	1	ZU-LT-91	M. PARSONS	1973
ZU-LT-207	Hamlet	Lakeshore Plain	1.7	30	0	0	0	0	0	0	0	0	0	1	ZU-LT-68	M. PARSONS	1973
ZU-LT-208	Hamlet	Lakeshore Plain	2.8	60	0	0	0	0	0	0	0	0	0	1	ZU-LT-69	M. PARSONS	1973
ZU-LT-209	Sm Disp Village	Lakeshore Plain	10.6	300	0	0	0	0	0	0	0	0	0	0	ZU-LT-81	J. PARSONS	1973
ZU-LT-210	Sm Nucl Village	Lower Piedmont	9.5	400	0	0	0	0	0	0	0	0	0	0	ZU-LT-84	J. PARSONS	1973

Site Number	Environmental Zone	UTM Coordinates East	UTM Coordinates North	Elev (in m)	Rainfall (in mm)	Modern Soil Depth	Modern Erosion	Modern Land use
							ZUMPANGO REGION - ENVIRONMENTAL DATA	
							Late Toltec Sites	
ZU-LT-211	Lakeshore Plain	484.80	2175.70	2245	630	Deep	None	Agricultural
ZU-LT-212	Lakeshore Plain	487.55	2174.22	2245	620	Deep	None	Agricultural
ZU-LT-213	Lakeshore Plain	488.00	2173.65	2245	620	Deep	None	Grazing & Agri

ZUMPANGO REGION - PREHISPANIC SETTLEMENT DATA
Late Toltec Sites

SITE NUMBER	CLASSIFICATION	ENVIRONMENTAL ZONE	AREA (in ha)	POP.	OTHER OCCUPATIONS										SURVEY RECORDS		
					EF	MF	LF	TF	EC	LC	ET	LT	EA	LA	TEMPORARY SITE NO.	SUPERVISOR	YEAR
ZU-LT-211	Local Center	Lakeshore Plain	97.5	3000	0	0	0	0	0	0	1	0	0	0	ZU-LT-70	M. PARSONS	1973
ZU-LT-212	Hamlet	Lakeshore Plain	1.4	60	0	0	0	0	1	1	1	0	0	1	ZU-LT-83	J. PARSONS	1973
ZU-LT-213	Sm Disp Village	Lakeshore Plain	4.4	130	0	0	0	0	0	0	0	0	0	1	ZU-LT-82	J. PARSONS	1973

ZUMPANGO REGION - ENVIRONMENTAL DATA
Aztec Sites

Site Number	Environmental Zone	UTM Coordinates East	UTM Coordinates North	Elev (in m)	Rainfall (in mm)	Modern Soil Depth	Modern Erosion	Modern Land use
ZU-AZ-1	Lower Piedmont	494.32	2210.85	2420	600	Shallow	Deep	Grazing
ZU-AZ-2	Lower Piedmont	496.05	2210.72	2400	600	Shallow	Deep	Grazing
ZU-AZ-3	Upper Piedmont	495.65	2210.80	2500	600	Shallow	Moderate	Grazing
ZU-AZ-4	Lower Piedmont	495.53	2210.70	2465	600	Shallow	Moderate	Agricultural
ZU-AZ-5	Lower Piedmont	495.38	2209.80	2438	600	Shallow	Moderate	Agricultural
ZU-AZ-6	Lower Piedmont	495.00	2209.57	2400	600	Shallow	Moderate	Agricultural
ZU-AZ-7	Lower Piedmont	495.03	2207.65	2340	600	Medium	None	Agricultural
ZU-AZ-8	Lower Piedmont	493.72	2208.10	2355	600	Deep	None	Agricultural
ZU-AZ-9	Lower Piedmont	497.05	2207.30	2405	600	Shallow	Deep	Grazing
ZU-AZ-10	Lower Piedmont	496.70	2206.80	2380	600	Shallow	Slight	Grazing
ZU-AZ-11	Lower Piedmont	495.85	2206.75	2355	600	Medium	Deep	Agricultural
ZU-AZ-12	Lower Piedmont	495.03	2206.57	2340	600	Medium	None	Agricultural
ZU-AZ-13	Lower Piedmont	494.80	2206.38	2340	600	Shallow	Moderate	None
ZU-AZ-14	Lower Piedmont	494.90	2206.07	2330	600	Shallow	Deep	None
ZU-AZ-15	Lower Piedmont	494.60	2206.10	2340	600	Shallow	Moderate	Agricultural
ZU-AZ-16	Lower Piedmont	495.90	2206.00	2345	600	Shallow	Moderate	Agricultural
ZU-AZ-17	Lower Piedmont	497.00	2205.45	2375	600	Shallow	Slight	Grazing
ZU-AZ-18	Lower Piedmont	497.90	2203.68	2353	600	Medium	Deep	Agricultural
ZU-AZ-19	Lower Piedmont	497.53	2203.07	2330	600	Deep	None	Agricultural
ZU-AZ-20	Lower Piedmont	496.63	2204.55	2345	600	Shallow	Deep	Agricultural
ZU-AZ-21	Lower Piedmont	495.13	2205.05	2325	600	Shallow	Moderate	Agricultural
ZU-AZ-22	Lower Piedmont	495.22	2205.28	2325	600	Shallow	Moderate	Agricultural
ZU-AZ-23	Lower Piedmont	494.75	2205.45	2325	600	Shallow	Moderate	Agricultural
ZU-AZ-24	Lower Piedmont	494.10	2204.85	2330	600	Medium	Moderate	Agricultural
ZU-AZ-25	Lower Piedmont	490.95	2206.85	2370	600	Shallow	Moderate	Agricultural
ZU-AZ-26	Lower Piedmont	490.45	2207.55	2380	600	Shallow	Moderate	Agricultural
ZU-AZ-27	Lower Piedmont	490.03	2206.10	2325	600	Shallow	Moderate	Agricultural
ZU-AZ-28	Lower Piedmont	489.90	2205.63	2320	600	Shallow	Deep	Grazing
ZU-AZ-29	Lower Piedmont	489.25	2205.90	2315	600	Shallow	Deep	Agricultural
ZU-AZ-30	Lower Piedmont	489.07	2206.32	2325	600	Medium	None	Agricultural
ZU-AZ-31	Lower Piedmont	489.43	2206.95	2345	600	Medium	None	Agricultural
ZU-AZ-32	Lower Piedmont	489.53	2207.40	2345	600	Medium	None	Agricultural
ZU-AZ-33	Lower Piedmont	489.05	2208.18	2375	600	Shallow	Deep	None
ZU-AZ-34	Lower Piedmont	489.35	2208.75	2410	600	Shallow	Deep	None
ZU-AZ-35	Lower Piedmont	488.85	2208.63	2395	600	Shallow	Deep	None
ZU-AZ-36	Lower Piedmont	488.75	2208.85	2400	600	Shallow	Deep	None
ZU-AZ-37	Lower Piedmont	487.20	2208.85	2295	600	Medium	None	Agricultural
ZU-AZ-38	Lower Piedmont	487.97	2207.63	2330	600	Medium	Moderate	Agricultural
ZU-AZ-39	Lower Piedmont	488.30	2207.10	2320	600	Medium	None	Grazing & Agri
ZU-AZ-40	Lower Piedmont	487.15	2207.10	2300	600	Medium	Deep	Agricultural
ZU-AZ-41	Lower Piedmont	487.90	2205.15	2300	600	Medium	None	Agricultural
ZU-AZ-42	Lower Piedmont	487.15	2205.22	2285	600	Medium	None	Agricultural

ZUMPANGO REGION - PREHISPANIC SETTLEMENT DATA
Aztec Sites

SITE NUMBER	CLASSIFICATION	ENVIRONMENTAL ZONE	AREA (in ha)	POP.	EF	MF	LF	TF	EC	LC	ET	LT	EA	LA	TEMPORARY SITE NO.	SUPERVISOR	YEAR
ZU-AZ-1	Small Hamlet	Lower Piedmont	0.5	5	0	0	0	0	0	0	0	0	0	1		J. PARSONS	1973
ZU-AZ-2	Small Hamlet	Lower Piedmont	0.1	5	0	0	0	0	0	0	0	0	0	1	ZU-AZ-19	J. PARSONS	1973
ZU-AZ-3	Small Hamlet	Upper Piedmont	0.4	10	0	0	0	0	0	0	0	0	0	1		J. PARSONS	1973
ZU-AZ-4	Small Hamlet	Lower Piedmont	1.1	20	0	0	0	0	0	0	0	0	0	1	ZU-AZ-18	J. PARSONS	1973
ZU-AZ-5	Lg Disp Village	Lower Piedmont	52.4	1200	0	0	0	0	0	0	0	3	0	1	ZU-AZ-17	J. PARSONS	1973
ZU-AZ-6	Small Hamlet	Lower Piedmont	0.7	10	0	0	0	0	0	0	0	0	0	1	ZU-AZ-17	J. PARSONS	1973
ZU-AZ-7	Sm Disp Village	Lower Piedmont	9.7	200	0	0	0	0	0	0	0	0	0	1	ZU-AZ-16	J. PARSONS	1973
ZU-AZ-8	Small Hamlet	Lower Piedmont	0.1	5	0	0	0	0	0	0	0	0	0	1	ZU-AZ-20	J. PARSONS	1973
ZU-AZ-9	Hamlet	Lower Piedmont	3.7	70	0	0	0	0	0	0	0	0	0	0	ZU-AZ-15	J. PARSONS	1973
ZU-AZ-10	Small Hamlet	Lower Piedmont	1.1	20	0	0	0	0	0	0	0	0	0	1	ZU-AZ-14	J. PARSONS	1973
ZU-AZ-11	Small Hamlet	Lower Piedmont	0.5	5	0	0	0	0	0	0	0	0	0	1		J. PARSONS	1973
ZU-AZ-12	Small Hamlet	Lower Piedmont	0.5	10	0	0	0	0	0	0	0	0	0	1	ZU-AZ-1	J. PARSONS	1973
ZU-AZ-13	Small Hamlet	Lower Piedmont	0.7	10	0	0	0	0	0	0	0	0	0	1	ZU-AZ-2	J. PARSONS	1973
ZU-AZ-14	Small Hamlet	Lower Piedmont	0.7	10	0	0	0	0	0	0	0	0	0	1	ZU-AZ-3	J. PARSONS	1973
ZU-AZ-15	Small Hamlet	Lower Piedmont	0.6	20	0	0	0	0	0	0	0	0	0	1	ZU-AZ-4	J. PARSONS	1973
ZU-AZ-16	Small Hamlet	Lower Piedmont	0.7	5	0	0	0	0	0	0	0	0	0	1		J. PARSONS	1973
ZU-AZ-17	Hamlet	Lower Piedmont	1.6	30	0	0	0	0	0	0	0	0	0	1	ZU-AZ-13	J. PARSONS	1973
ZU-AZ-18	Lg Disp Village	Lower Piedmont	50.0	1000	0	0	0	0	0	1	0	2	0	1	ZU-AZ-12	J. PARSONS	1973
ZU-AZ-19	Small Hamlet	Lower Piedmont	1.2	20	0	0	0	0	0	1	0	1	0	1	ZU-AZ-11	J. PARSONS	1973
ZU-AZ-20	Small Hamlet	Lower Piedmont	0.4	5	0	0	0	0	0	0	0	0	0	1		J. PARSONS	1973
ZU-AZ-21	Hamlet	Lower Piedmont	3.0	60	0	0	0	0	0	0	0	1	0	1	ZU-AZ-6	J. PARSONS	1973
ZU-AZ-22	Hamlet	Lower Piedmont	1.4	60	0	0	0	0	0	0	0	1	0	1	ZU-AZ-5	J. PARSONS	1973
ZU-AZ-23	Small Hamlet	Lower Piedmont	0.4	10	0	0	0	0	0	0	0	0	0	1		J. PARSONS	1973
ZU-AZ-24	Hamlet	Lower Piedmont	1.0	20	0	0	0	0	0	0	0	0	0	1	ZU-AZ-7	J. PARSONS	1973
ZU-AZ-25	Small Hamlet	Lower Piedmont	0.1	10	0	0	0	0	0	0	0	0	0	1	ZU-AZ-29	J. PARSONS	1973
ZU-AZ-26	Small Hamlet	Lower Piedmont	1.1	20	0	0	0	0	0	0	0	0	0	1	ZU-AZ-30	J. PARSONS	1973
ZU-AZ-27	Small Hamlet	Lower Piedmont	0.4	10	0	0	0	0	0	0	0	0	0	1	ZU-AZ-28	J. PARSONS	1973
ZU-AZ-28	Small Hamlet	Lower Piedmont	1.0	10	0	0	0	1	0	0	1	0	0	1	ZU-AZ-17	J. PARSONS	1973
ZU-AZ-29	Small Hamlet	Lower Piedmont	0.9	20	0	0	0	1	0	0	1	0	0	1	ZU-AZ-40	M. PARSONS	1973
ZU-AZ-30	Small Hamlet	Lower Piedmont	0.6	10	0	0	0	0	0	0	0	0	0	1		M. PARSONS	1973
ZU-AZ-31	Small Hamlet	Lower Piedmont	1.0	10	0	0	0	0	0	0	0	0	0	1	ZU-AZ-34	M. PARSONS	1973
ZU-AZ-32	Small Hamlet	Lower Piedmont	0.7	10	0	0	0	0	0	0	0	0	0	1	ZU-AZ-33	M. PARSONS	1973
ZU-AZ-33	Small Hamlet	Lower Piedmont	1.3	20	0	0	0	0	0	0	0	0	0	1	ZU-AZ-32	M. PARSONS	1973
ZU-AZ-34	Hamlet	Lower Piedmont	3.0	30	0	0	0	0	0	0	0	0	0	1	ZU-AZ-30	M. PARSONS	1973
ZU-AZ-35	Small Hamlet	Lower Piedmont	0.7	10	0	0	0	0	0	0	0	0	0	1	ZU-AZ-31	M. PARSONS	1973
ZU-AZ-36	Small Hamlet	Lower Piedmont	1.3	10	0	0	0	0	0	0	0	0	0	1	ZU-AZ-29	M. PARSONS	1973
ZU-AZ-37	Hamlet	Lower Piedmont	1.6	40	0	0	0	0	0	0	0	0	0	1	ZU-AZ-25	M. PARSONS	1973
ZU-AZ-38	Hamlet	Lower Piedmont	1.7	30	0	0	0	0	0	0	0	0	0	1	ZU-AZ-28	M. PARSONS	1973
ZU-AZ-39	Small Hamlet	Lower Piedmont	1.1	20	0	0	0	0	0	0	0	0	0	1	ZU-AZ-27	M. PARSONS	1973
ZU-AZ-40	Sm Disp Village	Lower Piedmont	8.6	170	0	0	0	0	0	0	0	0	0	1	ZU-AZ-26	M. PARSONS	1973
ZU-AZ-41	Small Hamlet	Lower Piedmont	0.8	10	0	0	0	0	0	0	0	0	0	1	ZU-AZ-16	M. PARSONS	1973
ZU-AZ-42	Hamlet	Lower Piedmont	1.8	40	0	0	0	0	0	0	0	0	0	1	ZU-AZ-15	M. PARSONS	1973

(Columns EF–LA are grouped under "OTHER OCCUPATIONS"; SUPERVISOR and YEAR are grouped under "SURVEY RECORDS".)

Early Aztec and Late Aztec occupations are tabulated on a presence-absence basis.

ZUMPANGO REGION - ENVIRONMENTAL DATA
Aztec Sites

Site Number	Environmental Zone	UTM Coordinates East	UTM Coordinates North	Elev (in m)	Rainfall (in mm)	Modern Soil Depth	Modern Erosion	Modern Land use
ZU-AZ-43	Lower Piedmont	485.70	2204.47	2250	600	Medium	None	Agricultural
ZU-AZ-44	Lower Piedmont	485.35	2204.05	2235	600	Medium	None	Agricultural
ZU-AZ-45	Lower Piedmont	484.85	2205.18	2245	600	Medium	None	Agricultural
ZU-AZ-46	Lower Piedmont	483.45	2206.50	2225	600	Shallow	None	Agricultural
ZU-AZ-47	Lower Piedmont	482.45	2206.93	2205	600	Medium	None	Agricultural
ZU-AZ-48	Lower Piedmont	481.57	2209.22	2175	600	Deep	None	Agricultural
ZU-AZ-49	Lower Piedmont	481.25	2206.03	2200	600	Medium	None	None
ZU-AZ-50	Lower Piedmont	482.47	2204.60	2205	610	Medium	Slight-Moderate	Agricultural
ZU-AZ-51	Lower Piedmont	481.57	2206.25	2200	600	Shallow	Slight	Agricultural
ZU-AZ-52	Lower Piedmont	481.55	2205.18	2195	610	Medium	None	Agricultural
ZU-AZ-53	Lower Piedmont	479.78	2206.10	2225	610	Medium	Slight-Moderate	Agricultural
ZU-AZ-54	Lower Piedmont	477.57	2206.32	2355	620	Shallow	Moderate	Grazing
ZU-AZ-55	Lower Piedmont	476.07	2205.03	2295	650	Medium	Slight	Agricultural
ZU-AZ-56	Lower Piedmont	475.70	2203.97	2280	680	Shallow	Deep	Agricultural
ZU-AZ-57	Lower Piedmont	476.65	2205.07	2275	700	Shallow	Slight	Agricultural
ZU-AZ-58	Lower Piedmont	477.82	2205.07	2260	680	Shallow	Slight	Grazing & Agri
ZU-AZ-59	Lower Piedmont	478.70	2203.50	2250	660	Shallow	Moderate	Agricultural
ZU-AZ-60	Lower Piedmont	481.22	2204.30	2200	620	Shallow	Slight	Agricultural
ZU-AZ-61	Lower Piedmont	483.30	2203.00	2240	630	Medium	None	Agricultural
ZU-AZ-62	Lower Piedmont	482.70	2201.35	2245	670	Medium	Moderate	Agricultural
ZU-AZ-63	Lower Piedmont	483.88	2202.25	2210	640	Medium	None	Agricultural
ZU-AZ-64	Lower Piedmont	484.13	2202.57	2215	630	Medium	None	Agricultural
ZU-AZ-65	Lower Piedmont	484.68	2202.63	2210	620	Medium	None	Agricultural
ZU-AZ-66	Lower Piedmont	486.20	2203.53	2225	600	Deep	None	Agricultural
ZU-AZ-67	Lower Piedmont	486.68	2203.55	2230	600	Deep	None	Agricultural
ZU-AZ-68	Lower Piedmont	487.72	2203.95	2250	600	Medium	None	Agricultural
ZU-AZ-69	Lower Piedmont	488.10	2203.97	2250	600	Medium	Slight	Agricultural
ZU-AZ-70	Lower Piedmont	488.40	2204.13	2255	600	Medium	Slight	Agricultural
ZU-AZ-71	Lower Piedmont	488.78	2204.32	2260	600	Deep	None	Agricultural
ZU-AZ-72	Lower Piedmont	489.07	2203.10	2288	600	Medium	Moderate	Agricultural
ZU-AZ-73	Lower Piedmont	488.28	2203.18	2285	600	Medium	Moderate	Agricultural
ZU-AZ-74	Lower Piedmont	491.35	2204.40	2360	600	Medium	None	Agricultural
ZU-AZ-75	Lower Piedmont	491.13	2203.90	2350	600	Shallow	Deep	None
ZU-AZ-76	Lower Piedmont	490.85	2203.47	2325	600	Shallow	Deep	Agricultural
ZU-AZ-77	Lower Piedmont	492.57	2204.15	2345	600	Medium	None	Agricultural
ZU-AZ-78	Lower Piedmont	493.53	2203.20	2325	600	Medium	None	Agricultural
ZU-AZ-79	Lower Piedmont	495.13	2202.95	2313	600	Medium	Deep	Agricultural
ZU-AZ-80	Lower Piedmont	495.47	2202.97	2315	600	Medium	None	Agricultural
ZU-AZ-81	Lower Piedmont	495.90	2201.88	2308	600	Deep	None	Agricultural
ZU-AZ-82	Lower Piedmont	495.38	2201.78	2300	600	Medium	Deep	None
ZU-AZ-83	Lower Piedmont	494.97	2201.00	2325	600	Medium	Moderate	Agricultural
ZU-AZ-84	Lower Piedmont	495.22	2200.75	2305	600	Shallow	Deep	Grazing

ZUMPANGO REGION – PREHISPANIC SETTLEMENT DATA

Aztec Sites

SITE NUMBER	CLASSIFICATION	ENVIRONMENTAL ZONE	AREA (in ha)	POP.	OTHER OCCUPATIONS										SURVEY RECORDS		
					EF	MF	LF	TF	EC	LC	ET	LT	EA	LA	TEMPORARY SITE NO.	SUPERVISOR	YEAR
ZU-AZ-43	Small Hamlet	Lower Piedmont	0.6	5	0	0	0	0	0	0	0	0	0	1	ZU-AZ-12	M. PARSONS	1973
ZU-AZ-44	Small Hamlet	Lower Piedmont	0.1	5	0	0	0	0	0	0	0	0	0	1	ZU-AZ-39	M. PARSONS	1973
ZU-AZ-45	Hamlet	Lower Piedmont	1.8	40	0	0	0	0	0	0	0	0	0	1	ZU-AZ-11	M. PARSONS	1973
ZU-AZ-46	Sm Disp Village	Lower Piedmont	8.1	160	0	0	0	0	0	0	0	1	0	1	ZU-AZ-9	M. PARSONS	1973
ZU-AZ-47	Ceremonial Ctr	Lower Piedmont	1.0	0	0	0	0	0	0	1	0	0	0	1	ZU-AZ-10	M. PARSONS	1973
ZU-AZ-48	Small Hamlet	Lower Piedmont	1.9	20	0	0	0	0	1	1	1	0	0	1	ZU-AZ-24	M. PARSONS	1973
ZU-AZ-49	Hamlet	Lower Piedmont	3.9	40	0	0	0	0	0	0	0	0	0	1	ZU-AZ-8	M. PARSONS	1973
ZU-AZ-50	Small Hamlet	Lower Piedmont	2.0	20	0	0	0	0	0	0	0	0	0	1	ZU-AZ-7	M. PARSONS	1973
ZU-AZ-51	Small Hamlet	Lower Piedmont	0.5	5	0	0	0	0	0	0	0	0	0	1	ZU-AZ-6	M. PARSONS	1973
ZU-AZ-52	Hamlet	Lower Piedmont	1.4	30	0	0	0	0	0	0	0	0	0	1	ZU-AZ-35	M. PARSONS	1973
ZU-AZ-53	Hamlet	Lower Piedmont	1.3	30	0	0	0	0	0	0	0	0	0	1	ZU-AZ-5	M. PARSONS	1973
ZU-AZ-54	Ceremonial Ctr	Lower Piedmont	0.1	0	0	0	0	0	0	0	0	0	0	1	ZU-AZ-3	M. PARSONS	1973
ZU-AZ-55	Small Hamlet	Lower Piedmont	2.0	20	0	0	0	0	0	0	0	0	0	1	ZU-AZ-1	M. PARSONS	1973
ZU-AZ-56	Hamlet	Lower Piedmont	4.5	90	0	0	0	0	0	0	0	0	0	1	ZU-AZ-2	M. PARSONS	1973
ZU-AZ-57	Small Hamlet	Lower Piedmont	1.5	10	0	0	0	0	0	0	0	0	0	1	ZU-AZ-44	M. PARSONS	1973
ZU-AZ-58	Lg Disp Village	Lower Piedmont	21.0	600	0	0	0	0	0	0	0	1	0	1	ZU-AZ-44	M. PARSONS	1973
ZU-AZ-59	Small Hamlet	Lower Piedmont	0.3	5	0	0	0	0	0	0	0	0	0	1	ZU-AZ-43	M. PARSONS	1973
ZU-AZ-60	Sm Disp Village	Lower Piedmont	10.4	210	0	0	0	0	0	0	1	0	0	1	ZU-AZ-4	M. PARSONS	1973
ZU-AZ-61	Small Hamlet	Lower Piedmont	1.4	10	0	0	0	0	0	1	0	0	0	1	ZU-AZ-66	M. PARSONS	1973
ZU-AZ-62	Small Hamlet	Lower Piedmont	1.5	10	0	0	0	0	0	0	0	0	0	1	ZU-AZ-70	M. PARSONS	1973
ZU-AZ-63	Small Hamlet	Lower Piedmont	2.1	40	0	0	0	0	1	0	0	0	0	1	ZU-AZ-67	M. PARSONS	1973
ZU-AZ-64	Small Hamlet	Lower Piedmont	2.4	20	0	0	0	0	0	0	0	0	0	1	ZU-AZ-68	M. PARSONS	1973
ZU-AZ-65	Hamlet	Lower Piedmont	2.8	60	0	0	0	0	0	0	0	0	0	1	ZU-AZ-69	M. PARSONS	1973
ZU-AZ-66	Hamlet	Lower Piedmont	1.9	30	0	0	0	0	1	0	1	0	0	1	ZU-AZ-13	M. PARSONS	1973
ZU-AZ-67	Small Hamlet	Lower Piedmont	0.5	5	0	0	0	0	0	0	0	0	0	1	ZU-AZ-14	M. PARSONS	1973
ZU-AZ-68	Small Hamlet	Lower Piedmont	1.1	20	0	0	0	0	0	0	0	1	0	1	ZU-AZ-21	M. PARSONS	1973
ZU-AZ-69	Small Hamlet	Lower Piedmont	0.4	10	0	0	0	0	0	0	0	0	0	1	ZU-AZ-20	M. PARSONS	1973
ZU-AZ-70	Small Hamlet	Lower Piedmont	0.9	20	0	0	0	0	0	0	0	0	0	1	ZU-AZ-19	M. PARSONS	1973
ZU-AZ-71	Hamlet	Lower Piedmont	1.4	30	0	0	0	0	1	0	0	1	0	1	ZU-AZ-18	M. PARSONS	1973
ZU-AZ-72	Sm Disp Village	Lower Piedmont	17.2	340	0	0	0	0	0	0	0	0	0	1	ZU-AZ-22	M. PARSONS	1973
ZU-AZ-73	Sm Disp Village	Lower Piedmont	15.2	300	0	0	0	0	0	0	0	1	0	1	ZU-AZ-23	M. PARSONS	1973
ZU-AZ-74	Hamlet	Lower Piedmont	5.1	50	0	0	0	0	0	0	0	0	0	1	ZU-AZ-25	J. PARSONS	1973
ZU-AZ-75	Small Hamlet	Lower Piedmont	0.1	5	0	0	0	0	0	0	0	0	0	1	ZU-AZ-23	J. PARSONS	1973
ZU-AZ-76	Hamlet	Lower Piedmont	2.6	30	0	0	0	0	0	0	0	1	0	1	ZU-AZ-22	J. PARSONS	1973
ZU-AZ-77	Hamlet	Lower Piedmont	0.9	30	0	0	0	0	0	0	0	0	0	1	ZU-AZ-24	J. PARSONS	1973
ZU-AZ-78	Hamlet	Lower Piedmont	1.8	40	0	0	0	0	0	0	0	0	0	0	ZU-AZ-8	J. PARSONS	1973
ZU-AZ-79	Lg Nucl Village	Lower Piedmont	19.8	800	0	0	0	0	0	0	0	1	0	1	ZU-AZ-9	J. PARSONS	1973
ZU-AZ-80	Hamlet	Lower Piedmont	2.8	60	0	0	0	0	0	1	0	0	0	1	ZU-AZ-10	J. PARSONS	1973
ZU-AZ-81	Sm Disp Village	Lower Piedmont	20.3	400	0	0	0	0	0	0	0	0	0	1	ZU-AZ-65	J. PARSONS	1973
ZU-AZ-82	Hamlet	Lower Piedmont	5.2	100	0	0	0	0	0	0	0	1	0	1	ZU-AZ-66	J. PARSONS	1973
ZU-AZ-83	Small Hamlet	Lower Piedmont	1.8	20	0	0	0	0	0	1	0	0	0	1	ZU-AZ-63	J. PARSONS	1973
ZU-AZ-84	Hamlet	Lower Piedmont	3.1	60	0	0	0	0	0	0	0	1	0	1	ZU-AZ-63	J. PARSONS	1973

Early Aztec and Late Aztec occupations are tabulated on a presence-absence basis.

ZUMPANGO REGION - ENVIRONMENTAL DATA
Aztec Sites

Site Number	Environmental Zone	UTM Coordinates East	North	Elev (in m)	Rainfall (in mm)	Modern Soil Depth	Modern Erosion	Modern Land use
ZU-AZ-85	Lower Piedmont	495.45	2200.13	2330	600	Shallow	Slight	Agricultural
ZU-AZ-86	Lower Piedmont	494.40	2202.03	2350	600	Shallow	Moderate	Grazing
ZU-AZ-87	Lower Piedmont	493.50	2202.72	2360	600	Shallow	Deep	Grazing
ZU-AZ-88	Lower Piedmont	494.18	2200.30	2320	600	Shallow	Deep	Grazing
ZU-AZ-89	Lower Piedmont	494.22	2200.47	2310	600	Shallow	Deep	Grazing
ZU-AZ-90	Lower Piedmont	494.18	2200.60	2303	600	Shallow	Deep	Grazing
ZU-AZ-91	Lower Piedmont	493.53	2201.10	2300	600	Shallow	Deep	Grazing
ZU-AZ-92	Lower Piedmont	493.18	2200.50	2300	600	Shallow	Deep	Grazing
ZU-AZ-93	Lower Piedmont	493.18	2200.55	2300	600	Shallow	Deep	Grazing
ZU-AZ-94	Lower Piedmont	492.93	2201.72	2320	600	Shallow	Deep	Grazing & Agri
ZU-AZ-95	Lower Piedmont	492.90	2202.18	2325	600	Shallow	Deep	Grazing & Agri
ZU-AZ-96	Lower Piedmont	491.90	2202.20	2335	600	Shallow	Deep	Agricultural
ZU-AZ-97	Lower Piedmont	491.68	2201.78	2325	600	Shallow	Deep	Grazing & Agri
ZU-AZ-98	Lower Piedmont	491.13	2201.90	2310	600	Shallow	Deep	Grazing & Agri
ZU-AZ-99	Lower Piedmont	492.78	2200.40	2325	600	Shallow	Deep	None
ZU-AZ-100	Lower Piedmont	489.25	2205.63	2350	600	Shallow	Deep	Grazing
ZU-AZ-101	Lower Piedmont	489.25	2202.90	2348	600	Shallow	Deep	Grazing
ZU-AZ-102	Lower Piedmont	490.95	2202.75	2310	600	Shallow	Moderate-Deep	Agricultural
ZU-AZ-103	Lower Piedmont	490.45	2201.90	2295	600	Shallow	Deep	Agricultural
ZU-AZ-104	Lower Piedmont	489.93	2202.22	2298	600	Shallow	Deep	Agricultural
ZU-AZ-105	Lower Piedmont	489.65	2201.93	2305	600	Shallow	Deep	Grazing & Agri
ZU-AZ-106	Lower Piedmont	488.75	2201.75	2310	610	Medium	Slight	Agricultural
ZU-AZ-107	Lower Piedmont	487.93	2202.43	2305	600	Shallow	Moderate-Deep	Agricultural
ZU-AZ-108	Lower Piedmont	487.60	2202.13	2280	620	Shallow	None	Agricultural
ZU-AZ-109	Lower Piedmont	487.00	2202.07	2270	620	Shallow	None	Agricultural
ZU-AZ-110	Lower Piedmont	486.45	2202.05	2255	620	Shallow	None	Agricultural
ZU-AZ-111	Lower Piedmont	486.72	2201.35	2245	630	Medium	Slight	Agricultural
ZU-AZ-112	Lower Piedmont	487.07	2200.88	2355	640	Medium	Slight	Agricultural
ZU-AZ-113	Lower Piedmont	488.18	2200.82	2285	630	Shallow	Deep	Grazing & Agri
ZU-AZ-114	Lower Piedmont	488.47	2200.60	2320	630	Shallow	Deep	Grazing
ZU-AZ-115	Lower Piedmont	487.00	2200.13	2275	650	Medium	None	Agricultural
ZU-AZ-116	Lower Piedmont	485.35	2200.78	2250	650	Medium	None	Agricultural
ZU-AZ-117	Lower Piedmont	485.47	2200.30	2300	660	Medium	None	Agricultural
ZU-AZ-118	Lower Piedmont	484.30	2199.82	2245	680	Shallow	Deep	Agricultural
ZU-AZ-119	Lower Piedmont	483.43	2199.07	2285	700	Medium	Deep	Agricultural
ZU-AZ-120	Lower Piedmont	483.88	2198.30	2265	700	Deep	Slight	Agricultural
ZU-AZ-121	Lower Piedmont	484.90	2198.50	2275	700	Medium	Moderate	Agricultural
ZU-AZ-122	Lower Piedmont	485.88	2199.32	2275	680	Medium	Deep	Agricultural
ZU-AZ-123	Lower Piedmont	485.82	2199.82	2280	670	Medium	Deep	Agricultural
ZU-AZ-124	Lower Piedmont	486.28	2200.03	2300	660	Medium	Deep	Agricultural
ZU-AZ-125	Lower Piedmont	487.25	2199.10	2290	670	Medium	Moderate	Agricultural
ZU-AZ-126	Lower Piedmont	487.93	2199.32	2293	650	Shallow	Deep	Grazing

ZUMPANGO REGION - PREHISPANIC SETTLEMENT DATA
Aztec Sites

SITE NUMBER	CLASSIFICATION	ENVIRONMENTAL ZONE	AREA (in ha)	POP.	EF	MF	LF	TF	EC	LC	ET	LT	EA	LA	TEMPORARY SITE NO.	SUPERVISOR	YEAR
									OTHER OCCUPATIONS							SURVEY RECORDS	
ZU-AZ-85	Small Hamlet	Lower Piedmont	0.4	10	0	0	0	0	1	1	0	0	0	1	ZU-AZ-69	J. PARSONS	1973
ZU-AZ-86	Small Hamlet	Lower Piedmont	1.0	20	0	0	0	0	0	1	0	0	0	1	ZU-AZ-31	J. PARSONS	1973
ZU-AZ-87	Sm Disp Village	Lower Piedmont	8.0	160	0	0	0	0	0	0	0	0	0	1	ZU-AZ-67	J. PARSONS	1973
ZU-AZ-88	Hamlet	Lower Piedmont	2.0	40	0	0	0	0	0	0	0	0	0	1	ZU-AZ-67	J. PARSONS	1973
ZU-AZ-89	Small Hamlet	Lower Piedmont	0.9	10	0	0	0	0	0	0	0	0	0	1	ZU-AZ-64	J. PARSONS	1973
ZU-AZ-90	Hamlet	Lower Piedmont	2.0	40	0	0	0	0	0	0	0	0	0	1	ZU-AZ-64	J. PARSONS	1973
ZU-AZ-91	Small Hamlet	Lower Piedmont	0.4	10	0	0	0	0	0	0	0	0	0	1	ZU-AZ-36	J. PARSONS	1973
ZU-AZ-92	Hamlet	Lower Piedmont	1.6	30	0	0	0	0	0	0	0	0	0	1	ZU-AZ-32	J. PARSONS	1973
ZU-AZ-93	Small Hamlet	Lower Piedmont	0.6	5	0	0	0	0	0	0	0	0	0	1	ZU-AZ-38	J. PARSONS	1973
ZU-AZ-94	Hamlet	Lower Piedmont	2.2	50	0	0	0	0	0	0	1	0	0	1	ZU-AZ-13	J. PARSONS	1973
ZU-AZ-95	Hamlet	Lower Piedmont	2.0	50	0	0	0	0	0	0	0	0	0	1	ZU-AZ-13	J. PARSONS	1973
ZU-AZ-96	Hamlet	Lower Piedmont	2.7	60	0	0	0	0	0	0	0	0	0	1	ZU-AZ-13	J. PARSONS	1973
ZU-AZ-97	Small Hamlet	Lower Piedmont	1.0	20	0	0	0	0	0	0	0	0	0	1	ZU-AZ-13	J. PARSONS	1973
ZU-AZ-98	Hamlet	Lower Piedmont	3.0	60	0	0	0	0	1	0	0	0	0	1	ZU-AZ-13	J. PARSONS	1973
ZU-AZ-99	Sm Disp Village	Lower Piedmont	15.7	310	0	0	0	0	1	1	0	2	0	1	ZU-AZ-34	J. PARSONS	1973
ZU-AZ-100	Hamlet	Lower Piedmont	4.5	90	0	0	0	0	0	0	0	0	0	1	ZU-AZ-26	J. PARSONS	1973
ZU-AZ-101	Sm Disp Village	Lower Piedmont	6.0	120	0	0	0	0	0	0	1	0	0	1	ZU-AZ-21	J. PARSONS	1973
ZU-AZ-102	Hamlet	Lower Piedmont	4.7	100	0	0	0	0	0	1	0	0	0	1	ZU-AZ-13	J. PARSONS	1973
ZU-AZ-103	Small Hamlet	Lower Piedmont	0.8	20	0	0	0	0	0	0	0	0	0	1	ZU-AZ-14	J. PARSONS	1973
ZU-AZ-104	Sm Disp Village	Lower Piedmont	8.3	160	0	0	0	0	0	0	1	0	0	1	ZU-AZ-14	J. PARSONS	1973
ZU-AZ-105	Hamlet	Lower Piedmont	5.0	100	0	0	0	0	0	1	0	0	0	1	ZU-AZ-14	J. PARSONS	1973
ZU-AZ-106	Hamlet	Lower Piedmont	2.0	40	0	0	0	0	0	0	1	0	0	1	ZU-AZ-50	J. PARSONS	1973
ZU-AZ-107	Small Hamlet	Lower Piedmont	1.4	20	0	0	0	0	0	0	0	0	0	1	ZU-AZ-14	J. PARSONS	1973
ZU-AZ-108	Small Hamlet	Lower Piedmont	1.0	20	0	0	0	0	0	0	0	0	0	1	ZU-AZ-51	M. PARSONS	1973
ZU-AZ-109	Hamlet	Lower Piedmont	1.4	30	0	0	0	0	0	0	1	0	0	1	ZU-AZ-50	M. PARSONS	1973
ZU-AZ-110	Small Hamlet	Lower Piedmont	0.6	5	0	0	0	0	0	0	0	0	0	1	ZU-AZ-49	M. PARSONS	1973
ZU-AZ-111	Small Hamlet	Lower Piedmont	0.6	5	0	0	0	0	0	0	0	0	0	1	ZU-AZ-52	M. PARSONS	1973
ZU-AZ-112	Small Hamlet	Lower Piedmont	0.9	10	0	0	0	0	0	0	0	0	0	1	ZU-AZ-53	M. PARSONS	1973
ZU-AZ-113	Small Hamlet	Lower Piedmont	0.7	10	0	0	0	0	1	1	0	0	0	1	ZU-AZ-54	J. PARSONS	1973
ZU-AZ-114	Sm Disp Village	Lower Piedmont	15.1	300	0	0	0	0	1	1	1	0	0	1	ZU-AZ-53	J. PARSONS	1973
ZU-AZ-115	Hamlet	Lower Piedmont	7.3	70	0	0	0	0	0	0	1	0	0	1	ZU-AZ-48	M. PARSONS	1973
ZU-AZ-116	Sm Disp Village	Lower Piedmont	11.2	220	0	0	0	0	0	0	1	0	0	1	ZU-AZ-46	M. PARSONS	1973
ZU-AZ-117	Hamlet	Lower Piedmont	2.9	30	0	0	0	0	0	0	1	0	0	1	ZU-AZ-47	M. PARSONS	1973
ZU-AZ-118	Sm Disp Village	Lower Piedmont	6.6	130	0	0	0	0	0	0	2	0	0	1	ZU-AZ-37	M. PARSONS	1973
ZU-AZ-119	Sm Disp Village	Lower Piedmont	6.4	130	0	0	0	0	0	0	1	0	0	1	ZU-AZ-36	M. PARSONS	1973
ZU-AZ-120	Small Hamlet	Lower Piedmont	0.8	20	0	0	0	0	0	0	1	0	0	1	ZU-AZ-38	M. PARSONS	1973
ZU-AZ-121	Sm Disp Village	Lower Piedmont	8.7	260	0	0	0	0	0	0	0	0	0	1	ZU-AZ-61	M. PARSONS	1973
ZU-AZ-122	Sm Disp Village	Lower Piedmont	6.1	120	0	0	0	0	0	0	0	0	0	1	ZU-AZ-62	M. PARSONS	1973
ZU-AZ-123	Sm Disp Village	Lower Piedmont	5.4	110	0	0	0	0	0	0	0	0	0	1	ZU-AZ-63	M. PARSONS	1973
ZU-AZ-124	Hamlet	Lower Piedmont	1.5	30	0	0	0	0	0	0	0	0	0	1	ZU-AZ-64	M. PARSONS	1973
ZU-AZ-125	Small Hamlet	Lower Piedmont	0.6	5	0	0	0	0	0	0	0	0	0	1	ZU-AZ-65	M. PARSONS	1973
ZU-AZ-126	Sm Disp Village	Lower Piedmont	10.2	200	0	0	0	0	0	0	0	0	0	1	ZU-AZ-56	J. PARSONS	1973

Early Aztec and Late Aztec occupations are tabulated on a presence-absence basis.

ZUMPANGO REGION - ENVIRONMENTAL DATA
Aztec Sites

Site Number	Environmental Zone	UTM Coordinates East	North	Elev (in m)	Rainfall (in mm)	Modern Soil Depth	Modern Erosion	Modern Land use
ZU-AZ-127	Lower Piedmont	488.75	2200.03	2305	640	Shallow	Deep	Grazing
ZU-AZ-128	Lower Piedmont	489.05	2200.80	2350	630	Medium	Slight	Agricultural
ZU-AZ-129	Lower Piedmont	489.38	2200.85	2350	620	Medium	Slight	Agricultural
ZU-AZ-130	Lower Piedmont	491.00	2201.00	2328	610	Shallow	Deep	Grazing
ZU-AZ-131	Lower Piedmont	491.50	2201.75	2305	610	Shallow	Deep	Grazing
ZU-AZ-132	Lower Piedmont	491.82	2199.88	2325	600	Shallow	Deep	Agricultural
ZU-AZ-133	Lower Piedmont	493.15	2200.05	2380	600	Shallow	Deep	Grazing
ZU-AZ-134	Lower Piedmont	493.13	2199.85	2365	600	Shallow	Deep	Grazing
ZU-AZ-135	Lower Piedmont	493.10	2199.25	2350	600	Shallow	Deep	Grazing
ZU-AZ-136	Lower Piedmont	492.40	2198.97	2353	600	Shallow	Deep	Grazing & Agri
ZU-AZ-137	Lower Piedmont	492.95	2205.95	2350	600	Shallow	Deep	Grazing & Agri
ZU-AZ-138	Lower Piedmont	493.53	2198.68	2355	600	Shallow	Deep	Grazing & Agri
ZU-AZ-139	Lower Piedmont	494.13	2198.70	2355	600	Shallow	Moderate	Agricultural
ZU-AZ-140	Lower Piedmont	494.47	2198.70	2355	600	Shallow	Deep	Agricultural
ZU-AZ-141	Lower Piedmont	494.72	2198.13	2345	600	Shallow	Deep	Grazing & Agri
ZU-AZ-142	Lower Piedmont	495.90	2198.65	2340	600	Shallow	Moderate	Agricultural
ZU-AZ-143	Lower Piedmont	495.47	2198.25	2340	600	Shallow	Deep	Grazing & Agri
ZU-AZ-144	Lower Piedmont	495.40	2197.80	2340	600	Shallow	Deep	Grazing & Agri
ZU-AZ-145	Lower Piedmont	494.57	2197.68	2345	600	Shallow	Deep	None
ZU-AZ-146	Lower Piedmont	494.20	2197.72	2350	600	Shallow	Deep	None
ZU-AZ-147	Lower Piedmont	492.63	2204.75	2400	620	Shallow	Deep	Agricultural
ZU-AZ-148	Lower Piedmont	492.93	2196.97	2275	620	Shallow	Deep	Grazing
ZU-AZ-149	Lower Piedmont	492.30	2196.50	2375	630	Shallow	Deep	Grazing
ZU-AZ-150	Lower Piedmont	492.03	2197.10	2393	630	Shallow	Deep	Agricultural
ZU-AZ-151	Lower Piedmont	491.47	2200.45	2405	630	Shallow	Moderate	Agricultural
ZU-AZ-152	Lower Piedmont	491.60	2198.40	2390	610	Shallow	Deep	Grazing
ZU-AZ-153	Lower Piedmont	491.20	2198.57	2375	610	Medium	Slight	Agricultural
ZU-AZ-154	Lower Piedmont	491.00	2198.35	2383	620	Medium	Slight	Agricultural
ZU-AZ-155	Lower Piedmont	491.53	2199.05	2345	610	Shallow	Deep	Grazing & Agri
ZU-AZ-156	Lower Piedmont	491.18	2199.65	2325	610	Shallow	Moderate	Agricultural
ZU-AZ-157	Lower Piedmont	490.82	2199.25	2348	620	Shallow	Deep	Grazing
ZU-AZ-158	Lower Piedmont	490.38	2198.72	2355	630	Shallow	Deep	Grazing
ZU-AZ-159	Lower Piedmont	489.63	2198.55	2340	640	Shallow	Deep	Grazing
ZU-AZ-160	Lower Piedmont	489.15	2198.97	2340	650	Shallow	Deep	Grazing
ZU-AZ-161	Lower Piedmont	489.65	2200.00	2348	630	Shallow	Moderate	Grazing & Agri
ZU-AZ-162	Lower Piedmont	489.03	2199.60	2310	640	Shallow	Deep	Grazing
ZU-AZ-163	Lower Piedmont	488.47	2198.90	2320	660	Shallow	Deep	Grazing
ZU-AZ-164	Lower Piedmont	490.10	2198.13	2365	650	Shallow	Deep	Agricultural
ZU-AZ-165	Lower Piedmont	489.55	2198.10	2360	650	Shallow	Deep	Agricultural
ZU-AZ-166	Lower Piedmont	489.13	2198.22	2355	640	Shallow	Deep	Agricultural
ZU-AZ-167	Lower Piedmont	488.35	2197.82	2350	670	Shallow	Moderate	Grazing
ZU-AZ-168	Lower Piedmont	487.68	2197.97	2300	680	Shallow	Deep	Grazing

ZUMPANGO REGION - PREHISPANIC SETTLEMENT DATA
Aztec Sites

SITE NUMBER	CLASSIFICATION	ENVIRONMENTAL ZONE	AREA (in ha)	POP.	EF	MF	LF	TF	EC	LC	ET	LT	EA	LA	TEMPORARY SITE NO.	SUPERVISOR	YEAR
ZU-AZ-127	Small Hamlet	Lower Piedmont	0.5	10	0	0	0	0	0	0	0	0	0	1	ZU-AZ-62	J. PARSONS	1973
ZU-AZ-128	Small Hamlet	Lower Piedmont	1.0	10	0	0	0	0	0	0	0	1	0	1	ZU-AZ-52	J. PARSONS	1973
ZU-AZ-129	Hamlet	Lower Piedmont	4.3	80	0	0	0	0	0	0	0	1	0	1	ZU-AZ-51	J. PARSONS	1973
ZU-AZ-130	Local Center	Lower Piedmont	103.8	2200	0	0	0	0	0	0	0	2	0	1	ZU-AZ-41	J. PARSONS	1973
ZU-AZ-131	Hamlet	Lower Piedmont	4.0	80	0	0	0	0	0	0	0	0	0	1	ZU-AZ-41	J. PARSONS	1973
ZU-AZ-132	Lg Disp Village	Lower Piedmont	53.6	1500	0	0	0	0	0	0	0	3	0	1	ZU-AZ-35	J. PARSONS	1973
ZU-AZ-133	Small Hamlet	Lower Piedmont	0.5	10	0	0	0	0	0	0	0	0	0	1	ZU-AZ-37	J. PARSONS	1973
ZU-AZ-134	Hamlet	Lower Piedmont	1.3	30	0	0	0	0	0	0	0	0	0	1	ZU-AZ-33	J. PARSONS	1973
ZU-AZ-135	Sm Disp Village	Lower Piedmont	6.1	120	0	0	0	0	0	0	0	1	0	1	ZU-AZ-42	J. PARSONS	1973
ZU-AZ-136	Sm Disp Village	Lower Piedmont	18.6	400	0	0	0	0	0	0	0	3	0	1	ZU-AZ-43	J. PARSONS	1973
ZU-AZ-137	Sm Disp Village	Lower Piedmont	6.3	120	0	0	0	0	0	0	0	0	0	1	ZU-AZ-44	J. PARSONS	1973
ZU-AZ-138	Hamlet	Lower Piedmont	3.7	80	0	0	0	0	0	0	0	0	0	1	ZU-AZ-74	J. PARSONS	1973
ZU-AZ-139	Small Hamlet	Lower Piedmont	0.8	10	0	0	0	0	0	0	0	0	0	1	ZU-AZ-73	J. PARSONS	1973
ZU-AZ-140	Small Hamlet	Lower Piedmont	1.9	20	0	0	0	0	0	0	0	0	0	1	ZU-AZ-71	J. PARSONS	1973
ZU-AZ-141	Lg Disp Village	Lower Piedmont	45.2	900	0	0	0	0	0	0	0	0	0	1	ZU-AZ-70	J. PARSONS	1973
ZU-AZ-142	Small Hamlet	Lower Piedmont	0.4	10	0	0	0	0	0	0	0	0	0	1	ZU-AZ-72	J. PARSONS	1973
ZU-AZ-143	Small Hamlet	Lower Piedmont	1.3	10	0	0	0	0	0	0	0	0	0	1	ZU-AZ-70	J. PARSONS	1973
ZU-AZ-144	Small Hamlet	Lower Piedmont	0.5	5	0	0	0	0	0	0	0	0	0	1	ZU-AZ-70	J. PARSONS	1973
ZU-AZ-145	Hamlet	Lower Piedmont	1.8	40	0	0	0	0	0	0	0	0	0	1	ZU-AZ-75	J. PARSONS	1973
ZU-AZ-146	Small Hamlet	Lower Piedmont	2.2	20	0	0	0	0	0	0	0	0	0	1	ZU-AZ-75	J. PARSONS	1973
ZU-AZ-147	Lg Disp Village	Lower Piedmont	73.4	1500	0	0	0	0	0	0	0	1	0	1	ZU-AZ-45	J. PARSONS	1973
ZU-AZ-148	Small Hamlet	Lower Piedmont	1.9	20	0	0	0	0	0	0	0	0	0	1		J. PARSONS	1973
ZU-AZ-149	Lg Disp Village	Lower Piedmont	25.2	600	0	0	0	0	0	0	0	1	0	1	ZU-AZ-93	J. PARSONS	1973
ZU-AZ-150	Hamlet	Lower Piedmont	2.9	30	0	0	0	0	0	0	0	0	0	1	ZU-AZ-91	J. PARSONS	1973
ZU-AZ-151	Hamlet	Lower Piedmont	1.8	40	0	0	0	0	0	0	0	0	0	1	ZU-AZ-47	J. PARSONS	1973
ZU-AZ-152	Hamlet	Lower Piedmont	1.0	40	0	0	0	0	0	0	0	0	0	1	ZU-AZ-46	J. PARSONS	1973
ZU-AZ-153	Hamlet	Lower Piedmont	1.5	40	0	0	0	0	0	0	0	0	0	1	ZU-AZ-46	J. PARSONS	1973
ZU-AZ-154	Sm Disp Village	Lower Piedmont	5.5	120	0	0	0	0	0	0	0	0	0	1	ZU-AZ-46	J. PARSONS	1973
ZU-AZ-155	Lg Disp Village	Lower Piedmont	28.7	600	0	0	0	0	0	0	0	1	0	1	ZU-AZ-39	J. PARSONS	1973
ZU-AZ-156	Small Hamlet	Lower Piedmont	0.8	10	0	0	0	0	0	0	0	1	0	1	ZU-AZ-40	J. PARSONS	1973
ZU-AZ-157	Sm Disp Village	Lower Piedmont	8.8	180	0	0	0	0	0	0	0	0	0	1	ZU-AZ-49	J. PARSONS	1973
ZU-AZ-158	Hamlet	Lower Piedmont	2.6	50	0	0	0	0	0	0	0	0	0	1	ZU-AZ-48	J. PARSONS	1973
ZU-AZ-159	Small Hamlet	Lower Piedmont	1.0	10	0	0	0	0	0	0	0	0	0	1		J. PARSONS	1973
ZU-AZ-160	Hamlet	Lower Piedmont	1.7	30	0	0	0	0	0	0	0	1	0	1	ZU-AZ-59	J. PARSONS	1973
ZU-AZ-161	Sm Disp Village	Lower Piedmont	6.4	130	0	0	0	0	0	0	0	0	0	1	ZU-AZ-55	J. PARSONS	1973
ZU-AZ-162	Hamlet	Lower Piedmont	2.4	50	0	0	0	0	0	0	0	0	0	1	ZU-AZ-57	J. PARSONS	1973
ZU-AZ-163	Hamlet	Lower Piedmont	4.8	40	0	0	0	0	0	0	0	0	0	1	ZU-AZ-58	J. PARSONS	1973
ZU-AZ-164	Small Hamlet	Lower Piedmont	0.7	5	0	0	0	0	0	0	0	0	0	1		J. PARSONS	1973
ZU-AZ-165	Small Hamlet	Lower Piedmont	0.6	5	0	0	0	0	0	0	0	0	0	1		J. PARSONS	1973
ZU-AZ-166	Small Hamlet	Lower Piedmont	0.8	10	0	0	0	0	0	0	0	0	0	1	ZU-AZ-61	J. PARSONS	1973
ZU-AZ-167	Small Hamlet	Lower Piedmont	1.4	10	0	0	0	0	0	0	0	0	0	1	ZU-AZ-60	J. PARSONS	1973
ZU-AZ-168	Small Hamlet	Lower Piedmont	0.6	5	0	0	0	0	0	0	0	0	0	1		J. PARSONS	1973

Early Aztec and Late Aztec occupations are tabulated on a presence-absence basis.

140

ZUMPANGO REGION - ENVIRONMENTAL DATA
Aztec Sites

Site Number	Environmental Zone	UTM Coordinates East	North	Elev (in m)	Rainfall (in mm)	Modern Soil Depth	Modern Erosion	Modern Land use
ZU-AZ-169	Lower Piedmont	490.20	2195.25	2335	680	Shallow	Deep	Grazing
ZU-AZ-170	Lower Piedmont	490.72	2195.30	2355	670	Shallow	Moderate	Grazing & Agri
ZU-AZ-171	Lower Piedmont	491.45	2195.32	2365	660	Shallow	Moderate	Agricultural
ZU-AZ-172	Lower Piedmont	493.13	2195.13	2370	650	Shallow	Deep	None
ZU-AZ-173	Lower Piedmont	492.00	2195.05	2385	660	Shallow	Deep	Agricultural
ZU-AZ-174	Lower Piedmont	493.57	2195.95	2348	630	Shallow	Deep	Grazing
ZU-AZ-175	Lower Piedmont	493.85	2195.80	2340	630	Shallow	Deep	Grazing
ZU-AZ-176	Lower Piedmont	494.13	2195.72	2340	630	Shallow	Deep	Grazing
ZU-AZ-177	Lower Piedmont	493.70	2195.43	2355	640	Shallow	Deep	Grazing
ZU-AZ-178	Lower Piedmont	493.97	2194.50	2330	650	Shallow	Deep	Grazing
ZU-AZ-179	Lower Piedmont	493.40	2194.38	2340	650	Shallow	Deep	Grazing
ZU-AZ-180	Lower Piedmont	492.47	2194.65	2373	660	Shallow	Deep	Grazing & Agri
ZU-AZ-181	Lower Piedmont	492.25	2193.80	2350	670	Shallow	Deep	Agricultural
ZU-AZ-182	Lower Piedmont	491.70	2195.13	2333	670	Shallow	Deep	Agricultural
ZU-AZ-183	Lower Piedmont	491.70	2193.13	2323	670	Shallow	Deep	Agricultural
ZU-AZ-184	Lower Piedmont	491.65	2192.72	2320	680	Shallow	Deep	Agricultural
ZU-AZ-185	Lower Piedmont	493.65	2193.03	2325	650	Medium	Slight	Agricultural
ZU-AZ-186	Lower Piedmont	494.18	2192.38	2315	660	Shallow	Moderate	Agricultural
ZU-AZ-187	Lower Piedmont	494.18	2192.22	2310	660	Shallow	Moderate	Agricultural
ZU-AZ-188	Lower Piedmont	494.03	2191.75	2315	670	Shallow	Moderate	Agricultural
ZU-AZ-189	Lower Piedmont	494.13	2191.40	2308	670	Medium	Moderate	None
ZU-AZ-190	Lower Piedmont	494.03	2191.20	2300	670	Medium	Moderate	Agricultural
ZU-AZ-191	Lower Piedmont	493.72	2191.30	2300	670	Medium	Moderate	Agricultural
ZU-AZ-192	Lower Piedmont	493.53	2191.00	2290	680	Medium	Moderate	Agricultural
ZU-AZ-193	Lower Piedmont	493.43	2191.00	2290	680	Medium	Moderate	Agricultural
ZU-AZ-194	Lower Piedmont	492.88	2191.57	2305	680	Shallow	Deep	Agricultural
ZU-AZ-195	Lower Piedmont	491.88	2191.90	2303	690	Shallow	Deep	Agricultural
ZU-AZ-196	Lower Piedmont	491.32	2192.25	2300	690	Shallow	Deep	Grazing & Agri
ZU-AZ-197	Lower Piedmont	491.18	2194.32	2350	680	Shallow	Moderate	Agricultural
ZU-AZ-198	Lower Piedmont	490.25	2194.53	2335	680	Shallow	Deep	Grazing
ZU-AZ-199	Lower Piedmont	489.82	2194.47	2315	690	Shallow	Deep	Grazing & Agri
ZU-AZ-200	Lower Piedmont	479.88	2195.13	2330	700	Shallow	Moderate	Agricultural
ZU-AZ-201	Lower Piedmont	479.65	2195.25	2335	700	Shallow	Moderate	Agricultural
ZU-AZ-202	Lower Piedmont	486.55	2194.07	2350	700	Shallow	Deep	Grazing
ZU-AZ-203	Lower Piedmont	486.28	2193.78	2345	700	Shallow	Deep	None
ZU-AZ-204	Lower Piedmont	485.38	2195.57	2390	700	Medium	None	Agricultural
ZU-AZ-205	Lower Piedmont	485.15	2195.55	2400	700	Shallow	None	Grazing
ZU-AZ-206	Lower Piedmont	485.00	2195.43	2400	700	Medium	None	Grazing
ZU-AZ-207	Lower Piedmont	483.90	2195.90	2365	700	Shallow	None	Grazing
ZU-AZ-208	Lower Piedmont	483.10	2195.93	2325	700	Medium	None	Agricultural
ZU-AZ-209	Lower Piedmont	482.38	2196.00	2300	700	Medium	None	Agricultural
ZU-AZ-210	Lower Piedmont	482.38	2196.25	2300	700	Medium	None	Agricultural

ZUMPANGO REGION - PREHISPANIC SETTLEMENT DATA
Aztec Sites

SITE NUMBER	CLASSIFICATION	ENVIRONMENTAL ZONE	AREA (in ha)	POP.	OTHER OCCUPATIONS										SURVEY RECORDS		
					EF	MF	LF	TF	EC	LC	ET	LT	EA	LA	TEMPORARY SITE NO.	SUPERVISOR	YEAR
ZU-AZ-169	Sm Disp Village	Lower Piedmont	18.1	400	0	0	0	0	0	0	0	0	0	1	ZU-AZ-10	J. PARSONS	1973
ZU-AZ-170	Hamlet	Lower Piedmont	3.6	70	0	0	0	0	0	0	0	2	0	1	ZU-AZ-10	J. PARSONS	1973
ZU-AZ-171	Small Hamlet	Lower Piedmont	1.0	20	0	0	0	0	0	0	0	0	0	1	ZU-AZ-10	J. PARSONS	1973
ZU-AZ-172	Local Center	Lower Piedmont	115.3	2400	0	0	0	0	1	1	0	3	0	1	ZU-AZ-76	J. PARSONS	1973
ZU-AZ-173	Hamlet	Lower Piedmont	6.3	60	0	0	0	0	0	0	0	0	0	1	ZU-AZ-95	J. PARSONS	1973
ZU-AZ-174	Hamlet	Lower Piedmont	1.6	30	0	0	0	0	0	0	0	0	0	1	ZU-AZ-81	J. PARSONS	1973
ZU-AZ-175	Small Hamlet	Lower Piedmont	0.6	5	0	0	0	0	0	0	0	0	0	1	ZU-AZ-80	J. PARSONS	1973
ZU-AZ-176	Small Hamlet	Lower Piedmont	1.3	10	0	0	0	0	0	0	0	0	0	1	ZU-AZ-79	J. PARSONS	1973
ZU-AZ-177	Small Hamlet	Lower Piedmont	0.7	10	0	0	0	0	0	0	0	0	0	1	ZU-AZ-78	J. PARSONS	1973
ZU-AZ-178	Hamlet	Lower Piedmont	4.1	40	0	0	0	0	0	0	0	0	0	1	ZU-AZ-82	J. PARSONS	1973
ZU-AZ-179	Hamlet	Lower Piedmont	2.4	50	0	0	0	0	0	0	0	0	0	1	ZU-AZ-83	J. PARSONS	1973
ZU-AZ-180	Hamlet	Lower Piedmont	9.2	100	0	0	0	0	0	0	0	1	0	1	ZU-AZ-94	J. PARSONS	1973
ZU-AZ-181	Sm Disp Village	Lower Piedmont	11.2	200	0	0	0	1	1	0	0	1	0	1	ZU-AZ-97	J. PARSONS	1973
ZU-AZ-182	Sm Disp Village	Lower Piedmont	6.2	120	0	0	0	0	0	0	0	0	0	1	ZU-AZ-96	J. PARSONS	1973
ZU-AZ-183	Hamlet	Lower Piedmont	3.6	70	0	0	0	0	0	0	0	0	0	1	ZU-AZ-98	J. PARSONS	1973
ZU-AZ-184	Sm Disp Village	Lower Piedmont	6.2	120	0	0	0	0	0	0	0	0	0	1	ZU-AZ-99	J. PARSONS	1973
ZU-AZ-185	Small Hamlet	Lower Piedmont	0.5	5	0	0	0	0	0	0	0	0	0	1	ZU-AZ-84	J. PARSONS	1973
ZU-AZ-186	Small Hamlet	Lower Piedmont	0.4	5	0	0	0	0	0	0	0	0	0	1	ZU-AZ-85	J. PARSONS	1973
ZU-AZ-187	Small Hamlet	Lower Piedmont	0.7	10	0	0	0	0	0	0	0	0	0	1	ZU-AZ-85	J. PARSONS	1973
ZU-AZ-188	Small Hamlet	Lower Piedmont	1.5	20	0	0	0	0	0	0	0	0	0	1	ZU-AZ-86	J. PARSONS	1973
ZU-AZ-189	Small Hamlet	Lower Piedmont	2.1	20	0	0	0	1	0	0	0	0	0	1	ZU-AZ-87	J. PARSONS	1973
ZU-AZ-190	Small Hamlet	Lower Piedmont	0.9	10	0	0	0	1	0	0	0	0	0	1	ZU-AZ-89	J. PARSONS	1973
ZU-AZ-191	Small Hamlet	Lower Piedmont	0.4	5	0	0	0	1	0	0	0	0	0	1	ZU-AZ-88	J. PARSONS	1973
ZU-AZ-192	Small Hamlet	Lower Piedmont	0.5	10	0	0	0	0	0	0	0	0	0	1	ZU-AZ-90	J. PARSONS	1973
ZU-AZ-193	Small Hamlet	Lower Piedmont	0.6	10	0	0	0	0	0	0	0	0	0	1	ZU-AZ-90	J. PARSONS	1973
ZU-AZ-194	Sm Disp Village	Lower Piedmont	10.8	220	0	0	0	0	0	0	0	0	0	1	ZU-AZ-10	J. PARSONS	1973
ZU-AZ-195	Sm Disp Village	Lower Piedmont	15.4	310	0	0	0	0	0	0	0	0	0	1	ZU-AZ-10	J. PARSONS	1973
ZU-AZ-196	Sm Disp Village	Lower Piedmont	8.1	160	0	0	0	0	0	0	0	0	0	1	ZU-AZ-11	J. PARSONS	1973
ZU-AZ-197	Small Hamlet	Lower Piedmont	0.5	10	0	0	0	0	0	0	0	0	0	1	ZU-AZ-10	J. PARSONS	1973
ZU-AZ-198	Hamlet	Lower Piedmont	2.9	60	0	0	0	0	0	0	0	0	0	1	ZU-AZ-10	J. PARSONS	1973
ZU-AZ-199	Small Hamlet	Lower Piedmont	1.7	20	0	0	0	0	0	0	0	0	0	1	ZU-AZ-10	J. PARSONS	1973
ZU-AZ-200	Small Hamlet	Lower Piedmont	0.8	20	0	0	0	0	0	0	0	0	0	1	ZU-AZ-59	M. PARSONS	1973
ZU-AZ-201	Small Hamlet	Lower Piedmont	0.6	10	0	0	0	0	0	0	0	0	0	1	ZU-AZ-60	M. PARSONS	1973
ZU-AZ-202	Hamlet	Lower Piedmont	2.3	50	0	0	0	0	0	0	0	0	0	1	ZU-AZ-58	M. PARSONS	1973
ZU-AZ-203	Small Hamlet	Lower Piedmont	0.1	5	0	0	0	0	0	0	0	1	0	1	ZU-AZ-87	M. PARSONS	1973
ZU-AZ-204	Small Hamlet	Lower Piedmont	0.4	5	0	0	0	0	0	0	0	0	0	1	ZU-AZ-56	M. PARSONS	1973
ZU-AZ-205	Small Hamlet	Lower Piedmont	0.9	20	0	0	0	0	0	0	0	1	0	1	ZU-AZ-55	M. PARSONS	1973
ZU-AZ-206	Small Hamlet	Lower Piedmont	0.1	5	0	0	0	0	0	0	0	1	0	1	ZU-AZ-57	M. PARSONS	1973
ZU-AZ-207	Small Hamlet	Lower Piedmont	0.4	5	0	0	0	0	0	0	0	0	0	1	ZU-AZ-75	M. PARSONS	1973
ZU-AZ-208	Hamlet	Lower Piedmont	2.8	60	0	0	0	0	1	1	0	0	0	1	ZU-AZ-72	M. PARSONS	1973
ZU-AZ-209	Small Hamlet	Lower Piedmont	1.5	5	0	0	0	0	0	0	0	0	0	1	ZU-AZ-73	M. PARSONS	1973
ZU-AZ-210	Small Hamlet	Lower Piedmont	0.7	5	0	0	0	0	0	0	0	0	0	1	ZU-AZ-74	M. PARSONS	1973

Early Aztec and Late Aztec occupations are tabulated on a presence-absence basis.

ZUMPANGO REGION – ENVIRONMENTAL DATA
Aztec Sites

Site Number	Environmental Zone	UTM Coordinates East	North	Elev (in m)	Rainfall (in mm)	Modern Soil Depth	Modern Erosion	Modern Land use
ZU-AZ-211	Lower Piedmont	479.57	2196.60	2280	700	Medium	Moderate-Deep	Agricultural
ZU-AZ-212	Lower Piedmont	479.32	2205.10	2375	700	Medium	None	Grazing
ZU-AZ-213	Lower Piedmont	479.00	2200.50	2305	700	Medium	Deep	Grazing
ZU-AZ-214	Lower Piedmont	478.30	2202.90	2300	700	Shallow	Deep	Grazing
ZU-AZ-215	Lower Piedmont	477.85	2197.78	2275	700	Medium	Moderate-Deep	Agricultural
ZU-AZ-216	Lower Piedmont	476.88	2197.72	2270	700	Shallow	Deep	Grazing
ZU-AZ-217	Lower Piedmont	476.32	2196.57	2265	700	Shallow	Deep	Grazing
ZU-AZ-218	Lower Piedmont	474.93	2193.22	2290	700	Shallow	Deep	Grazing & Agri
ZU-AZ-219	Lower Piedmont	480.95	2194.65	2290	700	Medium	Moderate	Agricultural
ZU-AZ-220	Lower Piedmont	481.25	2194.53	2295	700	Shallow	Deep	Agricultural
ZU-AZ-221	Lower Piedmont	481.28	2193.18	2305	700	Shallow	Deep	Agricultural
ZU-AZ-222	Lower Piedmont	482.10	2192.97	2340	700	Medium	Slight	Agricultural
ZU-AZ-223	Lower Piedmont	482.38	2194.03	2350	700	Medium	None	Agricultural
ZU-AZ-224	Upper Piedmont	487.28	2194.35	2550	700	Shallow	Slight	None
ZU-AZ-225	Lower Piedmont	482.05	2192.43	2340	700	Deep	None	Agricultural
ZU-AZ-226	Lower Piedmont	482.28	2192.50	2350	700	Deep	None	Agricultural
ZU-AZ-227	Lower Piedmont	482.60	2190.78	2300	700	Deep	None	Agricultural
ZU-AZ-228	Lower Piedmont	484.07	2192.03	2340	700	Medium	None	Grazing
ZU-AZ-229	Lower Piedmont	485.07	2192.32	2391	700	Shallow	Deep	None
ZU-AZ-230	Lower Piedmont	485.30	2191.75	2400	700	Shallow	Moderate	Grazing
ZU-AZ-231	Lower Piedmont	485.88	2191.60	2330	700	Medium	None	Agricultural
ZU-AZ-232	Lower Piedmont	485.88	2191.80	2330	700	Medium	None	Agricultural
ZU-AZ-233	Lower Piedmont	484.95	2190.88	2323	700	Medium	None	Agricultural
ZU-AZ-234	Lakeshore Plain	487.68	2192.00	2295	700	Deep	Slight	Agricultural
ZU-AZ-235	Lower Piedmont	486.65	2190.72	2275	700	Medium	None	Agricultural
ZU-AZ-236	Lower Piedmont	487.68	2191.13	2260	700	Deep	None	Agricultural
ZU-AZ-237	Lakeshore Plain	488.50	2191.18	2250	700	Medium	None	Agricultural
ZU-AZ-238	Lakeshore Plain	489.57	2189.63	2255	700	Medium	None	Agricultural
ZU-AZ-239	Lakeshore Plain	491.25	2190.35	2280	700	Medium	None	Agricultural
ZU-AZ-240	Lakeshore Plain	491.95	2190.72	2280	690	Medium	None	Agricultural
ZU-AZ-241	Lakeshore Plain	492.90	2190.43	2280	680	Medium	None	Grazing & Agri
ZU-AZ-242	Lakeshore Plain	492.57	2189.93	2270	690	Medium	None	Agricultural
ZU-AZ-243	Lakeshore Plain	497.45	2188.38	2275	640	Shallow	Slight	Agricultural
ZU-AZ-244	Lakeshore Plain	498.00	2187.38	2260	630	Shallow	None	Agricultural
ZU-AZ-245	Lakeshore Plain	491.95	2187.43	2260	700	Deep	None	Agricultural
ZU-AZ-246	Lakeshore Plain	491.68	2186.93	2250	700	Deep	None	Agricultural
ZU-AZ-247	Lakeshore Plain	489.28	2185.43	2245	680	Deep	None	Agricultural
ZU-AZ-248	Lakeshore Plain	488.25	2185.63	2245	680	Deep	None	Agricultural
ZU-AZ-249	Lakeshore Plain	488.00	2185.30	2245	680	Deep	None	Agricultural
ZU-AZ-250	Lakeshore Plain	487.63	2185.63	2245	680	Deep	None	Agricultural
ZU-AZ-251	Lakeshore Plain	487.50	2185.75	2245	680	Deep	None	Agricultural
ZU-AZ-252	Lakeshore Plain	487.50	2185.82	2245	680	Deep	None	Agricultural

ZUMPANGO REGION - PREHISPANIC SETTLEMENT DATA
Aztec Sites

SITE NUMBER	CLASSIFICATION	ENVIRONMENTAL ZONE	AREA (in ha)	POP.	EF	MF	LF	TF	EC	LC	ET	LT	EA	LA	TEMPORARY SITE NO.	SUPERVISOR	YEAR
ZU-AZ-211	Small Hamlet	Lower Piedmont	1.4	20	0	0	0	0	0	0	0	0	1	0	ZU-AZ-10	M. PARSONS	1973
ZU-AZ-212	Small Hamlet	Lower Piedmont	0.6	10	0	0	0	0	0	0	0	0	0	1	ZU-AZ-41	M. PARSONS	1973
ZU-AZ-213	Small Hamlet	Lower Piedmont	0.8	20	0	0	0	0	0	0	0	0	0	1	ZU-AZ-42	M. PARSONS	1973
ZU-AZ-214	Small Hamlet	Lower Piedmont	1.0	20	0	0	0	0	0	0	0	0	0	1	ZU-AZ-45	M. PARSONS	1973
ZU-AZ-215	Small Hamlet	Lower Piedmont	2.5	40	0	0	0	0	0	0	0	1	0	1	ZU-AZ-97	M. PARSONS	1973
ZU-AZ-216	Hamlet	Lower Piedmont	7.4	70	0	0	0	0	0	0	0	1	0	1	ZU-AZ-98	M. PARSONS	1973
ZU-AZ-217	Lg Disp Village	Lower Piedmont	31.8	600	0	0	0	0	0	0	0	0	0	1	ZU-AZ-99	M. PARSONS	1973
ZU-AZ-218	Lg Disp Village	Lower Piedmont	38.0	800	0	0	0	0	0	0	0	4	0	1	ZU-AZ-10	M. PARSONS	1973
ZU-AZ-219	Hamlet	Lower Piedmont	3.5	70	0	0	0	0	0	0	1	0	0	0	ZU-CL-41	M. PARSONS	1973
ZU-AZ-220	Small Hamlet	Lower Piedmont	2.4	30	0	0	0	0	0	0	0	0	0	1	ZU-AZ-10	M. PARSONS	1973
ZU-AZ-221	Hamlet	Lower Piedmont	7.8	80	0	0	0	0	0	0	0	0	0	1	ZU-AZ-77	M. PARSONS	1973
ZU-AZ-222	Small Hamlet	Lower Piedmont	0.8	10	0	0	0	0	0	0	0	0	0	1		M. PARSONS	1973
ZU-AZ-223	Hamlet	Lower Piedmont	1.2	30	0	0	0	0	0	0	0	0	0	1	ZU-AZ-76	M. PARSONS	1973
ZU-AZ-224	Ceremonial Ctr	Upper Piedmont	0.1	0	0	0	0	0	0	0	0	0	0	1	ZU-AZ-54	M. PARSONS	1973
ZU-AZ-225	Small Hamlet	Lower Piedmont	1.0	10	0	0	0	0	0	0	0	0	0	1	ZU-AZ-78	M. PARSONS	1973
ZU-AZ-226	Small Hamlet	Lower Piedmont	0.8	10	0	0	0	0	0	0	0	0	0	1	ZU-AZ-79	M. PARSONS	1973
ZU-AZ-227	Small Hamlet	Lower Piedmont	0.9	10	0	0	0	0	0	0	0	1	0	1	ZU-LT-67	M. PARSONS	1973
ZU-AZ-228	Small Hamlet	Lower Piedmont	0.1	5	0	0	0	0	0	0	1	0	0	1	ZU-AZ-80	M. PARSONS	1973
ZU-AZ-229	Small Hamlet	Lower Piedmont	0.5	10	0	0	0	0	0	0	0	0	0	1	ZU-AZ-81	M. PARSONS	1973
ZU-AZ-230	Ceremonial Ctr	Lower Piedmont	0.1	0	0	0	0	0	0	0	0	0	0	1	ZU-AZ-85	M. PARSONS	1973
ZU-AZ-231	Small Hamlet	Lower Piedmont	0.6	10	0	0	0	0	0	0	0	0	0	1	ZU-AZ-82	M. PARSONS	1973
ZU-AZ-232	Small Hamlet	Lower Piedmont	0.3	5	0	0	0	0	0	0	0	0	0	1	ZU-AZ-82	M. PARSONS	1973
ZU-AZ-233	Hamlet	Lower Piedmont	5.4	100	0	0	0	0	0	0	0	0	0	1	ZU-AZ-92	M. PARSONS	1973
ZU-AZ-234	Small Hamlet	Lakeshore Plain	0.5	5	0	0	0	0	0	0	0	0	0	1	ZU-AZ-11	J. PARSONS	1973
ZU-AZ-235	Hamlet	Lower Piedmont	1.2	20	0	0	0	0	0	0	0	0	0	1	ZU-AZ-86	M. PARSONS	1973
ZU-AZ-236	Sm Disp Village	Lower Piedmont	11.8	240	0	0	0	0	0	0	0	0	0	1	ZU-AZ-83	M. PARSONS	1973
ZU-AZ-237	Hamlet	Lakeshore Plain	2.6	50	0	0	0	0	0	0	0	0	0	1	ZU-AZ-12	J. PARSONS	1973
ZU-AZ-238	Questionable	Lakeshore Plain	0.0	0	0	0	0	0	0	0	0	0	0	1	ZU-AZ-12	J. PARSONS	1973
ZU-AZ-239	Small Hamlet	Lakeshore Plain	1.1	10	0	0	0	0	0	0	0	0	0	1	ZU-AZ-13	J. PARSONS	1973
ZU-AZ-240	Small Hamlet	Lakeshore Plain	1.8	20	0	0	0	0	0	0	0	2	0	1	ZU-AZ-13	J. PARSONS	1973
ZU-AZ-241	Hamlet	Lakeshore Plain	1.9	40	0	0	0	0	0	0	0	0	0	1	ZU-AZ-13	J. PARSONS	1973
ZU-AZ-242	Hamlet	Lakeshore Plain	2.5	50	0	0	0	0	0	0	0	0	0	1	ZU-AZ-13	J. PARSONS	1973
ZU-AZ-243	Small Hamlet	Lakeshore Plain	1.0	10	0	0	0	0	0	0	0	0	0	1	ZU-AZ-13	J. PARSONS	1973
ZU-AZ-244	Small Hamlet	Lakeshore Plain	0.6	20	0	0	0	1	0	0	0	0	0	1	ZU-AZ-13	J. PARSONS	1973
ZU-AZ-245	Hamlet	Lakeshore Plain	3.5	70	0	0	0	1	0	0	0	0	0	1	ZU-AZ-13	J. PARSONS	1973
ZU-AZ-246	Small Hamlet	Lakeshore Plain	1.0	10	0	0	0	0	0	0	0	0	0	1	ZU-AZ-13	J. PARSONS	1973
ZU-AZ-247	Hamlet	Lakeshore Plain	1.3	30	0	0	0	0	0	0	0	0	0	1	ZU-AZ-11	J. PARSONS	1973
ZU-AZ-248	Small Hamlet	Lakeshore Plain	0.3	5	0	0	0	0	0	0	0	0	0	1		J. PARSONS	1973
ZU-AZ-249	Hamlet	Lakeshore Plain	5.1	100	0	0	0	0	0	0	1	0	0	1	ZU-AZ-11	J. PARSONS	1973
ZU-AZ-250	Small Hamlet	Lakeshore Plain	0.9	20	0	0	0	0	0	0	0	1	0	1	ZU-AZ-10	J. PARSONS	1973
ZU-AZ-251	Small Hamlet	Lakeshore Plain	0.4	10	0	0	0	0	0	0	0	1	0	1	ZU-AZ-10	J. PARSONS	1973
ZU-AZ-252	Small Hamlet	Lakeshore Plain	0.3	10	0	0	0	0	0	0	0	0	0	1	ZU-AZ-10	J. PARSONS	1973

Early Aztec and Late Aztec occupations are tabulated on a presence-absence basis.

ZUMPANGO REGION - ENVIRONMENTAL DATA
Aztec Sites

Site Number	Environmental Zone	UTM Coordinates East	UTM Coordinates North	Elev (in m)	Rainfall (in mm)	Modern Soil Depth	Modern Erosion	Modern Land use
ZU-AZ-253	Lakebed	487.22	2185.65	2245	690	Deep	None	Agricultural
ZU-AZ-254	Lakeshore Plain	484.88	2189.88	2290	700	Medium-Deep	None	Agricultural
ZU-AZ-255	Lakeshore Plain	483.93	2190.38	2300	700	Medium-Deep	None	Agricultural
ZU-AZ-256	Lakeshore Plain	483.60	2186.60	2250	680	Deep	None	Agricultural
ZU-AZ-257	Lakeshore Plain	482.80	2186.65	2245	680	Deep	None	Agricultural
ZU-AZ-258	Lakeshore Plain	481.47	2188.85	2255	680	Deep	Slight	Agricultural
ZU-AZ-259	Lakeshore Plain	481.18	2189.25	2255	680	Deep	Very Slight	Agricultural
ZU-AZ-260	Lakeshore Plain	480.88	2189.25	2255	680	Deep	None	Agricultural
ZU-AZ-261	Lakeshore Plain	479.10	2188.85	2250	680	Deep	None	Agricultural
ZU-AZ-262	Lakeshore Plain	478.57	2189.30	2255	680	Deep	None	Agricultural
ZU-AZ-263	Lakeshore Plain	478.43	2189.55	2255	680	Deep	None	Agricultural
ZU-AZ-264	Lower Piedmont	477.15	2189.10	2275	680	Deep	Deep	Agricultural
ZU-AZ-265	Lower Piedmont	476.88	2190.35	2263	680	Shallow	Moderate	Agricultural
ZU-AZ-266	Lower Piedmont	476.50	2189.57	2298	680	Shallow	Deep	Agricultural
ZU-AZ-267	Lower Piedmont	476.32	2189.05	2305	680	Medium	None	Agricultural
ZU-AZ-268	Lower Piedmont	475.82	2189.00	2305	680	Shallow	Moderate-Deep	Agricultural
ZU-AZ-269	Lower Piedmont	474.95	2189.43	2293	680	Medium	Moderate	Agricultural
ZU-AZ-270	Lower Piedmont	478.80	2185.05	2288	680	Shallow	Deep	Grazing & Agri
ZU-AZ-271	Lower Piedmont	478.45	2185.05	2280	670	Medium	Moderate	Agricultural
ZU-AZ-272	Lower Piedmont	479.55	2187.55	2275	670	Medium	Moderate-Deep	Agricultural
ZU-AZ-273	Lakeshore Plain	485.05	2185.28	2250	670	Deep	None	Agricultural
ZU-AZ-274	Lakeshore Plain	493.00	2181.32	2245	600	Deep	None	Grazing
ZU-AZ-275	Lakeshore Plain	493.32	2180.80	2245	600	Deep	None	Grazing
ZU-AZ-276	Lakebed	494.90	2180.50	2250	600	Medium	Moderate	Grazing
ZU-AZ-277	Lakeshore Plain	485.80	2182.30	2245	650	Deep	None	Agricultural
ZU-AZ-278	Lakeshore Plain	488.80	2179.15	2275	610	Shallow	Slight	Grazing & Agri
ZU-AZ-279	Lakeshore Plain	487.50	2179.20	2275	620	Shallow	Moderate	Grazing
ZU-AZ-280	Lakeshore Plain	487.80	2178.75	2275	620	Shallow	Moderate	Grazing
ZU-AZ-281	Lower Piedmont	486.82	2179.28	2285	620	Shallow	Moderate	Grazing
ZU-AZ-282	Lower Piedmont	485.93	2179.03	2315	630	Medium	None	Agricultural
ZU-AZ-283	Lower Piedmont	486.07	2178.60	2315	630	Medium	None	Agricultural
ZU-AZ-284	Lakeshore Plain	484.80	2179.00	2260	630	Deep	None	Agricultural
ZU-AZ-285	Lakeshore Plain	484.28	2178.63	2250	630	Deep	None	Agricultural
ZU-AZ-286	Lower Piedmont	486.75	2178.28	2340	620	Medium	Moderate	Agricultural
ZU-AZ-287	Lower Piedmont	487.93	2177.72	2293	620	Shallow	Moderate	Agricultural
ZU-AZ-288	Lower Piedmont	487.15	2177.65	2293	620	Shallow	Moderate	Agricultural
ZU-AZ-289	Lower Piedmont	486.45	2178.00	2340	620	Medium	Slight	Grazing
ZU-AZ-290	Lower Piedmont	486.43	2177.60	2315	620	Medium	None	Grazing & Agri
ZU-AZ-291	Lower Piedmont	485.95	2177.60	2315	630	Medium	None	Grazing & Agri
ZU-AZ-292	Lower Piedmont	485.63	2177.25	2300	630	Medium	None	Agricultural
ZU-AZ-293	Lower Piedmont	485.78	2176.93	2280	630	Medium	None	Agricultural
ZU-AZ-294	Lower Piedmont	486.45	2177.00	2288	620	Medium	None	Agricultural

ZUMPANGO REGION - PREHISPANIC SETTLEMENT DATA
Aztec Sites

SITE NUMBER	CLASSIFICATION	ENVIRONMENTAL ZONE	AREA (in ha)	POP.	OTHER OCCUPATIONS EF	MF	LF	TF	EC	LC	ET	LT	EA	LA	TEMPORARY SITE NO.	SURVEY RECORDS SUPERVISOR	YEAR
ZU-AZ-253	Small Hamlet	Lakebed	0.1	5	0	0	0	0	0	0	0	0	0	1	ZU-AZ-12	J. PARSONS	1973
ZU-AZ-254	Hamlet	Lakeshore Plain	1.8	40	0	0	0	0	0	0	1	0	0	1	ZU-AZ-92	M. PARSONS	1973
ZU-AZ-255	Local Center	Lakeshore Plain	13.8	400	0	0	0	0	1	1	1	0	0	1	ZU-AZ-92	M. PARSONS	1973
ZU-AZ-256	Questionable	Lakeshore Plain	0.4	0	0	0	0	0	0	0	0	0	0	1	ZU-AZ-89	M. PARSONS	1973
ZU-AZ-257	Small Hamlet	Lakeshore Plain	0.6	10	0	0	0	0	0	0	0	0	0	1	ZU-AZ-88	M. PARSONS	1973
ZU-AZ-258	Small Hamlet	Lakeshore Plain	1.0	10	0	0	0	0	0	0	0	0	0	1	ZU-AZ-11	M. PARSONS	1973
ZU-AZ-259	Small Hamlet	Lakeshore Plain	0.4	10	0	0	0	0	1	1	1	1	1	1	ZU-AZ-11	M. PARSONS	1973
ZU-AZ-260	Small Hamlet	Lakeshore Plain	1.3	20	0	0	0	0	1	1	1	1	0	1	ZU-AZ-11	M. PARSONS	1973
ZU-AZ-261	Small Hamlet	Lakeshore Plain	1.5	15	0	0	0	0	0	0	1	1	0	1	ZU-AZ-11	M. PARSONS	1973
ZU-AZ-262	Small Hamlet	Lakeshore Plain	0.3	5	0	0	0	0	0	0	0	1	0	1	ZU-AZ-11	M. PARSONS	1973
ZU-AZ-263	Small Hamlet	Lakeshore Plain	0.8	20	0	0	0	0	0	0	0	0	0	1	ZU-AZ-11	M. PARSONS	1973
ZU-AZ-264	Hamlet	Lower Piedmont	1.7	30	0	0	0	0	0	0	0	0	0	1	ZU-AZ-10	M. PARSONS	1973
ZU-AZ-265	Hamlet	Lower Piedmont	3.0	30	0	0	0	0	0	0	0	0	0	1	ZU-AZ-10	M. PARSONS	1973
ZU-AZ-266	Hamlet	Lower Piedmont	5.3	100	0	0	0	0	1	0	0	1	0	1	ZU-AZ-10	M. PARSONS	1973
ZU-AZ-267	Small Hamlet	Lower Piedmont	1.7	10	0	0	0	0	0	0	0	0	0	1	ZU-AZ-10	M. PARSONS	1973
ZU-AZ-268	Hamlet	Lower Piedmont	1.5	30	0	0	0	0	0	0	0	0	0	1	ZU-AZ-10	M. PARSONS	1973
ZU-AZ-269	Sm Disp Village	Lower Piedmont	13.6	200	0	0	0	0	0	0	1	1	0	1	ZU-AZ-10	M. PARSONS	1973
ZU-AZ-270	Hamlet	Lower Piedmont	2.8	80	0	0	0	0	0	1	0	0	0	1	ZU-CL-46	M. PARSONS	1973
ZU-AZ-271	Sm Disp Village	Lower Piedmont	6.5	130	0	0	0	0	0	0	0	0	0	1	ZU-AZ-11	M. PARSONS	1973
ZU-AZ-272	Hamlet	Lower Piedmont	3.1	30	0	0	0	0	0	0	0	1	0	1	ZU-AZ-11	M. PARSONS	1973
ZU-AZ-273	Small Hamlet	Lakeshore Plain	1.4	10	0	0	0	0	0	0	0	0	0	1	ZU-AZ-90	M. PARSONS	1973
ZU-AZ-274	Hamlet	Lakeshore Plain	3.2	60	0	0	0	0	0	0	0	0	0	1	ZU-AZ-14	J. PARSONS	1973
ZU-AZ-275	Hamlet	Lakeshore Plain	3.2	60	0	0	0	0	0	0	0	0	0	1	ZU-AZ-14	J. PARSONS	1973
ZU-AZ-276	Local Center	Lakebed	69.3	3500	0	0	0	0	0	0	0	0	1	1	ZU-AZ-14	J. PARSONS	1973
ZU-AZ-277	Small Hamlet	Lakeshore Plain	1.3	10	0	0	0	0	0	0	0	0	0	1	ZU-AZ-91	M. PARSONS	1973
ZU-AZ-278	Sm Disp Village	Lakeshore Plain	5.7	120	0	0	0	0	0	0	0	1	0	1	ZU-AZ-11	J. PARSONS	1973
ZU-AZ-279	Small Hamlet	Lakeshore Plain	0.8	10	0	0	0	0	0	0	0	0	0	1		J. PARSONS	1973
ZU-AZ-280	Small Hamlet	Lakeshore Plain	0.8	10	0	0	0	0	0	0	0	0	0	1	ZU-AZ-11	J. PARSONS	1973
ZU-AZ-281	Sm Disp Village	Lower Piedmont	7.5	150	0	0	0	0	0	0	0	0	0	1	ZU-AZ-94	J. PARSONS	1973
ZU-AZ-282	Hamlet	Lower Piedmont	2.9	60	0	0	0	0	0	0	0	0	0	1		M. PARSONS	1973
ZU-AZ-283	Small Hamlet	Lower Piedmont	1.6	10	0	0	0	0	0	1	0	1	0	1	ZU-AZ-94	M. PARSONS	1973
ZU-AZ-284	Hamlet	Lakeshore Plain	5.4	60	0	0	0	0	0	0	0	0	0	1	ZU-AZ-93	M. PARSONS	1973
ZU-AZ-285	Small Hamlet	Lakeshore Plain	0.1	5	0	0	0	0	0	0	0	1	0	1	ZU-LT-68	M. PARSONS	1973
ZU-AZ-286	Sm Disp Village	Lower Piedmont	10.1	150	0	0	0	0	1	1	0	0	0	1	ZU-AZ-95	M. PARSONS	1973
ZU-AZ-287	Sm Disp Village	Lower Piedmont	8.5	170	0	0	0	0	0	0	0	0	0	1	ZU-AZ-11	J. PARSONS	1973
ZU-AZ-288	Sm Disp Village	Lower Piedmont	14.5	300	0	0	0	0	0	0	0	0	0	1	ZU-AZ-11	J. PARSONS	1973
ZU-AZ-289	Hamlet	Lower Piedmont	1.5	30	0	0	0	0	0	0	0	0	0	1	ZU-AZ-12	J. PARSONS	1973
ZU-AZ-290	Hamlet	Lower Piedmont	1.7	40	0	0	0	0	0	0	0	0	0	1	ZU-AZ-12	J. PARSONS	1973
ZU-AZ-291	Small Hamlet	Lower Piedmont	2.0	20	0	0	0	0	0	0	0	0	0	1	ZU-AZ-12	J. PARSONS	1973
ZU-AZ-292	Hamlet	Lower Piedmont	2.9	60	0	0	0	0	0	0	0	0	0	1	ZU-AZ-96	M. PARSONS	1973
ZU-AZ-293	Small Hamlet	Lower Piedmont	1.6	10	0	0	0	0	0	0	0	0	0	1	ZU-AZ-96	M. PARSONS	1973
ZU-AZ-294	Sm Disp Village	Lower Piedmont	15.2	400	0	0	0	0	0	0	0	0	0	1	ZU-AZ-96	M. PARSONS	1973

Early Aztec and Late Aztec occupations are tabulated on a presence-absence basis.

ZUMPANGO REGION - ENVIRONMENTAL DATA
Aztec Sites

Site Number	Environmental Zone	UTM Coordinates East	North	Elev (in m)	Rainfall (in mm)	Modern Soil Depth	Modern Erosion	Modern Land use
ZU-AZ-295	Lakeshore Plain	487.70	2177.15	2255	620	Shallow	Moderate	Agricultural
ZU-AZ-296	Lakeshore Plain	487.38	2175.55	2245	620	Shallow	None	Agricultural
ZU-AZ-297	Lakebed	487.65	2174.32	2245	620	Deep	None	Grazing & Agri
ZU-AZ-298	Lakeshore Plain	487.38	2173.97	2245	620	Deep	None	Agricultural
ZU-AZ-299	Lakebed	489.05	2173.60	2245	610	Deep	None	Agricultural
ZU-AZ-300	Lakebed	488.68	2173.40	2245	610	Deep	None	Grazing
ZU-AZ-301	Lakebed	488.95	2173.35	2245	610	Deep	None	Agricultural
ZU-AZ-302	Lower Piedmont	479.80	2201.32	2350	690	Medium	Moderate	Grazing

ZUMPANGO REGION – PREHISPANIC SETTLEMENT DATA
Aztec Sites

SITE NUMBER	CLASSIFICATION	ENVIRONMENTAL ZONE	AREA (in ha)	POP.	OTHER OCCUPATIONS										TEMPORARY SITE NO.	SURVEY RECORDS	
					EF	MF	LF	TF	EC	LC	ET	LT	EA	LA		SUPERVISOR	YEAR
ZU-AZ-295	Hamlet	Lakeshore Plain	4.1	80	0	0	0	0	0	0	0	0	0	1	ZU-AZ-11	J. PARSONS	1973
ZU-AZ-296	Small Hamlet	Lakeshore Plain	0.6	5	0	0	0	0	0	0	0	0	0	1	ZU-AZ-11	J. PARSONS	1973
ZU-AZ-297	Small Hamlet	Lakebed	4.6	20	0	0	0	0	1	1	0	1	0	1	ZU-AZ-12	J. PARSONS	1973
ZU-AZ-298	Lg Disp Village	Lakeshore Plain	23.7	500	0	0	0	0	1	1	1	1	0	1	ZU-AZ-12	J. PARSONS	1973
ZU-AZ-299	Questionable	Lakebed	0.1	0	0	0	0	0	0	0	0	0	0	1		J. PARSONS	1973
ZU-AZ-300	Questionable	Lakebed	1.4	0	0	0	0	0	0	0	0	0	0	1	ZU-AZ-12	J. PARSONS	1973
ZU-AZ-301	Questionable	Lakebed	1.0	0	0	0	0	0	0	0	0	0	0	1	ZU-AZ-12	J. PARSONS	1973
ZU-AZ-302	Small Hamlet	Lower Piedmont	0.1	5	0	0	0	0	0	0	0	0	0	0	ZU-AZ-71	M. PARSONS	1973

Early Aztec and Late Aztec occupations are tabulated on a presence-absence basis.

COMPUTER PROGRAMS USED FOR DATA ANALYSIS

Through a consistent tabular presentation, this report is intended to facilitate analysis of these settlement data. Computer programs that have been used in the analysis and presentation of these data are provided here so that they too may be used in additional analyses.

The Valley of Mexico data were originally encoded for the purpose of facilitating quantitative analysis for the Chalco-Xochimilco and Zumpango Regions (Kintigh 1982: 463-74). Considerable manipulation of these data was required to answer archaeological questions discussed in these reports. Much of the quantitative analysis was accomplished using a packaged statistical system. However, certain kinds of analytical requests could not be satisfied using available packages, and additional computer programs had to be written.

Although these programs were written with the immediate goal of answering analytical questions relevant to the analysis of settlement patterns in the Valley of Mexico, the programs were written for general archaeological use and are in no way specialized to these particular data. The basic capabilities of the programs are described in the following sections. Listings of these programs, including basic program documentation, are included as Appendices I, II, and III. All of these programs will require some adaptation to run at non-MTS (Michigan Terminal System) computer installations. In general, if the facilities provided by the programs are otherwise obtainable at the available computer system, these other facilities should be used. However, in many cases no other such facilities may be available, in which case these programs may prove useful.

Map Plotting Program

Settlement pattern analysis obviously requires the analysis of distributions of points in space. A map plotting program was written in order to easily produce maps for analysis and publication. The program has relatively rigid requirements for its input but is very flexible in formatting maps. The maps included in this report were all produced by the program. These maps are simply reduced versions of the computer plots, with the exceptions that the legend, which is normally produced to the side of the map, was moved onto the map, and stippling was added to increase the clarity.

The maps produced by this program consist of a pair of labeled axes, a two line map title, a set of reference lines and a set of points, each of which has an associated type that determines what symbol is plotted for the point, and a legend for the different symbols. In the maps produced here, the axis units are UTM kilometers, the reference lines are the survey area outlines and the approximate lakeshore, the points represent archaeological sites, and the point types are the site classifications described above. The program is capable of producing several maps with the same basic layout (but different data) in a single run. For example, one map for each different time period could be produced in a single run.

Input to the program consists of several parts. First the set of maps to be produced in a given run of the program is described, including size of the map, the scaling of the input data, axis labels, map labels, the number of reference lines, the number of different point types, and the number of maps to be produced (the number of different sets of point data to be processed). Next the point types are defined by the symbol height, the symbol shape (either a special symbol or a letter or number), and the label to be associated with that symbol in the legend. Each reference line is described by the number of points that define the line, and the way in which the line is to be plotted (for example, straight lines connecting the points, curved lines connecting the points, or dashed lines connecting the points). Finally, each different plot (each separate set of point data) is described by the number of points in the plot and title lines specific to that plot. The set of data for the reference lines is simply a sequential set of $(\underline{x}, \underline{y})$ coordinates for the points (to make a closed line, the first point of the list and the last should be the same). The data for the points to be plotted on a single map consists of a set of lines, each of which has $\underline{x}$ and $\underline{y}$ coordinates of the point and an integer point type.

Using the options provided by the program, complex sets of publishable-quality maps can be produced with relative ease. Generally, some experimentation is required to determine the best scale and use of symbols, although default values for most parameters will usually produce acceptable results. However, once one map has been produced with an acceptable layout, any number of additional maps can be very easily produced. Using this program, basic maps, such as those reproduced here were made. However, during the analysis many kinds of additional maps were desired. For example, we produced maps of all sites in a given time period that were also occupied in the succeeding and previous time period. In our analysis, we used the statistical package to do appropriate selections of data and then output a set of point corrdinates and point types, which was read by the plotting program.

This program has proved useful in settlement pattern analysis and in plotting the distributions of piece-plotted artifacts in a site, and it was designed to produce publishable quality output, with archaeological data in mind. Packaged plotting programs that can produce maps adequate for many of the analytical purposes for which this program is designed may be available in some installations. In addition, these programs offer powerful manipulations of spatial data that this program does not provide. However, many of these programs will not produce output that is suitable for publication.

The map plotting program (Appendix I) is written in PL/I (F) using the MTS plot system FORTRAN plotter calls. Conversion of this program to run on other systems with PL/I compilers should be very simple. Few, if any changes will be required to compile the PL/I code using the IBM optimizing compiler. Changes to the FORTRAN plot calls will be required to run the program at non-MTS installations, however, in most cases, these changes should be relatively minor. (A basic description of the MTS plot routines used is given in the appendix to aid in this conversion.)

Nearest Neighbor Analysis Program

Nearest neighbor analysis is a widely used technique for the analysis of spatial patterns, and the computation of the statistic is relatively straightforward (Whallon 1974). Analysis of the Valley of Mexico data suggested that it might be useful to not only have the statistic computed within and between different types of sites in an area, but also to have a listing of the first few nearest neighbors to each site. A program was written to allow the computation of nearest neighbors under a variety of conditions, to list the nearest neighbors to each point, and to independently analyze multiple sets of data (e.g., sites from different periods) in a single run (Appendix II). Although the program is discussed in terms of settlement pattern studies, it has also been used in a spatial analysis of archaeological living floors.

The data consist of a character label (site number) for each point, a stratum (period) number that determines the independently analyzed sets of data, a point type (such as the site classification of hamlet, village, center, etc.), and location expressed in x and y coordinates. Parameters required to run the program include the total area of the region, any desired grouping together of the point types, and whether nearest neighbors within or between these groups' point types are desired. The program will optionally produce an output file with the nearest neighbors to each point and the distance to the neighbor so that these data can be subjected to further statistical manipulation.

For example, we might wish to group hamlets and dispersed villages together, and nucleated villages and centers together. In this case, the within-group nearest neighbor statistic would be computed separately for hamlets and dispersed villages and for the nucleated villages and centers. However, using between-group computation, the nearest neighbor to a given small dispersed village is the closest nucleated village or center, while the nearest neighbor to a given large nucleated village would be the closest hamlet or dispersed village.

A few points should be made about the interpretation of the output of this program. One must be aware of the limitations of the nearest neighbor statistic discussed by Whallon (1974), Hodder and Orton (1976), and Pinder et al. (1979). In light of these problems, it is often preferable to look at changes in the nearest neighbor statistic between periods, as opposed to examining the absolute values as indicative of random, clustered, or uniform distributions. It should be noted that the nearest neighbor statistic is not strictly defined when computed between groups and, in this case, the absolute value of the statistic cannot be interpreted in the standard way. However, it may be useful to look at changes in these values between periods. In any event, the listing of the actual nearest neighbors to a site may be analytically useful, independent of the nearest neighbor statistic per se.

Although the program was written to have considerable general utility, making it easy to transfer to another computer system was not a major consideration while writing it. The program is written in the version of ALGOL W running under MTS. Because this language is not widely available, the program will not be directly usable at non-MTS installations. However, it could be translated to a block-structured language, such as Pascal or PL/I, without great difficulty, and thus be made to work elsewhere.

Program for the Production of Tabular Output

During the course of analysis, it was often desirable to produce complex, but readable, tables of site information. In order to check the data, we wanted to translate the encoded description of a site (contained on three computer card images) into a readable site description in outline form. Various analytical requests required tabular output. And, for efficient publication of the data, well-labeled, and well-formatted publishable output was desired. The tables produced by standard statistical packages were generally too inflexible in their format and produced output that was too cryptic for these purposes. Therefore, a table-formatting program was developed (Appendix III). This program was used to produce all tables of data in this report.

The program takes as input: a description of the format of the variables to be read in; a description of any transformations to be done to the input data; a description of the table to be produced; and a set of actual data to be tabulated. The output of the program is a printed table of the data in the specified format. The program provides great flexibility in reading and transforming data and in formatting complex tables. Among others, the program has the following input and transformation capabilities: any fixed format numeric and character data can be read in; numeric values can be scaled (i.e., multiplied or divided by any power of ten); numeric values can be translated into character strings (e.g., an input value of 11 can be translated to "small hamlet" on output); leading and trailing labels can be added to a value (e.g., the value "2204" can be output as "Elevation 2204 meters").

Although the program does not provide any facilities to select from a data file the observations to be printed, this can be accomplished by using a packaged statistical or data management program to select the observations to be printed and to produce an output file with the necessary data. This file can then be processed by the table program just like any other data file.

The program produces output tables in two layouts, which are called block layout and table layout. The tables produced in this report were produced using the table layout. Using this option, each line of the table represents a single observation, in this case, an archaeological site. An arbitrarily complex multi-line heading can be specified, and if desired, a new page will be started when a specified variable changes in the data (and, that variable's value may occur in the heading). In the tables produced here, new pages were begun for each chronological period, and the period name is put in the first line of the heading. The table may optionally be enclosed in a box (like those produced in this report).

In contrast to the table layout, the block layout is used to produce output in which multiple lines are to be used for each observation. This layout is used to display more data than can fit on a single line of text, and it proved particularly useful for checking the data coding, because the variables can be clearly labeled and because numeric codes can be translated into meaningful English phrases.

The program has a relatively large number of interrelated parameters that must be specified to produce any table. The flexibility provided by the program allows the production of complex tables. However, the investment in time that is involved in laying out a table using this program is not warranted if the table desired is a relatively simple one that can be produced using a statistical package. Finally, it may also be noted that some of the more powerful general purpose database management systems and document formatting provide complex formatting facilities like those provided by the program.

Like the nearest neighbor program, the table program is written in MTS ALGOL W which is not readily transported to computers with other operating systems. However, the code provided could be converted to run in another high-level language.

Appendix I

PLOT PROGRAM

PROGRAM: PLOT

AUTHOR: KEITH W KINTIGH
MUSEUM OF ANTHROPOLOGY
UNIVERSITY OF MICHIGAN
ANN ARBOR. MI 48109

PURPOSE: PLOT IS A PROGRAM WHICH PRODUCES BOTH PRINTER AND PLOTTER
PLOTS OF POINT AND LINE DATA. EACH POINT HAS ASSOCIATED
X AND Y COORDINATES AND AN INTEGER POINT "TYPE". ON THE
PLOTS EACH TYPE OF POINT CAN BE REPRESENTED BY A
DIFFERENT, USER SPECIFIED SYMBOL. A KEY FOR THESE
SYMBOLS IS PLOTTED. OTHER OPTIONS FOR REFERENCE LINES AND
POINTS ARE DESCRIBED BELOW.

```
PARAMETERS IN EFFECT FOR ALL PLOTS:
    OUTPUT      - 'PRINTER', 'PLOTTER' OR 'BOTH' - TYPE OF OUTPUT
                  (DEFAULT 'BOTH') - MAY BE ABBREVIATED TO 2 CHARS
    PLOTS       - NUMBER OF DIFFERENT PLOTS TO BE MADE
                  (DEFAULT 1)
    LINES       - NUMBER OF REFERENCE LINES TO BE PLOTTED ON EACH PLOT.
                  (DEFAULT 0).
    TYPES       - NUMBER OF DIFFERENT SYMBOL TYPES USED IN PLOT
                  (DEFAULT 1)
    XMIN, YMIN  - MIN OF X AND Y VALUES IN DATA UNITS   (DEFAULT 0)
    XMAX, YMAX  - MAX OF X AND Y VALUES IN DATA UNITS NO DEFAULT
                  POINTS OUTSIDE PLOT AREA DEFINED BY XMIN, YMIN
                  XMAX, YMAX WILL NOT BE PLOTTED.
    FACT,XFACT,YFACT - DATA UNITS/PLOT CM  (DEFAULT 1)
                  IF FACT IS SPECIFIED, XFACT=YFACT=FACT.
    SCALE       - PRINT CM/PLOT CM
                  (DEFAULT .635=2.54/4 - IE 1 PLOT CM = .25 PRNT INCHES)
    TITLE1      - FIRST TITLE LINE AT BOTTOM OF PLOT (80 CHAR MAX)
    TITLE2      - SECOND TITLE LINE AT BOTTOM OF PLOT (80 CHAR MAX)
    XTITLE, YTITLE - TITLES ON COORDINATE AXES (80 AND 60 CHARS MAX).
    DV, DXV, DYV- PLOT CM BETWEEN AXIS TIC MARKS    (DEFAULT 2)
                  IF DV IS SPECIFIED, DXV=DYV=DV.
    XWID,XDEC   - FORMAT OF X AXIS LABELS = PLI F(XWID,XDEC)
                  DEFAULT F(5.2) PRINTER PLOT ONLY
    YWID,YDEC   - FORMAT OF Y AXIS LABELS = PLI F(YWID,YDEC)
                  DEFAULT F(5.2) PRINTER PLOT ONLY
    XORG, YORG  - COORD. IN INCHES OF AXIS ORIGIN ON PLOT.  (DEFAULT
    COMPUTED)
    TITLE!_HT   - TITLE CHAR HEIGHT (INCHES) (DEFAULT .25)
    AXIS!_T!_HT - HEIGHT (INCHES) OF AXIS TITLES (DEFAULT .2)
    AXIS!_V!_HT - HEIGHT (INCHES) OF AXIS VALUE LABELS (DEFAULT .15)
    DESC!_HT    - DESC CHAR HEIGHT (INCHES) (DEFAULT .2)
    IGNORE      - NUMBER OF NUMERIC VARS TO IGNORE BEFORE X IN POINTIN
    STREAM
    DESCLEN     - UPPER BOUND FOR NUMBER OF CHARACTERS IN LONGEST
                  DESCRIPTION OF A SYMBOL IN THE KEY  (DEFAULT 30)
    LINEPOINTS  - UPPER BOUND OF NUMBER OF TOTAL POINTS DEFINING
                  REFERENCE LINES (DEFAULT 250)
    MAXWARN     - MAXIMUM NUMBER OF PLOT WARNINGS PRINTED (20).
    PAGESIZE    - MAXIMUM NUMBER OF LINES PER PAGE (DEFAULT 60)
    LINESIZE    - MAXIMUM NUMBER OF CHARACTERS IN A LINE
                  LINESIZE AND PAGESIZE MAY BE CHANGED TO GET
                  BETTER SIZE OUTPUT TO INCLUDE IN TEXT.  (DEFAULT 132)
    LPI         - LINES PER INCH ON PRINTED OUTPUT (DEFAULT 6)
```

```
PARAMETERS DESCRIBING A SPECIFIC POINT TYPE ('TYPES', ENTRIES)
SYMB      - A 1 CHAR SYMBOL FOR PLOTS, USED ON BOTH PRINTER
            AND PLOTTER PLOTS UNLESS INDX IS SPECIFIED.  ANY
            UPPER OR LOWER CASE TN SYMBOL ALLOWED. SEE PSYM VOL 11.
            (DEFAULT '+')

INDX      - INTEGER INDEX FOR SYMBOL FOR PLOTTER PLOT.
            SYMBOLS 0-13 ARE DESCRIBED UNDER LINESYMB BELOW.
            OTHERS ARE GIVEN IN MTS VOL 11 UNDER PSYMB.
            IF THE DEFAULT SYMB ('+') IS GIVEN OR ASSUMED AND INDX
            IS
            UNSPECIFIED, INDX WILL DEFAULT TO 3, A CENTERED '+'.
            IF INDX IS NEGATIVE, THE CHARACTER SPECIFIED BY SYMB
            WILL BE PLOTTED, OTHERWISE THE SYMBOL INDEXED BY
            INDX WILL BE USED.

HGHT      - HEIGHT IN INCHES FOR SYMBOL ON PLOTTER PLOT.
            (DEFAULT .1)

DESC      - DESCRIPTION OF THE SYMBOL VALUE.  LENGTH LESS THAN
            DESCLEN SPECIFIED IN PLOT PARAMETERS.
            E.G. DESC='SMALL HAMLET'.
            (DEFAULT '')  NOTE: IF MAXIMUM LENGTH FOR ANY TYPE
            IS > DESCLEN THEN DESCLEN MUST BE SPECIFIED

-PARAMETERS DESCRIBING A GIVEN LINE ('LINES', ENTRIES)
LINEPTS   - NUMBER OF POINTS IN THIS LINE
LINETYPE  - 'LINE', DRAW STRAIGHT LINE SEGMENTS BETWEEN POINTS
            'VERTEX' DRAW LINES AND PLOT LINESYMB SYMBOL AT
               AT EACH VERTEX.
            'POINT' PLOT LINESYMB AT VERTICES BUT DO NOT CONNECT
               VERTICES WITH LINES.
            'CURVE' DRAW A SMOOTH CURVE BETWEEN VERTICES.
            'DASH'  DRAW DASHED STRAIGHT LINE SEGMENTS BETWEEN
               POINTS ON THE LINE.  DASHES HAVE LENGTH
               DASHLEN.
            'SHADE' SHADE ARBITRARY POLYGON DEFINED BY LINE. SHADE
               ANGLE GIVEN BY S!_ANGLE, DISTANCE BETWEEN HATCH
               LINES
               GIVEN BY S!_DIST.
            NOTE (DEFAULT='LINE').  PARAMETER VALUES MAY BE
            TRUNCATED TO ANY UNAMBIGUOUS ABBREVIATION.
            I.E. 'L','V','P','C','D','S'.
LINESYMB  - CENTERED SYMBOL TO PLOT ON LINE (DEFAULT 3 (='+'))
            NO EFFECT UNLESS LINETYPE='POINT' OR 'DATA'.
            MUST BE INTEGER NUMBER 0-13.  SEE PLINE MTS VOL 11.
            0=SQUARE          5=DIAMOND          10=X WITH SQUARE
                                                    CENTER
            1=HEXAGON         6=ARROW            11=*
            2=TRIANGLE        7=X CLOSED TOP     12=X CLOSED TOP !&
                                                    BOTTOM
            3=+               8=Z                13=|
            4=X               9=Y

SKIP      - USE EVERY SKIP'TH POINT IN LINE (DEFAULT 1)
DASHLEN   - LENGTH IN INCHES OF LINE DASHES (DEFAULT .1") NOTE
            0 HAS THE EFFECT OF .1".  NO EFFECT UNLESS
            LINETYPE='DASH'.
S!_ANGLE  - ANGLE OF SHADING + COUNTERCLOCKWISE DEGREES.  NO EFFECT
            UNLESS LINETYPE='SHADE'.  (DEFAULT 45.)
S!_DIST   - DISTANCE BETWEEN SHADE HATCHING LINES IN INCHES.  NO
            EFFECT UNLESS LINETYPE='SHADE'.  (DEFAULT .1)
```

PARAMETERS DESCRIBING A SPECIFIC PLOT ('PLOTS' ENTRIES)
NOTE: IF ANY OR ALL OF THESE PARAMETERS DO NOT VARY BETWEEN PLOTS,
      OR IF PLOT=1 THESE PARAMETERS MAY BE SPECIFIED WITH THE
      INITIAL PLOT PARAMETERS.

POINTS   - NUMBER OF POINTS TO BE PLOTTED ON THIS PLOT
           IF THERE IS ONLY ONE PLOT IN A RUN THIS NEED
           NOT BE SPECIFIED DEFAULT(9999 OR EOF).

TITLE1   - FIRST TITLE LINE AT BOTTOM OF PLOT (80 CHAR MAX)
TITLE2   - SECOND TITLE LINE AT BOTTOM OF PLOT (80 CHAR MAX)
-PROGRAM FILE ASSIGNMENTS AND DATA SEQUENCES
BECAUSE OF THE WAY MTS HANDLES FREE FORMAT, FILE SPECIFICATIONS
SHOULD HAVE A @F(L) WHERE L IS GREATER THAN THE MAX LINELENGTH. ALL
DATA ENTRY IS FREE FORMAT.

SERCOM   - TERMINAL LOG MESSAGES !& ERRORS

SPRINT   - PRINTED OUTPUT

9   - SEQUENTIAL PLOT FILE

SCARDS   - FILE WITH PROGRAM PARAMETERS AND SYMBOL DESCRIPTIONS
           PARAMETERS ARE ENTERED IN KEYWORD FORMAT IN ANY ORDER.
           NO ABBREVIATIONS OF PARAMETER NAMES ARE ALLOWED. LISTS MAY
           BE
           SPACED IN ANY WAY BUT EACH LIST MUST END WITH A SEMICOLON.
           1) PARAMETER LISTS FOR FOR ALL PLOTS FOLLOWED BY ';'
           2) 'TYPES' PARAMETER LISTS WITH KEYWORD DESCRIPTIONS OF
              EACH POINT TYPE, EACH LIST FOLLOWED BY A ';'
              IF DEFAULTS ARE DESIRED ONLY A SEMICOLON NEED BE GIVEN.
              NOTE: THE FIRST OF THESE SETS OF VALUES IS ASSOCIATED
              WITH TYPE 1 OF THE DATA CARDS, THE SECOND WITH
              TYPE 2, ETC. INSERT SEMICOLONS IF TYPES ARE MISSING
              IN A SEQUENCE.
           3) 'LINES' PARAMETER LISTS WITH KEYWORD DESCRIPTIONS OF
              EACH LINE, EACH LIST FOLLOWED BY A ';'
           4) 'PLOTS' PARAMETER LISTS WITH KEYWORD DESCRIPTIONS OF
              EACH PLOT, EACH LIST FOLLOWED BY A ';'
              NOTE - IF PLOTS=1 THEN 4) MAY BE OMITTED AND THE
              PARAMETERS
              SPECIFIED WITH 1). IF PLOTS>1 THEN AT LEAST 'POINTS'
              MUST
              BE GIVEN IN EACH OF LINES DESCRIBED IN 4)

LINEIN   - FILE WITH INFORMATION ON REFERENCE LINES. FREE
           FORMAT LIST OF X,Y VALUES FOR ALL LINES EACH ONE NEED NOT
           START
           A NEW LINE IN THE FILE. VALUES FOR SUM OF 'LINEPTS' OF
           'LINES'
           LINES. NOTE: IF THE SUM ALL LINEPTS IS GREATER THAN
           THE DEFAULT LINEPOINTS, THEN LINEPOINTS MUST BE
           SPECIFIED GREATER THAN OR EQUAL TO THIS SUM IN
           SCARDS RUN PARAMETER INPUT (1).

```
POINTIN - LIST OF POINTS POINT DESCRIPTIONS FOR EACH PLOT.
          FREE FORMAT LIST OF 'X Y TYPE' - EACH POINT STARTS A NEW
          LINE
          NOTE THE NUMBER OF LINES IN THIS FILE, EACH WITH 3
          VALUES SHOULD BE THE SUM OF THE POINTS PARAMETERS IN
          SCARDS INPUT (4) - OR IF POINTS IS NOT SPECIFIED ALL
          POINTS IN POINTIN WILL BE READ AND PLOTTED ON ONE PLOT.
          'IGNORE' NUMERIC VALUES WILL BE READ AND IGNORED BEFORE
          EACH X.

END OF PROGRAM DOCUMENTATION */

/* FIXED POINT VARIABLES */

DCL (
FO INIT(O),F1 INIT(1),F5 INIT(5),F6 INIT(6),F7 INIT(7),F9 INIT(9),
LINESIZE INIT(132),
PAGESIZE INIT(60),
TYPE!_PT INIT(O),
XWID INIT(5),
XDEC INIT(2),
YWID INIT(5),
YDEC INIT(2),
WID INIT(O),
DEC INIT(-1),
LPI INIT(6),
P INIT(O),
NCHAR INIT(O),
DESCLEN INIT(30),
XTCHAR INIT(O),
YTCHAR INIT(O),
T1CHAR INIT(O),
T2CHAR INIT(O),
LINEPOINTS INIT(250),
LINES INIT(O),
TYPES INIT(1),
TYPE INIT(O),
POINT INIT(O),
POINTS INIT(-9999),
PLOTTED INIT(O),
IGNORE INIT(O),
ERROR INIT(O),
WARN INIT(O),
MAXWARN INIT(20),
PLOTS INIT(1)) FIXED BIN(31);
```

```
/* FLOATING POINT VARIABLES */

DCL (
PGXWTH INIT(0),
CMPI INIT(2.54000508),
TITLE!_HT INIT(.25),
AXIS!_T!_HT INIT(.20),
AXIS!_V!_HT INIT(.15),
DESC!_HT   INIT(.2),
DV INIT(0),
DXV INIT(2),
DYV INIT(2),
SCALE INIT(.635),
SCO INIT(0),
SC1 INIT(1),
VERT INIT(90),
HORIZ INIT(0),
XPT INIT(0),
YPT INIT(0),
XMIN INIT(0),
YMIN INIT(0),
XMAX INIT(0),
YMAX INIT(0),
XORG INIT(3),
YORG INIT(-99),
SPACE INIT(.5),
FACT INIT(0),
XFACT INIT(1),
YFACT INIT(1),
XAXLTH INIT(0),
YAXLTH INIT(0) )   FLOAT BIN;


/* ARRAY VARIABLES */

DCL
1 ARRAY CONTROLLED,
2 SYMBINDX(0:TYPES) FIXED BIN(31),
2 SYMBCHAR(0:TYPES) CHAR(1),
2 SYMBHGHT(0:TYPES) FLOAT BIN,
2 SYMBDESC(0:TYPES) CHAR(DESCLEN),
2 TYPEUSED(0:TYPES) FIXED BIN,
2 XLINE(0:LINEPOINTS) FLOAT BIN,
2 YLINE(0:LINEPOINTS) FLOAT BIN,
2 K(0:LINES) FIXED BIN(31),
2 ITYP(0:LINES) FIXED BIN(31),
2 ISYM(0:LINES) FIXED BIN(31),
2 DASLTH(0:LINES) FLOAT BIN,
2 SANGLE(0:LINES) FLOAT BIN,
2 SDIST(0:LINES) FLOAT BIN,
2 N!_LINE(0:LINES) FIXED BIN(31) ;
```

163

```
/* BIT STRING VARIABLES */

DCL
TRUE BIT(1) INIT('1'B),
FALSE BIT(1) INIT('O'B),
EOF BIT(1) INIT('O'B),
PLT BIT(1) INIT('1'B),
PRNT BIT(1) INIT('1'B);

/* CHARACTER VARIABLES */

DCL
TITLE1 CHAR(80) INIT(' '),
TITLE2A CHAR(80) INIT(' '),
TITLE2 CHAR(80) INIT(' '),
XTITLE CHAR(80) INIT('X COORDINATE '),
YTITLE CHAR(60) INIT('Y COORDINATE '),
PAGE(PAGESIZE) CHAR(LINESIZE) INIT((PAGESIZE)(' ')),
BLANKPAGE(PAGESIZE) CHAR(LINESIZE) INIT((PAGESIZE)(' ')),
NULL CHAR(1) INIT('') VARYING,
BLANK CHAR(1) INIT(' '),
OUTPUT CHAR(8) INIT('BOTH'),
SPECIAL CHAR(6) INIT(' +|-:.');

/* FILES !& PROCEDURES */

DCL
SERCOM FILE STREAM OUTPUT PRINT,
SCARDS FILE STREAM INPUT,
SPRINT FILE STREAM OUTPUT PRINT,
POINTIN FILE STREAM INPUT,
LINEIN FILE STREAM INPUT.

/* PLOTOUT FILE STREAM OUTPUT, */

PLCALL ENTRY (ENTRY,FIXED BIN(31),.,.,,,,,),
(PLTEND, PLTOFS, PLTXMX, PSYMB, PLINE, PDSHLN, PFLINE, PAXIS,
PSYM,PSHADE,PAXVAL,PAXTTL) ENTRY,
PPSYMB ENTRY (FLOAT BIN,FLOAT BIN,FLOAT BIN,CHAR(*),
FLOAT BIN,FIXED BIN(31),FLOAT BIN),
PPLINE ENTRY ((*) FLOAT BIN,(*) FLOAT BIN,FIXED BIN(31),
FIXED BIN(31),FIXED BIN(31),FLOAT BIN,FLOAT BIN,FIXED
BIN(31)),
PPAXIS ENTRY (FLOAT BIN,FLOAT BIN,CHAR(*),FIXED BIN(31),
FLOAT BIN,FLOAT BIN,FLOAT BIN,FLOAT BIN),
PPLTEND ENTRY,
ERRCHK ENTRY (FIXED BIN(31),FIXED BIN(31)),
LNGTH ENTRY (CHAR(*)) RETURNS (FIXED BIN(31)),
STRNGR ENTRY (FLOAT BIN,FIXED BIN(31),FIXED BIN(31))
RETURNS(CHAR(16) VARYING),
STRNGI ENTRY (FIXED BIN(31),FIXED BIN(31)) RETURNS (CHAR(16)
VARYING);

DCL (ABS,ADDR,CEIL,DATAFIELD,INDEX,LENGTH,MOD,ROUND,SUBSTR,TRUNC,
MIN,MAX,ONSOURCE) BUILTIN;
```

```
/* CONTROL PROCEDURE DECLARATIONS (IN CALLED ORDER) */

CONTROL: PROC;
    OPEN FILE(SCARDS),  FILE(SERCOM) LINESIZE(72);
    ON ENDFILE(SCARDS) BEGIN;
        PUT FILE(SERCOM) EDIT ('END OF FILE ON SCARDS')(A);
        CALL ERRCHK(1,0);
    END;
    ON ENDFILE(POINTIN) BEGIN;
        PUT FILE(SERCOM) EDIT ('END OF FILE ON POINTIN')(A);
        CALL ERRCHK(1,0);
    END;
    ON ENDFILE(LINEIN) BEGIN;
        PUT FILE(SERCOM) EDIT ('END OF FILE ON LINEIN')(A);
        CALL ERRCHK(1,0);
    END;
    CALL PROC1;  /* GET BASIC PROGRAM PARAMETERS */
    ALLOCATE ARRAY;
    /* IF PLT THEN OPEN FILE(PLOTOUT) TITLE('9') LINESIZE(256); */
    IF PRNT THEN OPEN FILE(SPRINT) LINESIZE(LINESIZE) PAGESIZE(PAGESIZE);
    CALL PROC2;  /* GET SYMBOLS TO PLOT AND HEIGHTS */
    IF LINES>0 THEN CALL PROC3;  /* GET OUTLINE POINTS */
    CALL ERRCHK(0,0);
    IF PRNT THEN CALL PLOTFMT1;  /* FORMAT PRINTER PLOT */
    DO P=1 TO PLOTS;
        IF ¬EOF THEN DO;
            IF PRNT THEN PAGE=BLANKPAGE;
            CALL PROC4;  /* READ INDIVIDUAL PLOT PARAMETERS */
            IF PLT THEN CALL PLOTFMT2;  /* FORMAT PEN PLOT */
            PUT FILE(SERCOM) EDIT ('START POINT PLOT') (SKIP(2),A);
            POINT=0;  PLOTTED=0;  TYPEUSED=0;
            DO WHILE ((POINT<POINTS) !& ¬EOF);
                CALL PROC5;  /* READ A POINT LOCATION AND TYPE */
                IF ¬EOF THEN DO;
                    IF TYPE!_PT>0 THEN DO;
                        CALL PROC6; /* PLOT POINT */
                        PLOTTED=PLOTTED+1;
                    END;
                    POINT=POINT+1;
                END;
            END;
            PUT FILE(SERCOM) EDIT('PLOT:', P,
               POINT,' POINTS PROCESSED',PLOTTED,' POINTS PLOTTED')
               (SKIP(2),A,F(4),SKIP,F(4),A,SKIP,F(4),A);
            CALL ERRCHK(0,0);
            CALL PLOTFMT3;
        END; ELSE PUT FILE(SERCOM) EDIT
            ('NO MORE DATA FOR SUBSEQUENT PLOTS') (SKIP(2),A);
    END;
    IF WARN>MAXWARN THEN PUT FILE(SERCOM) SKIP(2) EDIT
        ('WARNING MESSAGES SUPPRESSED:',WARN-MAXWARN)(A,F(5));
    PUT FILE(SERCOM) EDIT ('END PROGRAM') (SKIP(2),A);
END;
```

```
PLOTFMT1: PROC;
  DCL I FIXED BIN, ORG FIXED BIN(31);
  CALL PPAXIS(XORG,YORG,XTITLE,XTCHAR,XAXLTH,HORIZ,XMIN,XFACT,DXV);
  CALL PPAXIS(XORG,YORG,YTITLE,YTCHAR,YAXLTH,VERT,YMIN,YFACT,DYV);
  ORG=1;
  DO I=1 TO LINES;
    CALL PPLINE(XLINE,YLINE,N!_LINE(I),K(I),ITYP(I),ISYM(I),SC1,ORG);
    ORG=ORG+N!_LINE(I);
  END;
  BLANKPAGE=PAGE;
END;

PLOTFMT2: PROC;
  DCL (I,ORG) FIXED BIN;
  CALL PLCALL(PLTXMX,F1,ADDR(PGXWTH),FO,FO,FO,FO,FO,FO);
  CALL PLCALL(PLTOFS,F6,ADDR(XMIN),ADDR(XFACT),ADDR(YMIN),
    ADDR(YFACT),ADDR(XORG),ADDR(YORG),FO,FO,FO);
  CALL PLCALL(PAXTTL,F1,ADDR(AXIS!_T!_HT),FO,FO,FO,FO,FO,FO,FO);
  CALL PLCALL(PAXVAL,F1,ADDR(AXIS!_V!_HT),FO,FO,FO,FO,FO,FO,FO);
  CALL PLCALL(PAXIS,F9,ADDR(XORG),ADDR(YORG),XTITLE,ADDR(XTCHAR),
    ADDR(XAXLTH),ADDR(HORIZ),ADDR(XMIN),ADDR(XFACT),ADDR(DXV));
  CALL PLCALL(PAXIS,F9,ADDR(XORG),ADDR(YORG),YTITLE,ADDR(YTCHAR),
    ADDR(YAXLTH),ADDR(VERT),ADDR(YMIN),ADDR(YFACT),ADDR(DYV));
  ORG=1;
  DO I=1 TO LINES;
    IF ITYP(I)<2 THEN CALL PLCALL
      (PLINE,F7,ADDR(XLINE(ORG)),ADDR(YLINE(ORG)),ADDR(N!_LINE(I)),
      ADDR(K(I)),ADDR(ITYP(I)),ADDR(ISYM(I)),ADDR(SC1),FO,FO);
    ELSE IF ITYP(I)=2 THEN CALL PLCALL
      (PDSHLN,F6,ADDR(XLINE(ORG)),ADDR(YLINE(ORG)),
      ADDR(N!_LINE(I)),ADDR(K(I)),ADDR(DASLTH(I)),ADDR(SC1),FO,FO,FO);
    ELSE IF ITYP(I)=3 THEN CALL PLCALL
      (PFLINE,F5,ADDR(XLINE(ORG)),ADDR(YLINE(ORG)),
      ADDR(N!_LINE(I)),ADDR(K(I)),ADDR(SC1),FO,FO,FO);
    ELSE IF ITYP(I)=4 THEN CALL PLCALL
      (PSHADE,F7,ADDR(XLINE(ORG)),ADDR(YLINE(ORG)),
      ADDR(N!_LINE(I)),ADDR(K(I)),ADDR(SANGLE(I)),ADDR(SDIST(I)),
      ADDR(SC1),FO,FO);
    ORG=ORG+N!_LINE(I);
  END;
END;
```

```
PLOTFMT3: PROC;
 DCL (XO,YO,X1) FLOAT BIN;
 T1CHAR=LNGTH(TITLE1);
 T2CHAR=LNGTH(TITLE2);
 TITLE2A=
 SUBSTR(TITLE2,1,T2CHAR)||STRNGI(PLOTTED,6)||' Points Plotted';
 T2CHAR=LNGTH(TITLE2A);
 IF PLT THEN DO;
  XO=XORG+XAXLTH+1;   X1=XO+SPACE;
  YO=YAXLTH+YORG;
  DO TYPE=1 TO TYPES;
   IF TYPEUSED(TYPE)  THEN DO;
    YO=YO-MAX(DESC!_HT,SYMBHGHT(TYPE))-DESC!_HT/2;
    IF SYMBINDX(TYPE)>=0 THEN DO;
     IF SYMBINDX(TYPE)>=13 THEN NCHAR=-3; ELSE NCHAR=-1;
     CALL PLCALL(PSYMB,F7,ADDR(XO),ADDR(YO),ADDR(SYMBHGHT(TYPE)),
      ADDR(SYMBINDX(TYPE)),ADDR(HORIZ),ADDR(NCHAR),ADDR(SCO),
      FO,FO);

     END;
    ELSE
     CALL PLCALL(PSYM,F7,ADDR(XO),ADDR(YO),ADDR(SYMBHGHT(TYPE)),
      ADDR(SYMBCHAR(TYPE)),ADDR(HORIZ),ADDR(F1),ADDR(SCO),FO,FO);
    CALL PLCALL(PSYM,F7,ADDR(X1),ADDR(YO),ADDR(DESC!_HT),
     ADDR(SYMBDESC(TYPE)),ADDR(HORIZ),ADDR(DESCLEN),ADDR(SCO),FO,FO);
    IF YO<=0 THEN TYPE=9999;

    END;
  XO=XORG-1;   YO=YORG-AXIS!_T!_HT-AXIS!_V!_HT-TITLE!_HT-1.0;
  CALL PLCALL(PSYM,F7,ADDR(XO),ADDR(YO),ADDR(TITLE!_HT),ADDR(TITLE1),
   ADDR(HORIZ),ADDR(T1CHAR),ADDR(SCO),FO,FO);
  XO=XORG-1; YO=YO-TITLE!_HT*2;
  CALL PLCALL(PSYM,F7,ADDR(XO),ADDR(YO),ADDR(TITLE!_HT),ADDR(TITLE2A),
   ADDR(HORIZ),ADDR(T2CHAR),ADDR(SCO),FO,FO);
  CALL PLCALL(PLTEND,FO,FO,FO,FO,FO,FO,FO,FO);

  END;
 IF PRNT THEN  DO;
  CALL PPSYMB(3,2,0,TITLE1,HORIZ,LENGTH(TITLE1),SCO);
  CALL PPSYMB(3,1,0,TITLE2A,HORIZ,LENGTH(TITLE2A),SCO);
  CALL PPLTEND;
  END;
 END;
```

```
PROC1: PROC;

  ON CONVERSION BEGIN;
    PUT FILE(SERCOM) SKIP(2) EDIT ('INVALID PARAMETER VALUE -
    ',ONSOURCE)
      (A,A);
    CALL ERRCHK(1,5);
    ONSOURCE='O';
  END;

  ON NAME(SCARDS) BEGIN;
    PUT FILE(SERCOM) SKIP(2) EDIT ('INVALID PARAMETER - ',DATAFIELD)
      (A,A);
    CALL ERRCHK(1,5);
  END;
  PUT FILE(SERCOM) PAGE EDIT ('PLOT PROGRAM - KEITH KINTIGH')
    (SKIP(2),A);
  PUT FILE(SERCOM) EDIT ('READ PROGRAM INPUT PARAMETERS FROM SCARDS:',
    ' KEYWORD FORMAT - XMIN,XMAX,YMIN,YMAX REQUIRED')
    (SKIP(2),A,SKIP,A);
  PUT FILE(SERCOM) SKIP;
  GET FILE(SCARDS) DATA (XMIN,XMAX,YMIN,YMAX,XTITLE,YTITLE,
    XFACT,YFACT,DXV,DYV,SCALE,TITLE!_HT,DESC!_HT,XORG,YORG,
    PLOTS,TITLE1,TITLE2,TYPES,LINEPOINTS,LINES,POINTS,OUTPUT,
    DESCLEN,IGNORE,PAGESIZE,LINESIZE,LPI,XWID,XDEC,YWID,YDEC,
    WID,DEC,DV,FACT,MAXWARN,AXIS!_T!_HT,AXIS!_V!_HT);
  IF FACT¬=O THEN XFACT,YFACT=FACT;
  IF DV¬=O THEN DXV,DYV=DV;
  IF WID>O THEN XWID,YWID=WID;
  IF DEC>=O THEN XDEC,YDEC=DEC;
  IF XWID>5 THEN DO;
    XWID=5;    IF XDEC>4 THEN XDEC=4;
    PUT FILE(SERCOM) EDIT ('** WARNING ** XWID>5, SET TO 5')
      (SKIP(2),A);
  END;
  IF YWID>5 THEN DO;
    YWID=5;    IF YDEC>4 THEN YDEC=4;
    PUT FILE(SERCOM) EDIT ('** WARNING ** YWID>5, SET TO 5')
      (SKIP(2),A);
  END;
  IF SUBSTR(OUTPUT,1,2)='PR' THEN PLT=FALSE;
  ELSE IF SUBSTR(OUTPUT,1,2)='PL' THEN PRNT=FALSE;
  ELSE IF SUBSTR(OUTPUT,1,2)¬='BO' THEN
    PUT FILE(SERCOM) EDIT ('** WARNING ** INVALID OUTPUT OPTION:
    ',OUTPUT,
    '"BOTH" ASSUMED') (SKIP(2),A,A);
  XTCHAR=-LNGTH(XTITLE); YTCHAR=LNGTH(YTITLE);
  XFACT=XFACT*CMPI;  YFACT=YFACT*CMPI;  DXV=DXV/CMPI;  DYV=DYV/CMPI;
  XAXLTH=ROUND((XMAX-XMIN)/XFACT,O);
  YAXLTH=ROUND((YMAX-YMIN)/YFACT,O);
  PGXWTH=XORG+XAXLTH+DESCLEN*DESC!_HT+2;
  IF YORG=-99 THEN YORG=TITLE!_HT*4+AXIS!_T!_HT+AXIS!_V!_HT+1.O;
  PUT FILE(SERCOM) EDIT ('PLOTTER MAP:',XAXLTH,'x',YAXLTH,' INCHES',
    'PRINTER MAP:',XAXLTH*SCALE,'x',YAXLTH*SCALE,' INCHES')
    (SKIP(2),A,F(4,1),A,F(4,1),A,SKIP,A,F(4,1),A,SKIP,A,F(4,1),A);
  PUT FILE(SERCOM) SKIP;
END;
```

```
PROC2: PROC;
DCL I FIXED BIN;

ON CONVERSION BEGIN;
  PUT FILE(SERCOM) SKIP EDIT
    ('ERROR - INVALID NUMERIC FIELD - ',ONSOURCE) (2 A);
    CALL ERRCHK(1,5);
    ONSOURCE='O';
END;

ON NAME(SCARDS) BEGIN;
  PUT FILE(SERCOM) SKIP(2) EDIT ('INVALID PARAMETER - ',DATAFIELD)
    (A,A);
    CALL ERRCHK(1,5);
END;

PUT FILE(SERCOM) EDIT ('READ POINT TYPE INFORMATION FROM SCARDS:',
  ' KEYWORD FORMAT - POINT PARAMETERS FOR ',TYPES,' TYPES')
  (SKIP(2),A,SKIP,A,F(4),A);
PUT FILE(SERCOM) SKIP;
DO I=1 TO TYPES;
  DCL INDX FIXED BIN, HGHT FLOAT BIN, SYMB CHAR(1), DESC
    CHAR(DESCLEN);
  INDX=-9999; HGHT=0.1; SYMB='+'; DESC=' ';
  GET FILE(SCARDS) DATA (SYMB,INDX,HGHT,DESC);
  SYMBHGHT(I)=HGHT; SYMBDESC(I)=DESC;
  IF SYMB='+' !& INDX=-9999 THEN INDX=3;
  SYMBINDX(I)=INDX; SYMBCHAR(I)=SYMB;
  IF SYMBINDX(I)>=13 THEN SYMBHGHT(I)=SYMBHGHT(I)*.84;
  /* NOTE PSYMB FOR SINGLE SYMBOLS PRINTS LETTERS */
  /* HIGHER THAN NOMINAL HEIGHT - THIS LOOP ADJUSTS */
END;

PROC3: PROC;
DCL (I,II,TOT) FIXED BIN;

ON CONVERSION BEGIN;
  PUT FILE(SERCOM) SKIP(2) EDIT ('INVALID PARAMETER VALUE -
    ',ONSOURCE)
    (A,A);
    CALL ERRCHK(1,5);
    ONSOURCE='O';
END;

ON NAME(SCARDS) BEGIN;
  PUT FILE(SERCOM) SKIP(2) EDIT ('INVALID PARAMETER - ',DATAFIELD)
    (A,A);
    CALL ERRCHK(1,5);
END;
```

```
PUT FILE(SERCOM) EDIT ('READ LINE INFORMATION FROM SCARDS',
', KEYWORD FORMAT - LINE PARAMETERS FOR ',LINES,' LINES')
(SKIP(2),A,SKIP,A,F(4),A);
PUT FILE(SERCOM) SKIP;
DO I=1 TO LINES;
DCL (LINEPTS INIT(O),SKIP INIT(1),LINESYMB INIT(3)) FIXED BIN(31),
(S!_ANGLE INIT(45), S!_DIST INIT(.1), DASHLEN INIT(.1)) FLOAT BIN,
LINETYPE INIT('LINE') CHAR(6);
GET FILE(SCARDS) DATA
(LINETYPE,LINEPTS,SKIP,DASHLEN,LINESYMB,S!_ANGLE,S!_DIST);
N!_LINE(I)=LINEPTS; K(I)=SKIP; ISYM(I)=LINESYMB;
DASLTH(I)=DASHLEN; SANGLE(I)=S!_ANGLE; SDIST(I)=S!_DIST;
ITYP(I)=INDEX('PLVDCS',SUBSTR(LINETYPE,1,1))-2;
IF ITYP(I)<=-2 THEN DO;
PUT FILE(SERCOM) SKIP(2) EDIT ('INVALID LINETYPE: ',
LINETYPE) (A,A);
CALL ERRCHK(1,5);
END;

ON CONVERSION BEGIN;
PUT FILE(SERCOM) SKIP EDIT
('ERROR - INVALID NUMERIC FIELD - ',ONSOURCE) (2 A);
CALL ERRCHK(1,5);
ONSOURCE='O';
END;
TOT=O;
DO I=1 TO LINES;
TOT=TOT+N!_LINE(I);
IF K(I)<=O THEN K(I)=1;
END;
IF TOT>LINEPOINTS THEN DO;
PUT FILE(SERCOM) EDIT ('TOTAL OF LINEPTS > LINEPOINTS',
', INCREASE LINEPOINTS TO AT LEAST ',TOT,' AND RERUN')
(SKIP(2),A,F(4),A);
CALL ERRCHK(1,O);
END;
PUT FILE(SERCOM) EDIT ('READ LINE DATA FROM LINEIN',
', FREE FORMAT - X !& Y COORDINATES FOR ',TOT,' VERTICES')
(SKIP(2),A,SKIP,A,F(4),A);
PUT FILE(SERCOM) SKIP;
XLINE(O)=XMIN; YLINE(O)=YMIN;
GET FILE(LINEIN) LIST
((XLINE(I),YLINE(I) DO I=1 TO TOT));
DO I=1 TO TOT;
IF XLINE(I)<XMIN | XLINE(I)>XMAX |
YLINE(I)<YMIN | YLINE(I)>YMAX THEN DO;
IF WARN<MAXWARN THEN PUT FILE(SERCOM) EDIT
('LINE POINT, I,' OUT OF BOUNDS:',XLINE(I),YLINE(I))
(SKIP(2),A,F(5),A,2 F(12,2));
XLINE(I)=XLINE(I-1); YLINE(I)=YLINE(I-1); WARN=WARN+1;
END;
END;
END;
```

```
PROC4: PROC;

ON CONVERSION BEGIN;
   PUT FILE(SERCOM) SKIP(2) EDIT ('INVALID PARAMETER VALUE -
   ',ONSOURCE)
      (A,A);
   CALL ERRCHK(1,5);        ONSOURCE='O';
END;

ON NAME(SCARDS) BEGIN;
   PUT FILE(SERCOM) SKIP(2) EDIT ('INVALID PARAMETER - ',DATAFIELD)
      (A,A);
   CALL ERRCHK(1,5);
END;

ON ENDFILE(SCARDS) BEGIN; IF P>1 THEN PUT FILE(SERCOM)
   SKIP EDIT (' WARNING - MISSING PLOT PARAMETERS') (A);     END;

IF POINTS=-9999 THEN POINTS=-POINTS;
PUT FILE(SERCOM) EDIT ('READ PARAMETERS FOR PLOT ',P,' FROM SCARDS',
   ' KEYWORD FORMAT - POINTS, OUTPUT, TITLE1,TITLE2')
   (SKIP(2),A,F(3),A,SKIP,A);
PUT FILE(SERCOM) SKIP;
GET FILE(SCARDS) DATA (TITLE1,TITLE2,POINTS,OUTPUT,IGNORE);
PUT FILE(SERCOM) EDIT ('READ POINT DATA FROM POINTIN:',
   ' FREE FORMAT - X Y TYPE - FOR ',POINTS,' POINTS')
   (SKIP(2),A,SKIP,A,F(4),A);
PUT FILE(SERCOM) SKIP;
END;
```

```
PROC5: PROC;
DCL DUMMY FLOAT BIN, I FIXED BIN(15);

ON CONVERSION BEGIN;
   PUT FILE(SERCOM) SKIP EDIT
      ('ERROR - INVALID NUMERIC FIELD - ',ONSOURCE) (2 A);
   CALL ERRCHK(1,5);          ONSOURCE='O';
END;

ON ENDFILE(POINTIN) EOF=TRUE;

GET FILE(POINTIN) LIST ((DUMMY DO I=1 TO IGNORE));
GET FILE(POINTIN) LIST (XPT,YPT,TYPE!_PT);
ON ENDFILE(POINTIN) BEGIN;
   IF EOF=TRUE THEN EOF=TRUE; ELSE EOF=FALSE;
END;
GET FILE(POINTIN) SKIP;
IF XPT<XMIN | XPT>XMAX | YPT<YMIN | YPT>YMAX THEN DO;
   IF WARN<MAXWARN THEN PUT FILE(SERCOM) EDIT
      ('POINT NUMBER:',POINT,' OUT OF BOUNDS:',XPT,YPT)
      (SKIP(1),A,F(5),A,2 F(12,2));
   XPT=XMIN; YPT=YMIN; TYPE!_PT=O; WARN=WARN+1;
END;
IF TYPE!_PT<O | TYPE!_PT>TYPES THEN DO;
   IF WARN<MAXWARN THEN PUT FILE(SERCOM) EDIT
      ('INVALID TYPE:',TYPE!_PT,' POINT NUMBER:',POINT)
      (SKIP(1),A,F(12,2),A,F(5));
   TYPE!_PT=O;  WARN=WARN+1;
END;
TYPEUSED(TYPE!_PT)=TYPEUSED(TYPE!_PT)+1;
END;

PROC6: PROC;
IF TYPE!_PT¬=O THEN DO;
   NCHAR=-1;
   IF PLT THEN DO;
      IF SYMBINDX(TYPE!_PT)>=O THEN CALL
         PLCALL(PSYMB,F7,ADDR(XPT),ADDR(YPT),
         ADDR(SYMBHGHT(TYPE!_PT)),ADDR(SYMBINDX(TYPE!_PT)),
         ADDR(HORIZ),ADDR(NCHAR),ADDR(SC1),FO,FO);
      ELSE CALL PLCALL(PSYM,F7,ADDR(XPT),ADDR(YPT),
         ADDR(SYMBHGHT(TYPE!_PT)),ADDR(SYMBCHAR(TYPE!_PT)),
         ADDR(HORIZ),ADDR(F1),ADDR(SC1),FO,FO);
   END;
   IF PRNT THEN CALL PPSYMB(XPT,YPT,SYMBHGHT(TYPE!_PT),
      SYMBCHAR(TYPE!_PT),HORIZ,NCHAR,SC1);
END;
END;
```

```
/* PRINTER PLOT ROUTINES */

PPSYMB: PROC(XO,YO,MULT,CHA,THETA,NCHAR,SC);
    /* IF SC=0 XO=COL POSITION, YO=LINE FROM BOTTOM */
    DCL (XO,YO,MULT,THETA,SC) FLOAT BIN, CHA CHAR(*),
        (X,Y,X1,Y1) FIXED BIN(15), NCHAR FIXED BIN(31);
    IF SC=0 THEN SUBSTR(PAGE(TRUNC(YO)),TRUNC(XO),NCHAR)=CHA;
    ELSE DO;
        Y=6+TRUNC((YO-YMIN)/YFACT*SCALE*LPI+.5);
        X=YWID+4+TRUNC((XO-XMIN)/XFACT*SCALE*10+.5);
        IF X<(YWID+4) | X>(LINESIZE-1) | Y<6 | Y>(PAGESIZE-1) THEN DO;
            IF WARN<MAXWARN THEN PUT FILE(SERCOM) SKIP(2) EDIT
            ('PLOT WARNING: POINT OUT OF BOUNDS -',XO,',',YO)
            (SKIP,A,F(XWID,XDEC),A,F(YWID,YDEC));
            WARN=WARN+1;
            GO TO OUT;
        END;
        IF MULT<0 | INDEX(SPECIAL,SUBSTR(PAGE(Y),X,1))>0 THEN
            SUBSTR(PAGE(Y),X,1)=CHA;
        ELSE IF MULT=0 THEN SUBSTR(PAGE(Y),X,1)='#'; /* PRINT '#' */
        ELSE DO; /* PRINT SYMBOL IN ADJACENT SPOT */
            DO Y1=0,1,-1;
                DO X1=0,1,-1;
                    IF INDEX(SPECIAL,SUBSTR(PAGE(Y+Y1),X+X1,1))>0 THEN DO;
                        SUBSTR(PAGE(Y+Y1),X+X1,1)=CHA;
                        GO TO OUT;

            END; END; END;
            IF WARN<MAXWARN THEN PUT FILE(SERCOM) SKIP(2) EDIT
            ('PLOT WARNING: NO ROOM TO PLOT POINT -',XO,',',YO)
            (SKIP,A,F(XWID,XDEC),A,F(YWID,YDEC));
            WARN=WARN+1;
        END;
    OUT: END;
END PPSYMB;

PPLINE: PROC(X,Y,N,K,ITYP,ISYM,SC,LN);
    DCL ((X(*),Y(*)),SC,D,DX,DY,M,X2,Y2) FLOAT BIN. (N,K,I,ITYP,ISYM,LN)
        FIXED BIN(31);
    DO I=LN TO LN+N-2 BY K;
        DX=X(I+1)-X(I);  DY=Y(I+1)-Y(I);
        IF DX=0 THEN M=100000; ELSE M=DY/DX;
        IF ABS(M)>1 THEN DO;
            IF DY>0 THEN D=YFACT/(SCALE*LPI) ; ELSE D=-YFACT/(SCALE*LPI);
            DO Y2=Y(I) TO Y(I+1) BY D;
                CALL PPSYMB(X(I)+(Y2-Y(I))/M,Y2,-1,'.',0.0,1,1.0);
        END; END;
        ELSE DO;
            IF DX>0 THEN D=XFACT/(SCALE*10) ; ELSE D=-XFACT/(SCALE*10);
            DO X2=X(I) TO X(I+1) BY D;
                CALL PPSYMB(X2,Y(I)+(X2-X(I))*M,-1,'.',0.0,1,1.0);
    END; END; END;
END PPLINE;
```

```
PPAXIS: PROC(XO,YO,TITLE,NCHR,AXLN,THETA,XMIN,DX1,DV1);
  DCL(XO,YO,AXLN,AXLTH,THETA,XMIN,DX,DX1,DV,DV1,DV2) FLOAT BIN,
    (M,N,MX,MN,INC,PFACT) FIXED BIN(31),
    TITLE CHAR(*)    , (NCHR,NCHAR) FIXED BIN(31),
    DX=DX1; DV=DV1; NCHAR=NCHR; AXLTH=AXLN;    LAB CHAR(12);
  /* SET UP HORIZ AND VERTICAL PARMS */
    /* MX=MAX AXIS LEN IN CHAR POS */
    /* INC=MIN SPACES BETWEEN TICS */
    /* PFACT=CHAR POS PER INCH    */
    /* DV=UNITS BETWEEN TICS      */
    /* DV2=CHAR POS BETWEEN TICS  */
  IF THETA=0 THEN DO; MX=LINESIZE-YWID-3; INC=XWID+2;
    MN=YWID+4; PFACT=10; END;
  ELSE DO; MX=PAGESIZE-5; MN=6; PFACT=LPI;  INC=2; END;
  AXLTH=TRUNC(AXLTH*PFACT*SCALE+.5);
  IF AXLTH>MX THEN DO;
    PUT FILE(SERCOM) SKIP(2) LIST
      ('PRINTER MAP AXIS WILL NOT FIT - RECALCULATE SCALE OR FACT');
    CALL ERRCHK(1,0);
  END;
  NCHAR=MIN(MX,ABS(NCHAR));
  DV2=DV*PFACT*SCALE;
  DO WHILE(DV2<INC); DV=DV*2; DV2=DV*PFACT*SCALE; END;
  IF THETA=0 THEN DO;
    SUBSTR(PAGE(3),MN,NCHAR)=TITLE;
    DO N=0 TO AXLTH;   SUBSTR(PAGE(5),N+MN,1)='-';    END;
    N=0;  M=0;
    DO WHILE (N<=AXLTH);
      SUBSTR(PAGE(5),N+MN,1)='+';
      LAB=STRNGR((XMIN+DX*DV*M),XWID,XDEC);
      SUBSTR(PAGE(4),N+MN-XWID+1,XWID)=LAB;
      M=M+1;  N=TRUNC(DV2*M+.5);
    END;
  END; ELSE DO;
    IF NCHAR<=AXLTH THEN M=AXLTH+7;  ELSE M=NCHAR+7;
    DO N=1 TO NCHAR;  SUBSTR(PAGE(M-N),1,1)=SUBSTR(TITLE,N,1);  END;
    DO N=0 TO AXLTH;  SUBSTR(PAGE(MN+N),YWID+3,1)='|'; END;
    N=0;  M=0;
    DO WHILE (N<=AXLTH);
      SUBSTR(PAGE(MN+N),YWID+3,1)='+';
      LAB=STRNGR((XMIN+DX*DV*M),YWID,YDEC);
      SUBSTR(PAGE(MN+N),3,YWID)=LAB;
      M=M+1;  N=TRUNC(DV2*M+.5);
    END; END;
END PPAXIS;

PPLTEND: PROC;
  DCL I FIXED BIN(15);
  PUT FILE(SPRINT) PAGE;
  DO I=PAGESIZE TO 1 BY -1;
    IF PAGE(I)¬=' ' THEN PUT FILE(SPRINT) EDIT (PAGE(I)) (COL(1).A);
  END;
END PPLTEND;
```

```
/* AUXILLIARY PROCEDURES */

LNGTH: PROC(STR) RETURNS (FIXED BIN(31));
  DCL STR CHAR(*), LEN FIXED BIN(31);
  LEN=LENGTH(STR);
  DO WHILE((SUBSTR(STR,LEN,1)=' ') !& (LEN>=2));
    LEN=LEN-1;
  END;
  RETURN (LEN);
END;

STRNGI: PROC(NUM,LEN) RETURNS (CHAR(16) VARYING);
  /* RETURNS RIGHT JUSTIFIED STRING OF LENGTH=LEN */
  DCL LEN FIXED BIN(31), NUM FIXED BIN(31), STR CHAR(16);
  PUT STRING (STR) EDIT (NUM)(F(16));
  IF SUBSTR(STR,1,16-LEN)¬=' ', THEN STR='****************';
  RETURN(SUBSTR(STR,17-LEN,LEN));
END;

STRNGR: PROC(NUM,LEN,DEC) RETURNS (CHAR(16) VARYING);
  /* RETURNS RIGHT JUSTIFIED STRING OF LENGTH=LEN */
  DCL (LEN,DEC) FIXED BIN(31), NUM FLOAT BIN, STR CHAR(16);
  PUT STRING (STR) EDIT (NUM)(F(16,DEC));
  IF SUBSTR(STR,1,16-LEN)¬=' ', THEN STR='****************';
  RETURN(SUBSTR(STR,17-LEN,LEN));
END;

ERRCHK: PROC(PLUSERR,MAXERR) FIXED BIN(31);
  DCL (PLUSERR,MAXERR) FIXED BIN(31);
  ERROR=ERROR+PLUSERR;
  IF ERROR>MAXERR THEN DO:
    PUT FILE(SERCOM) EDIT (('PROGRAM ENDS DUE TO ',ERROR,' ERRORS')
      (SKIP(2),A,F(4),A);
    SIGNAL ERROR;
  END;
END;

/* BEGIN EXECUTION HERE!! CALL CONTROL ROUTINE */

CALL CONTROL;
END PLOT;
```

SAMPLE RUN COMMAND AND FILE SETUP
=== === =======

The run command:
=== === =======

```
$RUN K8UH:PLOT.OBJ+*PL1LIB+*PLOTSYS -
 SCARDS=*SOURCE* SPRINT=-LIST SERCOM=-MSG -
 PAR=LINEIN=K8UH:PLOT.TESTLINE@F(80) -
 POINTIN=K8UH:PLOT.TESTDATA@F(80) 9=PLOTFILE

XMIN=500 XMAX=530 YMIN=2140 YMAX=2170 PLOTS=1 LINES=4
TITLE1='Valley of Mexico Survey - Texcoco Region'
XTITLE='UTM East Coordinate (km)' YTITLE='UTM North Coordinate (km)'
TYPES=13 OUTPUT='BOTH' DV=5 WID=4 DEC=0 SCALE=.635;

SYMB='h' HGHT=.15 DESC='Small Hamlet';
SYMB='H' HGHT=.15 DESC='Hamlet';
SYMB='d' HGHT=.15 DESC='Small Dispersed Village';
SYMB='D' HGHT=.20 DESC='Large Dispersed Village';
SYMB='n' HGHT=.15 DESC='Small Nucleated Village';
SYMB='N' HGHT=.20 DESC='Large Nucleated Village';
SYMB='L' HGHT=.30 DESC='Local Center';
SYMB='R' HGHT=.30 DESC='Regional Center';
SYMB='S' HGHT=.30 DESC='Supraregional Center';
SYMB='C' HGHT=.15 DESC='Isolated Ceremonial Center';
SYMB='e' HGHT=.15 DESC='Small Elite District';
SYMB='E' HGHT=.15 DESC='Large Elite District';
SYMB='?' HGHT=.15 DESC='Questionable';

LINEPTS=3;
LINEPTS=29 LINETYPE='LINE';
LINEPTS=46 LINETYPE='LINE';
LINEPTS=56 LINETYPE='LINE';

POINTS=59 TITLE2='Late Toltec Sites';
```

FILE SET UP

The Data
=== ====

The following is the
K8UH:PLOT.TESTLINE data
used in the sample run.

	(Testline Data) (Continued)	(Testline Data) (Continued)
530.00 2140.00	513.42 2152.60	514.33 2160.47
530.00 2170.00	513.60 2152.05	516.71 2160.47
500.00 2170.00	518.72 2152.05	516.71 2161.93
504.63 2141.07	518.72 2152.42	517.08 2161.93
508.11 2141.07	520.74 2152.42	517.08 2162.11
508.11 2144.00	520.92 2152.96	518.36 2162.30
510.31 2144.00	522.57 2152.96	519.27 2162.48
510.31 2143.40	522.57 2153.33	520.74 2162.30
510.86 2142.72	523.30 2153.33	521.65 2162.66
513.23 2142.72	523.85 2152.78	521.65 2163.03
514.15 2141.07	524.40 2153.15	522.93 2163.03
519.09 2141.07	524.21 2153.51	523.30 2162.66
519.09 2144.18	523.30 2153.70	523.30 2162.11
517.44 2144.18	523.12 2155.53	524.40 2161.57
517.44 2145.64	524.40 2155.16	525.50 2162.30
510.49 2145.64	524.58 2155.53	525.50 2165.04
510.49 2148.76	524.21 2155.71	524.21 2165.04
509.21 2148.76	524.21 2156.44	524.21 2165.23
509.21 2149.49	524.58 2156.44	524.40 2165.41
507.01 2149.49	524.76 2156.99	524.03 2165.59
507.01 2150.40	523.85 2157.36	523.85 2165.59
505.73 2150.40	523.85 2157.72	522.93 2167.06
505.73 2149.67	524.21 2157.91	522.93 2167.42
504.82 2149.67	524.03 2158.27	522.20 2167.60
504.82 2150.40	524.03 2158.27	522.02 2167.24
503.54 2150.40	523.30 2158.64	521.10 2167.79
503.54 2149.49	523.30 2158.64	520.01 2167.42
501.89 2149.49	523.67 2158.82	519.27 2167.79
501.89 2146.01	523.67 2159.37	518.36 2167.79
502.25 2144.18	523.67 2159.55	518.36 2168.52
504.63 2142.90	524.03 2160.47	517.81 2168.52
504.63 2141.07	524.21 2160.47	517.81 2168.89
503.72 2156.44	517.99 2158.82	517.26 2168.89
504.27 2154.06	516.89 2158.82	516.71 2168.52
506.46 2153.43	516.89 2158.27	516.71 2168.15
510.31 2153.51	514.52 2158.27	514.33 2167.97
510.31 2152.60	514.52 2158.64	514.15 2167.06
	511.22 2158.64	513.78 2166.69
	511.22 2158.45	513.78 2166.32
	506.46 2158.45	509.21 2165.96
	506.46 2157.72	505.91 2164.86
	504.82 2157.72	505.91 2163.76
	503.72 2156.44	505.00 2163.58
	503.90 2160.65	505.00 2162.11
	505.00 2160.65	505.00 2161.93
	505.00 2161.38	504.45 2161.93
	506.83 2161.57	503.90 2160.65
	506.83 2160.65	
	508.84 2160.65	
	508.66 2161.75	
	512.32 2162.11	
	513.42 2161.57	
	514.33 2161.57	

K8UH:PLOT.TESTDATA
==================

The following is the
K8UH:PLOT.TESTDATA used
in the sample run command.

504.20	2160.50	2.	TX-LT-1
504.80	2160.90	2.	TX-LT-2
505.50	2162.60	1.	TX-LT-3
507.70	2161.20	1.	TX-LT-4
508.90	2164.10	1.	TX-LT-5
510.20	2163.60	2.	TX-LT-6
510.20	2162.40	2.	TX-LT-7
511.40	2163.30	1.	TX-LT-8
511.70	2162.20	1.	TX-LT-9
513.40	2162.00	2.	TX-LT-10
514.80	2161.80	1.	TX-LT-11
514.50	2163.90	4.	TX-LT-12
512.70	2163.80	1.	TX-LT-13
513.60	2165.80	10.	TX-LT-14
513.50	2164.70	1.	TX-LT-15
515.40	2164.70	1.	TX-LT-16
515.20	2165.80	1.	TX-LT-17
517.20	2167.30	2.	TX-LT-18
517.40	2167.70	1.	TX-LT-19
517.90	2166.50	1.	TX-LT-20
518.40	2164.60	1.	TX-LT-21
517.60	2165.20	1.	TX-LT-22
516.40	2165.10	1.	TX-LT-23
516.60	2164.10	2.	TX-LT-24
516.00	2162.60	13.	TX-LT-25
516.70	2161.90	2.	TX-LT-26
516.90	2162.70	1.	TX-LT-27
518.00	2163.00	3.	TX-LT-28
519.80	2164.30	2.	TX-LT-29
520.70	2164.30	1.	TX-LT-30
523.10	2164.80	2.	TX-LT-31
507.80	2157.10	2.	TX-LT-32
508.50	2156.20	2.	TX-LT-33
509.10	2155.50	3.	TX-LT-34
506.60	2156.10	3.	TX-LT-35
506.90	2155.00	2.	TX-LT-36
505.10	2154.30	13.	TX-LT-37
509.40	2153.90	2.	TX-LT-38
511.50	2157.90	2.	TX-LT-39
511.90	2156.90	13.	TX-LT-40

(Testdata Data Continued)

514.20	2157.50	1.	TX-LT-41
515.90	2156.80	1.	TX-LT-42
517.50	2157.70	1.	TX-LT-43
520.10	2155.20	1.	TX-LT-44
521.60	2155.00	1.	TX-LT-45
519.90	2154.50	1.	TX-LT-46
520.80	2154.80	1.	TX-LT-47
520.20	2154.50	1.	TX-LT-48
513.20	2152.90	1.	TX-LT-49
517.80	2151.50	1.	TX-LT-50
514.20	2144.30	1.	TX-LT-51
513.40	2143.80	2.	TX-LT-52
511.10	2144.30	7.	TX-LT-53
505.70	2146.60	3.	TX-LT-54
504.70	2144.50	10.	TX-LT-55
503.00	2144.50	3.	TX-LT-56
505.00	2142.80	3.	TX-LT-57
506.00	2142.40	3.	TX-LT-58
505.50	2141.50	3.	TX-LT-59

```
MESSAGES PRINTED OUT FROM THE PROGRAM
======== ======= === ==== === ======

PLOT PROGRAM - KEITH KINTIGH

READ PROGRAM INPUT PARAMETERS FROM SCARDS:
   KEYWORD FORMAT - XMIN,XMAX,YMIN,YMAX REQUIRED

PLOTTER MAP: 11.8x11.8 INCHES
PRINTER MAP:  7.5x 7.5 INCHES

READ POINT TYPE INFORMATION FROM SCARDS:
   KEYWORD FORMAT - POINT PARAMETERS FOR    13 TYPES

READ LINE INFORMATION FROM SCARDS
   KEYWORD FORMAT - LINE PARAMETERS FOR     4 LINES

READ LINE DATA FROM LINEIN
   FREE FORMAT - X & Y COORDINATES FOR   134 VERTICES

READ PARAMETERS FOR PLOT    1 FROM SCARDS
   KEYWORD FORMAT - POINTS, OUTPUT, TITLE1,TITLE2

READ POINT DATA FROM POINTIN:
   FREE FORMAT - X Y TYPE - FOR   59 POINTS
-PDS: PLOT DESCRIPTION GENERATION BEGINS.

START POINT PLOT

PLOT:    1
   59 POINTS PROCESSED
   59 POINTS PLOTTED

END PROGRAM
```

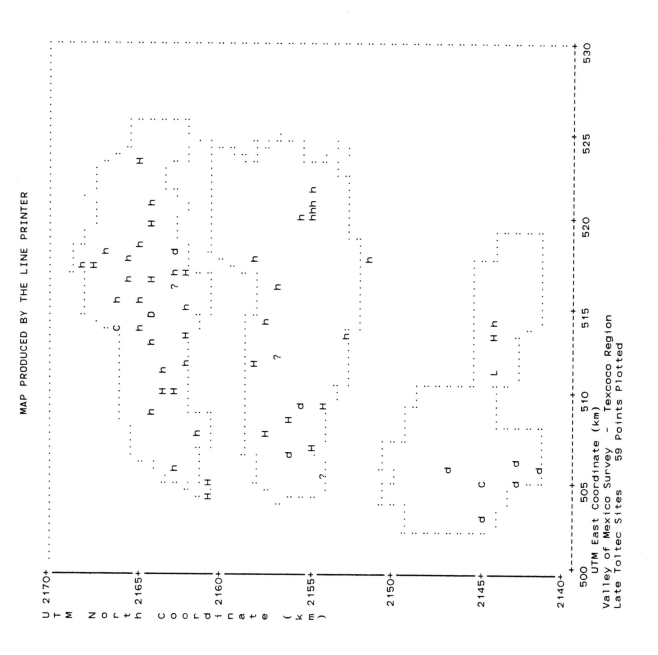

Appendix II

NEAREST NEIGHBOR PROGRAM

```
COMMENT PROGRAM DOCUMENTATION
TO RUN PROGRAM ENTER:
$RUN K8UH:NEIGH.OBJ SPRINT=-MESSAGES
THE PROGRAM WILL PROMPT FOR OTHER FILE ASSIGNMENTS
AND THE PROGRAM PARAMETERS DESCRIBED BELOW

PROGRAM PARAMETERS
   AREA    AREA (IN UNITS IN WHICH DISTANCE IS MEASURED)
   NSTRATA MAXIMUM STRATUM NUMBER IN DATA
   NTYPE   NUMBER OF DIFFERENT TYPES OF UNITS W/I STRATUM
   NNEIG   NUMBER OF NEIGHBORS TO BE PRINTED - O FOR NO LIST
   MATCH   "WITHIN" OR "BETWEEN" TO LOOK FOR WITHIN OR BETWEEN GROUP
           NEIGHBORS.  USUALLY WILL BE "WITHIN".  IF "BETWEEN" IS
           THE NEAREST NEIGHBOR WILL BE THE CLOSEST POINT WHICH IS
           NOT IN THE SAME GROUP AS THE SUBJECT POINT.

TYPE IDENTIFICATION CHARACTERS - 1 LINE
   NTYPE   NONBLANK CHARACTERS USED TO IDENTIFY TYPES
           MUST ALL BE ON ONE LINE AND MAY (BUT NEED NOT)
           BE SEPARATED BY ONE OR MORE BLANKS.

GROUP COMPOSITION
   GROUP(TYPE) LIST OF GROUP VALUES, 1 PER TYPE (NTYPE VALUES)
ITEM DATA - NITEM ITEMS, FREE FORMAT, ITEM STARTS A NEW LINE
   ID      CHARACTER VALUE ID FOR ITEM IN "'S - MAX 1O CHAR
   STRATA  INTEGER STRATUM (PERIOD) OF ITEM 1-NSTRATA
   TYPE    INTEGER TYPE OF ITEM 1-NTYPE
   XVAL    X COORD (EAST)
   YVAL    Y COORD (NORTH)

THE PROGRAM READS THE ITEM DATA AND WITHIN EACH STRATUM
(PERIOD) COMPUTES THE NEAREST NEIGHBOR COEFFICIENT FOR
EACH GROUP OF ITEM TYPES WITHIN THE STRATUM.  THE GROUP
MAY BE COMPOSED OF ANY (NONOVERLAPPING) SUBSET OF THE
ITEM TYPES.  (TO GET OVERLAPPING SUBSETS RUN PROGRAM
MORE THAN ONCE.)  FOR EASE OF READING THE OUTPUT, EACH
TYPE IS IDENTIFIED BY A SPECIAL CHARACTER.  TO GET
SIMPLE NEAREST NEIGHBOR COEFF OF A GROUP OF DATA, SPECIFY
1 STRATA, 1 GROUP AND 1 TYPE.

THE PROGRAM ALSO WRITES A FILE OF NEAREST NEIGHBOR DATA WHICH
CAN BE PROCESSED FURTHER (E.G. BY MIDAS) IF DESIRED.  THE
OUTPUT FORMAT IS AS FOLLOWS:
   1X
   I2 - STRATA OF ITEM
   1X,A1O - ITEM ID
   1X,I2  - GROUP OF ITEM
   1X,I2  - TYPE OF ITEM
   REPEATED FOR EACH OF NNEIG NEIGHBORS:
   1X,I2  - NEIGHBOR NUMBER E.G. 1,2,3...
   1X,A1O - ID OF NEIGHBOR
   1X,I2  - GROUP OF NEIGHBOR
   1X,I2  - TYPE OF NEIGHBOR
   1X,F8.2 - DISTANCE FROM ITEM

END DOCUMENTATION;
```

COMMENT SAMPLE RUN PARAMETER INPUT AND SAMPLE DATA:

SAMPLE RUN:

```
$RUN NEIGH.OBJ SPRINT=-MESSAGES PAR=SIZE=100K
>FILE CONTAINING DATA ?
NEIGHBOR.DATA
>LISTING FILE (WILL BE EMPTIED) ?
*PRINT*
>PUNCH FILE (WILL BE EMPTIED) ?
-NEIGHBOR.OUT
>AREA ?
812.0000
>NUMBER OF STRATA ?
2
>NUMBER OF POINT TYPES ?
6
>NUMBER OF NEIGHBORS PRINTED ?
3
>WITHIN OR BETWEEN ?
WITHIN
>NTYPE ID CHARACTERS (ON ONE LINE) ?
h H dD n N
>NTYPE GROUP ASSIGNMENTS (ONE PER LINE) ?
>h ?
1
>H ?
1
>d ?
1
>D ?
2
>n ?
1
>N ?
2
```

```
FILE NEIGHBOR.DATA
"CH-EF-1  " 1 5 2114.79 527.64
"CH-EF-2  " 1 5 2114.71 527.99
"XO-EF-1  " 1 1 2132.60 497.23
"XO-EF-2  " 1 2 2132.06 497.51
"CH-MF-1  " 2 3 2136.13 518.35
"CH-MF-2  " 2 1 2135.35 518.65
"CH-MF-3  " 2 2 2133.75 514.05
"CH-MF-4  " 2 3 2131.47 516.07
"CH-MF-5  " 2 6 2130.43 518.00
"CH-MF-6  " 2 2 2125.38 520.72
"CH-MF-7  " 2 2 2125.47 521.30
"CH-MF-8  " 2 3 2125.70 517.95
"CH-MF-9  " 2 6 2122.83 512.20
"CH-MF-10 " 2 1 2124.56 512.95
```

```
IF THE PROGRAM FAILS WITH RUN ERROR 5007, RECORD STORAGE AREA
OVERFLOW, RERUN WITH A LARGER SIZE PARAMETER ON THE RUN
COMMAND EG. SIZE=250K.

END SAMPLE INPUT;

PROCEDURE ASSIGN!_FILES;
BEGIN
   STRING(80) STR80;
   STR80:=PROMPTS("FILE CONTAINING DATA ?");
   ASSIGN("DATA",STR80(0|30));
   STR80:=PROMPTS("LISTING FILE (WILL BE EMPTIED) ?");
   ASSIGN("LISTING",STR80(0|30));
   IF STR80(0|1)¬="*" THEN EMPTY("LISTING");
   STR80:=PROMPTS("PUNCH FILE (WILL BE EMPTIED) ?");
   ASSIGN("FILE",STR80(0|30));
   IF STR80(0|1)¬="*" THEN EMPTY("FILE");
END;

INTEGER PROCEDURE PROMPTI(STRING(80) VALUE MSG);
BEGIN
   INTEGER RSLT;
   PROMPT(MSG);
   READER("USER");   READ(RSLT);   WRITE(RSLT);
   RSLT
END;

REAL PROCEDURE PROMPTR(STRING(80) VALUE MSG);
BEGIN
   REAL RSLT;
   PROMPT(MSG);
   READER("USER");   READ(RSLT);   WRITE(RSLT);
   RSLT
END;

LOGICAL PROCEDURE PROMPTL(STRING(80) VALUE MSG);
BEGIN
   STRING(1) ANSWER;
   PROMPT(MSG);
   READER("USER");   ANSWER:="X";
   WHILE ANSWER¬="Y" AND ANSWER¬="N" AND ANSWER¬="O" DO
   BEGIN
      READCARD(ANSWER);
      IF ANSWER¬="Y" AND ANSWER¬="N" AND ANSWER¬="O" THEN
         PROMPT("REPLY YES OR NO?");
   END;
   WRITE(ANSWER);
   IF ANSWER="Y" OR ANSWER="O" THEN TRUE ELSE FALSE
END;
```

```
STRING(80) PROCEDURE PROMPTS(STRING(80) VALUE MSG);
BEGIN
    STRING(80) RSLT;
    PROMPT(MSG);
    READER("USER");        READCARD(RSLT);        WRITE(RSLT);
    RSLT
END;

PROCEDURE PROMPT(STRING(80) VALUE MSG);
BEGIN
    WRITER("ERROR");    SKIP(1);    WRITE(MSG);
    WRITER("PRINT");    SKIP(1);    WRITE(MSG);
END;

PROCEDURE SKIP(INTEGER VALUE N);
BEGIN INTEGER I;
    FOR I:=1 UNTIL N DO WRITE(" ");
END;

INTEGER NITEM,NTYPE,NNEIG,PNEIG,NSTRATA,LSTRATA,FSTRATA,NGROUP;
REAL AREA;
STRING(80) CARD;
STRING(81) TYPES;
STRING(132) LINE;
STRING(1) CHAR1,CHAR2;
STRING(80) DEVICE,MATCH;
LOGICAL WITHIN;

ASSIGN!_FILES;

READER("USER");  WRITER("ERROR");  WRITE!_CC:=TRUE;
I!_W:=4;
AREA:=PROMPTR("AREA ?");
NSTRATA:=PROMPTI("NUMBER OF STRATA ?");
NTYPE:=PROMPTI("NUMBER OF POINT TYPES ?");
NNEIG:=PROMPTI("NUMBER OF NEIGHBORS PRINTED ?");
PNEIG:=NNEIG;
IF NNEIG<1 THEN NNEIG:=1;
MATCH:="??";
WHILE MATCH(0|2)¬="WI" AND MATCH(0|2)¬="wi" AND MATCH(0|2)¬="BE" AND
    MATCH(0|2)¬="be" DO MATCH:=PROMPTS("WITHIN OR BETWEEN ?");
COMMENT DEVICE:=PROMPTS("PRINTER OR TERMINAL ?");

ASSERT NNEIG<=5;

BEGIN

RECORD ITEM (STRING(10) ID; INTEGER TYPE,STRATA; REAL YVAL,XVAL;
    REFERENCE(ITEM) SREF; REFERENCE(NEIGHBOR) NREF);
RECORD NEIGHBOR (REFERENCE(ITEM) NEIG; REAL DIST;
    REFERENCE(NEIGHBOR)NEXT);
REFERENCE(ITEM) ARRAY FIRST,LAST(1::NSTRATA);
INTEGER ARRAY GROUP(1::NTYPE);
INTEGER ARRAY MATRIX(1::NNEIG,1::NTYPE,1::NTYPE);
COMMENT ACTUAL BOUNDS ARE NGROUP NOT NNEIG BUT NNEIG<NGROUP;
```

```
LOGICAL PROCEDURE DECIDE(INTEGER VALUE G1,G2);
   IF WITHIN THEN G1=G2 ELSE G1¬=G2;
PROCEDURE INIT;
BEGIN
   INTEGER COL1,COL2;
   STRING(3) CHAR3;
   FOR P:=1 UNTIL NSTRATA DO
      FIRST(P):=LAST(P):=ITEM(" ",O,P,O,O,NULL,NULL);
   CARD:=PROMPTS("NTYPE ID CHARACTERS (ON ONE LINE) ?");
   TYPES:=" ";
   COL1:=O;
   FOR COL2:=O UNTIL 79 DO
      IF CARD(COL2|1)¬=" " THEN BEGIN
         COL1:=COL1+1;
         TYPES(COL1|1):=CARD(COL2|1);
      END;
   IF COL1<NTYPE THEN BEGIN
      PROMPT("NOT ENOUGH TYPE ID CHARACTERS");
      ASSERT FALSE;
   END;
   NGROUP:=1;
   PROMPT("NTYPE GROUP ASSIGNMENTS (ONE PER LINE) ?");
   FOR T:=1 UNTIL NTYPE DO BEGIN
      CHAR3:=" ?"; CHAR3(O|1):=TYPES(T|1);
      GROUP(T):=PROMPTI(CHAR3);
      IF GROUP(T)>NGROUP THEN NGROUP:=GROUP(T);
   END;
   IF MATCH(O|2)="WI" OR MATCH(O|2)="wi" THEN WITHIN:=TRUE
   ELSE IF MATCH(O|2)="BE" OR MATCH(O|2)="be" THEN WITHIN:=FALSE
   ELSE BEGIN
      PROMPT("INVALID MATCH SPECIFICATION: ");
      ASSERT FALSE;
   END;
   IF NGROUP=1 AND ¬WITHIN THEN BEGIN
      PROMPT("ERROR - BETWEEN - BUT 1 GROUP");
      ASSERT FALSE;
   END;
   CHAR1:="-";  CHAR2:="+";
   COMMENT IF DEVICE(O|2)="PR" THEN CHAR1:=CODE(191);
   COMMENT IF DEVICE(O|2)="PR" THEN CHAR2:=CODE(143);
   LINE:=" ";
   FOR I:=1 UNTIL NNEIG*23+15 DO LINE(I|1):=CHAR1;
   LINE(O|1):=CHAR2;  LINE(NNEIG*23+16|1):=CHAR2;
   S!_W:=1; I!_W:=4; R!_FORMAT:="A"; R!_W:=8; R!_D:=2;
END;
```

188

```
PROCEDURE ITEMDATA;
BEGIN
  REFERENCE(ITEM) DUMMY;
  REFERENCE(NEIGHBOR) NEAREST,FARTHEST;
  REAL RSTRATA,RTYPE;
  FSTRATA:=10000;  LSTRATA:=-10000;  NITEM:=0;   ENDFILE:=NULL;
  WHILE ¬FILEMARK DO
  BEGIN
    FARTHEST:=NEIGHBOR(NULL,MAXREAL,NULL);
    NEAREST:= NEIGHBOR(NULL,-MAXREAL,FARTHEST);
    DUMMY:=ITEM(" ",0,0,0,NULL,NEAREST);
    READ(ID(DUMMY),RSTRATA,RTYPE,YVAL(DUMMY),XVAL(DUMMY));
    IF ¬FILEMARK THEN BEGIN
      NITEM:=NITEM+1;
      STRATA(DUMMY):=TRUNCATE(RSTRATA);
      IF STRATA(DUMMY)<FSTRATA THEN FSTRATA:=STRATA(DUMMY);
      IF STRATA(DUMMY)>LSTRATA THEN LSTRATA:=STRATA(DUMMY);
      IF FSTRATA<1 OR LSTRATA>NSTRATA THEN BEGIN
        PROMPT("OSTRATA IN DATA IS < 1 OR > NSTRATA");
        ASSERT FALSE;
      END;
      TYPE(DUMMY):=TRUNCATE(RTYPE);
      LAST(STRATA(DUMMY)):=SREF(LAST(STRATA(DUMMY))):=DUMMY;
    END;
  END;
END;

PROCEDURE ITEMDIST;
BEGIN
  REAL DSTNCE;
  REFERENCE(ITEM) FROM,TO;
  FOR P:=FSTRATA UNTIL LSTRATA DO
  BEGIN
    FROM:=SREF(FIRST(P));
    WHILE FROM¬=NULL DO
    BEGIN
      TO:=SREF(FROM);
      WHILE TO¬=NULL DO
      BEGIN
        IF DECIDE(GROUP(TYPE(FROM)),GROUP(TYPE(TO))) THEN
        BEGIN
          DSTNCE:=SQRT((YVAL(FROM)-YVAL(TO))**2+
            (XVAL(FROM)-XVAL(TO))**2);
          INSERT(DSTNCE,FROM,TO);
          INSERT(DSTNCE,TO,FROM);
        END;
        TO:=SREF(TO);
      END;
      FROM:=SREF(FROM);
    END;
  END;
END;
```

```
PROCEDURE INSERT(REAL VALUE DSTNCE; REFERENCE(ITEM) VALUE FROM,TO);
BEGIN
    REFERENCE(NEIGHBOR) PNTR;
    INTEGER CNT;
    PNTR:=NREF(FROM);
    CNT:=1;
    WHILE (CNT<=NNEIG) AND (DSTNCE>DIST(NEXT(PNTR))) DO
    BEGIN
        PNTR:=NEXT(PNTR);
        CNT:=CNT+1;
    END;
    IF CNT<NNEIG THEN
        NEXT(PNTR):=NEIGHBOR(TO,DSTNCE,NEXT(PNTR))
    ELSE IF CNT=NNEIG THEN
        NEXT(PNTR):=NEIGHBOR(TO,DSTNCE,NULL);
END;

PROCEDURE SUMHEAD(INTEGER VALUE P);
BEGIN
    INTEGER M;
    WRITE("1",LINE); I!_W:=2; S!_W:=1;
    WRITE(" | STRATUM _",P,"||");
    I!_W:=1;
    FOR M:=1 UNTIL NNEIG DO
        WRITEON("        NEIGHBOR ",M,"        |");
    WRITE(" | ITEM     TYPE ||");
    FOR M:=1 UNTIL NNEIG DO WRITEON(" NEIGHBOR TYPE     DIST |");
END;

PROCEDURE SUMMARY;
BEGIN
    INTEGER I,J,K,S,G;
    INTEGER ARRAY N(1::NGROUP);
    REAL ARRAY SUM!_R,DENSITY,R!_OBS,R!_EXP,CAP!_R,STD!_ERR,CAP!_C,
        R!_STD,SUM!_RSQ (1::NGROUP);
    REFERENCE(ITEM) PNTR;
    FOR P:=FSTRATA UNTIL LSTRATA DO
    BEGIN
        S:=1;
        PNTR:=SREF(FIRST(P));
        FOR I:=1 UNTIL NNEIG DO FOR J:=1 UNTIL NTYPE DO
            FOR K:=1 UNTIL NTYPE DO MATRIX(I,J,K):=0;
        FOR G:=1 UNTIL NGROUP DO
        BEGIN
            N(G):=0;
            SUM!_R(G):=0;
            SUM!_RSQ(G):=0;
        END;
```

```
WHILE PNTR¬=NULL DO
BEGIN
  IF NNEIG>O THEN BEGIN
    IF ((S-1) REM 50)=O AND PNEIG>O THEN BEGIN
      IF S>1 THEN WRITE(" ",LINE);
      SUMHEAD(P);
    END;
    IF ((S-1) REM 10)=O AND PNEIG>O THEN WRITE(" ",LINE);
    IF PNEIG>O THEN PRINTNEIG(PNTR);
    PUNCHNEIG(PNTR);
  END;
  G:=GROUP(TYPE(PNTR));
  N(G):=N(G)+1;
  IF NEIG(NEXT(NREF(PNTR)))¬=NULL THEN BEGIN
    SUM!_R(G):=SUM!_R(G)+DIST(NEXT(NREF(PNTR)));
    SUM!_RSQ(G):=SUM!_RSQ(G)+DIST(NEXT(NREF(PNTR)))**2;
  END;
  PNTR:=SREF(PNTR);
  S:=S+1;
END;
IF PNEIG>O AND SREF(FIRST(P))¬=NULL THEN WRITE(" ",LINE);
I! W:=2;
WRITE("1");
WRITE("OSTRATUM",P);
FOR G:=1 UNTIL NGROUP DO
  IF N(G)>1 THEN
  BEGIN
    DENSITY(G):=(N(G)-1)/AREA;
    R!_OBS(G):=SUM!_R(G)/N(G);
    R!_STD(G):=SQRT(SUM!_RSQ(G)/N(G)) - R!_OBS(G)**2);
    R!_EXP(G):=1/(2*SQRT(DENSITY(G)));
    CAP!_R(G):=R!_OBS(G)/R!_EXP(G);
    STD!_ERR(G):=.26136/SQRT(N(G)*DENSITY(G));
    CAP!_C(G):=(R!_OBS(G)-R!_EXP(G))/STD!_ERR(G);
    I! W:=2;
    WRITE("OGROUP ",G);
    WRITEON(" <");
    FOR T:=1 UNTIL NTYPE DO IF GROUP(T)=G THEN
      WRITEON(TYPES(T|1));
    WRITEON(">");
    I! W:=4;
    WRITE("         N =         ",N(G)," ");
    WRITEON("    AREA =         ",AREA);
    R! D:=4;
    WRITEON("         DENSITY =        ",DENSITY(G));
    R! D:=2;
    WRITE("         robs =       ",R!_OBS(G));
    WRITEON("         rexp =       ",R!_EXP(G));
    WRITEON("         stddev(robs) = ",R!_STD(G));
    WRITE("         NN Coeff = ",CAP!_R(G));
```

```
            WRITEON("    std error =",STD!_ERR(G));
            WRITEON("   Test Stat:  C = ",CAP!_C(G));
    COMMENT CHANGE 100 TO MIN SIZE IN NEXT COMMAND;
    IF N(G)>=100 THEN
      BEGIN
        IF ABS(CAP!_C(G))<1.960 THEN WRITE("    p>.05")
        ELSE WRITE("    p<.05");
      END;
    IF NTYPE>1 THEN PRINTMATRIX(G);

  END;
END;

PROCEDURE PRINTNEIG(REFERENCE(ITEM) VALUE SPNTR);
BEGIN
  INTEGER ITP,NTP;
  REFERENCE(NEIGHBOR) NPNTR;
  WRITE("  ","|  ",ID(SPNTR)," ",TYPES(TYPE(SPNTR)|1),"  ||");
  ITP:=TYPE(SPNTR);
  NPNTR:=NEXT(NREF(SPNTR));
  FOR N:=1 UNTIL NNEIG DO
  IF NEIG(NPNTR)=NULL THEN
    WRITEON("                              |")
  ELSE
  BEGIN
    WRITEON(" ",ID(NEIG(NPNTR))," ",TYPES(TYPE(NEIG(NPNTR))|1),
      DIST(NPNTR),"|");
    NTP:=TYPE(NEIG(NPNTR));
    MATRIX(N,ITP,NTP):=MATRIX(N,ITP,NTP)+1;
    NPNTR:=NEXT(NPNTR);
  END;

END;

PROCEDURE PUNCHNEIG(REFERENCE(ITEM) VALUE SPNTR);
BEGIN
  REFERENCE(NEIGHBOR) NPNTR;
  STRING(10) BLANK;
  BLANK:=" ";
  WRITER("FILE"); I! W:=2; S! W:=1;
  WRITE(" ",STRATA(SPNTR),ID(SPNTR),"
    ",GROUP(TYPE(SPNTR)),TYPE(SPNTR));
  NPNTR:=NEXT(NREF(SPNTR));
  FOR N:=1 UNTIL NNEIG DO
  IF NEIG(NPNTR)=NULL THEN
    WRITEON(N,BLANK," ",.0,.0,.0,.0)
  ELSE BEGIN
    WRITEON(N,ID(NEIG(NPNTR))," ",GROUP(TYPE(NEIG(NPNTR))),
      TYPE(NEIG(NPNTR)),DIST(NPNTR));
    NPNTR:=NEXT(NPNTR);
  END;
  WRITER("LISTING"); I! W:=2;
END;
```

```
PROCEDURE PRINTMATRIX(INTEGER VALUE G);
BEGIN
COMMENT PRINT NEIGHBOR GROUP MATRIX;
INTEGER N,T1,T2,CLINE,NLINE;
S!_W:=0;  CLINE:=8;  NLINE:=0;
COMMENT POINTS TO CURRENT LINE, NLINE IS LINES NEEDED FOR A TABLE;
FOR N:=1 UNTIL NNEIG DO
BEGIN
   IF CLINE+NLINE>60 THEN BEGIN
      WRITE("1");  CLINE:=1;

   END;
   NLINE:=7;
   I!_W:=2;
   WRITE("-GROUP",G," NEIGHBOR",N," ITEM-NEIGHBOR TYPE MATRIX");
   WRITE("OITEM | NEIGHBOR TYPE");
   WRITE(" TYPE | ");
   I!_W:=4;
   FOR T2:=1 UNTIL NTYPE DO
      IF DECIDE(GROUP(T2),G) THEN WRITEON("   ",TYPES(T2|1));
   WRITE(" ------+--");
   FOR T2:=1 UNTIL NTYPE DO
      IF DECIDE(GROUP(T2),G) THEN WRITEON("----");
   FOR T1:=1 UNTIL NTYPE DO
   BEGIN
      IF GROUP(T1)=G THEN BEGIN
         WRITE("   ",TYPES(T1|1)," | ");
         FOR T2:=1 UNTIL NTYPE DO IF DECIDE(GROUP(T2),G) THEN
            WRITEON(MATRIX(N,T1,T2));
         NLINE:=NLINE+1;
      END;
   END;
   CLINE:=CLINE+NLINE;
   I!_W:=4; S!_W:=1;
END;

COMMENT CONTROL PROCEDURES;

INIT;
READER("DATA");
ITEMDATA;
ITEMDIST;
WRITER("LISTING"); WRITE!_CC:=FALSE;
SUMMARY;
WRITE("1");

END
END.
```

Appendix III

TABULATE PROGRAM

PROGRAM TABULATE - KEITH KINTIGH

TO RUN THE PROGRAM:
$SET PRINT=TN
$R TABL.OBJ
THE PROGRAM PROMPTS FOR INPUT AND OUTPUT FILES.
IF THE PROGRAM HAS A LARGE NUMBER OF TAG VARIABLES WITH
MANY VALUES AND FAILS BECAUSE OF RUNNING OUT OF SPACE
ADD TO THE REN COMMAND: PAR=SIZE=NNNK WHERE NNN=100 OR
LARGER AS NECESSARY.

FILES REFERENCED:
SERCOM   PROMPTS TO TERMINAL
GUSER   INPUT FROM TERMINAL
COMMAND VARIABLE DESCRIPTIONS AND TABLE LAYOUT
DATA   INPUT DATA FILE
FILE   OUTPUT FILE E.G. -PRINT, *PRINT*, *SINK*
THESE FILES NEED NOT BE SPECIFIED ON THE RUN COMMAND
ALL WILL DEFAULT OR BE PROMPTED FOR.

PROGRAM INPUT:

PROGRAM PARAMETERS (FREE FORMAT 1 OR MORE LINES)
VARS   NUMBER OF VARIABLES DESCRIBED AND READ
OUTVAR   NUMBER OF VARIABLES IN OUTPUT TABLE - MAY BE < VARS
STRATA   VNUM FOR A STRATUM VARIABLE. EACH TIME VNUM CHANGES
            IN VALUE A NEW PAGE WILL BE STARTED.
            IF NO STRATUM VARIABLE ENTER NUMBER <=0
MAXVAR   UPPER BOUND FOR VARIABLE,NUMBER (E.G. 100)
TAGVARS   NUMBER OF VARIABLES FOR WHICH TAGS ARE
            TO BE SUBSTITUTED FOR INTEGER VALUES
MAXTAG   UPPER BOUND FOR A TAG INDEX (E.G. 25)
CARDS   NUMBER OF INPUT RECORDS PER CASE
PAGESIZE   NUMBER OF LINES TOTAL PER PAGE
HEADING   NUMBER OF HEADING LINES
CASESPERPAGE NUMBER OF CASES TO BE PRINTED ON A PAGE
SEPARATE   NUMBER OF CASES BETWEEN SEPARATING LINES OF ----- EG 10.
            SEPARATE MUST DIVIDE EVENLY INTO CASESPERPAGE
LINESIZE   NUMBER OF CHARS PER LINE INCL MARGIN, NOT INCL CC
MARGIN   LEFT MARGIN SPACES USUALLY 0 (0<=MARGIN<=80)
LAYOUT   "TABLE" FOR STANDARD TABLE WITH COLUMNS OF DATA.
            "BLOCK" FOR BLOCKS OF DATA - USUALLY USES LABEL1
            AND HAS MULTIPLE LINES PER CASE.
            MAY BE ABBREVIATED TO "T" OR "B".
DEVICE   "PRINTER" FOR TN PRINTER OR "TERMINAL"
            FOR OTHER PRINTER OR TERMINAL.
            USE "X9700" FOR XEROX PRINTER.
            MAY BE ABBREVIATED TO "T", "P" OR "X".

196

HEADING LINES - HEADING (AS ABOVE) LINES READ
HEAD   HEADING LINES OF DESIRED LENGTH (MAY BE >80 CHARS LONG).
            $BOXTOP MAY APPEAR IN THE FIRST 7 CHARS OF A
            HEADING LINE. IF LAYOUT="TABLE", A BOXTOP IS FORMED
            AT THIS POINT IN THE HEADING. HOWEVER, IF LAYOUT
            IS "TABLE", $BOXTOP SHOULD NOT BE USED AS THE LAST LINE
            OF A HEADING, SINCE A BOXTOP IS FORMED THERE ANYWAY.
            IF LAYOUT=TABLE, $BOXTOP IS USED IN THE HEADING TO MAKE
            LINES OF DASHES AT THE LINE OF THE HEADING. IN THIS
            CASE $BOXTOP MAY BE USED AT ANY POINT IN THE HEADING.
            IF LAYOUT=TABLE AND $BOXTOP OCCURS AT LEAST ONCE IN THE
            HEADING, AT THE BOTTOM OF THE PAGE A LINE OF DASHES
            IS ALSO PRINTED. LINES OF DASHES SEPARATING CASES ARE
            GOVERNED BY THE SEPARATE PARAMETER.
            IF $STRATA OCCURS IN THE FIRST 7 COLUMNS OF A
            HEADING LINE, THE VALUE OF THE STRATA VARIABLE,
            INCL LEADING AND TRAILING LABELS WILL BE
            PRINTED FOR THAT HEADING LINE.

            $BOXTOP and $STRATA MUST BE IN UPPER CASE.

VARIABLE DESCRIPTIONS - EACH VAR STARTS A LINE - FREE FORMAT
VNUM   INTEGER VARIABLE NUMBER 0<=VNUM<=100
            REFERENCE NUMBER USED TO IDENTIFY VARIABLE.
TYPE   "N" NUMERIC DATA (REAL OR INTEGER)
            "C" CHARACTER DATA (MAX LENGTH 80 CHARS)
            "T" TAGS (UP TO 80 CHARS) TO BE PRINTED
                FOR INTEGER VALUES - VALUES MUST BE
                IN THE RANGE 0-MAXTAG. VALUE 0=MISSING.
            "D" DUMMY VARIABLE - USE TO ADD HEADINGS AND OTHER
                CONSTANT DATA. FORMAT SHOULD BE 0 HOWEVER
                LABEL1 AND LABEL2 MAY BE USED TO INSERT CONSTANT
                INFORMATION AT THE PROPER POSITION.
                INPUT COLUMN AND CARD MAY BE 0.
            DATATYPE MUST BE GIVEN BETWEEN "" AS
            SHOWN.
CARD   SEQUENTIAL INPUT RECORD OF VARIABLE
COLUMN   BEGINNING INPUT COLUMN
LENGTH   NUMBER OF COLUMNS OCCUPIED BY INPUT FIELD
SCALE   SCALE FACTOR APPLIED TO INPUT VALUE
            OUTPUT VAL=INPUT VAL*10**SCALE
FORMAT   OUTPUT FORMAT: FIELD WIDTH.NUMBER OF DECIMALS
            NO MORE THAN 9 DECIMALS MAY BE SPECIFIED.
            FIELD WIDTH INCLUDES SIGN & DECIMAL PT.
LABEL1LEN   NUMBER OF CHARACTERS IN LABEL WHICH WILL ALWAYS
            PRECEDE VALUE ON OUTPUT.
            CURRENTLY LIMITED TO 80 CHARACTERS.
LABEL1   STRING WHICH WILL ALWAYS PRECEDE VALUE - MUST BE GIVEN
            BUT IF LABEL1LEN<=0 WILL BE IGNORED - EG "AREA=".
LABEL2LEN   NUMBER OF CHARACTERS IN LABEL WHICH WILL ALWAYS
            FOLLOW VALUE ON OUTPUT.
            CURRENTLY LIMITED TO 80 CHARACTERS.
LABEL2   STRING WHICH WILL ALWAYS FOLLOW VALUE - MUST BE GIVEN
            BUT IF LABEL2LEN<=0 WILL BE IGNORED - EG "KM.".

197

```
PARAMETERS REQUIRED ONLY!!! FOR TYPE="T" VARS:
NTAG    MAX VALUE FOR WHICH A LABEL IS ASSIGNED.
        NTAG<=100.
TAG     LIST OF NTAG TAGS IN "" EG "LABL VAL".
        NTAG LABELS MUST BE GIVEN. IF SOME ARE
        UNDEFINED ENTER AS " ".

TABLE DESCRIPTION - FREE FORMAT 1 OR MORE LINES
   IN ORDER OF APPEARANCE IN OUTPUT - READ FOR VARSPERTABLE VARS:
   VNUM      VARIABLE NUMBER AS IN INPUT LIST
   IF LAYOUT="TABLE" THEN USE FOLLOWING PARAMETERS:
     FIELDWIDTH WIDTH OF OUTPUT FIELD INCLUDING BLANKS
             THE FORMATTED DATA WILL BE CENTERED IN FIELD
             FIELDWIDTH MUST BE >= FORMAT+LABEL1LEN+LABEL2LEN.
     SEPCHAR    THE SINGLE CHAR IN QUOTES WHICH IS
             USED TO SEPARATE THE VAR COLUMNS
             IN THE TABLE. USUALLY "|" OR " ".
   IF LAYOUT="BLOCK" THEN USE FOLLOWING PARAMETERS:
     LINE       RELATIVE LINE NUMBER WITHING CASE OUTPUT
     POSITION   STARTING PRINT POSITION FOR FIELD
   NOTE: THE OUTPUT LINE LENGTH = 1+VARSPERTABLE+ SUM OF
         FIELDWIDTHS OF VARS IN TABLE MUST NOT EXCEED LINESIZE.
         ALL VARIABLES DESCRIBED NEED NOT BE IN THE TABLE.

DATA - FOR EACH CASE READ VARS VARIABLES (IN ORDER DESCRIBED)
       DATA IS FIXED FORMAT, EACH CASE STARTS A NEW LINE.
       A BLANK NUMERIC FIELD IS READ AS 0.  NO EXPONENTIAL
       NOTATION ALLOWED ON INPUT OR OUTPUT.

PROGRAM OPERATION:

==> LAYOUT="TABLE"
PROGRAM READS ALL PARAMETERS DESCRIBED ABOVE AND WRITES
TABLES WITH THE SPECIFIED LISTS OF VARIABLES IN THE
SPECIFIED ORDER AND FORMAT.  VARIABLE FIELDS ARE SEPARATED
AND SETS OF SEPARATE CASES ARE SEPARATED BY LINES OF ----.
USER MUST ARRANGE HEADINGS ACCORDINGLY.

==> LAYOUT="BLOCK"
ONE OR MORE LINES OF INFORMATION ARE WRITTEN FOR EACH CASE.
THE USER SPECIFIES THE LOCATION ON THE PAGE (IGNORING THE
MARGIN WHERE A VALUE IS TO OCCUR.  THE LABEL1 AND LABEL2
OPTIONS CAN BE USED TO NICELY FORMAT THE DATA (ALTHOUGH THEY
MAY ALSO BE USED IN "TABLE" LAYOUT.  NO BOX IS DRAWN.
```

```
==> BOTH LAYOUTS
    IF A RECORD WITH $PAGE IN COLS 1-5 OCCURS IN THE
    DATA A NEW PAGE IS STARTED.  THE PROGRAM PROMPTS FOR THE
    FILE WITH THE VARIABLE AND TABLE DESCRIPTIONS, THE FILE
    WITH THE DATA, AND THE OUTPUT FILE OR DEVICE (NOTE *PRINT*
    MAY BE USED).  ALSO NOTE THAT LOWER CASE CHARACTERS MAY BE
    USED IN THE LABELS AND TAGS.
    IN READING THE DATA ONE COLUMN OR SET OF COLUMNS CAN BE
    REFERENCED ANY NUMBER OF TIMES IN DEFINING DIFFERENT
    VARIABLES.

END OF COMMENT;

INTEGER VARS,HEADING,LEFT,TOPLINES,RIGHT,
CARDS,LINESIZE,CASESPERPAGE,PAGESIZE,STRATA,
SEPARATE,MARGIN,MAXTAG,TAGVARS,MAXVAR,LEN,TOT_LEN.
OUTVAR,LAYOUTN,BLOCK,TABLE;
STRING(9) LAYOUT,DEVICE;
STRING(64) STR64;
PROCEDURE ASSIGN_FILES;
BEGIN
  STR64:=PROMPTS("FILE DESCRIBING VARIABLES AND TABLE ?");
  ASSIGN("COMMAND",STR64(0|30));
  STR64:=PROMPTS("FILE CONTAINING INPUT DATA ?");
  ASSIGN("DATA",STR64(0|30));
  STR64:=PROMPTS("OUTPUT FILE (WILL BE EMPTIED) ?");
  ASSIGN("FILE",STR64(0|30));
  IF STR64(0|1)-="*" THEN EMPTY("FILE");
END;
STRING(64) PROCEDURE PROMPTS(STRING(64) VALUE MSG);
BEGIN
  STRING(64) RSLT;
  WRITER("ERROR");    WRITE(MSG);   WRITE(" ");
  READER("USER");     READCARD(RSLT);
  RSLT
END;
PROCEDURE READ_PARMS;
BEGIN
  READ(VARS,OUTVAR,STRATA,MAXVAR,TAGVARS,MAXTAG,CARDS,
  PAGESIZE,HEADING,CASESPERPAGE,SEPARATE,LINESIZE,MARGIN,
  LAYOUT,DEVICE);

  WRITE("PROGRAM PARAMETERS READ");
  IF LAYOUT(0|1)="T" THEN LAYOUTN:=TABLE
  ELSE IF LAYOUT(0|1)="B" THEN LAYOUTN:=BLOCK
  ELSE BEGIN
    WRITE("LAYOUT:",LAYOUT," INVALID"); ASSERT(FALSE);
  END;
END;
```

```
ASSIGN_FILES;

TABLE:=1;  BLOCK:=2;  S_W:=O;  I_W:=4;  R_FORMAT:="A";  R_D:=2;
READER("COMMAND"); WRITER("ERROR");

READ_PARMS;

BEGIN
  INTEGER ARRAY XREF(O::MAXVAR);
  INTEGER ARRAY
    BREF,TAGREF,FIELDWIDTH,CARD,COLUMN,POSITION,LINE,
    LENGTH,SCALE,LABEL1LEN,LABEL2LEN,NTAG,TABLEVAR(1::VARS);
  INTEGER ARRAY TYP (O::VARS);
  STRING(1) ARRAY TYPE(1::VARS);
  STRING(80) ARRAY STRDATA(1::VARS);
  REAL ARRAY REALDATA(1::VARS);
  STRING(80) ARRAY LABEL1,LABEL2(1::VARS);
  REAL ARRAY FORMAT(1::VARS);
  STRING(201) ARRAY HEAD(-HEADING-2::HEADING+2);
  STRING(1) ARRAY SEPCHAR(1::VARS);
  STRING(81) ARRAY INPUT(1::CARDS);
  STRING(1) LLC,ULC,LRC,URC,INTER,DASH;
  INTEGER TOP,BETWEEN,BOTTOM,CAS,SEQ,DEV,TN,PN,X9700;
  REAL STVALN;
  STRING(80) STVALC;
  STRING(80) ARRAY TAG(1::TAGVARS, -1::MAXTAG);
PROCEDURE CHARSET;
BEGIN
  TN:=O;    PN:=1;  X9700:=-1;  DEV:=100;
  IF DEVICE(O,1)="T" THEN DEV:=PN;
  IF DEVICE(O,1)="P" THEN DEV:=TN;
  IF DEVICE(O,1)="X" THEN DEV:=X9700;
  IF DEV=100 THEN ERROR("INVALID DEVICE, MUST BE ""P"",""T"", OR ""X"" ");
  IF DEV=TN THEN BEGIN
    INTER:=CODE(143);    LLC:=CODE(171);   ULC:=CODE(172);
    LRC:=CODE(187);  URC:=CODE(188);   DASH:=CODE(191);
  END;
  IF DEV=PN THEN BEGIN
    INTER:="+";  LLC:="+";  ULC:="+";    LRC:="+";   URC:="+";
    DASH:="-";
  END;
  IF DEV=X9700 THEN BEGIN
    INTER:=CODE(191);   DASH:=CODE(191);
    LLC:=" ";   LRC:=" ";   ULC:=" ";   URC:=" ";
  END;
END;
PROCEDURE ERROR(STRING(6O) VALUE STR);
BEGIN
  WRITE_CC:=TRUE;   WRITER("ERROR");
  WRITE(STR);  WRITE("PROGRAM FAILS");
  ASSERT(FALSE);
END;
PROCEDURE FORMATHEAD;
BEGIN
```

```
IF LAYOUTN=TABLE THEN BEGIN
  INTEGER I,K,V,VAR,POS;
  STRING(201) OUT1,OUT2;

  TOP:=O;  OUT1:=" ";  OUT1(O|1):="+";
  OUT1(1+MARGIN|1):=ULC; OUT1(LEN+2+MARGIN|1):=URC;
  FOR I:=2 UNTIL LEN+1 DO OUT1(I+MARGIN|1):=DASH;
  HEAD(TOP):=OUT1;

  OUT1:=" ";  OUT2:=" ";
  POS:=MARGIN+2;
  FOR V:=1 UNTIL OUTVAR DO
  BEGIN
    VAR:=TABLEVAR(V);
    FOR K:=1 UNTIL FIELDWIDTH(VAR) DO
    BEGIN
      OUT1(POS|1):=DASH;   POS:=POS+1;
    END;
    IF SEPCHAR(V)=" " THEN OUT1(POS|1):=DASH
    ELSE OUT1(POS|1):=INTER;
    POS:=POS+1;
  END;
  OUT1(1+MARGIN|1):=LLC;   OUT1(LEN+2+MARGIN|1):=LRC;
  HEAD(BETWEEN):=OUT1;
  IF DEV=TN THEN BEGIN
    OUT2(1+MARGIN|1):=ULC;  OUT2(LEN+2+MARGIN|1):=URC;
    OUT2(O|1):="+";       HEAD(-BETWEEN):=OUT2;
  END ELSE
  IF DEV=X9700 THEN HEAD(BETWEEN)(O|1):="+";

  OUT2:=" ";
  IF DEV¬=X9700 THEN
    FOR POS:=MARGIN+2 UNTIL LEN+MARGIN+1 DO
      IF OUT1(POS|1)=INTER THEN
      BEGIN
        OUT1(POS|1):=LLC;   OUT2(POS|1):=LRC;
      END;
  HEAD(BOTTOM):=OUT1;
  IF DEV=TN THEN BEGIN       HEAD(-BOTTOM):=OUT2;
    OUT2(O|1):="+";
  END ELSE
  IF DEV=X9700 THEN HEAD(BOTTOM)(O|1):="+";
```

```
COMMENT FORMAT IMBEDDED $BOXTOPS;
FOR I:=1 UNTIL HEADING DO
BEGIN
    HEAD(I)(1+MARGIN|1):="|";
    HEAD(I)(LEN+2+MARGIN|1):="|";
    IF HEAD(I)(2+MARGIN|7)="$BOXTOP" THEN
    BEGIN
        OUT2:=" ";
        OUT2(1+MARGIN|1):=ULC;
        OUT2(LEN+2+MARGIN|1):=URC;
        FOR POS:=MARGIN+2 UNTIL LEN+MARGIN+1 DO
            IF (DEV¬=X9700) AND (HEAD(I+1)(POS|1)="|") THEN
            BEGIN
                OUT1(POS|1):=ULC; OUT2(POS|1):=URC;
            END ELSE OUT1(POS|1):=DASH;
        HEAD(I):=OUT1;
        IF DEV=TN THEN BEGIN
            OUT2(O|1):="+";        HEAD(-I):=OUT2;
        END ELSE
        IF DEV=X9700 THEN HEAD(I)(O|1):="+";
    END;
    HEADING:=BETWEEN;

END ELSE BEGIN
    TOP:=1;
    HEAD(BETWEEN):=" "; HEAD(BOTTOM):=" ";
    FOR I:=MARGIN+LEFT UNTIL LEN+MARGIN DO HEAD(BETWEEN)(I|1):=DASH;
    FOR I:=1 UNTIL HEADING DO
        IF HEAD(I)(LEFT+MARGIN|7)="$BOXTOP" THEN BEGIN
            HEAD(BOTTOM):=HEAD(BETWEEN);
            HEAD(I):=HEAD(BETWEEN);
        END;
    HEAD(TOP)(O|1):="+";

END;
PROCEDURE INITIALIZE;
BEGIN
    INTEGER VAR;
    IF LAYOUTN=TABLE THEN BEGIN LEFT:=2; RIGHT:=LINESIZE-1; END
    ELSE BEGIN LEFT:=1; RIGHT:=LINESIZE; END;
    FOR VAR:=O UNTIL MAXVAR DO XREF(VAR):=O;

    FOR VAR:=1 UNTIL VARS DO BREF(VAR):=NTAG(VAR):=O;

    FOR I:=1 UNTIL TAGVARS DO BEGIN
        FOR J:=1 UNTIL MAXTAG DO TAG(I,J):=" ";
        TAG(I,O):=" ";
        TAG(I,-1):="?????????????????????";
    END;
```

```
          STVALN:=O;  STVALC:=" ";
     LEN:=O; TOT_LEN:=O;
     CAS:=O; SEQ:=O;
     I_W:=6;  R_FORMAT:="A";
     TOP:=O;  BETWEEN:=HEADING+1;  BOTTOM:=HEADING+2;
     FOR J:=-BOTTOM UNTIL BOTTOM DO HEAD(J):="$";
END;
PROCEDURE PRINT(INTEGER VALUE LINE);
BEGIN
     IF HEAD(LINE)(LEFT+MARGIN|7)="$STRATA" THEN BEGIN
        WRITE(" "); FOR I:=1 UNTIL MARGIN DO WRITEON(" ");
        IF LAYOUTN=TABLE THEN BEGIN
           WRITEON("|");  PRINTVAL(STRATA);
           FOR I:=1 UNTIL LEN-(LABEL1LEN(STRATA)+LABEL2LEN(STRATA)+
              TRUNCATE(FORMAT(STRATA))) DO WRITEON(" ");
           WRITEON("|");
        END ELSE PRINTVAL(STRATA);
     IF LINE¬=O AND HEAD(-LINE)(O|1)¬="$" THEN WRITE(HEAD(-LINE));
END;
PROCEDURE PRINTBLOCK;
BEGIN
     INTEGER VAR,V,LNE,COL;
     LNE:=1; COL:=1; WRITE(" ");
     FOR I:=1 UNTIL MARGIN DO WRITEON(" ");
     FOR V:=1 UNTIL OUTVAR DO BEGIN
        VAR:=TABLEVAR(V);
        WHILE LNE<LINE(VAR) DO BEGIN
           WRITE(" "); LNE:=LNE+1; COL:=1;
           FOR I:=1 UNTIL MARGIN DO WRITEON(" ");
        END;
        IF COL>POSITION(VAR) THEN BEGIN
           WRITER("ERROR");
           WRITE("OUTPUT FIELDS OVERLAP: VAR ",
           BREF(VAR));
           ASSERT(FALSE);
        END;
        FOR I:=COL UNTIL POSITION(VAR)-1 DO WRITEON(" ");
        COL:=POSITION(VAR);
        PRINTVAL(VAR);
        COL:=COL+FIELDWIDTH(VAR);
     END;
END;
```

```
PROCEDURE PRINTTABLE;
BEGIN
  INTEGER VAR,V,WIDTH,SPCBEF,SPCAFT;
  WRITE(" ");
  FOR I:=1 UNTIL MARGIN DO WRITEON(" ");
  WRITEON("|");
  FOR V:=1 UNTIL OUTVAR DO BEGIN
    VAR:=TABLEVAR(V);
    WIDTH:=TRUNCATE(FORMAT(VAR))+LABEL1LEN(VAR)+LABEL2LEN(VAR);
    SPCAFT:=(FIELDWIDTH(VAR)-WIDTH) DIV 2;
    SPCBEF:=(FIELDWIDTH(VAR)-WIDTH-SPCAFT;
    FOR I:=1 UNTIL SPCBEF DO WRITEON(" ");
    PRINTVAL(VAR);
    FOR I:=1 UNTIL SPCAFT DO WRITEON(" ");
    WRITEON(SEPCHAR(V));
  END;
END;
PROCEDURE PRINTVAL(INTEGER VALUE VAR);
BEGIN
  INTEGER FMTWID;
  FMTWID:=TRUNCATE(FORMAT(VAR));
  FOR I:=1 UNTIL LABEL1LEN(VAR) DO WRITEON(LABEL1(VAR)(I-1|1));
  CASE TYP(VAR) OF BEGIN
    IF (FORMAT(VAR)-FMTWID)=O THEN WRITEON
        (I_W:=FMTWID,TRUNCATE(REALDATA(VAR)))
    ELSE WRITEON(R_W:=FMTWID,
        R_D:=ROUND((FORMAT(VAR)-FMTWID)*10),REALDATA(VAR));
    FOR I:=1 UNTIL FMTWID DO
        WRITEON(STRDATA(VAR)(I-1|1));
    FOR I:=1 UNTIL FMTWID DO
        WRITEON(TAG(TAGREF(VAR),TRUNCATE(REALDATA(VAR)))(I-1|1));
    COMMENT DUMMY VARS HAVE NO VALUE;
  END;
  FOR I:=1 UNTIL LABEL2LEN(VAR) DO WRITEON(LABEL2(VAR)(I-1|1));
END;
LOGICAL PROCEDURE READ_DATA;
BEGIN
  INTEGER VAR;
  FOR CRD:=1 UNTIL CARDS DO
  IF ¬FILEMARK THEN BEGIN
    READCARD(INPUT(CRD));
    IF INPUT(CRD)(O|4)="$PAGE" THEN BEGIN
      SEQ:=O;  READCARD(INPUT(CRD));
    END;
  IF FILEMARK THEN BEGIN
    WRITER("ERROR");  I_W:=6;
    WRITE("END OF FILE READING CASE",CAS+1," RECORD",CRD);
    WRITER("FILE");
  END;
```

204

```
      IF ¬FILEMARK THEN BEGIN CAS:=CAS+1; SEQ:=SEQ+1;
        FOR VAR:=1 UNTIL VARS DO
          CASE TYP(VAR) OF BEGIN
            READ_REAL(VAR);
            READ_STR(VAR);
            READ_REAL(VAR);
          END;

      END;
      CASE TYP(STRATA) OF BEGIN
        IF STVALN¬=REALDATA(STRATA)  THEN BEGIN
          STVALN:=REALDATA(STRATA);   SEQ:=1;
        END;
        IF STVALC¬=STRDATA(STRATA) THEN BEGIN
          STVALC:=STRDATA(STRATA);  SEQ:=1;
        END;
        IF STVALN¬=REALDATA(STRATA) THEN BEGIN
          STVALN:=REALDATA(STRATA);  SEQ:=1;
        END; COMMENT NO ACTION FOR DUMMY;

      END;
      ¬FILEMARK

    END;
    PROCEDURE READ_HEAD;
    BEGIN
      STRING(200) HEADER;
      FOR J:=1 UNTIL HEADING DO
      BEGIN
        READCARD(HEADER);
        HEAD(J):=" ";
        FOR K:=LEFT+MARGIN UNTIL RIGHT DO
          HEAD(J)(K|1):=HEADER(K-MARGIN-LEFT|1);

      END;
      WRITE("HEADING READ COMPLETED");

    END;
    PROCEDURE READ_REAL(INTEGER VALUE VAR);
    BEGIN
      REAL RSLT,SIGN;
      LOGICAL DEC;
      INTEGER LOC,SC;
      STRING(1) DIG;
      DEC:=FALSE;    RSLT:=0;        SC:=0;       SIGN:=1.0;
      LOC:=COLUMN(VAR)-1;
      WHILE(LOC<=LENGTH(VAR)-1) AND (INPUT(CARD(VAR))(LOC|1)=" ") DO
        LOC:=LOC+1;
      IF INPUT(CARD(VAR))(LOC|1)="-" THEN BEGIN
        SIGN:=-1.0;  LOC:=LOC+1;  END
      ELSE IF INPUT(CARD(VAR))(LOC|1)="+" THEN LOC:=LOC+1;
      WHILE(LOC<=LENGTH(VAR)-1) AND INPUT(CARD(VAR))(LOC|1)¬="." AND
      (INPUT(CARD(VAR))(LOC|1)¬=" ") DO
        BEGIN
```

```
        DIG:=INPUT(CARD(VAR))(LOC|1);
        IF DIG<"0" OR DIG>"9" THEN BEGIN
            I_W:=3;
            WRITE("CARD=",CARD(VAR),"   COLUMN=",LOC+1);
            FOR I:=1 UNTIL CARDS DO WRITE(INPUT(I));
            WRITER("FILE");   ASSERT(FALSE);
            WRITER("ERROR");   WRITE("INVALID DIGIT IN INPUT:",DIG);

        END;
        RSLT:=RSLT*10+DECODE(DIG)-240;
        LOC:=LOC+1

    END;
    IF INPUT(CARD(VAR))(LOC|1)="." THEN
    BEGIN
        LOC:=LOC+1;
        DEC:=TRUE;
        WHILE(LOC<=LENGTH(VAR)-1) AND INPUT(CARD(VAR))(LOC|1)¬=" " DO
        BEGIN
            DIG:=INPUT(CARD(VAR))(LOC|1);
            IF DIG<"0" OR DIG>"9" THEN BEGIN
                WRITER("ERROR");   WRITE("INVALID DIGIT IN INPUT:",DIG);
                I_W:=3;
                WRITE("CARD=",CARD(VAR),"   COLUMN=",LOC+1);
                FOR I:=1 UNTIL CARDS DO WRITE(INPUT(I));
                WRITER("FILE");   ASSERT(FALSE);

            END;
            RSLT:=RSLT*10+DECODE(DIG)-240;
            LOC:=LOC+1;
            SC:=SC+1;

        END;
    IF DEC=TRUE THEN RSLT:=RSLT*10**(-SC);
    RSLT:=SIGN*RSLT*10**SCALE(VAR);
    IF TYPE(VAR)="T" THEN BEGIN
        RSLT:=TRUNCATE(RSLT);
        IF RSLT<0 OR RSLT>NTAG(VAR) THEN BEGIN
            WRITER("ERROR");
            WRITE("TAG VAR",BREF(VAR)," CASE",CAS," VALUE",RSLT,
            "OUT OF TAG BOUNDS, ???? WILL BE PRINTED");
            WRITER("FILE");

        END;
    REALDATA(VAR):=RSLT;
END;
PROCEDURE READ_STR(INTEGER VALUE VAR);
    FOR I:=0 UNTIL LENGTH(VAR)-COLUMN(VAR) DO
        STRDATA(VAR)(I|1):=
        INPUT(CARD(VAR))(COLUMN(VAR)+I-1|1);
PROCEDURE READ_TABLE_LAYOUT;
BEGIN
    INTEGER VAR,VREF,CUR_LEN,TOT_LIN;
```

```
WRITE("READ TABLE LAYOUT - VARIABLES:"); WRITE("    ");
FOR K:=1 UNTIL OUTVAR DO BEGIN
   READON(VREF);   WRITEON(VREF);
   IF VREF<0 OR VREF>MAXVAR OR XREF(VREF)=0 THEN BEGIN
      WRITER("ERROR");
      WRITE("INVALID VARIABLE NUMBER IN TABLE:",VREF);
      ASSERT FALSE;
   END;
   VAR:=XREF(VREF);   TABLEVAR(K):=VAR;
   IF LAYOUTN=TABLE THEN BEGIN
      READON(FIELDWIDTH(VAR));
      IF TRUNCATE(FORMAT(VAR))+LABEL1LEN(VAR)+LABEL2LEN(VAR)
      > FIELDWIDTH(VAR) THEN BEGIN
         WRITE("FIELDWIDTH TOO SMALL - VARIABLE:",VAR);
         ASSERT FALSE;
      END;
      IF K<OUTVAR THEN READON(SEPCHAR(K))
   END ELSE BEGIN
      READON(LINE(VAR),POSITION(VAR));
      FIELDWIDTH(VAR):=TRUNCATE(FORMAT(VAR))+LABEL1LEN(VAR)+LABEL2LEN(VAR);
   END;
END;
WRITE("TABLE LAYOUT READ COMPLETE");
IF LAYOUTN=TABLE THEN BEGIN
   SEPCHAR(OUTVAR):="|";
   FOR K:=1 UNTIL OUTVAR DO
      LEN:=LEN+FIELDWIDTH(TABLEVAR(K));
   LEN:=LEN+OUTVAR-1;
   TOT_LEN:=LEN+MARGIN+2;
   TOT_LIN:=CASESPERPAGE+((CASESPERPAGE-1) DIV SEPARATE)+3+HEADING;
END ELSE BEGIN
   FOR K:=1 UNTIL OUTVAR DO
   BEGIN
      CUR_LEN:=POSITION(TABLEVAR(K))+FIELDWIDTH(TABLEVAR(K))-1;
      IF CUR_LEN>LEN THEN LEN:=CUR_LEN;
   END;
   TOT_LEN:=LEN+MARGIN-1;
   TOT_LIN:=LINE(TABLEVAR(OUTVAR))*CASESPERPAGE+HEADING+3+
      ((CASESPERPAGE-1) DIV SEPARATE);
END;
IF TOT_LEN>LINESIZE THEN BEGIN
   WRITER("ERROR");
   WRITE("TABLE TOO WIDE",LEN,"CHARS");
   ASSERT(FALSE);
END;
IF TOT_LIN>PAGESIZE THEN BEGIN
   WRITER("ERROR");
   WRITE(TOT_LIN," LINES NEEDED: > PAGESIZE=",PAGESIZE);
   ASSERT(FALSE);
END ELSE TOPLINES:=(PAGESIZE-TOT_LIN) DIV 2;
```

```
        IF (CASESPERPAGE REM SEPARATE)¬=O THEN
          ERROR("SEPARATE MUST DIVIDE EVENLY INTO CASESPERPAGE");
      FORMATHEAD;
    END;
    PROCEDURE READ_VARIABLE_DESCRIPTION;
    BEGIN
      INTEGER VAR,VREF,TAGINDX,VARINDX;
      TAGINDX:=O;  VARINDX:=O;

      WRITE("READ VARIABLE DESCRIPTIONS - VARIABLES:");  WRITE("   ");
      FOR I:=1 UNTIL VARS DO
      BEGIN
        READ(VREF);   WRITEON(VREF);
        IF VREF<O OR VREF>MAXVAR THEN BEGIN
          WRITE("VNUM WRONG  - VAR=",VREF);
          ASSERT (FALSE);
        END;

        VARINDX:=VARINDX+1;  XREF(VREF):=VARINDX;  VAR:=VARINDX;
        BREF(VAR):=VREF;
        READON(TYPE(VAR),CARD(VAR),COLUMN(VAR),LENGTH(VAR),
          SCALE(VAR),FORMAT(VAR),LABEL1LEN(VAR),LABEL1(VAR),
          LABEL2LEN(VAR),LABEL2(VAR));
        LENGTH(VAR):=COLUMN(VAR)+LENGTH(VAR)-1;
        COMMENT LENGTH IS TRANSFORMED TO END COLUMN;
        IF TYPE(VAR)="I" OR TYPE(VAR)="R" OR TYPE(VAR)="N" THEN
          TYP(VAR):=1;
        IF TYPE(VAR)="S" OR TYPE(VAR)="C" THEN TYP(VAR):=2;
        IF TYPE(VAR)="D" THEN BEGIN
          TYP(VAR):=4;  FORMAT(VAR):=O;
        END;
        IF TYPE(VAR)="L" OR TYPE(VAR)="T" THEN BEGIN
          TYP(VAR):=3;
          TAGINDX:=TAGINDX+1;
          IF TAGINDX>TAGVARS THEN
            ERROR("MORE TAG VARIABLES THAN SPECIFIED BY TAGVARS");
          TAGREF(VAR):=TAGINDX;
          READON(NTAG(VAR));
          IF NTAG(VAR)>MAXTAG THEN
            ERROR("TAG VAR HAS NTAG > MAXTAG");
          IF NTAG(VAR)>O THEN FOR J:=1 UNTIL NTAG(VAR) DO
            READON(TAG(TAGINDX,J));
        END;
      END;
      FOR VAR:=1 UNTIL VARS DO IF NTAG(VAR)<O THEN BEGIN
        VREF:=XREF(-NTAG(VAR));
        NTAG(VAR):=NTAG(VREF);
        FOR J:=1 UNTIL NTAG(VAR) DO
          TAG(TAGREF(VAR),J):=TAG(TAGREF(VREF),J);
        COMMENT COPY TAGS FROM VREF;
      END;
```

```
        IF STRATA<=0 OR XREF(STRATA)=0 THEN BEGIN
            STRATA:=0; TYP(STRATA):=4;
        END ELSE STRATA:=XREF(STRATA);
        WRITE("VARIABLE DESCRIPTION READ COMPLETE");
END;
PROCEDURE WRITETABLE;
BEGIN
    INTEGER VAR,LNE;
    IF ((SEQ-1) REM CASESPERPAGE)=0 THEN
    BEGIN
        IF CAS¬=1  THEN PRINT(BOTTOM);
        WRITE("1");  FOR LNE:=1 UNTIL TOPLINES DO WRITE(" ");
        FOR LNE:=TOP UNTIL HEADING DO
            PRINT(LNE);
    END ELSE IF ((SEQ-1) REM SEPARATE)=0 THEN PRINT(BETWEEN);
    IF LAYOUTN=TABLE THEN PRINTTABLE ELSE PRINTBLOCK;
END;


COMMENT MAIN PROGRAM;

INITIALIZE;

CHARSET;

READ_HEAD;

READ_VARIABLE_DESCRIPTION;

READ_TABLE_LAYOUT;

WRITE("BEGIN READING DATA");
WRITER("FILE");  READER("DATA");  WRITE_CC:=FALSE;
ENDFILE:=NULL;
WHILE ¬FILEMARK DO
    IF READ_DATA THEN WRITETABLE;
    PRINT(BOTTOM);
END;
END.
```

```
SAMPLE FILE DESCRIBING VARIABLES AND TABLE
====== ==== =========== ========= === =====

TEST.TABLE describes the variables and table:

17 16 17 20 3 20 3 60 5 40 10 132 10 "TABLE" "PRINT"
       IXTAPALAPA REGION - TABULAR PRESENTATION OF PREHISPANIC SETTLEMENT DATA

$STRATA
$BOXTOP
 SITE                               |        |                     |RAINFALL| AREA      |          | OTHER OCCUPATIONS
NUMBER | CLASSIFICATION  | ELEV     |ENVIRONMENTAL ZONE   |(in mm)|(in ha.)|POPULATION|EF MF LF TF EC LC ET LT AZ
                         |(in m)    |
17 "T" 1  1 2 0 25.0 43 . O                   O " "
   12
      "  Early Formative Sites  "
      "  Middle Formative Sites "
      "  Late Formative Sites   "
      "Terminal Formative Sites "
             Classic Sites  "
      "  Early Classic Sites    "
      "  Late Classic Sites     "
      "  Early Toltec Sites     "
      "  Late Toltec Sites      "
             Aztec Sites   "
      "  Early Aztec Sites      "
             Late Aztec Sites   "

 1 "C" 1 18  9 0  9.00 "Site Number: "       O " "
 2 "L" 3 57  2 0 15.00 "Site Type: "         O " 13
      "Small Hamlet" "Hamlet" "Sm Disp Village"
      "Lg Disp Village" "Sm Nucl Village" "Lg Nucl Village" "Local Center"
      "Regional Center" "Supraregion Ctr" "Ceremonial Ctr" "Sm Elite Dist"
      "Lg Elite Dist" "Questionable"
 3 "N" 2 26  4 0  4.00 "Elevation:"          O " "
 4 "L" 2 42  2 0 20.00 "Environmental Zone: "  O " 20
      "Island" "Lakebed" "Lakebed" "Lakeshore Plain" "Lakeshore Plain"
      "Lakeshore Plain" "Lakeshore Plain" "Lakeshore Plain" "Lakeshore Plain"
      "Lakeshore Plain"
      "Lower Piedmont" "Lower Piedmont" "Low Piedmont-Rugged"
      "Upper Piedmont" "Upper Piedmont" "Upr Piedmont-Rugged"
      "Sierra" "Pedregal" "Amecameca Sub-Valley"
 5 "N" 2 57  4 0  4.0 0 "Rainfall: "         O "mm"
 6 "N" 3 11  6 0  6.1 0 "Site Area: "        O "ha"
 7 "N" 3 42  5 0  5.0 0 "Population: "       O " "
 8 "N" 3 63  1 0  1.0 0 "EF Occupations: "   O " "
 9 "N" 3 64  1 0  1.0 0 "MF Occupations: O   " "
10 "N" 3 65  1 0  1.0 0 "LF Occupations: "   O " "
11 "N" 3 66  1 0  1.0 0 "TF Occupations: "   O " "
12 "N" 3 68  1 0  1.0 0 "EC Occupations: "   O " "
13 "N" 3 69  1 0  1.0 0 "LC Occupations: "   O " "
14 "N" 3 70  1 0  1.0 0 "ET Occupations: "   O " "
15 "N" 3 71  1 0  1.0 0 "LT Occupations: "   O " "
16 "N" 3 72  1 0  1.0 0 "AZ Occupations: "   O " "

1 11 " "
2 17 " "
3  6 " "
4 22 " "
5  8 " "
```

```
6  8  "
7  10 "
8  2  "
9  2  "
10 2  "
11 2  "
12 2  "
13 2  "
14 2  "
15 2  "
16 3  "
```

TABLE.TESTDATA
==========

This file contains the data for the test run.

```
804001  IXET  1IX-ET-1              0          01304855   569-2  1 RB                  1
804001  12141.43 514.0023502350     0                     55  41 670                  2
804001  3.0  0  1  0  1 0253 2377   75         30  75 2012 000001101100 4              3
804002  IXET  2IX-ET-2              0          01304877   569-2  1 RB                  1
804002  02142.97 509.7244202420     0                     11  21 630                  2
804002  0.1  0  0  0 0003 2355      10          5  10 1011 000000000000 0              3
804003  IXET  3IX-ET-3              0          01304855   569-2  1 RB                  1
804003  02142.53 509.0524102410     0                     33  21 630                  2
804003  0.1  0  0  0 0003 2355      10          5  10 1011 000001000000 1              3
804004  IXET  4IX-ET-4              0          01304855   569-2  1 RB                  1
804004  02139.97 504.9722502250     0                     553741 610                  2
804004  3.5  0  0  0 0153 2300      88         35  88 2012 000001001100 3              3
804005  IXET  5IX-ET-5              0        0 603277     569-2  1 RB                  1
804005  02139.75 503.0322402240     0                     11  23 610                  2
804005  28.0  0  1  2  3 0003 2300  700       280 700 4022 000001101100 4              3
804006  IXET  6IX-ET-6              0          01404955   569-2  1 RB                  1
804006  02133.78 500.5522502250     0                     11  21 690                  2
804006  2.0  0  0  0  0 0003 2300   20         10  20 1011 000001001000 2              3
804007  IXET  7IX-ET-7              0        0 603277     569-2  1 RB                  1
804007  02140.03 501.7522502250     0                     33  55 610                  2
804007  5.0  0  0  0 0003 2355      125        50 125 3021 000000001100 2              3
```

```
SAMPLE SESSION AT THE TERMINAL
===== ======= == === ========

FILE DESCRIBING VARIABLES AND TABLE ?    TEST.TABLE

FILE CONTAINING INPUT DATA ?    TABLE.TESTDATA

OUTPUT FILE (WILL BE EMPTIED) ?    PRINTOUT

PROGRAM PARAMETERS READ
HEADING READ COMPLETED
READ VARIABLE DESCRIPTIONS - VARIABLES:
 50    1   2   3   4   5   6   7   8   9  10
      11  12  13  14  15  16  17  18  19  20
      21  22  23  24  25  26  27  28  29  30
      31  32  33  34  35  36  37  38  39  40
      41  42  43  44  45  46  47

VARIABLE DESCRIPTION READ COMPLETE
READ TABLE LAYOUT - VARIABLES:
       1   2   3   4   5   6   7   8   9  10
      11  12  13  14  15  16  17  18  19  20
      21  22  23  24  25  26  27  28  29  30
      31  32  33  34  35  36  37  38  39  40
      41  42  43  44  45  46  47

TABLE LAYOUT READ COMPLETE
BEGIN READING DATA
END OF FILE READING CASE    11 RECORD    1
00.221 seconds in execution


SAMPLE BLOCK AND TABLE PRINTOUT FOLLOWS:
```

PREHISTORIC SETTLEMENT PATTERNS - IXTAPALAPA REGION   (RB)
                    Early Toltec Sites

Site Number: IX-ET-1   Field Number:

Natural Setting
   Location (UTM): 514.00E 2141.43N   Zone 14
   Elevation: 2350 meters   range: 0-   0 meters
   Zone: Lower Piedmont, Smooth Terrain
   Rainfall: 670 mm
   Soil Depth: Medium
   Erosion: Moderate

Modern Utilization: Agriculture and Grazing
Modern Settlement Encroachment: None

Archaeological Remains   (Very Light-Light)
   Sherd Scatter: Light
   Rubble Density: Heavy
   Area of Scatter: 3.0 ha
   Mounds - Domestic: 0 Ceremonial: 1 Questionable: 0
   Other Occupations of Site Area
      EF 0   LF 0   EC 1   ET 0   AZ 1
      MF 0   TF 0   LC 1   LT 1

Classification: Hamlet
   Population: 30 to   75

Site Number: IX-ET-2   Field Number: (RB)

Natural Setting
   Location (UTM): 509.72E 2142.97N   Zone 14
   Elevation: 2420 meters   range: 0-   0 meters
   Zone: Lower Piedmont, Smooth Terrain
   Rainfall: 630 mm
   Soil Depth: Deep
   Erosion: None

Modern Utilization: Agriculture
Modern Settlement Encroachment: None

Archaeological Remains   (Very Light-Light)
   Sherd Scatter: Light
   Rubble Density: Moderate
   Area of Scatter: 0.1 ha
   Mounds - Domestic: 0 Ceremonial: 0 Questionable: 0
   Other Occupations of Site Area
      EF 0   LF 0   EC 0   ET 0   AZ 0
      MF 0   TF 0   LC 0   LT 0

Classification: Small Hamlet
   Population: 5 to   10

PREHISTORIC SETTLEMENT PATTERNS - IXTAPALAPA REGION
Early Toltec Sites

Site Number: IX-ET-3   Field Number: (RB)

Natural Setting
   Location (UTM): 509.05E 2142.53N   Zone 14
   Elevation: 2410 meters   range: 0-   0 meters
   Zone: Lower Piedmont, Smooth Terrain
   Rainfall: 630 mm
   Soil Depth: Medium
   Erosion: Slight

Modern Utilization: Agriculture
   Modern Settlement Encroachment: None

Archaeological Remains
   Sherd Scatter: Light   (Very Light-Light)
   Rubble Density: Moderate
   Area of Scatter: 0.1 ha
   Mounds - Domestic: O Ceremonial: O Questionable: O
   Other Occupations of Site Area
       EF O   LF O   EC 1   ET O   AZ O
       MF O   TF O   LC O   LT O

Classification: Small Hamlet
   Population: 5 to   10

Site Number: IX-ET-4   Field Number: (RB)

Natural Setting
   Location (UTM): 504.97E 2139.97N   Zone 14
   Elevation: 2250 meters   range: 0-   0 meters
   Zone: Lower Piedmont, Smooth Terrain
   Rainfall: 610 mm
   Soil Depth: Medium
   Erosion: Moderate   (Slight-Severe)

Modern Utilization: Agriculture and Grazing
   Modern Settlement Encroachment: None

Archaeological Remains
   Sherd Scatter: Light   (Very Light-Light)
   Rubble Density:
   Area of Scatter: 3.5 ha
   Mounds - Domestic: O Ceremonial: O Questionable: O
   Other Occupations of Site Area
       EF O   LF O   EC 1   ET O   AZ 1
       MF O   TF O   LC O   LT 1

Classification: Hamlet
   Population: 35 to   88

Appendix IV

MICHIGAN TERMINAL

SYSTEM DOCUMENTATION

MTS-SPECIFIC COMMANDS, PLOTTING SUBROUTINES, AND LANGUAGE FEATURES
by Keith Kintigh

This appendix provides a brief description MTS commands, plotting
subroutines, and non-standard ALGOL W variables and procedures that may
be useful in understanding the programs and examples provided in
Appendices I-III.   Additional information can be found in the standard
MTS documentation.

MTS Commands

$COMMENT <comment>: ignored by MTS.

$EMPTY <filename>: $EMPTY ($EMP) causes MTS to empty the file <filename>
so that any data written to the file is put at the beginning of the
file.

$RUN <object module>+<library> GUSER=<fdname> SERCOM=<fdname>
SCARDS=<fdname> SPRINT=<fdname> PAR=<parameters>:0$RUN ($R) causes MTS
to load and execute the program <object module> with any necessary
<library> modules.   The run command also makes input/output device
assignments to the appropriate files and devices (fdnames).   GUSER
indicates the source of interactive input (usually *source*, the
terminal).   SERCOM indicates the destination of error and log messages
and is usually also the terminal (*sink*).   SCARDS indicates the basic
input file or device.   SPRINT indicates the basic output file or device,
usually (*print*) or a temporary file (a file name starting with a "-")
that can later be printed.   Program parameters and non-standard device
assignments (using the logical file names defined in the program) are
passed to the program through the PAR option of the run command.   A
continuation of a command line is indicated by a "-" in the last
position of a line.

FORTRAN Subroutine Calls from PL/1

FORTRAN subroutines are called from PL/1 under MTS using the PLCALL
procedure.   PLCALL has as its first parameter the library subroutine
name (e.g. PSYM).   The second parameter is a integer variable containing
the number of parameters of the FORTRAN subroutine.   These two
parameters are followed 9 additional parameters.   These parameters are
the one word addresses of variables that have the values of the
parameters, followed by arbitrary dummy variables to fill out the list
of 9.

MTS Plotter Subroutines

PLTXMX (PGXWTH)   The PLTXMX sets the maximum plot length in inches as
PGXWTH.

PLTOFS(XMIN,XFACT,YMIN,YFACT,XORG,YORG)   The PLTOFS subroutine defines
the relative coordinate system.   XORG,YORG is the absolute origin in
inches of the coordinate system.   XMIN,YMIN is the value assigned to the
origin of the relative coordinate system.   XFACT and YFACT are scale

218

factors for X and Y values. The absolute (in inches) X coordinate is computed by dividing the difference between XREL and XMIN by XFACT.

PAXIS(XO,YO,TITLE,NCHAR,AXLTH,THETA,XMIN,DX,DV)   The PAXIS subroutine draws an axis with the origin at XO,YO and a length in inches of AXLEN at an angle of THETA in counter-clockwise degrees from the horizontal. The scale of the axis is DX units per inch. The origin of the axis is assigned the value XMIN, and tic marks are plotted along the axis each DV inches. A label is generally printed under each tic mark. The axis is printed with TITLE centered below it. NCHAR contains the number of characters in the title. The title and tic labels are printed on the clockwise side of the axis if NCHAR is negative, otherwise they are printed on the counter-clockwise side.

PAXTTL(TITLHT)   A call to this subroutine sets the height (in inches) of the axis title printed below the axis.

PAXVAL(VALHT)   A call to this subroutine sets the height (in inches) of the numeric values printed along an axis.

PSYM(XO,YO,HGHT,CHAR,THETA,NCHAR,SC)   Starting at the point XO,YO, this subroutine plots a symbol or string with length NCHAR at the angle THETA. THETA is in counter-clockwise degrees from the horizontal. If SC is 0.0 then the XO,YO coordinates are absolute, as measured from the origin of the plot area, otherwise, XO,YO is determined through coordinate transformations specified in PLTOFS. If NCHAR is -1, then the symbol is plotted with its center at XO,YO, otherwise, its lower left corner is plotted at that point.

PSYMB(XO,YO,HGHT,CHAR,THETA,NCHAR,SC)   PSYMB is like PSYM except that in PSYMB, if CHAR is an integer, it is interpreted as a special character.

PLINE(X,Y,N,K,J,L,SC)   This subroutine plots a data curve of N points in every Kth position of the X and Y arrays of coordinates. If J=0 then a straight line is drawn between each point in sequence. If J>0, then the special symbol with the index L (<14) is plotted at every Jth vertex. If J<0 then only symbols are plotted at every Jth vertex with no connecting lines. If SC=0.0 then the X,Y coordinates are considered absolute, otherwise they are considered relative and are operated upon as defined in PLTOFS to get absolute positions.

PDSHLN(X,Y,N,K,DSHLTH,SC)   PDSHLN plots a dashed line with dashes of length DSHLTH. Other parameters operate as described in PLINE.

PFLINE(X,Y,N,K,SC)   PFLINE plots a smooth (curved) line through the points in the array. Other parameters operate as described in PLINE.

PSHADE(X,Y,N,K,SANGLE,SDIST,SC)   Shades (hatches) the region defined by the array. Hatching lines are separated by SDIST inches at an angle of SANGLE. Other parameters operate as described in PLINE.

PLTEND   The PLTEND subroutine, with no parameters terminates a plot and establishes a new coordinate system for the next plot.

Non-standard ALGOL W Procedures and Variables

ASSIGN(<stream>,<fdname>)   This procedure assigns an file or device to the logical file name used in the program.

READER(<stream>)   this procedure changes the input stream so that subsequent READ and READCARD statements read from <stream>. Initially the input stream is set to SCARDS.

WRITER(<stream>)   This procedure changes the output stream so that subsequent WRITE and WRITEON statements write to <stream>. Initially, the output stream is set to SPRINT.

integer I_W: This integer supplies the field width used in integer output. If this field width is too small to print the number, it will be expanded. This variable replaces the standard ALGOL W variable intfieldsize.

string(1) R_Format: This string specifies the format to be used in the printing of real numbers. The value of "A" prints a fixed length field of width R_W with R_D digits to the right of the decimal point. If R_Format="A", R_W=6, R_D=2 and the value is 29.751, the value will print as " 29.75" (equivalent to FORTRAN format F6.2).

integer R_W: This integer supplies the field width used in the output of real numbers using R_Format="A". If R_W is too small to print the number, it will be overriden.

integer R_D: This integer supplies the decimal digit field width used for real output with R_Format="A".

integer S_W: The number of spaces following each numeric value output.

logical WRITE_CC: When this variable is set to true, each output line is assumed to start with a carriage control character. Otherwise, ALGOL W provides carriage control.

BIBLIOGRAPHY

Alden, John

    1979   A reconstruction of Toltec period political units in the Valley of Mexico. In <u>Transformations</u>: <u>mathematical approaches to cultural change</u>, edited by Colin Renfrew, pp. 169-200. New York: Academic Press.

Blanton, Richard E.

    1972   Prehispanic settlement patterns of the Ixtapalapa Peninsula Region, Mexico. <u>Pennsylvania State University Department of Anthropology, Occasional Papers in Anthropology</u> 6.

Blanton, Richard E., Stephen A. Kowalewski, Gary Feinman, and Jill Appel

    1982   <u>Ancient Mesoamerica</u>: <u>a comparison of change in three regions</u>. Cambridge: Cambridge University Press.

Brumfiel, Elizabeth

    1976   Regional growth in the eastern Valley of Mexico: a test of the "population pressure" hypothesis. In <u>The early Mesoamerican village</u>, edited by Kent V. Flannery, pp. 234-47. New York: Academic Press.

Comision de Estudios del Territorio Nacional y Planeacion

    1970   <u>Carta de climas, hoja Mexico, 14Q-V, escala 1: 500,000</u>. Mexico, D.F.: Secretaria de la Presidencia.

Earle, Timothy K.

    1976   A nearest-neighbor analysis of two Formative settlement systems. In <u>The early Mesoamerican village</u>, edited by Kent V. Flannery, pp. 196-221. New York: Academic Press.

Hirth, Kenneth

    1983   Review of Parsons et al. 1982. <u>Science</u> 220: 1041-42.

Hodder, Ian, and Clive Orton

    1976   <u>Spatial analysis in archaeology</u>. Cambridge: Cambridge University Press.

Kintigh, Keith W.

1982   A summary of the coding and computer analysis of the Valley of Mexico archaeological survey. "Appendix 3" in Parsons et al., Prehispanic settlement patterns in the southern Valley of Mexico: the Chalco-Xochimilco Region. Memoirs of the University of Michigan Museum of Anthropology, No. 14: 463-74.

Parsons, Jeffrey R.

1971   Prehistoric settlement patterns in the Texcoco Region, Mexico. Memoirs of the University of Michigan Museum of Anthropology, No. 3.

Parsons, Jeffrey R., Elizabeth Brumfiel, Mary Parsons, and David Wilson

1982   Prehispanic settlement patterns in the southern Valley of Mexico: the Chalco-Xochimilco Region. Memoirs of the University of Michigan Museum of Anthropology, No. 14.

Pinder, David, Izumi Shimada, and David Gregory

1979   The nearest-neighbor statistic: archaeological application and new developments. American Antiquity 44: 430-45.

Rattray, Evelyn

1968   A Tzacualli burial from Pueblo Perdido. American Antiquity 33: 103-05.

Sanders, William T., Jeffrey R. Parsons, and Robert S. Santley

1979   The Basin of Mexico: ecological processes in the evolution of a civilization. New York: Academic Press.

Secretaria de la Defensa Nacional

1959   Cartas topograficas, escala 1: 25,000. Mexico, D.F.: Departamento Cartografico Militar.

Steponaitis, Vincas P.

1981   Settlement hierarchies and political complexity in non-market societies: the Formative period of the Valley of Mexico. American Anthropologist 83: 320-63.

Tourtellot, Gair

1973   Review of Parsons 1971. American Anthropologist 75: 524-25.

Whallon, Robert

1974   Spatial analysis of occupation floors II: the application of nearest neighbor analysis. American Antiquity 39: 16-34.

(continued on back cover)